NEW GAME PLAN
FOR COLLEGE SPORT

Other Books by Richard Lapchick

100 Heroes: People in Sport Who Make This a Better World

Smashing Barriers: Race and Sport in the New Millennium

Never Before, Never Again: The Stirring Autobiography of Eddie Robinson, the Winningest Coach in the History of College Football

Sport in Society: Equal Opportunity or Business as Usual?

Five Minutes to Midnight: Race and Sport in the 1990s

Rules of the Game: Ethics in College Sport

On the Mark: Putting the Student Back in Student-athlete

Fractured Focus: Sport as a Reflection of Society

Broken Promises: Racism in American Sports

Oppression and Resistance: The Struggle of Women in Southern Africa

Politics of Race and International Sport: The Case of South Africa

NEW GAME PLAN
FOR COLLEGE SPORT

Edited by
Richard E. Lapchick

AMERICAN COUNCIL ON EDUCATION
PRAEGER
Series on Higher Education

Library of Congress Cataloging-in-Publication Data

New game plan for college sport / edited by Richard E. Lapchick.
    p.   cm. — (Ace/Praeger series on higher education)
    Includes bibliographical references and index.
    ISBN 0-275-98147-9 (alk. paper)
    1. College sports—Moral and ethical aspects—United States.   2. College
sports—Corrupt practices—United States.   I. Lapchick, Richard Edward.
II. American Council on Education/Praeger series on higher education.
    GV351.N48 2006
    796.04'30973—dc22   2005034803

British Library Cataloguing in Publication Data is available.

Library of Congress Catalog Card Number: 2005034803
ISBN: 0-275-98147-9

First published in 2006

Praeger Publishers, 88 Post Road West, Westport, CT 06881
An imprint of Greenwood Publishing Group, Inc.
www.praeger.com

Printed in the United States of America

The paper used in this book complies with the
Permanent Paper Standard issued by the National
Information Standards Organization (Z39.48-1984).

10 9 8 7 6 5 4 3 2 1

New Game Plan for College Sport is dedicated to the memory
of three dear friends.

First is Jim Murray, who for years was vice president of the American
Council on Education. He asked me to write this book, and it was
his inspiration that began the work.

Ralph Wiley was a gifted writer who helped shed light on many of the
issues covered in this book. I think he was one of America's finest
writers. Ralph died at the all-too-young age of 51 in 2004.

Finally, I dedicate this to Sam Lacy, the first renowned African-American sports
journalist who died at age 99 in 2003, after a brilliant career
and a lifetime of confronting racism in sport and in society.

CONTENTS

PREFACE

Richard E. Lapchick

As we look at the headlines in our newspapers about scandals in college sport, it is tempting to think nostalgically about the good old days. We often think that college sport was more fun, and comprised pure amateurism and the right perspective on academics and athletics back in those days.

However, if you look at the history of college sport, it begs the question: "Was it ever really that way?" Surely sport has become a big business. Athletic budgets have grown much more rapidly than the overall budgets for colleges. Athletic directors and power coaches earn more than presidents.

There is a belief among alumni and trustees that winning big in Division IA will lead to larger gifts from alumni and a larger and better applicant pool.

This belief is used to justify the increased expenditures in athletics, assuming that it will improve the university's bottom line in other areas. The Knight Foundation Commission on Intercollegiate Athletes issued a report on this subject in 2004. "Challenging the Myth: A Review of the Links Among College Athletics' Success of Student Quality and Donations," by Robert Frank, argues forcefully against that assumption. Athletics budgets have increased more than twice as fast as have university budgets in Division I institutions between 1995 and 2001.

Yet Frank's study shows there is really no link among winning, donations, and increased applications. It seems as though throughout the history of college sport we have sought a rationale for increasing the athletics arms race.

However, the escalation of the arms race in the last 20 years seems to indicate that history has not taught us as much as we would hope.

The problems that are being discussed in the *New Game Plan for College Sport* are not new. In fact, I coauthored a book that discussed the issues with John Slaughter in 1989. *The Rules of Game: Ethics in College Sport*, also published by the American Council on Education, included many of the same issues discussed here, including money in sport, race, gender, gambling, performance enhancing drugs, and agents on college campuses.

Likewise, one could pick up the *Chronicle of Higher Education* in 1980, 1990, 2000, or in 2005 and one would see stories about the same issues in college sport in each decade. The players might have changed with the increased power and influence of conference commissioners. Also, the focus at any given moment might change, and the specific cases may seem different. However, the same challenges to higher education seem always to be before those responsible for intercollegiate sport on their campuses.

New Game Plan covers the myriad challenges faced by college and university governing boards, presidents, coaches, administrators, and student-athletes. It explores in depth issues such as the commercialization of sport, race and gender, legal issues, gambling, performance enhancing drugs, and the academic peril faced by too many student-athletes. Intercollegiate sport has never existed in a vacuum, and so the book starts with Welch Suggs's historical analysis.

Part of the mission of *New Game Plan* is to be a forum for conflicting opinion on how to improve the way we run our college sports enterprise. It was not conceived to be a theoretical piece, but instead it relies on the wisdom and experience of those who have had significant roles in sport to discuss how far we may have come from the ideals of sport and what we have to do to correct our course.

After the historical overview, the book is divided into a section on the issues, a chapter on the influence of the media, and a section on what I call "the players"—that is, those most involved in, and with the most at stake in, the college sports enterprise. Finally, *New Game Plan* ends with a series of recommendations drawn from the authors of the respective chapters.

Welch Suggs joined the Knight Commission on Intercollegiate Athletics in 2005, after serving as senior editor of the *Chronicle of Higher Education*. He is one of the country's leading writers covering off-the-field issues in college sports. He is the author of *A Place on the Team: The Triumph and Tragedy of Title IX* (Princeton University Press, 2005).

Suggs traces the history of college sport in his chapter, "Historical Overview: At Play at America's Colleges." The United States is the only country in the world where academe and athletics are so closely linked. Nearly 500,000 student-athletes participate on varsity teams annually. They learn lessons about life that may be unavailable in the classroom. Winning teams can build campus spirit. In a few cases, they earn their universities extra income.

At the same time, there is a history of tensions between athletics departments and the rest of the campus. However, athletics officials continue to view themselves as educators even as the stakes rise year-by-year in the business of college sports.

Richard Lapchick's chapter on "The Integrity of the Enterprise" looks at, and beyond, the negative headlines of college sport. The headlines include two murders, two suicides, sex scandals in recruiting, coaches being fired after unethical behavior, the surrendering of national championships because of NCAA violations, and athletics directors and presidents resigning in 2003 and 2004, the two years prior to the completion of this book.

There are sections of *New Game Plan* on finances in college sport, on the attitudes of high school students and student-athletes who may end up on our college campuses, and a section on the crises faced by youth, which delineates some huge differences of future students from those who preceded them.

John R. Gerdy is a visiting professor in sports administration at Ohio University (Athens) and former All-American and professional basketball player, NCAA legislative assistant, and associate commissioner of the Southeastern Conference.

According to Gerdy, in his chapter, "Higher Education's Failed Experiment with Professional Athletics," it is no longer in doubt that Division IA athletics—particularly in football and basketball, but with other sports marching down the same road—have tried to become very expensive professional teams in college uniforms.

Gerdy challenges higher education leaders to meet what he considers may be their most important educational responsibility, and he provides the rationale and blueprint for colleges and universities to dismantle their departments of "professional athletics" by eliminating the current "pay (scholarship) for play" professional model of Division IA athletics.

"Ethical Dilemmas in College Sport" was written by Dr. Sharon K. Stoll and Dr. Jennifer M. Beller. Dr. Stoll is Professor and Director of the Center for ETHICS* at University of Idaho, and Dr. Beller is Associate Professor of Educational Psychology at Washington State University. The authors' purpose for this chapter is to argue for a better ethical education for all individuals involved in the athletic experience, from the athlete to the college/university president. The authors contend that the issue is not about dealing with or studying each case of cheating, but rather about the fact that we need to focus on addressing how we can better develop educational models to reduce the incidence of cheating.

In the chapter "Race in College Sport," Richard Lapchick focuses on sport's lingering problem of the lack of African-American head coaches, especially in football, and on poor graduation rates of football and basketball student-athletes, particularly African-American players. The author explores in this chapter the hiring practices in all of college sport beyond football, which is the special emphasis of the chapter that follows it. He examines the NCAA headquarters, student-athletes, coaching positions, and athletics directors, as well as all other professional personnel in athletics departments. The chapter also examines the roles of conference commissioners and the Black Coaches Association.

At the time his chapter, "The Impact of Race As It Relates to Employment Opportunities for Collegiate Football Coaches," was written, Dr. Fitzgerald Hill was one of five African-American head football coaches in Division IA at San Jose State and was one of a handful of coaches with a Ph.D. He writes not only from his experiences but also from his own unique research. At the end of the 2004 season, he was the first African-American head football coach to leave of his own volition when he became a visiting scholar at the DeVos Sport Business Management program.

In his chapter, Hill discusses the lack of opportunities for African-American football coaches. Dr. Hill focuses of four key points: (1) barriers restricting employment opportunities for African-American football coaches; (2) past and current collegiate football coaching opportunities as they relate to employment equity; (3) contrasting perceptions between African-American and white football coaches at Division IA institutions regarding employment opportunities; and (4) implications from studies of African-American football coaches employed at predominantly white colleges and universities. Additionally, Hill makes recommendations of ways to achieve equal opportunity for all coaches, regardless of race.

Dr. Donna A. Lopiano is currently the Chief Executive Officer of the Women's Sports Foundation and is listed as one of the "100 Most Influential People in Sports." She has been a college coach, director of women's athletics (17 years), and the president of the Association for Intercollegiate Athletics for Women.

In her chapter, "Gender and Sport," Dr. Lopiano shows how discrimination on the basis of gender still exists in intercollegiate athletics with regard to both employment and participation opportunities and treatment. According to Dr. Lopiano, the requirements of Title IX, the federal law prohibiting sex discrimination in education programs and activities receiving federal funds, are being ignored by many institutions that are moving at a snail's pace in fulfilling their compliance obligations. Females of color are in double jeopardy with regard to participation and employment discrimination. She discusses a range of challenges and issues related to gender and sport that require the immediate attention of educational leaders and outspoken criticism by sports professionals.

Bill Saum is the NCAA's Director of Agent, Gambling, and Amateur Activities and has been a dynamic leader for the NCAA on the issue of gambling. He has addressed the student-athletes on many of America's campuses about the dangers of being drawn into sports wagering.

His chapter, "National Collegiate Athletic Association and the Issue of Sports Wagering," gives depth to the concerns of the NCAA about this serious issue. Gambling, especially sports wagering, has been of significant importance to the NCAA membership throughout the existence of the Association. Intercollegiate football and basketball have both been marred by wagering-related incidents over the past half-century. According to Saum, these incidents threaten to undermine the integrity of all sports and cannot be tolerated by those entrusted with protecting the good of the game.

Dr. Yun-Oh Whang teaches in the marketing department at Kansas State University. He has written extensively about and taught sports marketing, and he knows the impact of performance enhancing drugs on the ability to market sports. His chapter, "Performance Enhancing Drugs (PED): The Wounds Behind the Glory," focuses on the issue as it affects college sport. He maintains that while the NCAA has been testing college athletes for illegal substances year-round since 1990 and has expanded the subject pool and banned substance list over the last few years, we have not seen any significant progress toward drug-free college sports. The chapter changes the focus of the discussion on performance enhancing drugs (PED) usage by college athletes, which, Whang holds, too often focuses on the athlete as the person to blame for making a wrong choice. The discussion frequently overlooks the fact that there are many entities involved other than the athletes themselves. This chapter attempts to provide a structure for the complex problem of PED usage in college athletics by looking at the different roles of the involved entities and the interrelationships among them.

Dr. Fritz G. Polite is a former player, coach, and sport administrator. He is now an assistant professor in the DeVos Sport Business Management Program. He is also the assistant director of the Institute for Diversity and Ethics in Sport at the University of Central Florida.

In his chapter, "Agents on Campus," Dr. Polite shares many of his past experiences and research in addressing the issues of agents on our university campuses. He focuses on several key areas: (1) the dramatic change in the world of sport and its impact on the status of amateur athletics; (2) the historical background of the college and professional issues; (3) the history, definitions, and role of agents; (4) effects on high school and college athletes; and (5) the legal issues facing athletes, universities, and administrators. Throughout the chapter, Dr. Polite addresses the many challenges of agents. The roles of the NCAA, coaches, agents, and administrators also are discussed in this chapter, which provides a framework for further discussions, research, and concerns of agents on our campuses.

Charles S. Farrell was the former sports editor of the *Chronicle of Higher Education* and deputy sports editor for the *Washington Post*. He directed Rainbow/PUSH Sports for Reverend Jesse Jackson for nearly a decade. He now is the senior consultant to Sports Perspectives International. In his chapter, "'Show Me the Money' Created a College Sportocracy: The Influence of the Media," Farrell discusses the current state of collegiate athletics and the impact money has had on media coverage of college sport.

Farrell believes that, for the most part, the media serves a valuable purpose to collegiate athletics. For example, the media is taking an increased interest in diversifying collegiate sport. However, he notes that sometimes the media crosses the line with negative publicity. The bottom line is that the media is all about business and will print what people want to read. Farrell offers several ways in which the media could make changes in order to have a more positive impact on collegiate athletics.

In today's corporate model of collegiate athletics, university presidents play an increasing role with their athletics departments. In the chapter entitled "Presidents' Forum" John DiBiaggio (Tufts University), Joe Crowley (University of Nevada), John Hitt (University of Central Florida), and Roger Webb (University of Central Oklahoma) discuss several of collegiate athletics' most compelling issues and their roles as presidents in helping to monitor future development. Major issues surrounding race, academics, ethical behaviors, and the commercialization of college sport are discussed in detail. Two of the themes discussed concern the current use of graduation rates in measuring student-athlete performance and the role of the president in the hiring of coaches and athletic administrators.

Conference commissioners have arguably become the most powerful voices in college sport. In the chapter entitled "Conference Commissioners' Forum," five of the leading commissioners share their views. Jim Delany (Big 10), Mike Slive (SEC), Patty Viverito (Gateway Football), Chris Monasch (American East), and Kevin Weiberg (Big 12) discuss their positions and recommendations regarding current issues in collegiate athletics. Topics covered include the unethical behaviors of student-athletes, coaches, agents, and other professionals within the collegiate athletics field. The commissioners also delve into racial issues, such as the importance of increasing diversity within the ranks of both coaches and administrators, and the constantly evolving scope of collegiate athletics in both positive and negative directions.

In the chapter entitled "Athletics Directors' Forum," Clarence Underwood (Michigan State), Don DiJulia (St. Joseph's), Dan Guerrero (UCLA), and Bill Byrne (Texas A&M) discuss their roles as athletics directors, examine current problems and controversial topics in collegiate athletics, and explore changes that may take place in the future. By addressing problems such as low graduation rates, the roles of academic advisors, and unethical recruiting practices, this forum leads to an increased understanding of the importance of the athletics director's role in collegiate athletics. Further, by discussing Title IX, racial hiring practices, stipends for student-athletes, and other controversial topics, we begin to understand the daily pressure and scrutiny placed on athletics directors as a result of working in the public eye.

Faculty leaders in college sport participated in the discussion in the chapter entitled "Faculty Forum." Percy Bates (Michigan), Murray Sperber (Indiana), Earl Smith (Wake Forest), Keith Harrison (Arizona State), and Ellen Staurowsky (Ithaca) discuss an array of issues involving the faculty's role in intercollegiate athletics. This chapter delves into such topics as faculty authority and involvement, the use of academic athletic advisors, time commitments of faculty and student-athletes, and mentoring. A major focus of "Faculty Forum" brings forward the question of the most appropriate involvement of faculty with athletics. It is argued by the faculty that they should have central authority relative to higher education, but often the relationship of faculty to athletics is either nonexistent, or exists in a manner that breaches ethical boundaries.

The views of eight former student-athletes are presented in the "Student-Athletes' Forum" chapter. Lindsay Beddow (LSU, gymnastics), Keri Boyce (Kentucky, soccer), Zach Falconer (Northeastern, football), Damone Jones (Penn State, football), Morgan Marr (Kentucky, softball), Brian O'Leary (Kentucky, soccer), Charece Williams (NCSU, volleyball), and Sarah Wong (Mississippi, soccer), are all former student-athletes who enrolled in the DeVos Sport Business Management Graduate Program at the University of Central Florida. They discuss what they believe would be the most effective incentives and disincentives, the most significant issues facing college athletics over the next five to ten years, the most important issues facing student-athletes themselves, and their views on the lack of minority head coaches in college sports.

Daniel Boggan worked for 18 years as the Vice Chancellor for Business and Administrative Services at the University of California, Berkeley, and as one of the two senior vice presidents at the NCAA. In both roles he worked to make the lives of the college student-athlete meaningful beyond the cheers and jeers that come with competition. Student-athlete success is his passion.

In his chapter, "The NCAA in 2010," Boggan discusses the future of collegiate athletics and the changes that will exist at the national level. The conflict that every university faces arises between those who believe that competition should be fair and within a set of principles and rules, and those who look for ways to win, no matter what. Boggan also notes that there are issues to be addressed beyond the field of competition. Fans, coaches, and administration alike must be responsible for creating a stronger, more united NCAA by 2010.

The final portion of the book compiles the recommendations made by the contributors.

ACKNOWLEDGMENTS

I would like to thank all the people involved in writing this book. It was a monumental effort on the part of many contributors. I would like to first thank those who wrote individual chapters, including Welch Suggs, John Gerdy, Sharon Stoll, Jennifer Beller, Fitz Hill, Donna Lopiano, Bill Saum, Yun-Oh Whang, Charles Farrell, Fritz Polite, and Dan Boggan. I would also like to thank all those who participated in what will hopefully be an innovative and insightful series of forums of presidents, conference commissioners, athletics directors, faculty, and student-athletes. The presidents were John DiBiaggio, Joe Crowley, John Hitt, and Roger Webb. The conference commissioners were Jim Delaney, Mike Slive, Patty Viverito, Chris Monasch, and Kevin Weiberg. The athletics directors were Clarence Underwood, Don DiJulia, Dan Guerrero, and Bill Byrne. The faculty included Percy Bates, Murray Sperber, Earl Smith, Keith Harrison, and Ellen Staurowsky. The student-athletes included Brian O'Leary, Zach Falconer, Lindsay Beddow, Keri Boyce, Charece Williams, Damone Jones, Morgan Marr, and Sarah Wong.

The entire staff of the Institute for the Study of Diversity and Ethics in Sport participated in this project in some fashion. In particular, I would like to thank Program Coordinator Philomena Pirolo, office assistant Maria Molina, and graduate assistants Tyechia Smith, Erin Alexander, Lindsay Beddow, Kate Troutman, Jennifer Frohm, and Keri Boyce.

However, if I had to single out one person who contributed the most to the overall effort, it would be Drew Tyler. Drew Tyler, who was a graduate assistant in the office of the Institute for the Study of Diverstiy and Ethics in Sport at the University of Central Florida, was my right hand in compiling all of the writings and providing wise advice. Drew will graduate from the DeVos Sport Business Management Program and help bring about some of the changes we talk about in this book as a senior administrator. He helped with the fine tuning of the entire manuscript and assisted in pulling together some of the research in individual chapters.

CHAPTER 1

Historical Overview: At Play at America's Colleges

Welch Suggs Associate Director, Knight Foundation Commission
on Intercollegiate Athletics

A merican college sports are a historical accident. Nearly 2,000 institutions of higher learning sponsor teams here, but this is the only country in the world where academe and athletics are so closely linked. Participating in college sports is usually a valuable educational experience for athletes, but the tension between the competitive mission of an athletics department and the academic mission of a college can be pernicious to both.

About half a million undergraduates compete on varsity teams every year, or roughly 4 percent of all enrolled undergraduates. All sorts of institutions field teams—research universities, liberal arts colleges, Bible colleges, and two-year colleges among them.

Participating in sports can teach a college student lessons unavailable in the classroom, such as the virtues of discipline and hard work, the necessity of sublimating individual aspirations in favor of team goals, and the values of a healthy lifestyle.

At the same time, winning teams in a variety of sports can whip college communities into a frenzy. They generate positive headlines; good feelings among alumni, donors, and potential students; and, for a handful of universities, a fair amount of money.

"Seven hundred years of Dominican scholarship, nobody ever heard of us until we put five kids on the floor at Madison Square Garden," the Rev. Robert J. Slavin, the president of Providence College, remarked in 1954. His basketball team had just won the National Invitation Tournament title, touching off a statewide celebration in Rhode Island.[1]

That's a powerful message to athletics directors, coaches, and athletes themselves. As important as educational ambitions and requirements may be to them, their jobs require them to think in terms of what their teams can do for their institutions.

This distinctly American ethos of college sports has evolved over the past 150 years, ever since the superintendent of the Boston, Concord, and Montreal rail line decided to promote a new route and a new resort in New Hampshire by staging a regatta featuring students from Harvard and Yale. Men's and women's sports have moved out of college physical education departments and into separate athletics departments, many of which sit far from academic buildings on their respective campuses.

In other countries, colleges may have sports teams, but athletes who are at all serious about their sports pursue their passions in local clubs and leagues, aspiring eventually to compete for national teams. In the United States, athletes compete for secondary-school teams (perhaps for "outside" clubs depending on the sport) and aspire to collegiate competition. In all but a few Olympic sports, colleges are the primary locus for elite athlete development.

This has led to any number of tensions between athletics departments and the rest of their campuses. Over the past century and a half, groups of faculty members or presidents have erupted in fits of indignation about every ten to fifteen years over the academic compromises made to allow players to compete, or over bribery scandals in which supposedly amateur athletes were paid off by win-craving boosters.

However, athletics officials have co-opted the goals of physical education and continue to promote themselves as educators, even as the stakes rise year by year in the business of college sports. Throughout the history of collegiate athletics, they have managed the tension between education and commercialism without prompting enough of an outcry to doom the enterprise.

This chapter will trace the extensive scholarship on the history of American college sports, focusing for the most part on elite colleges where athletics has colored institutional missions and public identities. These include the "big-time" members of the National Collegiate Athletic Association's Division IA, such as the University of California at Los Angeles and Michigan, as well as what we now know as members of the Ivy League. It will also touch on the role of sports at smaller regional institutions and liberal arts colleges and the way women's athletics was taken over by, and yet has reshaped, predominantly male athletics departments.

ORIGINS OF INTERCOLLEGIATE SPORT

The development of residential colleges in the Middle Ages in Europe gave students a fair amount of leisure time. They filled this time with games of all sorts, as well as hunting and other pursuits. Games like tennis, badminton, racquetball, and others trace their origins to British public schools, according to J.A. Mangan.[2] Such games, though, were unique to a given institution, and rules evolved among the insular societies that evolved at Eton, Westminster, and other schools. Other sports, such as rowing and cricket, developed in parallel to games among students and other people throughout the country.

Many of these games were adapted to American schools and colleges when they began attracting students in the 17th and 18th centuries. Furthermore, like the British, Americans became consumed with class contests, which often took the form of hazing and near-riots.

This represented a major shift from the Puritan tradition, which frowned upon sport and other forms of play as being frivolous. Early 19th-century Americans thought that playing sports was about as moral as dancing, thanks to the Calvinists who held sway, especially in colleges.[3]

At the same time, in the mid-Victorian era, British citizens and Americans were being led to question Victorian values. Theologians and authors like Charles Kingsley and Thomas Hughes thought the Anglican church was becoming "overly tolerant of physical weakness and effeminacy."[4] Clifford Putney notes "neurasthenia" as the most in-vogue malady of Victorian England and America.[5]

Kingsley notes that athletes would help Britain maintain its world supremacy and status as the chosen people "in covenant with God." The medical profession began to advocate mild physical activity, physical well-being, and the proper eugenics. WASPs feared an influx of the new "breeds" among immigrants, and healthy women were to be the best guard against the dilution of the bloodlines by the mongrel hordes.[6]

Physical education became an integral part of the curriculum at most Northeastern colleges at that time, and school officials quickly realized that traditional forms of exercise, such as German and Swedish gymnastics and other forms of calisthenics, were never going to develop much of a following among the rich young rulers in attendance at Harvard, Yale, Princeton, and elsewhere.[7] According to an 1888 survey, 80 percent of Harvard students were exercising between one and three hours a day.[8]

Colleges developed departments of physical education, most notably Harvard under Dudley Allen Sargent. By century's end, an ethic of sport as a means of developing manhood was firmly entrenched throughout higher education and beyond, most notably in the persons of Theodore Roosevelt and Henry Cabot Lodge. "There is a tendency to underestimate or overlook the need of the virile, masterful qualities of the heart and mind," Roosevelt wrote in 1890. "There is no better way of counteracting this tendency than by encouraging bodily exercise and especially sports which develop such qualities as courage, resolution, and endurance."[9]

The Duke of Wellington's apocryphal comment about the Battle of Waterloo being won on the playing fields of Eton is echoed in a quotation from Henry

Cabot Lodge: "The injuries that occurred on the playing field are part of the price which the English-speaking race has paid for being world-conquerors."[10]

This emphasis on physical activity was not exclusive to men. In 1865, one of the board of governors of Vassar wrote in the college's first prospectus, "Good health is, in the first place, essential to success in study. A suitable portion of each day is set aside for physical exercise and every young lady is required to observe it as one of her duties."[11]

This says something about Vassar's status in American society, according to Boutilier and San Giovanni. Upper-crust sports were a form of conspicuous consumption, hailed as an art form in which those of lesser "breeding" had neither the time nor the money for participation.[12]

Women were encouraged to partake in physical activity as a way of staying healthy—healthy enough to bear children, specifically. This was fairly revolutionary by Victorian standards on both sides of the Atlantic. According to Reet Howell, "Women in the Victorian period were not to exert themselves in any way, and any vigorous physical activity was unthinkable. It was believed that injuries could result from vigorous activity, and doctors warned particularly of injury to the reproductive organs because it would seriously affect motherhood."[13]

For women of a certain social class, "gymnastics" was required as a way of staying fit for childbirth and maintaining the race's health, and participating in a bit of sport. Bicycling, tennis, and walking are all noted as acceptable activities for 19th-century women.[14]

As women's colleges took root and education for women became socially acceptable in itself, sports developed as well. Ellen Gerber describes three stages of sports development: Curricular sports, or gymnastics, evolved into intramural competitions in basketball, field hockey, baseball, and other sports that can be played between classes. They would then develop into extramural sports—but not until later.[15]

While physical education was becoming a discipline, sports were becoming an obsession. James Elkins, superintendent of the Boston, Concord, and Montreal railroad, brought up the idea of a regatta with James Whiton of the Yale Boat Club in 1851. (Whiton later became the first Ph.D. in America.) He offered to pay all the bills for a race between Yale and Harvard at Lake Winnipesaukee, where a new resort hotel had been built.[16]

It ended up being an eight-day affair in 1852, with very little training going on for either team except for the Harvard team abstaining from pastries. Amid much gambling, and for the prize of a silver plate, Harvard won the actual race. In 1855, the two universities raced each other again, with Harvard again prevailing. However, the Yale team protested the race because Harvard used a graduate student as its coxswain—the same man who had coxed the 1852 winning crew.

Thus, as many others have pointed out, virtually all the ills of college sports were present at the beginning: External corporations were using college sports to advertise their own services; teams were bending the rules on using academically eligible athletes; and everyone was gambling on everything. And colleges were trying to set up their own competitions that were somehow distinct from and purer than "professional" matches.

In this way, though, commercialized sports hijacked the idea of friendly, "amateur" competition in this country. Colleges began training athletes in earnest for competitions that by century's end were attracting thousands of spectators, and of course were accusing each other of under-the table payments, recruiting athletes off the street without forcing them to go to class, and committing all the other sins for which they are now criticized.

Amateurism in sport has a curious history. It is a British concept, drawn from the notion that manly qualities were inherited rather than being "the fruit of individually acquired merits."

The leisure time needed to pursue recreational sport was a mark of the gentry, while activities "associated with making a living" were thought to be inferior, the mark of a tradesman.[17] In Britain, the ideal of amateurism went into decline following the Britons' defeat in the Boer War in present-day South Africa. The lack of expertise and fitness that denotes the amateur athlete does not hold up well in war according to George C. Broderick, warden of Merton College, Oxford: "The English gentleman is no dandy and no coward, but he is an amateur born and bred, with an amateur's lack of training."[18]

However, the idea was eagerly embraced by American colleges in the last two decades of the 19th century, when college administrators took over rowing and football teams from student groups. Following the Civil War, college students began playing baseball and experimenting with the British sports of soccer (then known as "association football") and rugby in addition to rowing. These teams were generally student-led and managed, as had been the case in Great Britain.

When representatives of different colleges could agree on rules, they began having competitions. Princeton and what would become known as Rutgers organized the first game in 1869, and teams from the two schools met in New Brunswick. Only a hundred people showed up to see Rutgers defeat Princeton 8-0, but this was the start of a major obsession.

Not at first, though. In 1876, a group of Cornell students who had been playing football among themselves were challenged to a game against Michigan in Cleveland. As Mark Bernstein recounts in *Football: The Ivy League Origins of an American Obsession*, the president of Cornell, Andrew D. White, forbade it. "I will not permit thirty men to travel 400 miles to agitate a bag of wind."[19]

As Harvard, Yale, and other institutions began agreeing to general sets of rules for the field of play, though, the sport quickly became a spectacle—first in the Northeast, and spreading to larger universities throughout the country during the early years of the 20th century. Bernstein quotes a *New York Times* account of an 1877 game in New York between Princeton and Yale: "The hour set down for the game was 2 o'clock, and at that time the two rickety shanties provided for spectators were crowded with comely young women and portly old gentlemen, who together with innumerable young men with short hair and canes, and Scotch terriers, viewed the game from the beginning to the close, and expressed their interest in every new phase of the contest."[20]

African-American men were sprinkled on a handful of rosters in Northern colleges in the early days of football, and historically black colleges and universities began sponsoring intercollegiate sports of their own in the 1890s. Monroe Little cites the founding of an intercollegiate athletics council at Howard University as a major step in organized college sports, and says baseball was a dominant sport until football took hold in the 1920s.[21]

By the 1890s, the Yale-Princeton game at Manhattan Field in Harlem was the start of the winter social season, and all of New York was draped in school colors, according to Bernstein. The spectacle did not attract just alumni of Yale or Princeton, but "nearly every man who had ever been within hailing distance of a college diploma."[22]

The commercial potential of successful teams was impossible to miss. The University of Chicago hired Amos Alonzo Stagg to, in the words of its president, "develop teams which we can send around the country and knock out all the colleges. We will give them a palace car and a vacation, too."[23]

COMPETITION VERSUS PARTICIPATION

Dudley Allen Sargent, despite his enthusiasm for athleticism, had deep misgivings about "varsity" sport, particularly football:

> In consequences of the popular enthusiasm and the wide public interest in athletics, a large number of young men upon entering college are filled with the ambition to become athletes and get on university athletic teams. In many cases the zeal of these young men is greatly in excess of their abilities, and in their efforts to get into university form and keep pace with the stars, they often do themselves injury. In football especially a great deal of raw material is used as a temporary battering ram, or made to furnish a wall of temporary resistance to develop the defensive or attacking power of the more-stalwart rushers.
>
> The coaches cannot afford to use their time and energy in developing men, for their business is to develop football players; so they are anxious to weed out the weak ones, that they may give their undivided attention to the most promising candidates.[24]

Sargent's contrast between "developing men" and "developing football players" sums up the tension between advocates of physical education and those of athletics, though one might think them natural allies. Syracuse's rowing coach, James A. Ten Eyck, summarizes the coach's perspective in words that are true today:

> Who is it that gets "a hand" from the layman at the finish line? No thought is given to the losers, it is all for the victors, and no small boys are anxious to tote grips and satchels for losers, but hang close to the heels of their heroes. It is human nature, and things will not change until perhaps that far-off millennium is reached. The spirit which permeates the men in charge and the men participating, is to win by "all honourable means." There is no getting behind the fact that races are entered to be won. The men who make the crew do not endure the long months of training or subject themselves to the discipline of crew life just for the fun of the thing.[25]

Yet women's sports developed precisely for the "fun"—and education—of the thing. Stanford and Berkeley faced off in the first women's interscholastic basketball game in 1896, but female physical education teachers held and taught a deep suspicion of emphasizing competition. Senda Berenson, who invented the women's version of basketball at the same time as (and not far from) James Naismith developed the men's, sounds faintly amazed in a 1942 memoir recalling the first contest among her students at Smith College:

> We thought that just a few students would come out to watch, but the whole college with class colors and banners turned out. They filled the broad balcony.... They stood along the walls.... Except for the fact that we had nine on a side, we played the men's rules. The cheering and screaming... was a high pitched sound I do believe no one had ever heard before.... The next day the local paper [had] a lurid description that must have made the staid citizens of the Valley wonder whether Sophia Smith had been wise to found a college in which young women might receive an education equal to that accorded to young men.[26]

Basketball became the major sport and the font of most controversies in women's sports early on. Berenson published the first official rulebook for women in 1892, and on the far coast, the University of California at Berkeley launched the first team to take on rivals from other institutions.[27] After playing girls' schools in San Francisco, the Berkeley team played the first-ever intercollegiate game in 1896 against Stanford University, losing 2-1. Berkeley refused to play at Stanford or in front of "a mixed audience." "Playing in the open, before a lot of college men... [would] be lowering a certain standard of womanhood."[28] Later that year, the University of Washington's women's team competed against Ellensburg Normal School for Women, which is now Eastern Washington University.

But many women, especially physical education teachers, were extraordinarily suspicious of interscholastic or intercollegiate sports. As Karen Kenny puts it:

Extramural forms of competitions were introduced as an effort to stimulate a general interest in sports. Intercollegiate competition existed as a questionable endeavor during the final decade of the nineteenth century, particularly because it was felt that the strain placed upon the players would be too great. Among other reasons, it was thought that the tendency would be to narrow, rather than to increase, the number of players participating by raising the standards of play and thus discouraging less-expert players.[29]

This attitude was a blend of two beliefs: first, that women could not handle the rigors of male-style sports. "Girls are not suited for the same athletic program as boys," wrote Ethel Perrin of the National Amateur Athletic Federation in 1928. "Under prolonged and intense physical strain, a girl goes to pieces nervously. A boy may be physically so weak that he hasn't the strength to smash a creampuff but he still has the 'will' to play. A girl is the opposite."[30]

The second belief was that there was something inherently wrong with the way men were conducting intercollegiate sports. "We must guard carefully the chances for character training, not allowing a passion for superior technique to blind us to these more worthwhile efforts," wrote Mabel Lee in 1930. "The field of men's athletics is full of sorry instances of this mad worship at the shrine of technique. Now that women's athletics are developing so rapidly all over our land, let us caution all our leaders to hold fast to the ideals of worthy citizenship even if at the expense of fine technique."[31]

The participatory aims of women's sport were woven into every governing organization, every physical education meeting, and every mission statement for college sporting organizations from the late 19th century until 1982, when the National Collegiate Athletic Association (NCAA) took over women's sports and the Association of Intercollegiate Athletics for Women dissolved.

The NCAA was formed out of a reaction to an entirely different set of issues, namely, that football players were dying on the field in droves. In October 1905, Roosevelt summoned the presidents of Harvard, Yale, and Princeton to the White House to ask them to do something about the brutal style of play in college football, but unlike the commonly accepted history, he did not ask them to ban the sport.[32] Two months later, representatives of 61 colleges met in New York to form the Intercollegiate Athletic Association of the United States, which the following year changed its name to the National Collegiate Athletic Association.[33]

School and college sports were organized into formal associations such as the NCAA in the early decades of the 20th century, espousing similar values but developing very different models. Men's conferences and associations pronounced themselves dedicated to amateur sports and the educational development of what would be called "student-athletes" some decades later, but they had no power to back up the rules, and the incentives to cheat were too high for opportunists to be deterred.

In the early 1920s, colleges across the country began building megalithic stadiums, often named Memorial Stadium in remembrance of students who had died in World War I. College football, especially, as a focal point of campus life began spreading far beyond the elite Northeastern institutions, even to tiny colleges such as Centre in Kentucky and the University of the South at Sewanee, Tennessee, both of which had dominant barnstorming football teams in the 1920s. This was the age of the first generation of college athletes as folk heroes. The amateur code was not exactly an issue for the demigods of the gridiron. Jess Neely, a star at Vanderbilt, played alternate weekends up the road at Sewanee.[34]

In 1929, the Carnegie Foundation published Bulletin 23, the first systematic critique of college athletics and its relationship to educational goals. Its goal, in the words of the foundation's president Henry S. Pritchett, was to ask, "What relation has this astonishing athletic display to the work of an intellectual agency like a university?" and "How do students, devoted to study, find either the time or the money to stage so costly a performance?"[35]

Pritchett places the university's role in "the development of the intellectual life" at odds with its function as "an agency to promote business, industry, journalism, salesmanship, and organized athletics on an extensive basis." Howard J. Savage, the principal author of the bulletin, is heavily critical of the expenses universities incurred to mount big-time football programs, noting especially the "extravagance on special personnel, including budgets for coaches, publicity agents and expenses of newspapermen, and the fictitious exaggeration of the importance of athletics, especially football."[36]

Sport was still a huge part of undergraduate life at the time of the Carnegie study. According to the bulletin, between 18 and 25 percent of the student body at 112 institutions studied were varsity athletes, and as many as 63 percent of students participated in intramural sports.[37]

Moreover, two-thirds of the colleges practiced athletic recruiting in some form, as well as "soliciting and subsidizing" athletes by means of athletics scholarships. However, researchers found that despite the beliefs of alumni, enrollments did not fluctuate based on how sports teams did, and that participating in athletics constituted a "lack of intellectual challenge to the young and alert mind" and "fail[ed] to contribute appreciably to morals and conduct."[38]

Many educators at the time complained that extracurricular activities of every type, be they fraternities or sports teams, were dumbing down the undergraduate experience. At Howard University's commencement in 1930, W.E.B. DuBois complained that "our college man today, is, on the average, a man untouched by real culture. He deliberately surrenders to selfish and even silly ideals, swarming into semi-professional athletics and Greek-letter societies, and affecting to despise scholarship and the hard grind of study and research."[39]

PROFESSIONALIZATION OF AMATEUR SPORT

In the years after World War II, controversies over college sports mushroomed. The debate over whether athletes should be paid became a national controversy that propelled the NCAA into the business of enforcing its rules; colleges discovered how to make money from radio and television broadcasts, prompting the NCAA to get involved in that, too; and gambling scandals threatened the very survival of college basketball.

Meanwhile, the elite Northeastern colleges opted out of big-time football and formed the Ivy League, and the University of Chicago and a host of other institutions dropped football altogether.

Public debates over whether colleges ought to be awarding athletes scholarships and what were then known as "subsidies" had gotten truly tawdry after World War II. Southern schools such as Georgia Tech and Louisiana State had long sworn by the practice, whereas members of the Big 10 pronounced themselves above such outright bribery and, in the words of one University of Minnesota official, "The only thing we do for any athlete is to procure him a part-time job at a recognized business in Minneapolis or St. Paul."[40]

During this time, recruiting had become a fine art. Colleges had sent many of their football coaches into the military to coach at training centers. Murray Sperber tells the story of Bear Bryant, en route to his first collegiate head-coaching job at Maryland, forswearing recruiting in favor of marching his North Carolina Pre-Flight Training Center squad straight up to College Park, enrolling them, and putting them out on the field within a week.[41]

Controversies over bribery prompted a group of officials from conferences across the country to meet in 1946 in Chicago to come up with a 12-point code of ethics for college athletics. The Big 10's powerful commissioner, Kenneth "Tug" Wilson, urged reporters to call it the "Purity Code," but he settled for the "Sanity Code" when the press proved too skeptical.[42]

According to the NCAA's official history, by Jack Falla, the Sanity Code contained the following principles, ensuring that athletes be held to the same academic standards as the student body; the awarding of financial aid "on the basis of qualifications of which athletic ability is not one"; and a policy of recruiting that basically prohibits a coach or anyone representing a member institution from "soliciting attendance" of any prospective student with the offer of financial aid or equivalent inducement.[43]

The code was adopted in 1948, along with a three-member "Constitutional Compliance Committee" to hear cases. The following year, complaints were lodged against seven institutions—Boston College, Villanova, the Citadel, Maryland, Virginia Military Institute, Virginia Tech, and the University of Virginia.[44] The entire membership voted on the fate of those schools at the 1950 convention.

However, the only penalty available to levy under the NCAA's rules was to kick members out altogether. Motions to do so against the "Sinful Seven" passed 111-93, failing to muster the two-thirds majority needed to ratify them.[45] This prompted the association to come up with the rules-enforcement system that is still in place today: a "Committee on Infractions" composed of representatives of member institutions to act as a tribunal, a range of penalties from probation and public censure to the suspension of a team, and, somewhat later, a team of staff members to function as field investigators when complaints were made.

Just in time, too. College basketball was rocked in the early 1950s by point-shaving scandals originating with the gamblers in the corridors of Madison Square Garden and involving Long Island University, City College of New York, New York University, Manhattan College, Bradley University, and the University of Kentucky. The Wildcats, under their legendary coach Adolph Rupp, were hit particularly hard by the new enforcement mechanism, earning the NCAA's first "death penalty" for the 1952–53 season.[46]

Other reform efforts failed miserably. The NCAA tried several times to take over the bowl-game system but ultimately resigned itself to "certifying" bowls and requiring them to pay most of their money to participating institutions. Giving the bowls—which were then and are still put on by local tourism authorities to promote holiday vacationing among sports fans—that level of license set the stage for current battles over postseason play in top-level football.

The evolution of rules enforcement and the subsequent thickening of the NCAA rulebook were emblematic of the organization's transformation into a bureaucracy. Walter Byers, Wilson's right-hand man at the Big 10, was hired as the NCAA's first executive director in 1951, and the 29-year-old proceeded to start the association's first headquarters in the Kansas City suburbs.

Byers's early years at the NCAA were spent not just building the bureaucracy, but building the revenue streams to support it. The association had begun televising a "Game of the Week" in the late 1940s and forced the Universities of Notre Dame and Pennsylvania to abandon their own, independent television deals.[47] The NCAA also had started its own men's basketball tournament to compete with the much-older National Invitation Tournament (NIT) in the mid-1930s, and by the mid-1950s had supplanted the NIT as the national championship in the public's eye.

Falla's official history puts the association's annual revenue at $100,000 in 1947. By 1967 that figure had risen to $500,000, and topped $1 million only five years later. By 1981, the NCAA was making $22 million a year.[48]

The biggest names in college sports were the ones appearing on television, but the NCAA was expanding its offerings for what it called the "college division," which consisted of the institutions in what in the 1970s became Divisions II and III. The first college-division basketball tournament and cross-country championship were held in 1957, with track and other sports following in the 1960s.

Also during the 1960s and 1970s, the NCAA began experimenting with national academic standards for incoming athletes in an effort to head off persistent public criticism that college athletes were making a sham of their education. First came the "1.6 rule," in 1966, which required colleges to admit only those athletes whose high school grades suggested that they would be able to achieve at least a 1.6 grade-point average, or a C-minus, at the college they attended.[49]

At the time, the NCAA also forbade freshmen from competing in the "university" division, and most universities had "frosh" teams for prize recruits. The University of Kansas has pictures of Wilt Chamberlain and Jim Ryun, as freshmen already among the best in their sports in the world, wearing "Kansas Frosh" uniforms.

In 1971 the NCAA abandoned freshman ineligibility as a cost-saving measure, and in 1973 they got rid of the 1.6 rule in favor of the "2.0 rule," which simply set a floor of 2.0 for high school grade-point averages. John Watterson points out that this had the effect of allowing many more athletes with poor academic preparation in high school into college, especially black athletes from rural areas.[50]

In 1970, the University of Southern California brought its team to Tuscaloosa and proceeded to whip the University of Alabama 42-21, largely behind the running of tailback Sam "Bam" Cunningham, the first black player to take the field against a white team in a major contest in the state of Alabama. Cunningham's 212-yard performance compelled Bryant to invite the Trojan into the Crimson Tide's locker room following the game and to tell his team, "Men, this is what a football player looks like." Fans in the South dubbed the game the "Brown vs. Board of Education of college football."

The debate over how colleges ought to subsidize athletes continued well into the 1970s. In 1952, the association passed its "Principle Concerning Financial Aid," which stated that "any college athlete who receives financial assistance other than that administered by his institution, shall not be eligible for intercollegiate competition; provided, however, that this principle shall have no application to assistance received from anyone upon whom the athlete is naturally or legally dependent."[51]

At that point, scholarships consisted of room, board, books, tuition, and what was known with a wink and a nod as "laundry money," although that went out as a cost-saving measure in the early 1970s. In 1976, the NCAA convention voted on limiting the value of Division I scholarships to room, board, and books, with everything else determined by the athlete's need, but that measure failed 120–112.[52]

COLONIZATION OF WOMEN'S SPORT, 1967–82

At various times through the 20th century, competitive women's sports were very popular indeed. Barnstorming teams of basketball players traveled the country during the middle of the century. At historically black colleges in the South, such as the Tuskegee Institute and Tennessee State University, strong women's basketball and track squads were commonplace. Tennessee State's Tigerbelle sprinters, coached by Ed Temple, sent Wilma Rudolph, Wyomia Tyus, and others to the 1964 Olympics in Tokyo. Industrial leagues allowed women to compete professionally, albeit for pittances, in softball, basketball, volleyball, and other sports.

Within mainstream white colleges, though, intercollegiate sports for women were officially disdained for the most part through most of the century, and until the 1970s few women had a chance to compete in anything except "Play Days," in which female physical education (P.E.) majors from one college visited another and spent a day socializing and competing in various events—but never one school against another: Teams were chosen up on the spot.

This reflected the philosophy of female physical educators, summed up best as "a girl for every sport, and a sport for every girl." They viewed elite, Olympic-style competition with suspicion because it placed too much emphasis on the few individuals who had real athletic talent, on winning rather than developing skills and providing a rewarding experience for all.

By the mid-1960s, however, those P.E. teachers realized that varsity-style sports for women were coming, either from the NCAA or from leagues completely outside higher education. "It was a function of a number of things," says Donna Lopiano, a star athlete in the 1960s who is now executive director of the Women's Sports Foundation.[53] "If we [women physical educators] don't do it, the NCAA will." Another pressure point was the [Amateur Athletic Union] and so many outside opportunities. "For instance, I was playing almost semipro softball in the 1960s with the Raybestos Brakettes, and there were outside amateur teams in volleyball and basketball.

"The question was not whether women were going to play in national championships, at a high level, but whether it was going to happen in educational sport or outside of it."

In an attempt to control the destiny of women in sports, the Division of Girl's and Women's Sports of the American Association of Health, Physical Education, and Recreation empaneled the Commission on Intercollegiate Athletics for Women (CIAW), with the following warning:

> Although some women may be physiologically stronger than some men, research has shown that women will be at a physiological disadvantage in some areas of sport. Sports which depend largely on strength and endurance give the man a decided advantage. Therefore, unless women compete against women, an unequal contest results. For these reasons, as well as for cultural considerations, women should not compete as a team against a men's team in an interscholastic or intercollegiate contests. This is not intended to prohibit mixed teams in such activities as volleyball, tennis, badminton, and golf when there are equal numbers of participants of both sexes. While positive experiences for the exceptional girl competitor may occur through participation in boys' or men's competitive

groups, these instances are rare and should be judged acceptable only as
an interim procedure for use until girls' programs can be initiated.[54]

The CIAW, formed in 1967, evolved into the Association for Intercollegiate
Athletics for Women (AIAW) in 1972. With 275 charter members, the organization formed itself into local and regional bodies sponsoring their own
events as well as open-to-all national championships. The first such event,
a volleyball competition, featured an enormous range of types of colleges,
including Sul Ross State of Texas and the University of California at Los
Angeles. In fact, Sul Ross beat UCLA in the championship match.

Also in 1972 came the pivotal event in opening the doors of higher education, and certainly athletics, to women: the passage of Title IX of the Education Amendments of 1972. Modeled on Title VI of the Civil Rights Act of
1964, Title IX stated, "No person in the United States shall, on the basis of sex,
be excluded from participation in, be denied the benefits of, or be subjected to
discrimination under any education program or activity receiving Federal
financial assistance."[55]

The applicability of this new gender-equity law to sports was never even
mentioned during congressional hearings on the topic, except when Birch
Bayh, the Democratic senator from Indiana who co-sponsored the legislation,
assured one of his colleagues that the measure would not force colleges to put
women on football teams. However, athletic administrators quickly got the
message and, over the next few years, started a slew of sports programs for
women. They could not be considered equal to men's teams in any way, but
they offered women some of the first opportunities they had ever had to
develop their skills in an educational context.

According to the NCAA's records, in 1971–72 there were 29,977 women
competing in varsity collegiate sports. By 1976–77 that number had more
than doubled, to 62,886. The number of male athletes dropped from 170,384
in 1971–72 to 168,136 in 1976–77.[56]

The AIAW maintained very strict rules in comparison to the NCAA, as
a way of preserving the philosophy of sport in an educational context in
its organization. Coaches were not allowed to recruit off campus, although
they could conduct tryouts on campus. Athletes were given four years of
eligibility, with no possibility of redshirting, as permitted by the NCAA. And
perhaps strictest of all, they forbade athletic scholarships as part of their initial
rules.

That led to the first of several conflicts between the AIAW and Title IX, the
law that was supposed to promote sports and other educational opportunities
for women. Female tennis players at Marymount College and Broward
Community College in Florida sued the AIAW and assorted other entities in
1973 for forbidding scholarships when men were allowed to receive them.
The AIAW settled the case and changed its rules to avoid losing its members.[57]

When they were published in 1975, the U.S. Department of Health, Education, and Welfare's guidelines on Title IX in sports sowed the seeds of further conflicts. They specified that equal athletic opportunity must be available to members of both sexes in the following areas:

- selection of sports and levels of competition to "effectively accommodate the interests and abilities of members of both sexes"
- equipment and supplies
- scheduling games and practice time
- travel and per diems
- opportunity to receive coaching and academic tutoring
- assignment and compensation of coaches and tutors
- locker rooms, practice, and competitive facilities
- medical and training facilities and services
- housing and dining
- publicity[58]

In essence, the regulations pushed colleges toward adopting uniform policies for male and female athletes, the very situation that the AIAW was trying to avoid. The organization's leaders wanted the benefits accruing to men's teams—such as new uniforms, chartered transportation, and so on—but they wanted to nurture women's athletics to avoid the many problems that had beset men's programs for so many years.

"The women in the 60s were historians, students of what had happened in intercollegiate athletics," recalls Lopiano. "The one thing they all recognized was that men's sport had gotten to where it was because physical educators, male physical educators, had taken a hands-off approach and were saying, 'I don't want anything to do with that.' They were faced with repeating history."[59]

In the mid-1970s, many collegiate presidents began moving women's athletics programs out of physical education departments and into what were then men's athletics departments, much to the dismay of many women administrators.

"The program here in athletics was an outgrowth of that extramural-type program," one anonymous women administrator in the 1970s told a researcher.

> I think what started us actually doing anything about moving into "athletics" as such was a group of students in the early 1970s who said "We are world class and national class athletes. And when we are swimming in the summer, we are just as good as the guys and we get [the same competitive opportunities and benefits]. And now you're offering these guys scholarships to come to the university to swim and you're not even providing us with a program, much less offering us any scholarships." And it was those students who stirred up such a ruckus in the early 1970s. Then

the emphasis of Title IX started to come along in 1972. The combination
of the two got the attention of the administration in this school.[60]

The NCAA itself was taking more of an active interest in women's sports.
Letters and memoranda cited by Lopiano in her deposition for the AIAW's
subsequent lawsuit against the NCAA show Byers and his lieutenants making a
steady progression from being curious about the thought of women's national
championships to thinking (even before Title IX passed) that they might be
legally obligated to sponsor them to, by the mid-1970s, actively campaigning
an unenthusiastic membership to boost support for the NCAA starting its own
championships, undermining the AIAW's.

Lopiano and the rest of the AIAW saw this as an unabashed takeover
attempt. The NCAA had expanded its championships for smaller colleges to
disenfranchise the much-smaller National Association for Intercollegiate
Athletics (NAIA), she argues, and was in the process of wrapping up a 50-
year-old battle with the Amateur Athletic Union over control of bids for the
Olympics.

That was hardly the case, according to Chuck Neinas and Tom Jernstedt,
who were two of Byers's top assistants in the 1960s and 1970s, respectively.
Byers had "strong feelings about the school-college community, and more
specifically the NCAA, not being afforded representation within the U.S.
Olympic Committee commensurate with the breadth and depth of its programs,
specifically with regard to athletes, coaches, and facilities," says Jernstedt, still
an NCAA vice president and also president of the national governing body for
the sport of basketball. The debate over women's sports was completely separate from those battles, he says.[61]

The NCAA adopted an interesting combination of policies regarding
women's sports during this time. While deliberating whether to start its own
slate of championships, the association actively lobbied Congress to exclude
revenue-producing sports from Title IX (an amendment offered by Sen. John
Tower, Republican of Texas, which was deleted in a House-Senate conference
committee in 1975). When that did not work, the NCAA sued the Department
of Health, Education, and Welfare, claiming it lacked authority to govern
intercollegiate athletic programs. A federal judge dismissed the complaint,
saying the association lacked the legal standing to sue the government.

The 1975 regulations specified that colleges had three years to come into
compliance with them. College officials protested mightily that they didn't
understand what was required of them, and after a few investigations, some
case studies and field visits, and numerous complaints, HEW released a
"policy clarification" in 1979 that expanded the 1975 Title IX regulation in
several ways.[62] Most important, it split compliance with the law into three
separate sections.

First were rules governing how a college could verify that it was offering enough sports opportunities to women. This section consisted of what

became known as the "three-part test," allowing colleges to come into compliance in any of three ways:

1. Whether intercollegiate-level participation opportunities for male and female students are provided in numbers substantially proportionate to their respective enrollments (a condition that becomes known as "substantial proportionality"); or
2. Where the members of one sex have been and are underrepresented among intercollegiate athletes, whether the institution can show a history and continuing practice of program expansion which is demonstrably responsive to the developing interest and abilities of the members of that sex; or
3. Where the members of one sex are underrepresented among intercollegiate athletes, and the institution cannot show a continuing practice of program expansion such as that cited above, whether it can be demonstrated that the interests and abilities of the members of that sex have been fully and effectively accommodated by the present program.

The "substantial proportionality" test is a threshold test in many other areas of civil-rights law. If investigators for what is now the Education Department's Office for Civil Rights are examining whether a local school district is discriminating against members of minority groups, they first look at whether the demographics of the district mirror the demographics of the local population as a whole. If they don't, it doesn't mean that the district is necessarily discriminating, but it sends investigators to evaluate other factors.

Bernice (Bunny Sandler), who campaigned for Title IX and its regulations on behalf of the Women's Equity Action League, says the three-part test was proposed by officials from big-time football institutions as a counteroffer to women's groups, which wanted the regulations to specify that athletics departments had to be 50-50.[63] Football officials who were active at the time vehemently deny that, so nobody is sure where the three-part test came from.

The second section of the 1979 interpretation specified that colleges needed to offer athletic scholarships to women in the same proportion that female athletes were represented in an athletics department, so that colleges couldn't reserve sports-related financial aid for men's teams. The third section restated the remaining elements of an athletics department that investigators would evaluate for equity in a format that became known as the "laundry list."

Lawyers for women's groups express amazement that the government took the better part of a decade to issue rules and regulations for Title IX, noting that the regulatory process of implementing the Civil Rights Act of 1964 was a matter of a few years, and schools and colleges were required to comply with that immediately.

The net effect of the struggles at the federal level translated into colleges converting thousands of women's club and intramural programs into varsity sports, often increasing the number of students playing sports by a third or more, but giving them neither the funds nor the opportunities to match what men were receiving.

Sylvia Rhyne Hatchell, then the women's basketball coach at Francis Marion College and now the highly paid coach at the University of North Carolina, marched out of her office recently with a mop and rubber gloves to fix a leak. It's how she operated in the early days of her career and of Title IX, she says. "When I was at Francis Marion, I'd sweep the floor, wash the uniforms, and we'd always drive the bus," Hatchell says. "You couldn't be too good to do something."[64]

Also in 1979, Byers finally got enough votes together for his members to agree to sponsor women's championships in Divisions II and III sports for the 1980–81 academic year. A year later, they approved women's events for Division I, beginning in 1981–82. The NCAA could afford to fly teams to central locations for championships, relieving athletics departments of significant financial burdens.

The AIAW went out of business and sued the NCAA, claiming that it had formed a monopoly over women's sports. Its complaint was denied, and women's programs were fully absorbed into the larger organization. Coaches were thrown into recruiting wars and women's teams into a championship model completely different from the AIAW's.

In the aftermath, female officials say their particular way of governing athletics, by focusing on participation, education, and collegiality, was lost in favor of emphasizing athletic excellence. NCAA officials take credit for boosting the status of women's sports, giving them publicity far beyond anything the AIAW could have done. But many AIAW officials, who are now retired or nearing retirement, still hold grudges.

RISING STAKES OF INTERCOLLEGIATE
ATHLETICS, 1984–PRESENT

From the 1950s to the early 1980s, the NCAA controlled the business side of college sports. It owned the evermore profitable men's basketball tournament, expanding it to 48 teams in 1975 and becoming a national phenomenon when Larry Bird and the Indiana State Sycamores took on Magic Johnson and the Michigan State Spartans in 1979. For football, the NCAA still offered only a small number of national "Games of the Week" to fans on television.

The strict controls on televised contests had been designed to keep fans in the stands at regular-season games, which was where individual, big-time institutions made most of their money. Following World War II, some college and professional teams had seen attendance drop during broadcast games, prompting fears about retaining fans for both NCAA and National Football League teams.[65]

By the 1980s, though, the market had changed. Cable television was in its infancy but expanding quickly enough that stations were eager for programming. College football and basketball were cheap ways to begin building audiences, particularly for a small network based in Bristol, Connecticut.

In 1984, executives at ESPN saw an opportunity to put on the air an otherwise unremarkable game between Vanderbilt and the powerful University of Georgia. They called Roy F. Kramer, then Vanderbilt's athletics director.

"I had never heard of ESPN," Mr. Kramer said in a 2000 interview. "I don't know if anybody saw the game, but that was our very first TV negotiation. I think they put a banner down in the end zone, and that was about it.

"I sold the game for $7,500, and I didn't split any money," he said, chuckling. "Georgia tried to get 50 percent of it, and Vince Dooley probably still thinks I owe him."

Mr. Dooley, Georgia's former athletics director, got a laugh out of that story. He doesn't remember the game, but he has his own memories of Mr. Kramer's opportunism. ESPN had offered Mr. Dooley's program $100,000 to televise its game against Clemson University when both teams were competing for the national championship. This time, rather than let Georgia keep the money, Mr. Kramer—by then the Southeastern Conference's commissioner—"wanted to split that up among everybody in the conference," Mr. Dooley recalls.[66]

The country's largest football programs saw that they had the potential to strike their own television deals, and in 1983, the governing boards of the Universities of Georgia and Oklahoma sued the NCAA, claiming its television policy violated federal anti-trust laws.

In 1984, the U.S. Supreme Court agreed, handing the NCAA what is still its worst-ever court loss. The television policy was dissolved, and the football powers in the Atlantic Coast, Southwest, and Southeastern Conferences, as well as major independent institutions such as Notre Dame, formed the College Football Association (CFA) as both a professional association and, more significant, as an entity to negotiate with television networks.

Many outsiders feared the group of colleges would withdraw from the NCAA and form its own "super division." But lacking the rest of the country's powerhouse athletics programs from the Big 10 and Pacific-10, the CFA was never close to doing so, and its officials denied any such intentions.

The NCAA still had a cash cow in the Division I men's basketball tournament, signing the first billion-dollar broadcast contract in sports history in 1991. The money from that enabled the association to continue expanding championships for men and women in all three divisions, as well as to implement a catastrophic-injury insurance program for athletes. Those incentives prompted hundreds of small colleges to leave the NAIA in droves, despite a succession of NCAA moratoriums against new members.

In Division I, though, the Supreme Court decision redrew the economic landscape. The most prominent colleges were able to control the revenue streams for regular-season football television contracts, as well as access to the small number of lucrative bowl games and their own not-inconsiderable gate receipts. They could then invest those funds in larger stadiums, better weight rooms, and higher salaries for coaches, widening the gap with less prominent programs in other conferences.

The CFA held together until the early 1990s, injured first by the defection of Notre Dame in 1991 and then mortally wounded by the Southeastern Conference's (SEC) withdrawal in 1994 to sign its own contract with CBS Sports to broadcast regular-season football.

That decision touched off the first round of conference shakeups. Except for Notre Dame, which had signed its own exclusive broadcast deal with NBC Sports, colleges needed some form of conference affiliation to guarantee television income and access to bowl games, which did business exclusively with conference offices. So the University of Miami joined the Big East Conference, and the Atlantic Coast Conference picked up Florida State University.

Two of the older, storied conferences, the Big 8 and the Southwest, found themselves in unenviable positions, with powerhouse programs like the Universities of Nebraska and Texas but comparatively few television stations. So athletics directors orchestrated a merger, with Texas, Texas A&M University, Baylor University (brought along to secure the support of Texas's governor, Ann Richards, an alumna), and Texas Tech University joining the Big 8 to form the Big 12.

These moves have created three reasonably distinct tiers in big-time college sports. The top six Division IA conferences have lucrative television deals for both football and basketball, as well as bowl tie-ins and the majority of bids to what is now a 64-team basketball tournament. Because the NCAA distributes money based on both teams' performance in the tournament and on the number of teams and scholarships offered by athletics departments, the six "equity" leagues—the Atlantic Coast, Big East, Big 10, Big 12, Pacific-10, and Southeastern Conferences—and their commissioners have become the market movers in college sports.

The second tier consists of Division IA members outside the Bowl Championship Series (BCS), such as the rump of the Southwest Conference abandoned by the four universities that joined the Big 10. Rice, Southern Methodist, and Texas Christian Universities all joined the Western Athletic Conference to form an ungainly 16-team alignment that at times stretched from Ruston, Louisiana, to Honolulu. The University of Houston joined (and eventually was joined by Texas Christian in) Conference USA, which has members scattered across Texas, Louisiana, Alabama, Florida, Tennessee, North Carolina, Kentucky, Ohio, Illinois, Wisconsin, Missouri, and Mississippi. In 2005, Conference USA included Central Florida, East Carolina, Houston, Marshall, Memphis, Rice, Southern Methodist, Southern Mississippi, Tulane, Tulsa, University of Alabama–Birmingham, and University of Texas–El Paso.

These colleges have essentially no chance of generating enough money through television contracts, gate receipts, or other sources to cover the costs of operating their athletics programs. Nor do members of the third tier, which consists of colleges with Division IAA football teams and members of Division IAAA, with no football at all. Together, they form what Patty Viverito, commissioner of the Missouri Valley Conference, calls the ALAMO conferences— "A Loose Association of Monetary Outcasts."[67] They depend on general funds from their universities, student fees, and state appropriations to keep their athletics programs in business.

All three tiers have been marked by scandal throughout the 1980s and 1990s, including point-shaving scandals, cases of outright bribery of prospective athletes, and academic fraud. The NCAA has made various attempts to improve the academic standing of athletes by raising national minimum academic requirements for athletic eligibility, but these have been controversial and as yet have not produced a noticeable jump in the graduation rates—that is, the educational outcomes—of athletes in high-profile sports.

In 1982, the NCAA passed a rule known as Proposition 48, which required athletes to post a minimum 700 on the SAT and earn a grade-point average of 2.5. In a move deplored by basketball coaches, who believed it would drive black athletes out of Division I sports, the NCAA implemented "Prop-48" in 1986 and toughened its standards a decade later with Proposition 16.

The number of black athletes did indeed drop after the passage of Proposition 48, but it soon recovered. Graduation rates spiked for the first classes coming into college under the new rules but soon fell back to dismal levels. Of the class entering college in 1995–96, 43 percent of men's basketball players (including 35 percent of black players) and 52 percent of football players earned degrees within the next six years.[68]

Many Division I institutions established and even built new buildings for tutors for athletes during the 1990s. Though some of these "academic advisers" proved only too willing to help athletes find shortcuts in their classwork to stay eligible for their fieldwork, the majority have taken athletes from widely varying academic backgrounds and taught them how to be students and to do the work expected for college students. They have helped identify learning disabilities—although, again, not without abuse—and have formed a bridge between academic departments and athletics ones.

The proliferation of academic counselors is only one facet of the growing professionalization and, indeed, bureaucratization of college sports. Even as the NCAA has expanded to a staff of over 250, athletics departments themselves are beginning to look like mid-sized corporations. Major colleges have staffs of full-time employees as well as part-timers and graduate students to supervise compliance with NCAA rules. They have even larger staffs of marketing professionals and media-relations staffers, who used to be known as Sports Information Directors and, before that, Sports Publicity Directors. Professional auxiliary employees, such as trainers and strength coaches, have become bona fide professionals requiring certification and extensive educational work to work with college athletes.

And really for the first time, colleges began taking Title IX seriously in the mid-1990s. In a 1992 decision unrelated to athletics, *Franklin v. Gwinnett County*, the Supreme Court ruled that plaintiffs in Title IX cases could sue for monetary damages. That prompted female athletes, upset about the sports being offered and the quality of what experiences were available at their institutions, to threaten or initiate lawsuits to force expansion of athletic opportunities and to obtain treatment equitable or equal to men's teams.

Texas, Auburn University, Louisiana State University, and Colorado State University were among the institutions that settled such cases, often by starting new women's teams and restoring others that had been cut. Brown University, however, chose to challenge the Education Department's Title IX guidelines and especially the three-part test in a lawsuit filed by Amy Cohen and several other female athletes.[69]

Cohen was a gymnast at Brown when the university elected to demote two women's sports, gymnastics and volleyball, from varsity to club status as a cost-cutting measure. Brown officials also demoted two men's sports for the same reasons. Cohen and eight other plaintiffs represented by Trial Lawyers for Public Justice sued, claiming that the university failed to meet the three-part test: Not only did it not meet the substantial proportionality standard, but by dropping women's teams it clearly failed to demonstrate either a history of expanding opportunities for women or that it was effectively accommodating the interests of women undergraduates. Brown's counter was that Title IX guidelines violated the institutional autonomy to which colleges were entitled, and that it was meeting the other two tests.[70]

However, Cohen et al. prevailed at every level in the courts, until the Supreme Court decided not to hear the case. The Third Circuit wrote a ringing defense of the Education Department's standards that, along with a 1996 "policy clarification" from the department,[71] led many athletics directors and college attorneys to conclude that the first test was the surest and possibly most cost-effective means of complying with Title IX. Many of them have chosen to do so by limiting the number of male athletes on nonrevenue-producing teams while recruiting as many women as possible.

This has caused an outcry among male athletes in those nonrevenue sports, especially wrestling and gymnastics, which already lost many teams during the recessions of the 1970s and 1980s. Numerous men have sued colleges under Title IX saying their teams were dropped solely because of the gender of the participants, but no appeals court has been sympathetic. Thus far, they have deferred to the Education Department's ability to set its own guidelines. According to Judge Cynthia Holcomb Hall of the U.S. Court of Appeals for the Ninth Circuit, "Title IX has enhanced, and will continue to enhance, women's opportunities to enjoy the thrill of victory, the agony of defeat, and the many tangible benefits that flow from just being given a chance to participate in intercollegiate athletics."[72]

Wrestlers got their hopes up following the 2000 election, when George W. Bush said that education policy shouldn't include quotas, a vague reference to the proportionality test. However, the Education Department in 2003 set aside recommendations for changes to the law that came out of a blue-ribbon panel of college administrators. Fearing the political fallout from anything that could be seen as slowing the progress made by girls and women in sports, the department came out with an endorsement of current standards and a promise to enforce them vigorously and consistently across the country.

During the 1990s, the NCAA's Division II grew somewhat and Division III grew staggeringly fast, making the latter—with nearly 400 members—by far the largest sector of the NCAA's membership. The new members came mostly from the NAIA, as the NCAA continued to expand its subsidized championships program and insurance offerings for athletes.

This is not to say that either division gained any political clout within the association. In 1997 the NCAA moved to a federated system in which each division governs itself. Divisions II and III vote on policies and rules at the association's annual convention, whereas a hierarchy of committees and councils consisting of college officials votes on Division I issues.

Also losing ground throughout the 1980s and 1990s were the athletics programs of historically black colleges and universities. Facing budgetary shortfalls along with the rest of their universities, sports programs have long since lost their relevance as the best African-American athletes are now recruited heavily by mainstream institutions. However, many black-college football teams now compete in several "classic" football contests: Promoters in faraway cities, including Indianapolis and San Jose, invite prominent Southern black-college teams from places like Grambling State University in Louisiana and Florida A&M University to play games as part of a series of parties and events for the local African-American community. The better-run games generate funds for the athletics departments involved and have become major party weekends in the host cities.

INTERCOLLEGIATE ATHLETICS AND THE INDIVIDUAL ATHLETE

The second wave of conference realignments swept across the Division I map in 2003. The Atlantic Coast Conference acquired Boston College, the University of Miami, and Virginia Tech from the Big East, dooming the latter league to second-class status.

In 2004, the Bowl Championship Series (BCS) managed to save off public appeals for a playoff in Division IA football. The series consists of the six equity conferences and the Fiesta, Orange, Rose, and Sugar Bowls, which match the first- and second-place football teams according to a complex formula to determine a "true" national champion. The leagues outside the BCS won an important concession, though, by convincing the BCS to add a fifth game to its rotation, allowing a better chance for lower tier teams to sneak into the elite matchups.

The ACC's deal with Boston College, Miami, and Virginia Tech provided one of the first real tests of the NCAA's principal theme of the 1990s and early 2000s: that college presidents, not athletics departments, were in charge of college sports. This had been a step recommended by the high-profile Knight Foundation Commission on Intercollegiate Athletics, which published reports in 1991 and 2001 criticizing athletics departments for commercial excesses and neglect of academics.

As part of the NCAA's restructuring in 1997, it created governing boards consisting of campus CEOs for each division. The Division I Board of Directors, for example, is the final vote on any policy or rules change.

As of 2004, the presidents have not taken many decisive actions to address the problems of college sports. The ACC's decision to expand became public months before conference officials had a plan in place, and even once they did, the presidents of Duke University and North Carolina remained suspicious enough of the plan to vote against it. As statewide political pressure built on University of Virginia officials, the ACC was put in the embarrassing position of having to rescind informal invitations to Boston College and Syracuse University, pick up Virginia Tech in addition to Miami (the member it had sought all along), and then reinvite Boston College.

Presidents in some lower echelon leagues have not been so reticent to discuss sticky issues in academics and athletics. Several internal and external studies have shown that sports plays a much larger role than the public has thought in the admissions practices of Ivy League universities and the elite liberal arts colleges belonging to the New England Small College Athletic Conference (NESCAC). Athletes in both sets of colleges benefit from being on coaches' "preferred" lists sent to admissions offices, which reserve a certain number of slots in each incoming freshman class for athletes who would not have been able to get in otherwise.

Two influential studies by the Andrew W. Mellon Foundation, published as *The Game of Life* by William G. Bowen and James L. Shulman and *Reclaiming the Game* by Bowen and Sarah Levine [Princeton University Press, 2001 and 2003, respectively], also indicated that athletes at Ivy and NESCAC institutions tend to cluster in certain academic fields of study, primarily the social sciences. They also tend to have poorer academic records in college than their high school test scores and grades would indicate.

These facts have long been true at the sports factories, but that such disparities exist even at the nation's elite academic institutions came as a surprise to many observers. The Ivies do not make any appreciable revenue off their sports teams, and alumni and fans have long since stopped filling the Yale Bowl and other venues to cheer on football teams.

Yet large and strong athletics programs—Harvard has more varsity athletes than any university in the country, and Williams College dominates Division III—are part of the social fabric of most four-year colleges in this country, large and small. They are seen as being an essential component in establishing a college's legitimacy with the American public.

Christopher B. White raised money and cleared the way for Gardner-Webb University to rise into Division I of the NCAA while he was president there, noting that he wanted to get the college's game scores onto the ticker on ESPN, "like Duke and Harvard."

"We aspire to be like Davidson, Furman, and Wofford," Mr. White said, defending his actions in circumventing the college's honor code in 2001 to keep a star basketball player eligible. "Academically we're in their league, and athletically we want to be, too."

The fact that the president of a small Baptist college in the North Carolina piedmont feels this way explains why the stakes are so high everywhere. Winning teams create a mythology for themselves—so much that athletics officials are tempted to excesses that would be thought outrageous in other departments.

Mr. White helped create a campus brouhaha when he circumvented Gardner-Webb's honor code to allow a star basketball player to compete in the National Christian College Athletic Association tournament. He eventually lost his job in the scandal but was hired as president of Chowan College in North Carolina less than a year later.

Thus far, no one has come up with a way to, in the words of the NCAA's president, Myles Brand, "turn down the volume."

NOTES

1. "Sports in America: Rhode Island," untitled feature in *Sports Illustrated*, July 14, 2003, Vol. 99, No. 2, 42.

2. J. A. Mangan, *Athleticism in the Victorian and Edwardian Public School*, Cambridge University Press, 1981.

3. Clifford Putney, *Muscular Christianity: Manhood and Sports in Protestant America 1880–1920*, Harvard University Press, 2001, 20.

4. *Ibid.*, 22.

5. *Ibid.*, 26.

6. *Ibid.*, 29.

7. Donald J. Mrozek, *Sport and American Mentality, 1880–1910*, University of Tennessee Press, 1983, 38–39.

8. Cited in Mark F. Bernstein, *Football: The Ivy League Origins of an American Obsession*, University of Pennsylvania Press, 2001, 37.

9. *Ibid.*

10. Lodge, "Speech at the Alumni Dinner, Harvard Commencement, June 1896," in *Speeches and Addresses*, 239. Cited at Mrozek, 28.

11. Ellen Gerber, *The American Woman in Sport*, Reading, Mass.: Addison-Wesley Publishers, 1974, 51.

12. Mary A. Boutilier and Lucinda SanGiovanni, *The Sporting Women*, Champaign, Ill.: Human Kinetics Publishers, 1983, 33–34.

13. Reet Howell, "American Women, 1860–1880, Recreational Pursuits and Exercise" in *Her Story in Sport: A Historical Anthology of Women in Sport*, West Point: Leisure Press, 1982, Reet Howell, ed.

14. Mrozek, 141–42.

15. Gerber, 48.

16. Ronald A. Smith, *Sports and Freedom*, New York: Oxford University Press, 1988, 27–29.

17. Sack, Allen L. and Ellen Staurowsky, *College Athletes for Hire*, Westport, Conn.: Praeger Publishers, 1998, 15.

18. Sack, et al., 1998, 12.

19. *Princeton Alumni Weekly*, December 15, 1909, 6. Cited in Bernstein, 9.

20. Bernstein, 14.

21. Monroe H. Little, "The Extra-Curricular Activities of Black College Students 1868–1940," *Journal of Negro History*, Vol. 65, No. 2, Spring 1980, 143.

22. Bernstein, 42.

23. Sack, et al., 1998, 21.

24. Cited in Mrozek, 69.

25. Cited in Mrozek, 81.

26. *Her Story in Sport: A Historical Anthology of Women in Sport*, West Point: Leisure Press, 1982, Reet Howell, ed.

27. Joan Paul, "Heroines: Paving the Way" in Greta L. Cohen, *Women in Sport: Issues and Controversies*, Newbury Park, Ca.: Sage Publications, 1993, 28.

28. Cited in "The First Intercollegiate Contest for Women: Basketball, April 4, 1896," Lynne Emery, in Howell, *Her Story in Sport: A Historical Anthology of Women in Sport*, West Point: Leisure Press, 1982, Reet Howell, ed.

29. Karen Kenney, "The Realm of Sports and the Athletic Woman, 1850–1900," in Howell *Her Story in Sport: A Historical Anthology of Women in Sport*, West Point: Leisure Press, 1982, Reet Howell, ed.

30. Attributed to Ethel Perrin, National Amateur Athletic Federation, 1928, available at http://library.usask.ca/herstory/hockey.html.

31. Attributed to Mabel Lee, Director of Physical Education for Women at University of Nebraska, Lincoln, from a 1930 article titled "Sports and Games—an Educational Dynamic Force," available at http://library.usask.ca/herstory/hockey.html.

32. Watterson, 69.

33. *Ibid.*, 74–79.

34. Noted in 2001 interview with Roy F. Kramer, then commissioner of the Southeastern Conference and a former Vanderbilt athletics director.

35. Cited in "Athletics in American Colleges," W. H. Cowley, *Journal of Higher Education*, Vol. 1, No. 1., January 1930, 29–30. This was a summary of the Carnegie Commission report published, in the author's words, to "make for a more-widespread knowledge of the report's findings," given its being so "voluminous."

36. *Ibid.*, 31.

37. *Ibid.*, 32.

38. *Ibid.*, 34–35.

39. Cited in Harris, 140.

40. Cited in Murray A. Sperber, *Onward to Victory: The Crises that Shaped College Sport*, New York: Henry Holt Co., 1998, 181.

41. Sperber, 171.

42. Sperber, 174.

43. Jack Falla, *NCAA: The Voice of College Sports*, Mission, Kan: National Collegiate Athletic Association, 1981, 133.

44. Walter F. Byers, *Unsportsmanlike Conduct*, University of Michigan Press, 1995, 54.

45. Falla, 134.

46. Materials gathered from interviews for Welch Suggs, "Anti-Gambling Seminar at U. of Kentucky Stars Athlete Charged in Betting Scandal," *Chronicle of Higher Education*, March 12, 1999, A43.

47. Watterson, 266.

48. Falla, 228.

49. Falla, 145.

50. Watterson, 305.

51. Falla, 136.

52. Falla, 151.

53. From 2003 interview.

54. Cited in "The Athletic Director," newsletter of National Council of Secondary School Athletic Directors, Vol. 5, No. 4, 2/74.

55. Title 20 U.S.C., Section 1681.

56. NCAA, Corey Bray, principal researcher, Sports Participation Report, 1982–2002, available at http://www.ncaa.org/library/research.html#participation_rates, 219.

57. The lawsuit was styled *Kellmeyer, et al. v. NEA et al.* and filed in the Southern District of Florida in 1973. Cited in Ying Wu, "Margot Polivy, Legal Costs, and the Demise of the Association for Intercollegiate Athletics for Women," *Sport History Review*, No. 30, 1999, 134.

58. The regulations are codified at 34 CFR Part 106.41, and the full text of the regulations is available at http://www.ed.gov/offices/OCR/regs/34cfr106.html#S41.

59. Oral interview with Lopiano, June 2003.

60. Cited in Patricia Ann Rosenbrock, *Persistence and Accommodation in a Decade of Struggle and Change: The Case of Women Administrators in Division I-A Intercollegiate Athletics Programs*, University of Iowa, 1987, unpublished dissertation, 50–51.

61. Interview with Tom Jernstedt, July 2003.

62. Available at http://www.ed.gov/offices/OCR/docs/t9interp.html.

63. "Letters to the Editor," *Chronicle of Higher Education*, March 8, 2002.

64. Interview with Sylvia Hatchell, July 2003.

65. Watterson, 264–65.

66. Anecdote adapted from Welch Suggs, "Players Off the Field: How Jim Delany and Roy Kramer Took Over Big-Time College Sports," *Chronicle of Higher Education*, November 16, 2000, A59.

67. Viverito interview, 1998.

68. NCAA 2002 Graduation Rates Report, available at http://www.ncaa.org/grad_rates/2002/d1/aggregate/d1.html.

69. Debra E. Blum, "Brown U. Accused of Bias Against Female Athletes," *Chronicle of Higher Education*, April 15, 1992, page unavailable.

70. Douglas Lederman, "A Key Sports-Equity Case," *Chronicle of Higher Education*, October 5, 1994, page unavailable.

71. Available at http://www.ed.gov/offices/OCR/docs/clarific.html.

72. From opinion in *Stephen Neal, et al. vs. California State University at Bakersfield*. Cited in Welch Suggs, "2 Appeals Courts Uphold Right of Universities to Reduce Number of Male Athletes," *Chronicle of Higher Education*, January 7, 2000, A64.

PART I

The Issues

CHAPTER 2

The Integrity of the Enterprise

Richard E. Lapchick

Two murders, two suicides, sex scandals in recruiting, coaches being fired after unethical behaviors, the surrendering of national championships because of NCAA violations, and athletics directors and presidents resigning were among the negative headlines often before us in 2003 and 2004, the two years prior to the completion of *New Game Plan for College Sport.*

Having been involved in sport for most of my adult life, I am dismayed by the extensive nature of the negative headlines and know how hard the task at hand will be. There are some people involved in college sport who have lost their moral compass. But my experience also informs me that most athletes and coaches are good people with an understanding of what is right and wrong, are deeply family-centered and religious, and are generous with their time and money in serving the communities around them. I believe it is the system and not the people that demanded an overhaul.

The NCAA, under its president, Myles Brand, pushed hard for academic reform, against exclusionary hiring practices, and for more fiscal responsibility. Those reforms will be discussed throughout the book. College officials hope the reforms are in time to save the enterprise from the cumulative dismay of fans and alumni in the wake of a list of seemingly unending news of scandals.

Thus, headlines were continually made in those years that raised ethical issues. Information was drawn from Welch Suggs's "A Hard Year in College

Sport," in the *Chronicle of Higher Education*, and the weekly reports from the *Sports Law News*, edited by Joel Zand (http://sports.findlaw.com).

Coaches from 17 colleges and universities were charged with an array of offenses including driving under the influence, striking or threatening a player, academic fraud, gambling, selling drugs, and carousing with strippers and co-eds. Student-athletes from 19 colleges and universities were charged with an array of offenses including gambling, assault, sexual assault, soliciting sex, identity theft, burglary, underage drinking, possession of drugs, murder, and suicide. Seventeen colleges and universities were listed in the "programs in trouble" section. A total of 50 colleges and universities were cited. Among them were 28 Division IA schools, private and public, as well as religious-affiliated. There were athletic powerhouses, and there were schools like Lock Haven College, Loras College, and the University of the District of Columbia. Problems can and do happen anywhere. There is a substantial section on high schools toward the end of this chapter where attitudes and problems are also apparent and, too often, prevalent.

I have divided those problems into national developments, athletes in trouble, coaches in trouble, programs in trouble, and financial issues such as facilities expansion, dropped sports, and shifts in conference alignments. The extraordinary problems at the universities of Colorado, Baylor, and St. Bonaventure merited special attention at the end of the chapter.

NATIONAL DEVELOPMENTS

- The presidents of 44 colleges that were not members of the football Bowl Championship Series (BCS) formed the Coalition for College Athletics Reform to gain entree to the biggest postseason football games.*
- In a September 2003 hearing before the House of Representatives Judiciary Committee, members of Congress criticized the NCAA and the BCS. In October 2003, members of the Senate Judiciary Committee criticized the BCS in its own hearings. Controversy surrounding the BCS series was the focus of many 2004–05 football bowl stories.*
- The University of Utah became the only school from a non-BCS conference to make a BCS bowl game. The Utah coach, Urban Meyer, announced that he would not accept the head coaching job at Notre Dame but instead accepted the same position at the University of Florida.*
- The NCAA released a report concluding there is no connection between the amount spent on sports teams and won-lost records. Nonetheless, the 2005 NCAA Convention focused on the athletics arms race because spending was so out of control in Division IA.*
- The NCAA released a report showing that athletes who entered college in 1996–97 graduated at higher rates than did those in any previous

*Suggs, Welch, "A Hard Year in College Sports," *Chronicle of Higher Education*.

class. However, problems persisted in basketball and football, especially for African-American student-athletes.*

- The NCAA passed its first-ever, incentives/disincentives program to reward those schools that have good graduation rates and penalize those that do poorly. The proposals were introduced by NCAA President Myles Brand.*
- The NCAA announced plans to raise the academic standards that athletes must meet to be eligible to compete. At the same time, it modified standards so that incoming players with low SAT scores but good high school grades could meet the eligibility requirements.*
- Vanderbilt University announced that, while keeping all of its sports, it would dissolve many offices in its athletics department after transferring responsibility for facilities, academics, and other administrative functions to other university departments. Some reform advocates looked at Vanderbilt as a new model for college sport.*
- The American Football Coaches Association released a survey showing that most football players spend far more time at practice than is allowed under NCAA rules.*
- In *Reclaiming the Game*, William G. Bowen and Sarah A. Levin examined highly selective colleges' admissions policies and found the widespread admission of athletes with lesser academic credentials than those of non student-athletes. They concluded that student-athletes at these schools also underperformed in the classroom, even allowing for their poorer preparation.*
- In February 2003, after more than a year of deliberation, the U.S. Department of Education's Commission on Gender Equity in Sports released its report. Several members of the commission representing women's groups issued their own report calling for stronger enforcement of Title IX of the Education Amendments of 1972. In July 2003, the U.S. Secretary of Education announced that the department would not change guidelines for gender equity in sports issued under Title IX, despite the proposals from its Commission. Leaders who support Title IX were apprehensive about what President Bush might do in his second term of office.*
- In June 2003, Tulane University decided to keep the athletics department in Division IA, after discussions about dropping the football team or moving the entire sports program to Division III.*
- In May 2004, the U.S. Court of Appeals for the District of Columbia Circuit upheld a ruling that the National Wrestling Coaches Association (NWCA) and other athletic groups failed to show that Title IX directly caused a reduction in men's sports. The NWCA had introduced a law in August 2003 claiming officials discriminated against male athletes in enforcing equal opportunities for women.†

---

*Suggs, Welch, "A Hard Year in College Sports," *Chronicle of Higher Education*.
†*Sports Law News*, edited by Joel Zand, available at http://sports.findlaw.com.

- Also in May 2004, Andy Carroll, a former University of Washington football player who graduated in 2000, announced a suit against the NCAA, claiming it violated antitrust laws by limiting the number of scholarships that can be awarded. Carroll proposed a class-action lawsuit in federal court, claiming that he was led to believe he might receive a scholarship as a walk-on but was later told none were available.[†]
- The Southeastern Conference (SEC) unveiled a reform package in June 2004 that was intended to reduce cheating among SEC schools. Four SEC schools were on probation at the time, and two more faced that possibility.[†]
- Congress moved to impose tougher penalties on sports agents who unethically get student-athletes to sign contracts that compromise their amateur standing.[†]
- Jeremy Bloom, a University of Colorado football player battled the NCAA over whether he could be paid in his alternate career as a professional skier. Bloom published a "Student-Athlete's Bill of Rights" and called on states to challenge NCAA rules.[*] In September 2004, Bloom pled his case before a sympathetic congressional panel that the NCAA cut his college football career short without giving him a fair chance to argue his case. The NCAA ruled that he lost his football college eligibility because of the endorsement deals he received as a professional skier.[†]

COACHES IN TROUBLE

- In February 2003, the University of Rhode Island made an out-of-court settlement with a former secretary in its athletics department who had charged that the former men's basketball coach, Jim Harrick Sr., and his assistant coach, Mike Wilson, had improperly touched her and abused her with obscene language. Harrick had other problems at Georgia.[*]
- The University of Georgia fired Jim Harrick Jr. in March 2004 for giving players A's in his course on "Principles of Basketball Coaching" after a student-athlete told ESPN about the course and also accused Georgia coaches of paying his long-distance telephone bills and committing other violations of NCAA rules. Harrick Jr. was an assistant men's basketball coach to then head coach, Jim Harrick Sr. One week later, the university ruled the men's basketball team ineligible for the SEC and NCAA tournaments and suspended Harrick Sr. while investigators continued looking into charges of academic fraud and improper benefits given to athletes. Harrick Sr. resigned in late March, when an investigation uncovered evidence that coaches gave money to players. The investigation also found that someone took the SAT test for a

[†]*Sports Law News*, edited by Joel Zand, available at http://sports.findlaw.com.
[*]Suggs, Welch, "A Hard Year in College Sports," *Chronicle of Higher Education*.

Georgia recruit.* The NCAA placed Georgia on four years' probation in August 2004 but allowed it to play in the postseason for rules violations including academic fraud, unethical conduct, and improper benefits under Harrick.

- Georgia announced plans to appeal the sanctions imposed by the NCAA.[†]
- North Carolina State University's head wrestling coach, Bob Guzzo, faced assault charges after he allegedly grabbed one of his athletes by the arm and throat and shoved him into a wall in January 2003.*
- Jerome Souers, Northern Arizona University's head football coach, pled guilty to driving under the influence of alcohol. He kept his job.*
- Randy Brown, an assistant men's basketball coach at Iowa State, re-signed after being charged with possession of child pornography and with obstruction of justice in March 2003.*
- A University of Cincinnati broadcaster abused a referee during an NCAA Division I men's basketball tournament game after the referee ejected Bob Huggins, Cincinnati's coach. The NCAA removed the broad-caster.* Huggins had more problems in 2004, when he was arrested on charges of driving under the influence of alcohol after visiting with a recruit. Huggins pled no contest and was suspended for 10 weeks as basketball coach, all during the off-season.[†]
- When the University of Kansas fired athletics director Allen Bohl, he blamed the basketball coach, Roy Williams. Less than a week later, Williams agreed to coach at his alma mater, the University of North Carolina.*
- At the end of April 2003, the Des Moines Register published photos of Larry Eustachy, Iowa State University's men's basketball coach, at a party with University of Missouri students, including co-eds, with beer in hand, following a game. Although he admitted he had a problem with alcohol, Eustachy was forced to resign.*
- Days after the pictures of Eustachy appeared, the University of Alabama fired its newly hired football coach, Mike Price, after newspapers re-ported that he had visited a strip club and entertained a stripper in a Florida hotel room during a golf tournament.*
- In June 2003, the University of Washington fired Rick Neuheisel, its football coach, after he finally admitted to betting more than $6,000 on the NCAA Division I men's basketball tournament.* Neuheisel sued the university. Washington also had trouble with its men's bas-ketball program when it lost a scholarship and received two years of probation because of an assistant coach's violations of NCAA recruiting rules.* Washington's troubles did not end there: The Health Department in the State of Washington documented thousands of instances in which William Scheyer, an athletics department team

---

[†]*Sports Law News*, edited by Joel Zand, available at http://sports.findlaw.com.
*Suggs, Welch, "A Hard Year in College Sports," *Chronicle of Higher Education*.

physician, gave steroids and other banned drugs to athletes.* Scheyer agreed to stop practicing medicine in a settlement with the State in the fall of 2004. Long-time athletics director Barbara Hedges retired after a career filled with distinction.

- The NCAA also sanctioned the men's basketball program at the University of Utah when it concluded that the university "had failed to foster an atmosphere of compliance" because Rick Majerus, the coach, had bought meals for players at the hotel where he lives.*
- In August 2003, Alabama State fired L. C. Cole, its football coach. An internal investigation found allegations of players' being entertained by strippers during recruiting visits and receiving improper academic support. Cole threatened to sue the university.
- Montana State University football coach Joe O'Brien was charged with possessing and selling methamphetamine in September 2003.*
- Tennessee State and its former men's basketball coach, Nolan Richardson III, were cited by the NCAA for numerous rules violations. Richardson, the son of the former Arkansas coach, had been fired in late 2002 for pulling a gun on an assistant coach.*
- Kentucky State fired Winston Bennett, its basketball coach, for striking a player during practice in November 2003.*
- Ohio State fired Jim O'Brien in June 2004 because he admitted he had given a recruit $6,000 five years before. Ohio State self-imposed a one-year ban on postseason play by its men's basketball team in response.†
  Coupled with problems with the Ohio State football program—including charges by Maurice Clarret made in *ESPN The Magazine* and the conviction of a player for assaulting a fellow student and taking his wallet—all of this eventually led to the resignation of Andy Geiger, a veteran athletics director who had had an outstanding reputation throughout a long career.
- In the same month, the Associated Press reported that the University of Missouri paid more than $136,000 to associate head basketball coach Tony Harvey and assistant coach Lane Odom, who had been accused of breaking NCAA rules in exchange for their resignations and pledges never to sue. It was confirmed that Missouri had no legal obligation to pay them anything.†
- Also in June 2004, Oregon's football program was placed on NCAA probation for two years for recruiting violations by an assistant coach. Oregon did not lose its eligibility for postseason play and did not lose any scholarships. The NCAA said the case centered on a "series of impermissible" contacts by the assistant in January 2003 and the improper handling of a national letter of intent.†
- Desiree Orwig-Grammell, who was the men's and women's track and field coach at Loras College in Dubuque, Iowa, was arrested for drunken driving and resisting arrest in October 2004.†

---

*Suggs, Welch, "A Hard Year in College Sports," *Chronicle of Higher Education*.
†*Sports Law News*, edited by Joel Zand, available at http://sports.findlaw.com.

- A federal judge dismissed a sexual harassment lawsuit filed six years previously by a former player against Anson Dorrance, North Carolina women's soccer coach. U.S. District Court Judge N. Carlton Tilley Jr. wrote the "behavior at issue does not constitute severe, pervasive and objectively offensive sexual harassment."[†]
- In December 2004, former Barton County Community College head coach Ryan Wolf was indicted on charges that he provided false academic information about his athletes to Division I schools. The indictment also charged Wolf with getting his student-athletes grants they were not qualified to receive and no-show campus jobs that paid them.[†]

ATHLETES IN TROUBLE

- Adrian McPherson was thrown off Florida State's football team in 2002 after being charged with forgery by state officials. In March 2003, he was charged with gambling. Police said he owed one bookie $8,000. The bookie and a team equipment manager were charged with felony bookmaking.[*]
- A University of Cincinnati football player was arrested for the second time in four months on charges of assault. Police charged he hit an opponent during an intramural basketball game.[*]
- Police charged Anwar Philips, a Penn State football player, with sexual assault for an incident that occurred in November. He had been allowed to play in the Capital One Bowl despite being suspended from the university by a judicial board in December. He was acquitted in a jury trial.[*]
- In June 2004, Penn State wide receiver Maurice Humphrey was sentenced to 3 to 12 months in prison for assaulting his former girlfriend and her friend, both track athletes at the school.[†]
- In April 2003, a Marshall football player was arrested on charges of domestic assault and battery. A teammate was arrested for soliciting sex from an undercover police officer in the following week. One month previous to that, another teammate had been arrested for a second time in six months on charges of underage drinking.[*]
- Five Georgia football players and one basketball player were arrested on charges of marijuana possession. The NCAA decided not to punish nine Georgia football players who sold conference championship rings on eBay. Georgia decided not to punish them either but required them to purchase rings (instead of receiving them free) in the future.[*]
- The murder case at Baylor University, discussed below, was not the only one involving a former college student-athlete accused of murder. In October 2004, Fabian Desmond Smart, who played free safety at Lock Haven University, was convicted of first-degree murder,

[†]*Sports Law News*, edited by Joel Zand, available at http://sports.findlaw.com.
[*]Suggs, Welch, "A Hard Year in College Sports," *Chronicle of Higher Education*.

kidnapping, and two counts of conspiracy in the death of 21-year-old Jason McMann in 1999. McMann was the brother of Olympic wrestler Sara McMann.[†]

- Maurice Clarett, Ohio State University's star running back, was often in the news even after he stopped playing at Ohio State. The *New York Times* published a July 2003 story with claims by a teaching assistant that Clarett received improper help in a course in African-American and African studies. In September, Clarett was charged with filing a false report of stolen property.[*] Clarett sat out the next college season and subsequently decided to enter the NFL draft. After he won a lower court victory to be able to enter early, the U.S. Second Circuit Court of Appeals reversed the ruling by holding that the NFL's eligibility rules were the result of the NFL's bargaining agreement with unionized players and were therefore protected from anti-trust claims.[†]
- That decision also kept Southern California's All-American receiver Mike Williams out of the NFL draft. The NCAA rejected his request to rejoin USC at the start of the 2004 season.[†]
- In the summer of 2003, four Kansas State players were arrested in less than a month.[*]
- A Troy State football player was shot and wounded near the campus.
- Kent State quarterback Joshua Cribbs pled guilty to marijuana possession and was suspended from all football-related activity between the arrest in January and September 2004. He was reinstated and missed the team's season opener at Iowa.[†]
- Junior defensive lineman Brenton Kendrick and starting sophomore cornerback Steven Murphy of the University of Nevada's football team were dismissed from the team after being arrested on multiple felony drug charges in August 2004.[†]
- Virginia Tech quarterback Marcus Vick pled no contest to a misdemeanor charge of contributing to the delinquency of a minor after a night of drinking with underage girls.[†]
- Wide receiver Adarius Bowman, linebacker Fred Sparkman, and defensive tackle Isaiah Thomas were suspended by North Carolina indefinitely after they were cited for possession of marijuana in October.[†]
- Dwayne Smith, a sophomore tailback at Wisconsin, was charged with sexually assaulting a 19-year-old woman at a campus area apartment in February.[†]
- In June, Diamond Ferri, a Syracuse University football player, was accused of assaulting two men and resisted arrest.[†]
- Narles R. Yde-Layne, a redshirt freshman on the Carroll College football team who was about to be charged with rape, committed suicide in October 2004 shortly after learning that a justice of the peace had issued a warrant for his arrest, authorities said. Yde-Layne's attorney

[†]*Sports Law News*, edited by Joel Zand, available at http://sports.findlaw.com.
[*]Suggs, Welch, "A Hard Year in College Sports," *Chronicle of Higher Education.*

said he had told his parents "he had done nothing wrong, but that he could not face what the community would think of him."[†]

- In July 2004, Marcus Douthit, a second-round draft pick of the Los Angeles Lakers who played for Providence College, was charged with participating in an identity theft and embezzlement scam and pocketing several thousand dollars. The indictment accused him of being part of a phony car accident as part of a scheme to defraud insurance companies.[†]
- In August 2004, Southern Illinois players Stetson Hairston and Michael Dale were charged with felony trespassing and mob action and misdemeanor battery.
- Western Illinois football players William Penn and Michael Black were each charged with residential burglary near the WIU campus.[†]

FANS

- More than $100,000 in damage resulted from a riot in Minneapolis after the University of Minnesota's men's ice hockey team won the NCAA championship. Eighty-seven people were arrested in a hockey riot after the University of New Hampshire loss, and most of those arrested were UNH students.[*]
- The Ohio State University expelled or suspended seven students for their roles in a riot following a football game with Michigan in the fall of 2002.[*]
- Logan Young, a University of Alabama fan, was indicted by a federal grand jury and charged with paying a Memphis high school coach $150,000 to steer Albert Means, a star player, to Alabama.[*]
- The Southeastern Conference approved a policy that took effect on December 1, 2004, under which schools could face fines of as much as $50,000 if fans came onto the field or court during football or basketball games.[†]

COLLEGE PROGRAMS IN TROUBLE

- In February 2003, Salem State's men's soccer team was banned for one year from Division III playoffs for improper loans made to a player.[*]
- A team statistician said he was paid to write papers for members of the Fresno State men's basketball team. In March, Fresno's president pulled the men's basketball team out of postseason tournaments amid a continuing investigation into the allegations.[*]
- The NCAA punished San Diego State's football team for holding improper summer workouts.[*]

[†]*Sports Law News*, edited by Joel Zand, available at http://sports.findlaw.com.
[*]Suggs, Welch, "A Hard Year in College Sports," *Chronicle of Higher Education*.

- Miami's baseball team lost part of its recruiting budget for violating NCAA recruiting rules.*
- The University of Hawaii-Manoa was reprimanded and fined by the Western Athletic Conference for failing to certify that all of its football players had earned at least six course credits during the previous semester.*
- The NCAA took scholarships away from the University of Arkansas at Fayetteville's football teams after ruling that a booster had improperly paid players.*
- Georgia's president, Michael F. Adams, decided not to extend the contract of Vincent J. Dooley, the popular athletics director and legendary former football coach. Instead of remaining until 2008, as he had requested, the 70-year-old Dooley left office in 2004. He was replaced by Damon Evans, the Southeastern Conference's first African-American athletics director.*
- In June 2003, five female student-athletes at Colby College in Maine alleged violations of Title IX and filed a complaint with the U.S. Department of Education's Office for Civil Rights.*
- The NCAA gave minor punishments to Rutgers University's New Brunswick athletics department after the university discovered administrative oversights that led to ineligible athletes competing in previous years.*
- The University of Mississippi announced that it was retiring its Rebel mascot, a caricature of a white Southern gentleman, in favor of something more intimidating for football and basketball games.* It had banned the use of the Confederate flag in the late 1990s.
- Florida A&M tried to become the first historically black institution to go from Division IAA to Division IA when its board voted to do so in June 2003.* After significant controversy in its athletics department, FAMU dropped the idea in 2004.
- High-ranking officials at Florida State, including the president and vice president for student affairs, were named by a woman who said she had been sexually assaulted by a football player. She said the officials had asked her not to press charges.*
- The NCAA took away the 2002 men's volleyball national championship from Hawaii for using an ineligible player.*
- In November 2003, Morehouse College's soccer team was suspended by the NCAA for three years for recruiting professional players.*
- In a public relations fiasco, Wade Walker, Auburn's president, secretly visited the University of Louisville's head football coach to offer him the head coaching job at Auburn. Auburn then defeated Alabama. Current coach Tommy Tuberville had no knowledge of the meeting in Louisville until the media reported it the following week. Auburn finally decided to retain Tuberville, who was named Coach of the Year in 2004.*

*Suggs, Welch, "A Hard Year in College Sports," *Chronicle of Higher Education*.

- In February 2004, six members of the St. John's University basketball team were dismissed from the team after they took a stripper to a hotel to have sex. When they refused to pay her, she charged them with rape. The players were cleared criminally, but St. John's expelled three and suspended the other three players. This left St. John's with eight players for the season.
- La Salle men's basketball coach Billy Hahn and women's coach John Miller resigned after two separate rape allegations involving players from the men's team during the previous two seasons. The players faced criminal prosecution. Both coaches had been placed on administrative leave July 6 following the allegations after reportedly not informing Athletics Director Tom Brennan about the charges.
- In November 2004, the University of the District of Columbia was compelled to cancel its men's and women's basketball seasons, citing problems with recruitment, academic eligibility, and financial aid.[†]
- Lewis University surrendered its Division II men's volleyball national title and was put on four years' probation for an array of infractions. The NCAA's report cited "lack of attention ... from the president of the institution on down."[†]

UNIVERSITY OF COLORADO

For me, the decision by the University of Colorado to reinstate head football coach Gary Barnett was a huge psychological setback to all the NCAA's efforts at reform. Working on issues in sport for more than three decades, I am rarely surprised when bad decisions are made. However, I admit that I was stunned that Colorado decided to reinstate Barnett and to keep the administrative team responsible for the university intact.

I do not know what more information we needed than knowing that nine women have accused Colorado football players or recruits of rape. An independent commission studied the situation and released its report that clearly established that the University of Colorado and members of its athletic teams have used sex, strippers, and alcohol as recruiting tools for its football team. In fact, *after* the commission issued its report, the recruiting scandal had a potent charge leveled before a state grand jury that heard testimony from a woman who said that Nathan Maxcey, a Colorado recruiting aide, gave more than $2,000 to an escort service. Maxcey was indicted in August 2004 for solicitation for prostitution and embezzlement of public property and theft.

Barnett claimed that he was unaware that any of this was going on. But as head coach, the responsibility was his. Though it may have started under the watch of his predecessor, the climate clearly had been maintained under Barnett's watch. The decision to reinstate Barnett was the kind of stonewalling that sends chills through the psyches of women who have been sexually

---

[†]*Sports Law News*, edited by Joel Zand, available at http://sports.findlaw.com.

assaulted and who fear what happens next if they report those assaults. Time and again, police refuse to fully prosecute alleged perpetrators, cases rarely go to trial, convictions are rarely obtained, and perpetrators barely spend time in prison. In the role of special prosecutor appointed by Governor Bill Owens, the State's Attorney General, Ken Salazar, announced that he would not file sexual assault charges against any of the Colorado football players or recruits accused of the attacks.

The University of Colorado officials said that in spite of all that went on, they had faith in the leadership of their football program. I believe it was a wrong decision that hurt college sport in significant ways. The university talked about its new policies that would protect the program from recurrences. New policies are put in place all the time. Most are well intentioned. But there was a huge degree of skepticism among people across the country who believed that it would be "business as usual" once the fall football season started. If you were seated in Boulder's football stadium in the Fall of 2004, all seemed well. Things got even better in 2005 as Colorado got off to a fast 7-2 start. Mike Bohn, the new athletics director, was talking about a contract extension for Barnett.

At least in some other cases in the 2003–04 year, colleges and universities (see information on Alabama, Washington, Iowa State, St. Bonaventure, Baylor, and Georgia) had the courage to fire coaches as a sign that there was going to be a new beginning.

But the University of Colorado did not allow such a new beginning in spite of the scathing report indicting the culture that existed. Colorado continued to have the same look as it had throughout this tumultuous period. Barnett's long-term future seemed solid until the Buffaloes lost their last three games including a season-ending 70-3 loss to Texas in the Big 12 Championship. He survived one of college sport's biggest scandals, but not a three-game losing streak. The university, which by December 2005 had a new chancellor, president, and athletics director, finally was rid of Coach Gary Barnett. The departure was expensive for the university with a three-million dollar buy-out paid to Barnett.

But most important, the lives of the nine women have been irrevocably changed by the alleged violent acts of Colorado recruits and players. I recognize that the University of Colorado is not the only school that has used sex to recruit or that has athletes who have been sexual predators. But Colorado had the chance to take the high road and set an example for the nation. It was a chance to give credence to NCAA reform. Instead of standing up for victims and for ethical decisions, the university seemed to stand up for football. Stay while you are winning; leave when you lose.

The Colorado saga marked an extraordinarily sad period for college sport and those who want fundamental reform. It was even sadder for advocates who try to stop men's violence against women in a national culture where nearly four million women are battered or sexually assaulted in the course of each and every year.

BAYLOR UNIVERSITY

It would take a great deal to be called the most outrageous case in the history of college sport, but Baylor University and its basketball program might have that title. One teammate allegedly murdered another, and the coach tried to fabricate a version of the story to keep the police away from his program. These horrific episodes opened a Pandora's box of violations.

It all began when basketball player Patrick Dennehy was reported missing on June 19, 2003. His SUV was found in July in Virginia Beach. Carlton Dotson, who had been Dennehy's teammate and roommate, was arrested on July 21 in Maryland. On July 25, the beheaded body of Dennehy was found near the Baylor campus in Waco. Dotson was arrested in Hurlock, Maryland, and indicted in Texas for the murder of Dennehy one month later. Finally, Dotson was extradited to Texas, where he still awaits trial. In October 2004, Dotson was ruled incompetent to stand trial and was sent to a state mental hospital so his competence would be reevaluated. In January 2005, doctors at the hospital determined that he had regained his competence to stand trial.

But the murder led to other disclosures. In August 2003 head basketball coach Dave Bliss and athletics director Tom Stanton resigned after Baylor president Robert Sloan announced evidence of major violations in the men's basketball program. The president announced self-imposed punishments, including placing men's basketball on probation and banning it from postseason play for the 2003–04 season. All that preceded the most damaging news about how Bliss handled the situation. An assistant coach had secretly recorded Bliss telling his team to portray Dennehy as a drug dealer to make it appear that his death was drug related. He told the players that since Dennehy was dead, he could not challenge this.

Baylor released its own internal investigation in February 2004, finding six major NCAA violations. The report concluded that Bliss tried to cover up that he had paid the tuition of two players; that he had asked boosters to give money that would be used to violate NCAA rules; that coaches bought meals and clothes, and paid for the transportation of athletes; and that department policies were not followed when there was a positive drug test. It was hard to escape the fact that Baylor reported a lack of institutional control. What was surprising to many was that President Sloan did not step down in spite of a faculty vote of no confidence. The school did announce further self-imposed sanctions, including losing nine scholarships and three years' probation of the men's basketball team.

ST. BONAVENTURE UNIVERSITY

In August 2003, St. Bonaventure board chairman William Swan committed suicide, despondent over the events at the school. Though events leading up to this perhaps paled in comparison to Baylor and Colorado, Swan's death illustrates how serious we are about sport and how things can go so terribly wrong.

St. Bonaventure had a storied basketball program back in the 1960s and 1970s. School president Robert Wickenheiser apparently wanted to reclaim that glory. He facilitated the admission of center Jamil Terrell with only a welding certificate and not an associates degree from a junior college. In March 2003, the Atlantic 10 announced that St. Bonaventure would forfeit six conference wins and would be banned from the conference tournament for using Terrell, who should have been ineligible. The team refused to play its last two regular season games.

Wickenheiser admitted that he had helped with the admission of Terrell and resigned in March. Gothard Lane, the athletics director, was not offered a contract renewal. Basketball coach Jan van Breda Kolff was dismissed after the season. Both Van Breda Kolff and Lane sued the school. However, it was Swann's suicide that really put an exclamation point on how the pursuit of wins can lead to tragedy.

The NCAA placed St. Bonaventure on probation for three years and barred it from playing in the 2004 postseason. But that was obviously the smallest part of the anguish caused by the scandal.

FINANCES AND COLLEGE SPORT

During the same period, some schools were dropping sports, some Division IA schools were expanding capital projects, conferences were raiding each other, and new studies challenged the widespread belief that spending more led to more victories which led to better student applicants and increased revenues. Finances in college sport continued to be a very hot topic.

The NCAA focused a great deal of attention at their 2005 convention on the cost of athletics. President Brand faced this head-on in his state of the association address. I thought his speech was so important to the topic of this book and this chapter that I am quoting from it extensively.

Dr. Brand said that it was a myth with a modicum of truth that college sports is only about the money and the student-athlete is the forgotten pawn.

> According to this myth, college sport is big business in which the top personalities earn million-dollar salaries. It is the world of sports entertainment, indistinguishable from professional athletics. It has succumbed to the machinations of media networks and has sold its soul to corporate America.
>
> Has the drive for financing intercollegiate athletics pushed the enterprise off center from the mission of higher education? Have dollars replaced the student-athlete as the object of the entire effort? If true, how on earth did America's great universities get to this position?

Dr. Brand maintained that though college sport was an expensive item, the average Division IA program represented only 3–4 percent of university expenditures. He pointed out that the cost of athletics have risen to an average of $15 million and $27 million in Divisions I and IA, respectively, during a time when "higher education has gone through a series of economic downturns. The financial pressures of maintaining and enhancing large physical plants, competing for, hiring and retaining faculty and staff, and increased technology demands have exacerbated the problem."

All of this has led to a search for outside revenue sources. Brand credited more lucrative media agreements with helping to fill the void. But he readily acknowledged that that resulted in escalating costs in college sport to build better facilities, pay coaches extraordinary salaries, and to improve team's opportunities to win.

Brand warned:

> Worse, this mounting financial problem threatens the integrity of the university. When the public—both local and en masse—begin to believe that the value of the institution is to be measured by the success of its athletics teams, the core mission of the university is threatened. The central role of the faculty is ignored in favor of winning the big game or recruiting the next young man with athletics star potential. And the ability of the university to successfully educate and push forward the boundaries of knowledge and the creative arts is compromised.

He went on that such pressures are having an impact so that too many Division IAA and Division II schools are trying to move up to Division IA or I, respectively.

Brand emphasized, "This spiraling fiscal problem must be arrested," that he would focus a good deal of attention to this in the years ahead, and that he needed to "engage the interests and action of college and university presidents."

> In my view, we must develop a process for value- and mission-based budgeting of athletics that parallels the way budgets for other university programs are set. The central point is that the value of an athletics program must ultimately rest on its support of and integration into the educational mission and traditions of the university.
>
> We must arrest the slide toward professional athletics and the sports entertainment industry. And while the problem is not of crisis proportions right now, the time to avoid turning this myth into reality is now.

Brand maintained that "good business practices constitute only part of fiscal responsibility. The popular view is that you have to increase spending to increase wins, and you have to increase wins to increase revenues."

There had been two recent studies that showed how flawed the latter thinking was. The NCAA's own study concluded there was no connection between the amount spent on sports teams and won-lost records.

Dr. Robert H. Frank, the H. J. Louis Professor of Management and Economics at Cornell University, prepared *Challenging the Myth: A Review of the Links Among College Athletic Success, Student Quality, and Donations* for the Knight Foundation Commission on Intercollegiate Athletics in 2004.

In conducting the study, Frank went over 13 studies that had been conducted between 1979 and 2003. Seven examined whether success in big-time athletics has any effect on a college's alumni donations, whereas six others looked at whether or not such success elevated the academic quality of its applicants. He concluded that great success in athletics neither increased alumni donations nor elevated the academic standing of the applicants.

Frank argued that "individual institutions that decide to invest more money in their sports programs in the hope of raising more funds or improving their applicant pools may be throwing good money after bad, and would be wiser to spend the money in other ways."

He went on, perhaps naively, that "groups of institutions that compete against each other in sports could jointly agree to cut back on sports spending—to abandon the 'arms race' in which they are now engaged—without reducing either donations by alumni or applications by prospective students."

Dr Brand lamented that, "[t]he spending spiral has not abated, and the strong if mistaken belief that spending more than your competitors will lead to increased winning has propelled athletics departments to increase expenditures . . . no matter the facts."

Brand warned against relying on outside revenue streams as the solution to increased costs because "the practical effect has been to push athletics programs outside an institution's normal budgeting process, to put unparalleled pressure on athletics administrators to find revenue streams outside the university, including accommodating major donors, to increase the pressure on coaches—and student-athletes, I might add—to win, and to adopt an approach that views intercollegiate athletics as an ancillary enterprise."

Dr. Brand concluded this section of his speech with:

> It is far too risky to take athletics outside the normal lines of accountability at the university. When there are major problems or scandals in athletics, the entire university is affected. Athletics is too visible and influential to be ancillary and too enriching to the university experience to be ignored as a contribution to the mission of higher education. And if it has value in the university's meeting its mission, it deserves to be supported, if needed.
>
> Value-based budgeting depends on an athletics program contributing to the fulfillment of the university's missions. As I define it, fiscal responsibility in college sports is more than a financial strategy; it means

more than operating efficiently. It means using the resources provided in ways that go beyond winning. It means being committed in word and especially in deed to the goals and the reasons for which the university exists.

It means the integration of college sports within the academic mission of the university, and it means keeping student-athletes at the center of what we do.

Welch Suggs documented some of the financial impacts of college sport in "A Hard Year in College Sports" in the *Chronicle of Higher Education* at the end of 2003.

West Virginia, which announced it would drop men's cross-country, tennis, indoor and outdoor track and field, and co-ed rifle, was the only BCS Conference school that announced it would drop a sport(s) in 2003. The list of other schools that faced the cuts by cutting sports was hardly one of powerhouses in college sport:

- Hillsdale College: four sports
- Florida International: men's soccer
- Fairfield: football and men's ice-hockey
- U.S. Merchant Marine Academy: men's water polo, men's volleyball, and men's and women's rifle
- Michigan Technological University, New Jersey City University, and the University of Massachusetts at Lowell: football
- Iona College: men's ice hockey and men's and women's tennis
- Edinboro University of Pennsylvania: baseball and men's tennis
- Fresno State: men's cross-country, soccer, indoor track and field, and women's swimming
- Toledo: men's swimming and indoor and outdoor track
- Marshall: men's cross-country and track and field
- East Tennessee State: football
- Athens State (Alabama): all of its sports programs*

In marked contrast, according to Suggs, Delaware State, which announced a $30 million upgrade to its football stadium, was the only school outside of Division IA that announced major facilities expansions in 2003. The well-to-do programs expanded their spending to do even better:

- Auburn: $28-million expansion of its football stadium
- Oklahoma State: received a $55-million gift from alumnus T. Boone Pickens for stadium renovations
- Mississippi: build a $17-million indoor practice facility
- Penn State: raised $132 million in a capital campaign*

*Suggs, Welch, "A Hard Year in College Sports," *Chronicle of Higher Education*.

However, the biggest recent story about money in college sport had to be the conference shake-ups that began in 2003. It was all about the quest for a higher level of play and the money that would result, and it started when two BCS conferences went at it. In May, nine Atlantic Coast Conference presidents approved negotiations with Big East members Boston College (BC), Syracuse University, and the University of Miami about moving to the ACC. In a desperate measure to save the schools, the remaining Big East colleges announced a lawsuit against the ACC and the Big East schools considering switching. The governor of Connecticut got involved on the side of the Big East. The University of Connecticut, so successful in basketball, had invested heavily in a new football stadium.

With the prospect of a 12-team ACC super-conference allowing for a highly profitable championship game and extra ACC regular season football games, the dollar value of Miami in the ACC was clear. The appeal of getting the Boston and New York television markets that BC and Syracuse would bring could have helped the ACC negotiate a new TV deal when the ACC's current contract expired.

The Big East apparently offered Miami more money than the ACC but it did not matter in the end. Instead of BC or Syracuse, the ACC officially invited Miami and Virginia Tech in June. In doing so, the ACC gained the Big East's top football powers. Between them, they had won 9 of the 12 Big East football championships and had the two best cumulative records for Big East play.

No one looked good in the process. Virginia Tech had been part of the Big East lawsuit against the ACC. Upon accepting the ACC invitation, it dropped out of the suit. Syracuse and BC, shunned at the altar, switched sides as their presidents joined other Big East presidents pledging that the Big East would become even stronger. That was hard to see in June 2003.

Mike Tranghese and John Swofford, two of the most highly thought-of people in sports, did not add to the luster of their careers as they verbally duked it out in the power struggle. Former Secretary of Education and current Miami president, Donna Shalala, hardly sounded presidential when she told Clemson president James Barker, "Ready or not, here we come." Lawyers used words like "predatory" to describe the ACC and "conspiratorial" to characterize Miami (ESPN.com, June 30, 2003).

Myles Brand said he was "disappointed the issue has been as disagreeable as it has been" and that "[t]he integrity of intercollegiate athletics demands that we handle conference alignments and related matters in the future in a better way."

The Big East had to go into action when Boston College accepted an invitation to join the ACC in October. Their future in the Bowl Championship Series (BCS) was at stake when the BCS TV contract was up for negotiations in 2005.

The *Boston College Chronicle* published an interview with the BC president, Reverend William Leahy, on October 17, 2004. In it, he described the sequence that led BC to accept an invitation to become the ACC's 12th team, allowing for a football championship game. Father Leahy said:

> The presidents of Big East football schools at a meeting in Newark on July 9 voted unanimously to accept a recommendation from their directors of athletics that an 8–9 school, all-sports conference be established. But within a few weeks, I learned that the other presidents no longer were committed to the 8–9 school concept, but wanted to expand to a conference of 16 institutions. I opposed such a plan on numerous occasions because 14 schools in the conference had not worked and therefore going to 16 institutions seemed to only worsen the problem.
>
> In late September, the NCAA championships cabinet voted against allowing the ACC to hold a football championship game with only 11 schools. Press reports then suggested that this would cause the ACC to consider adding a 12th team, and speculation began that BC would be invited to join.
>
> On Oct. 1, the Big East subcommittee, working on reorganizing the conference, met in Newark, and I told the group that given stories in the press and because of my continued unhappiness with the proposed league structure, I intended to find out if the ACC was in fact interested in BC, and then make a decision. I also said that I realized the Big East needed to know soon about BC's status so that the Conference could complete restructuring plans for action at the Nov. 4 meeting of league presidents.
>
> On Oct. 12, we received and accepted an invitation to become a member of the ACC.

Expediency and money had won out again. When the NCAA ruled against an 11-school championship game, everyone's pace picked up. On the day the *Chronicle* ran this interview, Conference USA, feeling a massive raid by the Big East was close, announced it was recruiting Rice, Southern Methodist, and Tulsa away from the Western Athletic Conference (WAC).

But the chips really fell out in on November 4, when the Big East, Conference USA, and the WAC all announced a huge shift. The *Daily Orange*, Syracuse's paper, called it "Conference Judgment Day" in its November 5 edition.

The Big East converted from the hunted to the hunter and picked up five Conference USA schools: Marquette, Cincinnati, DePaul, South Florida, and Louisville. Though it might have still been weak in football, four of the new members added to the existing strength of Big East basketball.

Conference USA was ready and accepted two Mid-American Conference (MAC) colleges, Marshall and Central Florida, and the three WAC schools, Rice, Tulsa, and SMU, mentioned above.

The WAC was also ready and accepted New Mexico State and Utah State, which had been in the Sun Belt Conference. Idaho joined the WAC later.

All the troubles in college sport including coaches, athletes, and programs in ethical trouble, mirrored a disturbing situation at the high school level.

Was what existed in high school a reflection of the boys and their coaches trying to emulate the men and their coaches at the next level? Or was what was happening in high schools a pipeline to troubles in college. Either way, it was not good news for either.

HIGH SCHOOL SPORT

Ethical issues in college sport did not come out of nowhere. Anything we see at the college level could have been foretold by things that are happening in high school athletics and, to a smaller degree, in youth sport. Yet whereas so much recent attention has been placed on ethical issues in college and professional sport, what happens at the high school level is virtually ignored.

Until colleges put in new eligibility standards for college freshmen, we barely noticed that few high school systems had meaningful eligibility standards for their own student-athletes. With all the attention on college and professional athletes in trouble with the law, we rarely see what is going on in high schools that mirror that.

Parents redshirt eighth-graders. High school transcripts are reportedly altered to keep athletes eligible. Coaches talk to teachers about helping student-athletes with their grades so they can get the college scholarship and then make it in the pros. Agents are now on high school campuses. High school games get national attention from print and broadcast media.

America loves sports. Kids want to play. At the high school level, 4,038,253 boys and 2,865,299 girls play high school sports. There are 544,811 boys who play high school basketball and 1,032,682 who play high school football. There are 457,986 girls who play high school basketball (National Federation of State High School Associations, *2003–04 Participation Study*).

At the college level in Division I, 5,012 play men's basketball; 14,674 compete in Division I college football; and 4,731 women play Division I college basketball (NCAA, *2002–03 Participation Study*).

There are only 1,696 active roster slots in the National Football League, 438 players in the National Basketball Association, and 165 women who play in the Women's National Basketball Association.

Too many high school student-athletes surrender their chance to get an education to prepare them for professional life by focusing everything on their sport. That has been made easier in a hip-hop culture where being perceived as intelligent and getting good grades is not "cool." Layered on top of that is the pervasive cheating and unethical behavior of high school students and high school student-athletes and their coaches.

More than 4,200 high school student-athletes were surveyed by the Josephson Institute. The results are so disturbing that I felt compelled to include most of the reported highlights. It clearly shows how coaches can positively and negatively affect those who play for them on moral and ethical issues. Moreover, it shows that so many young people are ethically unhinged.

According to the Institute's president, Michael Josephson:

> The values of millions of youngsters are directly and dramatically influenced by the values conveyed in high school sports. This survey reveals that coaches and parents simply aren't doing enough to assure that the experience is a positive one. Too many youngsters are confused about the meaning of fair play and sportsmanship and they have no concept of honorable competition. As a result they engage in illegal conduct and employ doubtful gamesmanship techniques to gain a competitive advantage. It appears that today's playing fields are the breeding grounds for the next generation of corporate pirates and political scoundrels.

Among the key findings:

Girls are more sportsmanlike than boys.   The attitudes of boys and girls who participate in sports vary dramatically. Overall, males are far more likely to exhibit cynical attitudes and engage in illegal or unsporting conduct. The closest they came on any questions was 68 percent of both males and females cheated on a test in the last year.

Coaches don't always set a good example.   Though nearly 90 percent of high school athletes report that most of their coaches set a good example regarding ethics and sportsmanship, it is not clear they know what a good example is. Large portions of these same athletes endorse questionable actions of coaches including: (1) **arguing with an official intending to intimidate or influence future calls** (51% of males, 30% of females); (2) **instructing players how to illegally hold and push opponents without getting caught** (45% of males, 22% of females); (3) **using a stolen playbook** of another team (42% of males, 24% of females); (4) saying nothing when an official **declares the wrong score in favor of the coach's team** (a mathematical rather than a judgment error) (40% of males, 21% of females); (5) **instructing a player to fake an injury** to get a needed extra time out (39% of males, 22% of females); (6) ordering a pitcher to **throw at an opposing hitter in retaliation** after a key player was hit by a pitch (30% of males, 8% of females); (7) **swearing at an official to get thrown out of a game** in order to get a team worked up (38% of males, 12% of females); and (8) using **profanity and insults to motivate players** (37% of males, 15% of females).

Many high school athletes break rules and engage in unsporting conduct.   Judging by the conduct and attitudes of young athletes, it appears that many coaches place winning above the concept of honorable competition and sportsmanship by teaching or condoning illegal or unsporting conduct. Thus, high percentages think it is proper to: (1) **deliberately inflict pain in football to intimidate** an opponent (58% of males, 24% of females); (2) **trash talk a defender after every score** (47% of males, 19% of females); (3) **soak a football**

field to slow down an opponent (27% of males, 12% of females); (4) **build up a foul line in baseball to keep bunts fair** (28% of males, 21% of females); (5) **throw at a batter who homered last time up** (30% of males, 16% of females); and (6) **illegally alter a hockey stick** (25% of males, 14% of females).

Cynical attitudes about success.   Nearly half of the male athletes reveal cynical attitudes about the prevalence, necessity, and legitimacy of cheating in the real world. Thus, high percentages agree with the following statements: (1) "in sports, **people who break the rules are more likely to succeed**" (30% of males, 15% of females); (2) "in the real world, **successful people do what they have to do to win even if others consider it cheating**" (56% of males, 45% of females); and (3) "**a person has to lie or cheat sometimes in order to succeed**" (43% of males, 27% of females).

Winning more important than sportsmanship.   (1) More than one in three males (37%)—versus only 15% of females—agree that "when all is said and done, **it's more important to win than be considered a good sport.**" (2) Whereas 94 percent of females agree that "**playing the game fairly and honorably is more important than winning,**" 20 percent of the males disagree. (3) Whereas 87 percent of females believe that a high school **coach "should be more concerned with character building and teaching positive life skills than winning,**" more than one in four males (27%) disagree. (4) Thirty-one percent of males and 25 percent of females believe their **coach is more concerned with winning than in building character** and life skills.

Putting sports above all.   Only half of all athletes (52%) think it is improper to hold an academically successful student back a grade so he will be older and bigger when he plays high school football; 25 percent say they are unsure.

Performance enhancing drugs.   (1) Twelve percent of males and 3 percent of females **used performance enhancing drugs** in the past year. (2) Seventy-eight percent of males and 91 percent of females agree that "no athlete should use performance enhancing drugs because it is **unhealthy.**" (3) Seventy-eight percent of males and 87 percent of females agree that "no athlete should use performance enhancing drugs because it is **cheating.**"

Playing more important than winning.   As a counterpoint to the winning obsession, 72 percent of both males and females say they would rather play on a team with a losing record than sit on the bench for a winning team, and more than one-fourth of the males (28%)—as opposed to only 13 perccent of the females—say that winning is essential for them to enjoy the sports experience.

Whereas the results portrayed above are attitudinal, what follows shows actions taken as a result.

Cheating and theft.   In the past year: (1) Sixty-eight percent of both males and females admitted **cheating on a test** in school; (2) 26 percent of males and 19 percent of females said they **stole something from a store**; and (3) 43 percent of males and 31 percent of females said they **cheated or bent the rules to win**.

Hazing and bullying.   (1) Thirty-one percent of males and 17 percent of females report that **degrading hazing or initiation rituals** are common at their school. (2) Sixty-nine percent of males and 50 percent of females admit that they bullied, teased, or taunted someone in the past year. (3) Fifty-five percent of males and 29 percent of females said they used racial slurs or insults.

The Josephson Institute also published the *2004 Report Card on the Ethics of American Youth*, which surveyed nearly 24,763 high school students. It showed that the moral compass that seemed so adrift for high school student-athletes also applied to their classmates who did not play sports. The only encouraging part was that there were improvements from a 2002 survey the institute had conducted.

- 82% admit they lied to parent within the past 12 months about something significant—and 57% said they lied two or more times. In 2002, 93% said they lied to parents.
- 62% admit they lied to teacher within the past 12 months about something significant—and 35% said they lied two or more times. In 2002, 83% said they lied to teachers.
- 35% copied an Internet document within the past 12 months—and 18% did so two or more times. This question was not asked in 2002.
- 62% cheated during a test at school within the past 12 months—and 38% did so two or more times. This is a major decrease from the 74% who admitted cheating on an exam in 2002.
- 83% copied another's homework within the past 12 months—and 64% did so two or more times. This question was not asked in 2002.
- 22% stole something from a parent or other relative within the past 12 months—and 11% did so two or more times. In 2002, 28% admitted stealing from a parent or other relative.
- 18% stole something from a friend within the past 12 months—and 7% did so two or more times. In 2002, 22% admitted stealing from a friend.
- 27% stole something from a store within the past 12 months—and 13% did so two or more times. This is a huge drop from 2002, when 38% admitted stealing from a store.
- 23% cheated or bent the rules to win in sports within the past 12 months—and 12% did so two or more times. This question was not asked in 2002.

Many of those high school students and student-athletes will end up on our campuses and will further challenge faculty, coaches, and administrators in their attempt to chart an ethical course for the institutions they serve and the community that comprises the institutions.

CRISES FACED BY AMERICAN YOUTH

Are these young people somehow less moral than the previous generation? I think there is more pressure and more crises in their lives than in any previous generation. I hope that people now entering the profession of sports administration have a better grasp on the culture of our youth. Many think that hip-hop is an urban phenomenon. Some of the same people thought school violence was an urban phenomenon until school shootings started taking place in more than ten locations that were anything but urban—and that drugs were an urban phenomenon until wealthy prep schools and sub-urban and rural schools had their own serious problems with drug and alcohol abuse. We need to understand our culture today better than we do.

In 1996, I was a member of the National Commission on Society, Culture, and Community. On the commission were people like Derek Bok, President Emeritus of Harvard, Judith Rodin, then President of the University of Pennsylvania, Lannie Guinier, Harvard Law Professor, Amy Gutman, then Provost of Princeton and now President of Penn, Anthony Appiah, of Harvard's Afro-American Studies Department, and former Senator Bill Bradley, among others.

We had a meeting in the second week of September focusing on the lack of civility and the decline of ethical and moral principles in our society. A significant part of the first hour was centered on how Tupac Amaru Shakur had helped the decline along with other rap artists. One week earlier, Tupac had been murdered after a fight in Las Vegas. As a distant observer of gangsta rap, the discussion made some sense to me. One of our biggest programs at the Center for the Study of Sport in Society was MVP, a gender violence prevention program. I knew that women were not only objectified in this music but that violence against women was an open topic of the lyrics.

About two weeks later I was coming to the NBA's Rookie Transition Program, which was taking place in Virginia. I was picked up at Dulles Airport by the NBA in a luxury bus that also had five rookies on board—all African-American. The discussion centered on *what would they do without Tupac*. Each talked about how great Tupac was as a writer, singer, actor, and playwright. They identified with his time in jail and were aware that he was the son of Afeni Shakur, who was a Black Panther Party leader and was considered a political prisoner back in the day. In a lot of ways I was surprised they even knew there was a Black Panther Party, considering the lack of historical knowledge of many young people today.

It helped me realize how huge the gap was in how we could perceive the same person so very differently. I talked to Emily, my 15-year-old daughter, about it. She said, "I love Tupac!" Apparently he crossed race, gender, age, and class.

I know part of our concern with college sport in the years ahead will be, how do we better understand the athletes coming to our campuses? Will their self-images sometimes conflict with role model status? How will the public view them compared to what they may think of themselves, which could be in a totally different light? What is a positive image to a student-athlete compared to what it is to the college?

So what is the world of these student-athletes like? It is not only hip-hop. The last four years have been colored by the events of September 11, 2001, and two wars. The uncertainty of life has been added on top of complex adolescent years. For me, the film *Hoop Dreams*' most poignant moment was at Arthur Agee's 18th birthday party, when his Mom, Shelia, said, "He lived to get to see 18. That's good." Too many of Arthur's friends were dead or in jail.

Many live in a violent world. According to the Centers for Disease Control and Prevention, more than 400,000 youth ages 10 to 19 were injured as a result of violence in the year 2000 (CDC, 2001). On an average day, 12 children under the age of 16 are killed by a gun (Children's Defense Fund). More than one-third reported being in a physical fight in the past 12 months, and more than 6 percent of high school students surveyed had carried a weapon during the preceding 30 days (CDC, 2002).

Many live in a world where male-on-female youth violence is almost the norm. According to the Commonwealth Fund Survey for the Health of Adolescent Girls (Schoen, C., 1997), 26 percent of girls in grades 9 to 12 have been the victim of physical abuse, sexual abuse, or date rape. Among teenage girls between ages 14 and 17, 40 percent reported knowing someone their age who had been hit or beaten by a boyfriend (Children Now/Kaiser Permanente Poll, December 1995). Approximately one in five adolescent girls reported being physically or sexually hurt by a dating partner (Silverman, J.G., 2001, *Journal of American Medical Association*). One in seven college females are sexually assaulted while in college (Center for the Study of Sport in Society, Northeastern University).

Though teen pregnancy is decreasing, 34 percent of young women become pregnant at least once before they reach the age of 20 (National Campaign to Prevent Teen Pregnancy, 2004). Only one-third of teen mothers are likely to complete high school and 1.5 percent earn a college degree by age 30 (Maynard, R. A., 1996). The United States has the highest rates of teen pregnancy and births in the Western industrialized world. Teen pregnancy costs the United States at least $7 billion annually (National Campaign to Prevent Teen Pregnancy, 1997).

There is an epidemic of sexually transmitted diseases (STDs) among the nation's teenagers. Dr. David Hager reported that within the United States each year there are 7 million STD cases contracted by U.S. teens. According to the American Social Health Association, teens have the highest contraction rate within the general population and almost 45 percent of all teenagers and young adults contract at least one STD by their mid-20s. Approximately

40,000 new HIV infections occur each year in the United States. Of these newly infected people, half are younger than 25 years of age (CDC, 2001).

Is teenage drug use an issue? Though only 20 percent of teenagers admit using marijuana, a majority are concerned about the problem of drug abuse among friends. Seventy-two percent of teens characterize use of drugs such as marijuana and cocaine as either a "very serious" (52%) or "somewhat serious" (20%) health issue among their teenage friends (2004 Gallup Youth Survey).

According to the 2004 Monitoring the Future (MTF) survey (study of teen drug abuse by the University of Michigan's Institute for Social Research, sponsored by the National Institute on Drug Abuse), the proportions of high school students using any illicit drug in the previous 10 months, though declining, still represented 15, 31, and 39 percent in grades 8, 10, and 12, respectively.

There is a similar pattern regarding teenage drinking. Though only 27 percent of teens admit using alcohol, a majority are concerned about the problem of drug abuse among friends. Seventy-four percent of teens characterize alcohol abuse as either a "very serious" (42%) or "somewhat serious" (32%) problem among their teenage friends (2004 Gallup Youth Survey). As with drugs, alcohol use is also greater among older teens than younger teens (37% vs. 20%) (McMurray, C., 2004).

According to the National Clearinghouse for Alcohol and Drug Information, it is estimated that over 3 million teenagers are out-and-out alcoholics. Several million more have serious a drinking problem that they cannot manage on their own.

The average age when youth first try alcohol is at 11 years for boys and at 13 years for girls.

Obviously we do not know what applies to each of the athletes joining our college sports, but we do know that we have so much more to deal with to help them. Are our athletic departments equipped to help young people who arrive on campus already in some form of crisis?

CONCLUSION

Myles Brand has provided a breath of fresh air and a hard-driving charge on reforming many of the issues that will be covered in the next section, "The Issues." Those include money in sports, ethics, race in general in college sport, and a chapter on the special cases of football, gender, gambling, agents, performance enhancing drugs, and the influence of the media.

The views from "The Players" section, from presidents, conference commissioners, athletics directors, faculty, and student-athletes will give us an idea of the possibilities for the success of the reforms.

There is an army of moral and ethical coaches and student-athletes out there who are ready to help.

Yet the chase for the money at stake in college sport led to many of the long list of ethical and legal transgressions between 2003 and 2004. Sometimes it can be a battle of good versus evil, ignorance versus arrogance, or the powerful versus the powerless. But there is no doubt that there is a battle for the integrity of the enterprise of college sport.

CHAPTER 3

Higher Education's Failed Experiment with Professional Athletics

John R. Gerdy Ohio University

In the movie *Casablanca*, there is a scene where Louie, the chief of the local French police, is ordered by the commander of the occupying German army to shut down Rick's Café, a nightclub/casino frequented by French nationalists during World War II. Rick, played by Humphrey Bogart, protests. "On what grounds?" he asks. To which Louie replies, "I am shocked—shocked—to discover there is gambling going on in here." No sooner has he spoken than a casino runner approaches him, hand extended furtively, muttering, "Your winnings, sir."

Though humorously depicting the hypocrisy of publicly stated ideals versus actual practice, the scene could very well be describing the behavior of American higher education leaders regarding the role and impact of Division I athletics on our colleges and universities. Unfortunately, such behavior, which serves to erode higher education's values and integrity, is anything but funny. When educational leaders condemn the pervasive commercialism of college sport while extending their hands to collect the financial benefits such commercialism allegedly brings, the negative impact on educational values, academic integrity, and public trust in higher education is enormous.

It is extremely ironic that we increasingly bemoan the degree to which college athletics have become commercialized. What do we expect? After all, it was precisely *because* of its commercial value and potential that intercollegiate athletics was incorporated into the fabric of American higher education.

Until the late 1800s, university athletics were operated by student-run associations. Students were responsible for travel arrangements, equipment procurement, and the general administration of the teams. Athletics was simply an institutional afterthought, an activity to keep students amused but certainly not critical to the educational mission of the university. It was the ever-constant search for resources, coupled with the rapidly growing public interest in athletics and the resultant capability to generate revenue, that enticed presidents and boards to formally incorporate athletics into the structure of their institutions. In short, institutions began to assume full control over the administration of athletic programs specifically for the purpose of generating revenues and resources in the form of money, increased visibility, student enrollment, and alumni favor through its ability to unite the university and surrounding communities. Interestingly, it was later, after concerns began to surface over athletics' negative impact on institutional academic values, that the athletic establishment began to promote athletics' educational benefits for student-athletes.

From television's influence over starting times of games, to shoe companies supplementing coaches' contracts, to corporate logos plastered on fields and scoreboards, there is no denying that college athletics is impacted by an enormous corporate influence. But simply because corporate influence is so visible does not necessarily mean it is the big, bad ogre of college sports. Commercialism has become an easy target, primarily because it implies that the problems of college athletics result from external influences that cannot be kept at bay. This analysis of the ills of intercollegiate athletics is convenient and comfortable because it places the responsibility for the evolution of the enterprise on outside influences rather than on decades of a lack of engagement and resolve on the part of faculty, presidents, and trustees.

It is time, however, for the higher education community to face up to the fact that commercial and corporate influences have little to do with the failure of our current system of Division I athletics to meet not only its educational purposes but, most ironic of all, its commercial purposes. Rather, it is the model that American higher education has chosen to try to reap the commercial potential of athletics to advance higher education's mission that is the problem. It is no longer in doubt that Division I athletics, in particular football and basketball but with other sports marching down the same road, have attempted to become professional teams—very expensive professional teams—in college uniforms. And the responsibility for the evolution of that model lies not in corporate boardrooms but solely at the feet of American higher education.

Consider the essence of professional athletics: pay for play. Despite the idealist rhetoric of the athletic establishment, the reality is that the contract between the athlete and the institution no longer represents the ideal of "pay (scholarship) for education." It is not pay for education when it is plain to everyone—coaches, fans, faculty, media, and especially, the athletes—that they are on campus, first and foremost, to play ball. *That*, by any definition, is "pay for play."

The professional model is also about paying whatever you have to for coaches, staff, facilities, scouting, travel, and anything else that coaches believe might make the difference between winning and losing, regardless of how outrageous or remote the actual impact. This culture of spending to win has escalated to an absurd level to where it makes neither fiscal nor educational sense. Professional sports is also about playing anywhere at anytime to reap television revenues. And professional athletics is about the expectation that athletes train year-round and sacrifice their bodies for "the program." Division I athletics has evolved to a point where it has come to mirror these aspects of the professional model.

In short, it is not commercialism that has led to the failure of Division I to contribute in timely, relevant, and fiscally sound ways to institutional mission. Rather, it is the fact that the higher education community has allowed the professional sports model to develop on campus virtually unchecked. And higher education simply has no business being in the business of professional athletics.

THE FAILURE OF A SYSTEM

A first glance would suggest that, from a commercial standpoint, professionalized college athletics is booming. Basketball and football games can be seen on television virtually every night of the week. CBS paid the NCAA more than $6 billion for the rights to telecast the NCAA men's basketball tournament for 11 years. Conference championship and football bowl and basketball tournament games generate millions of dollars for participating institutions and their conferences. Corporations pay millions of dollars for sponsorship rights for events and for skyboxes in stadiums. There is now a 24-hour college sports cable network. Colleges also rake in millions from the sale of sports apparel and related merchandise. Corporate logos are plastered on fields, courts, equipment, and uniforms, and coaches are paid hundreds of thousands of dollars to hawk products. Athletics department budgets are bigger, as are stadiums, arenas, and athletic administration buildings.

But if all of these things are true, why is it that the vast majority of athletic programs lose money? And why is it that virtually all the commercial justifications for which athletics was incorporated into American higher education are not being realized? Most important, why does the higher education community refuse to confront the fact that its century-old experiment with using professional athletics as a commercial entity to advance educational values and institutional mission has failed?

At a time when college athletics has reached unprecedented levels of commercial popularity, how can it be said that its incorporation into higher education has failed? As mentioned, athletics was formally incorporated into higher education because it was believed it could be used as a vehicle to advance educational ideals and values and thus contribute to institutional mission. That being the case, it would follow that the "success" of such programs would be judged by how effective they are in meeting those goals. Unfortunately, the justifications upon which athletics was accepted within the walls of the academe are not the standards upon which we have come to judge them. Today, a college athletic program's "success" is measured by wins and losses, revenue generated, television appearances, and championship banners hung from gymnasium rafters. Such standards have very little relevance as they relate to the societal challenges that higher education is expected to provide leadership in addressing. Rather, these are the standards that are used to measure the success of professional sports franchises.

SHOW ME THE MONEY!

Consider, for example, the following trends, all of which lend strong credence to the claim that Division I athletics, as currently conducted, is failing to meet its purposes. The most fundamental justification for university-sponsored, professionally modeled athletics is its capacity to generate resources. But despite the widely held belief that athletic programs generate enormous revenue for colleges and universities, the fact is that nearly 80 percent of the programs actually *lose* money! According to a 1999 NCAA study, only 23 percent of Division I programs generate more revenues than they expend (Fulks, 29, 47, 65). And in the past two years alone, the number of Division I schools that operate at a profit declined from 48 to 40 and the average deficit size increased from $3.3 to $3.8 million. Though the profitability of an athletic department may not be a major concern at those schools in which athletics is an institutional budget item (largely NCAA Division II and III institutions), it does raise significant concern at institutions that have established programs intended to produce revenue.

More significant, these figures must be considered against the larger backdrop of higher education finances and our nation's economy. As universities continue to chase the holy grail of professional athletics at substantial cost, college tuition is rising dramatically. According to a 2002 study by the College Board, tuition and fees at public schools have increased by 38 percent over the past decade. For the 2002–03 academic year, the average tuition and fees charged by public four-year colleges and universities increased by 9.6 percent (College Board, 4). Further, public institutions are carrying greater debt. Three years ago, the average debt for a public institution was $87 million. Today, it is over $140 million (Schemo). The result is that at a time when our country desperately needs more high school graduates to continue on to college, it is becoming increasingly difficult for middle and lower class students to afford to do so.

Meanwhile, according to the National Governor's Association, state economies are experiencing their worst fiscal crisis since World War II. This will dramatically affect state spending on higher education. According to a survey conducted by Illinois State University's Center for the Study of Education Policy, colleges are facing the most sweeping spending cuts in a decade. In spending plans states have adopted for the 2002–03 fiscal year, aggregate appropriations for higher education only rose 1.2 percent, failing to keep pace with inflation, which was 2 percent for the 12 months ending in October 2002. That figure is about a quarter of the 4.6 percent increase in 2001–02 and the smallest such rise since the 1992–93 fiscal year, which saw a 0.09 percent drop (Arone). In short, states are hurting economically and higher education will feel the pinch in a dramatic way.

Given these trends, it is becoming more difficult to justify sinking increasingly large amounts of money, resources, and energy into maintaining professional athletic programs that, while entertaining, have lost virtually all connection to the central mission of the institution.

It is unfair, however, to evaluate an athletics department's performance on dollars alone. Athletics, it is said, generates resources in the form of student enrollment, alumni giving, visibility, and public relations. Though it is logical that it would benefit the institution in these ways, it is becoming increasingly clear that even in these areas, athletics is simply not delivering on its promise.

For example, recent data contradict one of the strongest myths about college athletics—that winning teams and especially winning football teams, have a large, positive impact on rates of philanthropic giving at universities that operate big-time programs (Bowen & Shulman, 220). In general, alumni favored *decreasing* their school's emphasis on intercollegiate competition, not increasing it. Those who made the biggest donations assigned lower priority to intercollegiate athletics than to nearly every other aspect of college or university life they were asked to rank (Bowen & Shulman, 204).

Further, the idea that athletics positively impacts a potential student's choice of institution is, apparently, a myth. Neither the quality nor divisional affiliation of a school's sports program were important to most students, as their awareness of intercollegiate sports was extremely superficial. Intramural and recreational sports, for example, have a much greater influence on college choice than intercollegiate athletics. Students rate jobs, internships, student clubs and organizations, and intramural sports as activities that are more important to them in college (Suggs). Most institutions will continue to attract quality students who, when they graduate, will donate money to their alma maters, with little regard to the quality or even existence of a big-time athletic program.

The claim that professional athletic programs serve a unifying function for an educational institution also can be disputed. There are just as many students, faculty, parents, and taxpayers who would rather see institutional resources and energy devoted to improving their school's art, science, theater, or English departments than to renovating a football stadium to include skyboxes that will be utilized less than ten games a year. Further, there are risks in relying on athletic teams to unify educational communities. Schools that use athletics to solve the problems of a fragmented community run the risk of making athletics, and not educational and academic excellence, the primary purpose of the institution. Although a football or basketball program can unite a high school in a way that an English department cannot, the primary purpose of the institution remains, as it always has been, educational. In short, a winning football team does not make a quality educational institution.

And perhaps most disturbing is the discovery that, despite the almost universal acceptance of the notion that issues of college athletic reform apply to big-time football and basketball only, a distinct "athletic culture" is appearing in essentially all sports at all levels of play, including Division III co-ed liberal arts colleges. This culture tends to separate athletes from other students and exacerbates the problem of academic performance, raising even more difficult questions of educational policy for small private colleges and highly selective universities than for big-time scholarship-granting schools (Bowen & Shulman, 82).

Moreover, in virtually every category, these negative athletic effects are becoming greater. This is so because the level of intensity of everything connected to the athletic experience, from recruiting, to individual commitment to the sport, to the level of play, has increased at all levels of sport, from pee-wee to professional leagues, all driven by the increasingly professionalized nature of the entire sports system. The result is that the chasm between athletics' values and priorities and those of the academic community, always palpable, is becoming greater.

Another justification for the use of athletics as a commercial vehicle to advance higher education's goals relates to the issue of visibility and public relations. Though there is no denying that the commercial function of athletics can generate significant public exposure and visibility for universities, the larger question is: What message is higher education sending to the public through its sponsorship of professional athletic programs? Is it a message that promotes positive educational and academic ideals and principles, or rather one that reeks of the hypocrisy of the pursuit of athletics glory and money at any cost?

The most obvious example of the negative visibility associated with our current professional model of college athletics is the national media coverage that accompanies an athletic scandal. Beyond that, however, there are indications that the public views athletics and the NCAA in ways that are harmful to higher education. For example, an NCAA study found that education is not strongly linked with the NCAA image and that most of the public believes that for the NCAA, assuring student-athletes get a degree is a low priority. Further, the image of the NCAA is directly linked with connotations of big business and money and that schools "cheat all the time" (NCAA, 22).

One needs only to watch a televised college football or basketball game to realize that Division I athletics visibility does little to promote educational values or higher education's mission. College sports is packaged, marketed, and projected purely as entertainment, with the promotion of educational themes, values, and information an afterthought at best. It is easy to see why televised college sports are overwhelmingly geared to promote athletics. The "management" of this aspect of athletic programs has always been left to coaches, athletics directors, conference commissioners, and television executives, the very people who are most personally vested in the professional model. As a result, televised college athletics have never been considered as an opportunity to interface with the public in an educational context. Instead, it is simply one game after another, all devoid of any larger educational purpose or vision—just like the pros.

In short, the use of professional athletics as a commercial vehicle to increase visibility and public relations comes at a cost to higher education, in the form of both repeated failures to promote education and the pervasive negative public opinion regarding the hypocrisy of claiming to be about education while operating a professional sports franchise.

GENIE OUT OF THE BOTTLE

If our current professional version of college athletics is failing, what can be done? First, we must acknowledge the fact that as long as we have athletics, commercialism will be a part of it. The genie of commercialism has long been out of the bottle and will never return to it.

Second, we must recognize that the financing of American higher education is radically different from how it was 20 years ago. As we have seen, higher education presidents are becoming less academic leaders than businessmen and fund raisers as colleges have become major financial engines. From corporate naming rights for business schools to corporate-sponsored research, the commercialism of higher education is here to stay. And given a future economic outlook of increasing costs and declining revenues and state funding, the pressure on institutions to partner with commercial entities to maintain academic excellence while balancing budgets will only increase. Against this backdrop, the commercialism of athletics will look increasingly less radical and out of line with the financing of higher education.

In this environment, athletics' potential to generate resources becomes increasingly important. Thus, the question is not whether athletics can or should be used as a commercial entity to advance institutional mission, but rather how to construct and operate athletics to maximize its commercial and educational value while minimizing its propensity to undermine academic values and drain institutional resources. This, coupled with the increasingly convincing case regarding athletics' failure as a commercial enterprise, calls into serious question whether the current professional model, with its runaway costs, its continued undermining of academic integrity, and its win-at-all-costs culture is the most effective way to do this.

CONFRONTING THE ELEPHANT IN THE CLOSET

Though a convincing case can be made that professional athletics should not be a part of our nation's system of higher education, it is not to say that intercollegiate athletics, or even commercialized athletics, should be eliminated from higher education. To the contrary, the benefits and positive influence of university-sponsored athletic programs that are fiscally responsible and consistent with institutional mission and academic values can be enormous. Such programs, even programs with commercial ties, can and should advance an academic agenda and contribute to institutional mission in meaningful ways. And it is not the value of elite athletics in our culture that is at issue, but whether our educational institutions should be saddled with the responsibility of developing elite athletes and sponsoring professional teams.

It is interesting to note that the United States is the only country in the world in which such programs are sponsored by educational institutions. In Europe, by contrast, the responsibility for the development of elite athletes and teams is borne by private sports clubs or professional teams. In the development and promotion of highly competitive, elite athletics, could it be that the Europeans, rather than we Americans, have it right?

In short, if Division I athletics, *as currently structured and conducted*, is not meeting the purposes for which it became a part of higher education, we have a responsibility to eliminate them or dramatically restructure them so they do. The history of American higher education offers many examples of programs or departments that were downsized or eliminated when it became apparent that they had become obsolete, had failed to meet their purpose, or had become a drain on institutional resources. Perhaps it is time for colleges and universities to eliminate their departments of professional athletics.

Though one of higher education's strengths is its tremendous diversity of services, programs, opportunities, and mission, it is time to face the fact that, in the case of athletics, higher education may not be able to have it all. Perhaps the sponsorship of highly competitive, commercialized, professionalized, elite athletics—in other words, the professional model of athletics— should be left to the professional leagues. Rather than trying to be all things to all people, perhaps higher education's responsibility in the cultural subject matter of athletics should be twofold: first, to positively impact the health and fitness of our populace with an aggressive commitment to involving the maximum number of participants in sports activities that can be enjoyed for a lifetime for purposes of promoting public health in this country, the most obese nation in the world; and second, to provide entertaining but educationally based intercollegiate athletics.

DECONSTRUCT IT AND THEY WILL STILL COME

For the past century, American higher education has rushed headlong down the road of making athletics bigger, better, and more professional. Unfortunately, that road has taken athletics to a point where they have become widely viewed as promoting values and practices that actually run counter to those of the academic community. Further, the competitive pressure to increase athletics department budgets has resulted in an "arms race" that threatens the fiscal integrity of a growing number of institutions. With almost 80 percent of Division I athletic programs losing money as a result of their attempt to keep pace in the fiscal arms race, perhaps it is time to take a new road—a road that would require not simply strengthening eligibility standards, but deconstructing the entire enterprise. Specifically, the professional model of intercollegiate athletics must be dismantled and rebuilt, not as a mirror of professional sports, but in the image of an educational institution. Such a model could and should include a commercial element. This, after all, was the primary reason athletics was originally incorporated into higher education. The first step in that process is to aggressively and directly challenge the prevailing notions regarding the relationship between the current model of the professionalization of athletics and public and commercial interest in college athletics.

Despite the self-serving rhetoric of coaches and athletics administrators, the popularity of college athletics is not driven by the requirement that it mirror the professional sports model. To the contrary, college athletics' appeal rests in the notion that it stands for something other than a win-at-all-costs business enterprise, where athletes are pieces of meat with no other purpose than to win games, generate revenue, and provide entertainment. What makes college athletics attractive is that there is a link to a higher purpose, specifically, education. In college, athletes are also supposed to be students, coaches are supposed to be educators, and the games, above all, are supposed to be about school spirit and fun.

Division I athletics—football and basketball in particular—has come to look, feel, and operate so much like the pros that there is very little to distinguish the values and principles of the two. If athletics is ever going to contribute effectively to institutional mission, higher education leaders must have the courage and confidence to halt the steady and destructive march toward the win-at-any-cost professional model. To do so will require a fundamental change in the collective mindset of the higher education community.

Specifically, it is the courage and will to act upon the fact that college athletics is higher education's property—not ESPN's or CBS's, not Nike's or

Adidas's, not corporate America's, not the sports talk show hosts, and not the crazed, face-painted fan in the stands. That being the case, it is the higher education community alone that must establish the rules of the game, the values of the enterprise, and the principles upon which it will be presented to the public. Higher education can make athletics look like and represent whatever it wants. And if higher education leaders are serious about reforming athletics, they must address not the commercial, but rather the professional, aspects of the enterprise.

To do this, the fundamental principle upon which the professional sports model is built upon—"pay for play"—must be changed. Specifically, the athletic scholarship must be eliminated in favor of institutional need-based aid.

FREEDOM TO PURSUE AN EDUCATION

At first glance, it would appear that eliminating athletic scholarships in favor of a need-based formula would not be in the best interest of student-athletes. However, if this proposal is judged upon what is in their best interest for the next 50 years of their lives rather than the 4 or 5 years they are on campus, it becomes clear that eliminating the athletic grant will contribute significantly to improving student-athletes' chances of obtaining a well-balanced academic, personal, and athletic experience while in college.

Athletic scholarships allow coaches to view students as employees, bought and paid-for by the athletics department. For coaches, an athletic scholarship has little to do with educational opportunity or financial need and everything to do with control. Athletic scholarships are a powerful means of keeping athletes focused on athletic performance. A need-based financial aid system would result in student-athletes being less beholden to athletics departments' competitive motives and thus more free to explore the wide diversity of experiences that college has to offer. And for those athletes who will not play for a school unless they receive a full ride, let them play elsewhere. The game, and the institution, will survive.

Not only would a need-based approach save money for our deficit-ridden athletic programs, it would bring the student-athlete ideal closer to reality. Such a change would have a significant public relations impact. The cynicism associated with the term *student-athlete* is widespread. Everyone knows the score: Division I participants are on campus to play ball, first and foremost. It is for this reason that the faculty-led athletic reform Drake Group has as one of its primary thrusts the elimination of the term *student-athlete*.

In keeping with higher education's responsibility to provide educational leadership in our society, the elimination of athletic scholarships will have a tremendous impact beyond the walls of the academe. As chronicled daily in our newspapers, high school and youth programs have become increasingly competitive and pressure packed: coaches screaming at 7-year-olds for committing an error; parents attacking Little League umpires or fatally beating each other at youth hockey practice; parents and coaches pushing their children to specialize in a sport at earlier and earlier ages; parents suing a coach because their son or daughter doesn't get enough playing time. It is sports, rather than education, that far too many parents and youngsters believe is their ticket to future success. This impact is particularly prevalent in the black community. In the vast majority of cases however, it is a cruel hoax. Much of this out-of-control behavior is justified in that it is the price necessary to earn a college scholarship that will then lead to a pro contract.

Though elimination of the athletic scholarship is the key, there are other aspects of the professional sports operation that must be changed. Freshman ineligibility should be adopted, and spring football and other out-of season practices should be eliminated, as should off-campus recruiting. Basketball and football coaching staffs should be cut in half. Seasons should be shortened, schedules reduced, and travel more restricted. And the NCAA should seek a congressional antitrust exemption with regard to coaches' salaries to keep them more in line with those of faculty rather than Hollywood movie stars.

These changes would significantly shrink the size, budgets, and campus influence of athletics departments. They address the major areas where the athletics "arms race" proliferates: recruiting, salaries, size of staff, and travel. In short, if you operate a business where expenses outpace revenue and will continue to do so in the future, and where revenue streams are close to being tapped out (how many more stadium boxes can you build and how much more stadium signage can you sell?), there is only one way to become solvent: Cut expenses and overhead. Shrink the operation.

Most reform efforts have been directed at academics, specifically the raising of eligibility standards. Though important, academic reform will not fundamentally alter the Division I landscape. History tells us that raising academic standards does not put athletes in the mainstream as intended. Rather, these changes result in a greater dependence on athletics department tutoring services, the creation of pseudo-majors to keep athletes eligible, and an arms race in the area of academic support programs. That aside, as long as athletes are getting paid to play, the professional model—complete with its escalating budgets, widening deficits, and attendant public skepticism—will remain. Though raising academic standards will result in a few more athletes graduating, the fundamental underpinnings, culture, and operating principles of the professional system will remain.

THE "QUALITY OF GAME" MYTH

Somewhere along the line we have bought into the notion,—a notion advanced by the athletic community—that what makes college athletics commercially viable is the quality of the game. This mentality has driven the cost structure of our programs to a level that no longer makes sense. Regardless, the mere suggestion of the above-mentioned changes will result in claims from coaches and athletic directors that the public will not accept the diminished "quality of game" that might result from such changes.

Prove it!

There is absolutely no evidence to suggest that changes such as those mentioned will adversely affect Florida's, Penn State's, or UCLA's long-term entertainment value in the marketplace. Ultimately, the Alabama fan who is watching the running back turn the corner to score a touchdown does not care whether that youngster runs the 40-yard dash in 4.4 or 4.8 seconds, or whether he participated in spring practice, or whether he is on an athletic scholarship, or whether the coach visited him at his home to recruit him, or how much his coach is paid. That fan cares about only two things: first, whether Auburn is abiding by the same rules and second, whether the player scores a touchdown for Alabama.

It has been the athletic establishment's rhetoric and propaganda about "the quality of the game," coupled with the academic community's lack of courage to confront their claims, that is most responsible for the fiscal excesses and professionalization of college athletics. College athletics' appeal rests not in how high the players jump or how fast they run, but rather in the fact that the activity is steeped in university, educational, and cultural tradition. Michigan vs. Ohio State, Texas vs. Texas A&M, Harvard vs. Yale, and Auburn vs. Alabama will always draw crowds, be covered by the media, and captivate the public's imagination, regardless of the level of play.

Given that higher education's most fundamental purpose is not to generate sports entertainment, but to provide educational, scientific, moral, medical, and ethical leadership in helping our society meet the many challenges it faces in today's rapidly changing, increasingly complex world, that property must be conducted and governed based upon not athletic but educational values and cultural norms. Despite what the power coach or rabid fan might think, when placed in the context of higher education's larger mission, ESPN highlights, championship trophies, and shoe contracts are virtually meaningless.

Even if there were a negative impact on revenues and public interest in college athletics, it would be a small price to pay for a return to a model of college athletics in which athletes are legitimate students, in which coaches are truly educators, and where the athletics department supplements, rather than undermines, academic values and institutional mission. More likely, however, such changes will increase college athletics' public appeal, as many who have lost interest in college athletics due to the hypocrisy inherent in the current system will regain respect for and interest in college sports. This is because most people want college athletic programs to stand for something more than simply turning a buck, preparing the next generation of professional stars, and winning at any cost. For these reasons, corporate interest in college athletics will also increase as companies prefer to associate their product with positive institutions.

In the end, not only the public but the corporate community and television networks will continue to be interested in and support college athletics, regardless of the form it takes. This, in large part, is due to the fact that college athletics is a monopoly. Because it is the only college game in town, people will continue to come to games, watch them on television, listen to them on the radio, and read about them in the newspapers. So why not spend half as much money on the enterprise and, in the process, reconnect it to the educational institution and academic values?

In short, if the operation is downsized, deconstructed, and refocused upon education, fans will continue to come.

A NATIONAL "TEACHING MOMENT"

The above assessment of athletics' failure to meet its institutional objectives is sobering and the prescriptions, for some, downright frightening. This, however, does not mean that the situation does not present an important opportunity for higher education. To visualize this opportunity, though, requires the consideration of the role that organized sports have come to play in our culture as they relate to higher education's historical mission.

It is no stretch to say that our country has lost perspective regarding the role of organized sport in our culture. We have come to glorify athletic accomplishment far more than academic achievement. And we in higher education have, in large part, been responsible for allowing this culture to evolve. Rather than fighting to maintain the academic and educational integrity of this, higher education's most visible resource, we have instead opted for passive resistance to the proliferation of the values and practices of the professional model of athletics and the resultant win-at-all-cost, keep-up-with-the-Joneses, spend, spend, spend mentality it perpetuates.

The result has been the grotesque distortion of educational priorities through the disproportionate resources and attention devoted to intercollegiate athletics. For 23 percent of the institutions, the distortion and losses may be limited to a destruction of academic values and educational mission. For the other 77 percent, the loss is far greater. These institutions not only lose significant amounts of money on the athletic enterprise, but they experience an even greater loss of academic values and mission because their unrealistic striving and emphasis to "be competitive" drives them to reallocate to athletics funds that rightfully belong to other departments or university functions that are far more closely linked to the core academic mission of the institution.

Given higher education's leadership role in our society, if we are ever going to begin the process of restoring our cultural consensus regarding the proper relationship between sport and education, it is up to the higher education community to initiate it. Perhaps this is an unfair burden. After all, most would argue, professional sports also bear some responsibility. Maybe so, but not nearly to the degree that we do. Our responsibility is greater because, in the case of the cultural subject matter of athletics, it is arguable that American higher education has failed in its public mission. We have not provided the necessary leadership in establishing a healthy societal attitude regarding athletics. Simply put, the real costs of American higher education's sponsorship of professional athletics on not only academic values and institutional mission, but society generally, have come to far outweigh the alleged benefits.

Though some may consider it a stretch, the way colleges and universities conduct athletic programs influences their ability to effectively address broader public concerns. Although our tendency has been to rationalize the current state of major college athletics as simply a reflection of societal values, the relationship has become symbiotic, with athletics greatly affecting cultural values as well. Regardless, an educational institution's fundamental purpose is to reinforce positive, not negative, values. It is also easy to say that the problems associated with Division I football and basketball affect only 2 or 3 percent of student-athletes. But again, because of their visibility and financial impact, the influence of these two sports is wildly disproportionate to the number of student-athletes involved in them.

Simply put, as the public comes to view the hypocrisies of major college athletics with a more critical eye, higher education pays a price, specifically in the form of declining credibility and public trust. Such a decline in public trust diminishes higher education's moral authority to address other important societal issues and challenges. If universities cannot conduct their athletic programs with integrity, how can it be expected that the public believe in their ability to effectively address issues such as poverty and illiteracy? Our colleges and universities can no longer afford to waste precious resources in the form of public trust and credibility on athletic programs that compromise these principles. The issues facing higher education and our society are simply too daunting to allow any institutional component, no matter how entertaining, to fall so far short of its intended purposes, particularly in these times of rising costs and tuition, declining state revenues, and economic recession.

In the final analysis, society looks to higher education to provide leadership on a broad array of issues, including the proper role of athletics in our culture. Perhaps the failing state of professionalized college athletics presents higher education a unique opportunity to exert educational leadership by having the courage to say, in the case of athletics, that being bigger and more like the pros is not necessarily better. Perhaps if positioned carefully, correctly, and artfully, higher education leaders could send a strong and much-needed message to our populace that as much as we love professional athletics, it is far more important that we love and value education more. Perhaps the failure of our current model of intercollegiate athletics to meet its purpose of contributing in timely, relevant, and direct ways to institutional mission presents higher education with a very rare and unique national teaching moment.

The issue is balance. Somewhere along the line, our cultural consensus regarding the importance of athletic performance versus intellectual achievement has become grotesquely distorted. And the societal consequences of our loss of perspective are becoming too great. If you accept the notion that higher education's most essential purpose is to provide leadership in addressing the critical issues of the day, its responsibility is clear.

In *Casablanca*'s final scene, as the two characters walk off into the foggy evening, Rick utters the memorable refrain, "Louie, I think this is the beginning of a beautiful relationship." When athletics was formally incorporated into American higher education, it was fully expected that the partnership would be as beautiful and mutually beneficial as Louie and Rick's. Unfortunately, a century later, a more fitting description is, "It's time to end this relationship and build a more sensible one."

The question is whether we have the courage to do so.

REFERENCES

Arnone, Michael. 2002. "State Spending on Colleges Increases at Lowest Rate in a Decade." *Chronicle of Higher Education*. December 13, A-28.

College Board. 2002. *Trends in College Pricing*. New York: College Board.

Fulks, Daniel L. 2000. *Revenues and Expenses of Intercollegiate Athletic Programs: Financial Trends and Relationships*. Indianapolis, Ind.: NCAA.

National Collegiate Athletic Association. 2002. *Will to Act*. Indianapolis, Ind.: NCAA.

Schemo, Diana Jean. 2002. "Public College Tuitions Rise 10% Amid Financing Cuts." *New York Times*. October 22, A-18.

Shulman, James L. and William G. Bowen. 2001. *The Game of Life: College Sports and Educational Values*. Princeton: Princeton University Press.

Suggs, Welch. 2001. "Study Casts Doubt on Idea That Winning Teams Yield More Applicants." *Chronicle of Higher Education*. March 30, A-51.

CHAPTER 4

Ethical Dilemmas in College Sport

Sharon K. Stoll University of Idaho
Jennifer M. Beller Washington State University

INTRODUCTION: DILEMMA? OR NO DILEMMAS?

On fear of trepidation into a world that has vast chasms and little illumination, this chapter is *not* about "ethical dilemmas in sport." From our pedagogical point of view, using ethical dilemmas to teach ethical conduct appears too often to be mired in hopeless and fruitless rhetoric, as individuals typically get lost in the hubris of the issues rather than being able to identify and solve the ethical issue through a principled perspective. It is not that ethical dilemmas do not exist, for ethical dilemmas are as old as sport itself,[1] or that ethical dilemmas could be useful in teaching ethics. The reality, from our point of view of over 40 years of teaching and researching sport ethics, is that without additional ethical study, few folks learn anything from reading about or even studying ethical dilemmas—or, in the jargon of university academe, case studies.[2]

The purpose of this chapter is a twofold argument that: (1) learning ethical principles rather than studying unethical practice and the concomitant consequences should be the basis of studying ethics in sport, and (2) better ethical education for all individuals involved in the athletic experience should be implemented, from the athlete to the president of the institution. It is clear that the present educational system has not prepared the athlete, the coach, or the college and university administrator about the problem of athletic misconduct or financial mismanagement at universities and colleges, for ethical dilemmas abound. Such is not a new or novel condition, for at the very first collegiate athletic event between Harvard and Yale, cheating and unethical misconduct occurred.[3] More than one hundred fifty years later, cheating still occurs and unethical violations or behaviors are the status quo of collegiate sport. Thus, to discuss ethical dilemmas seems rather fruitless, for we could spend a lifetime, and reams of paper, arguing against cheating and unethical practice by discussing the practice—in which the story and outcome is always about the same.

Rules exist and individuals, that is, administrators, coaches, fans, and athletes, knowingly violate the rules but argue that either they did not know or they rationalize that their action was misunderstood. The sordid story usually ends in contrite behaviors, good moral intentions[4] to solve the problem, but wholly naive expectations to mitigate the greater problem. That is: Someone is caught, she is sorry and says "people make mistakes," she is punished, everyone involved is embarrassed, administrative rhetoric is accusatory but contrite, people resign, the athletic program suffers, the program then appears to be clean for a while, new people come in to start the program again, and then the cycle repeats itself—that is, the new people suffer the same inabilities as the former "cheaters" to "be ethical." A case in point is found in any of the 15+ NCAA signature schools who have been sanctioned two or three times since 1992 by the NCAA for violations of rules and are on probation, or some variation of the above, including the University of Alabama, University of Wisconsin-Madison, Baylor, New Mexico State, University of Nevada-Las Vegas, and so forth.[5]

We, the authors, argue that the academic society involved in the study of sport has missed the whole point. Few folks learn anything from reading about or even studying ethical dilemmas—or, in the jargon of university academe, case studies.[6] For case studies miss the focus. The true focus of ethical education should be on the "flawed-ness" of our own humanity. The true dilemma lies in the following conditions: (1) Cheaters will always be with us; (2) all of us will cheat or be tempted to cheat; (3) not one human is above cheating; (4) can we ever expect better behavior; (5) and if so, what conditions will support better ethical behavior? Cheating is symptomatic of a greater malaise—the lack of character education within society.

CYNIC OR TEACHER?

The above comments sound a bit cynical, but such is not the case. The reality is that cheating and ethical violations occur and we are all guilty. It does not matter how righteous we are: We probably cheat or have cheated. How so? Cheating per se is about violating or not holding to an honor-bound promise that we make. That is, we make many promises to follow the rules, whether the rules are mandated and regulated by the state (i.e., speed laws), by an organization (the NCAA rules), or by an institution (i.e., scientific conduct guidelines). If we knowingly violate those rules, we are cheating.

Promise keeping is the key to it all and is premised on a set of principles—or first rules[7]—that we value and hold dear. These first rules stand by themselves and are not based on consequences, and they include the moral values of justice, beneficence, responsibility, and honesty, or in simpler terms, promise keeping. All of us have personal demons that we try to control by making promises. Most times, we keep those promises—but many times we do not. We make a promise to follow some sort of path or rule; then we knowingly choose not to keep our promise by weighing and/or justifying the consequences. Most of these promise violations are somewhat harmless and may *seem* to be trivial. For example, suppose you make a promise to your doctor that you will not eat chocolate because of the health problems it causes you, and then as you pass the candy store you buy a pound package of white chocolate kisses. You justify your action with some sort of intellectual two step: "I really didn't break my word, because I bought white chocolate, which really isn't chocolate after all." Right . . . except it is cheating. You broke a promise.

The chocolate promise appears to be benign and trivial. However, in ethical conduct and moral practice the trivial often defines our moral character. The little things help establish ethical behavior, for a history of little trivial things develop a pattern of moral justification, which later causes great harm. A trivial action that seems to cause no harm may indeed cause great harm—to the reasoning and principled thinking process as well as to how others view your moral actions. And today, promise keeping or not promise keeping is usually accompanied by moral two stepping.

A case in point is the comparison between Coach John Wooden and Coach Dennis Erickson. One took the issue of promise keeping as a spiritual imperative; the other dismissed it as not being expected.

John Wooden, the famous basketball coach at UCLA who won so many collegiate basketball titles, discusses the importance of making promises in his latest book, *Wooden*.[8] John Wooden had a successful career as a high school coach and was being offered excellent collegiate positions. He had been contacted by UCLA to become their basketball coach and was also contacted by the University of Minnesota.

Wooden's first choice was Minnesota, because his wife wanted to stay close to family in the Midwestern United States. Wooden interviewed at both places and was upfront with both schools about his dealings with the other. UCLA made the better offer. But, Wooden still wanted to go with Minnesota. He told Minnesota what he needed, and the individual who was doing the negotiations could not formalize the changes. He needed more time; hence the deal with Minnesota couldn't be finalized. UCLA was pushing Wooden to sign a contract, so finally, Wooden told UCLA that if he didn't hear from Minnesota by 5 p.m. on a specific date, he would sign their contract.

The day came and at 5 p.m., no word came from Minnesota. Wooden immediately called UCLA and told them he would accept their offer. An hour later, Minnesota called and gave him all of the conditions he had requested, plus more. They had tried to call him the entire day, but an ice storm in Minnesota had downed all of the lines. The first time they were able to get through was at 6 p.m.

Wooden turned down Minnesota and took the UCLA job. His simple statement was, "I had to—I had given my word." For Wooden, his character was who he was, as is this simple statement by him: "I am just a common man who is true to his beliefs."

Compare Wooden's story with the following about Dennis Erickson, as told by Mike Pattison.[9] Dennis Erickson ranks as the seventh winningest Division IA active college head coach in the nation, with a winning percentage of 0.722, and he is ninth for total victories with 136. Erickson was the head coach at Washington State University, Pullman, in 1988 and was in the middle of recruiting season. One of the local kids, Michael J. Pattison, in Moscow, Idaho—just eight miles across the Washington-Idaho border—was an outstanding high school quarterback who was being heavily recruited by University of California at Berkeley and Stanford University, as well as Washington State University.

On Friday before the final day of signing, rumors were flying in the community that Erickson was being considered for the next head coaching job at Miami. On Saturday, Erickson was in the living room of Mike's parents, who were very leery of their son attending Washington State University. They thought that Mike could get a better education at Berkeley, Mike's first choice for an engineering degree. However, Erickson was known as a quarterback's coach and Mike really wanted to play and learn under someone of his quality.

The family asked Erickson numerous times, "Will you be the coach at WSU next year?" Erickson gave them his word that he would be at WSU the next year and that Mike would be a starting quarterback for WSU. Mike signed his letter of intent that evening and was on his way to WSU.

The next afternoon, Erickson announced on national television that he had made a deal with Miami to be their head coach. When confronted with the promises that he had made to the WSU recruits, Erickson answered that it was a difficult decision but that he had to consider his family and his responsibilities to them. The amount of money to be earned was more important than the promise to the Pattisons.

At the time, NCAA rules did not permit a player to rescind a recruiting letter without losing a year of eligibility, so Mike Pattison was bound for WSU. His father later said that though his wife was irate with Erickson's behavior, it probably all turned out okay. Their son did get to play quarterback a few times during the career of Drew Bledsoe at WSU. Mike received a great education; he later studied law and today is a practicing attorney in Moscow, Idaho.

INTELLECTUAL TWO STEPS—MORAL JUSTIFICATION

The intellectual two step (moral justification) causes many of the ethical dilemmas that occur in athletic programs.[10] Basically, the two step stems from three different thought processes: (1) The unethical action was really ethical, that is, muddy the waters and make the wrong look like a right. (2) The unethical action was a non-issue in the sense that the action caused no harm to another individual or was unseen, that is, no foul, no harm, see above. (3) A rule was violated but the amount of good accomplished overshadowed the small amount of harm that occurred, that is, the ends justify the means. Many of these problems arise because individuals, as Bertrand Russell[11] states, just do not think. Rather, they react and deal with the consequences afterwards, which is a direct result of limited principled thinking education.

The Unethical Action Was Really Ethical (Muddy the Waters)

This form of moral justification is denying that any unethical action occurred, because the action did not exactly match the definition of cheating in the particular case. For example, the chocolate eater did not really eat chocolate, because white chocolate is not chocolate. Therefore, the promise was not violated and no cheating occurred. The logic resides in the argument that cheating only occurs if the behavior coincides directly to a one-to-one ratio of the exact wording used in the promise. Taken further, this is the typical and false belief that rules or laws can be formulated to define and proscribe ethical practice in each and every case. Therefore, a rule is written in a one-to-one ratio to the possible infraction, with individuals typically treating rules as synonymous with principles.[12]

The NCAA Division I Manual[13] is such an instrument. Rules are written in a retroactive fashion to address a practice that is found to be unethical. Each year more rules are written to cover the problems that occur. One of the results of such a practice, with more rules and more complicated rules books, is that each institution needs (1) compliance officers to monitor coaches and athletes, and (2) athletics directors with law degrees to interpret the rules. Rules, unfortunately, cannot accomplish the task at hand, for it is impossible to write a rule for every possible unethical action. The final interpretation for the athlete, coach, and often the administrator is that the moral view of the NCAA is impossible to follow, and thus begins the intellectual two step that supports the following mindset: (1) If there is no rule against the practice, then the practice must be ethical, and/or (2) the rule does not exactly say we cannot do it.

The Unethical Action Was Trivial, and No One
Saw Me—No Harm, No Foul

Often individuals believe that just as in the case of the chocolate cheater, if no harm occurred to another individual by violating a promise and/or if no one saw the infraction, then the action was acceptable. The logic is something like this: The action is good, that is, the chocolate tastes good, so why not violate the promise? It will only happen this one time, and no one saw me.

However, the truth of the matter is that such logic has a great deal to do with how we value ethical promises and how we will actually carry them out.[14]

Promise keeping is based on the premise that we (1) made the promise, (2) value the promise, and (3) carry out the promise. It *does not* matter if anyone else ever knows that we did or did not keep the promise. And, it *does not* matter how trivial, unimportant, or unsophisticated the promise is. The reality is that higher levels of moral development are dependent on "doing the right" for its own sake, not because people watch us do the right. Character is tied to anonymous ethical action—in this case, to follow-through on promise keeping, even when no one else ever sees or knows that we did.

The "ethics is only when you get caught" mentality is common reasoning in athletics. No harm, no foul. It is the perspective that wrong only occurs if the wrong is caught by an official, an administrator, a coach, and so on. Such little regard for promise keeping follows through in all that we do, and it results in making poor decisions that affect others. Examples of such poor principled thinking can be found daily on the sports page as athletes, coaches, and administrators violate a professional trust, break training rules, break contracts, and break agreements, ad infinitum. A good specific example is the following: A football player was once asked if holding is a violation, to which the player responded, "Only if the referee sees it." The player was then given this scenario: "Let us assume that you have a girlfriend. And let us assume that the two of you have made a commitment to one another. Let us also assume that she has an affair with another player; and, let us assume that you never find out that the affair occurred. Based on your logic about holding, can we assume then that the affair never happened?" Obviously, the player thought the logic didn't apply to the affair and his girlfriend.

Good Overshadows Harm

This form of moral justification is probably the classic "slippery slope"[15] of the intellectual two step. The argument is that rules are usually good, because rules give us direction on how we should act. However, rules can be bad if the rules violate people, or if the rules do more harm than good. The moral justification is based on a convoluted sense of utilitarian ethics, that is, measuring the amount of good done in relation to the amount of harm.[16] The problem with weighing harm is: How much harm is permissible in relation to the amount of good done? In the chocolate eater's case, the harm is rationalized that white chocolate is not chocolate, which is true, but the nutritional elements in white chocolate (i.e., cholesterol and sugar) may do the same amount of harm. Or, the chocolate eater may rationalize that the little bit of harm in not keeping the promise about eating chocolate will never be manifested, because no one will know that the promise was broken.

In most cases, weighing harm and good is the perception that the good done far outweighs the harm. That is, if the good helps others, then the little bit of harm done is acceptable. The chocolate eater's case would not apply because the chocolate eater eats for self appeasement, which is impossible to justify on the basis of good for others. Ethical egoism, or doing the good only for one's betterment, is not about ethics but about hedonism.[17] Ethics is *not* about what is good for me, or what pleasures me, or what I deserve. Ethics is about how we are motivated, how we are intentional, and how we act toward others. We must remember that to weigh the distribution of harm to good is a serious moral reasoning problem. The process most times is flawed, and the outcome could easily violate principles, individuals, and/or the system.[18]

In athletics, breaking rules based on the notion of doing good is a rather standard case. Examples are endless: violating eligibility rules to admit athletes with substandard academic credentials, writing papers for athletes (plagiarism), mitigating social and criminal actions with a "they just made a mistake" rational, and so forth. The argument is: The athletes are really good kids, they need a little help, and being at the university is a good thing for the students, so why not just overlook a rule and help them out?

The intellectual two step occurs, we believe, because as learned people we actually misunderstand or do not value the process of moral development and moral education. As a society, we have been seduced into a postmodernistic philosophy that (1) multiculturalism denies a universal standard of ethics,[19] (2) self gratification is more important than responsibility to others, and (3) because all people make mistakes, we have no right to judge. Doing good ethics is recognizing relativistic thought, "becoming sensitive to moral issues, respecting and loving oneself, looking for win-win solutions, respecting and loving your craft, and searching for moral excellence" (Kretchmar, 1994, 237–38).

To gain these skills demands active, continuing, lifelong education for all. Moral development is not innate by race or class, or by education or position. There is a mystical belief that formal ethics education—that is, seminars, discussions, lectures—is only for people who have problems or did not come from the "right" education or background. "They apparently weren't raised in a good home." "People who are educated know the right thing to do." Or, "obviously, they don't know what is right, look where they live." "We don't need ethics education because it is embedded in the parameters of the project, and a good leader will always be ethical and always ensure ethical actions of his/her followers." These stereotypical comments intimate that if one is white, educated, bright, a professional, and from the right side of the tracks, then one "knows" what is right—and one will not suffer from the malaise of cheating or dishonesty. Such is not reality.

A CASE IN POINT

In 2003, four college presidents—who are supposed to know what is right—found themselves in ethical quandaries by knowingly violating NCAA rules or mismanaging some form of athletic business within their institution.[20] All four matched our stereotypical population of folks who know better. Unfortunately, either they did not know the right or they were doing that proverbial intellectual two step. In two of the cases, outright cheating occurred when a president skirted the rules of his own organization and permitted an ineligible player to attend his institution. One president argued that he "had good intentions, but the NCAA didn't see it that way."[21] In the other two cases, the president hired a coach with a long history of unethical conduct. To their credit, the ethical lapse was not as great as in the former two cases, but they did suffer from the stereotypical arrogance that "in the right environment, the coach would do the right thing." A typical reasoning pattern is: "This coach is a really great guy; you can't help but like him. And in the right environment, he would be monitored and he would *do the 'right thing.'*"

THE ERROR OF ARROGANCE

Unfortunately, most of us are confused about "the right thing" most of the time, college presidents included. Expediency, another type of two step, befuddles all of us. We have not been educated to think morally; rather, we are educated to think globally. We have not been trained to value the right; rather, we have been trained to value efficiency. We have not been immersed in a society that values the right; rather, we are immersed in a society that values compromise. We are mortals who suffer all the vulgarities of being moral and immoral. That is why: (1) Moral education, moral discussion, and moral seminars are needed at all levels of business enterprise and should be held at the minimum of every other month, including at the NCAA; (2) moral criteria should be a part of every business vision and mission; and (3) moral behavior should be supported, expected, and mandated throughout the community, whether it is business or athletics.

TEACHING ETHICS

Of course, to state that ethics can be taught and should be taught to administrators, coaches, and even college presidents causes unrest. Moral education for students or athletes may be acceptable, but for administrators? Yes!

It's acceptable for all administrators—for the *error of arrogance* is to see oneself above the immorality of self. We all need constant education and reminders of the moral life. Moral development and moral behavior is not a finished project. Moral education is a lifelong endeavor. We are not necessarily born moral or immoral, and morality does not mysteriously occur in childhood and stay rooted in our psyches for life. Rather, all of us grow, mature, and develop or do not develop morally through our education and environment, and we are highly affected by moral or immoral role models. Currently, the professional world completely misunderstands the point that moral development is a lifelong endeavor.

Moral education is a combined lifelong informal and formal process of learning in which our own moral sense, personal values, and system of knowing about morality and moral issues influences our actual doing.[22] All of us are inculcated by our life's experiences, and the process culminates in developing what is otherwise known as our moral character, that is, moral development. No specific period of time is known as the end line of character development, though if left unchallenged moral character can become static and, in the right conditions, lost in a vacuum.

However, with challenges to our value systems through what we call moral reasoning, a psychological dissonance occurs in which we begin to ponder our own personal morality, even our professional ethics, and our social responsibility. It is at this juncture that all of us need continual education in morality and ethics. There is no end line for moral education, and the more stressful the profession or the more competitive the vocation, the more one needs active education in ethics (Darley & Batson, 1973; Beller & Stoll, S.K, 1995; Penny & Priest, 1990; Priest & Krause, 1999; Priest & Krause, 1993).

THE TEACHING AND LEARNING OF ETHICS

All of us need reflection and education about morality. Of course, to state that ethics can be taught and should be taught to administrators, coaches, and even college presidents causes unrest. The usual and very tired question is: Can we teach ethics?[23] Should morality be taught through an educational program?

The question is rather remarkable in and of itself. To ask the question is to ask if humans can be taught to value life, to value honor, to value decency, to value codes of conduct, to value honesty, and to value justice. Can humans be taught to take others into consideration before they act? If we honestly believe that ethics cannot be taught, or that individuals cannot be taught moral values, then the whole notion of education as ascribed by pedagogists from Socrates through Goodlad[24] is a lie, a farce. To say that ethics cannot be taught is to believe that goodness and decency cannot be learned. Hence, humankind is beyond help and humans can only react to avarice, violence, debauchery, and indecency. Yet this is not the case, for ethics can be taught and people can learn to care, to share, to give, and to love.

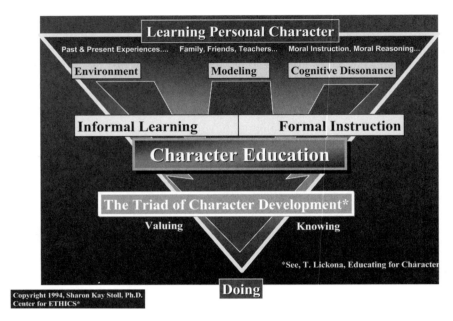

Figure 4.1. A Schematic of the Process of Character Education

Perhaps the question is not if ethics can be taught, but rather whose ethics should be taught? This question rests in fear of religious or political ideologies being forced on unsuspecting individuals. Critics argue that teaching ethics is about teaching individuals to parrot a prescribed religious or political philosophy, in which the human ability to think and reason becomes a programmed "brainwashed" response.

However, such also is not the case. The process of teaching ethics is about inspiring thought and giving tools to make difficult moral decisions—that is, moral reasoning. To teach moral reasoning is to offer the ability to critically assess the importance of moral values and to be able to make moral decisions based on a clearly "thought-out" philosophy of what is right and necessary in relation to both professional and societal principles, laws, and common practice.

The teaching of moral reasoning is about helping others develop a "thought-out" worldview in which one questions one's role, purpose, and responsibility to others. Moral reasoning pedagogy is directed toward reading, writing, and reflecting on personal values, social constructs, and global theories of honesty, fair play, respect, responsibility, and decency toward others. Specifically, the purpose of moral reasoning is to aid in developing a coherent philosophic base of values and ethical conduct. As individuals develop this philosophic base, they learn the skills of good argumentation and reasoning.

Specifically, they ask questions such as: What do they believe about honesty, justice, responsibility, and beneficence? How do those beliefs function globally as well as locally? What skills do they have to make ethical decisions using their value structure in the marketplace, in the businessplace, and in the home? How can they improve those skills to meet and address the difficult ethical decisions of life?

Does the teaching of moral reasoning result in an ethical individual?

No, not completely or totally. The learning of personal morality and the practice of personal ethics is a greater, multifaceted learned experience that is affected by the environment around us and the role models who influence us. Moral reasoning must be in place for consistent moral action to occur, as well as other factors for moral education to occur.

Moral education/character education refers to the deliberate and intentional activity of cultivating, modeling, and teaching moral growth and moral judgment. The resultant purpose of this deliberate and intentional activity is to build habitual patterns in which we have a willing disposition to act upon moral judgment.[25] In other words, moral education is about how one garners the ability not only to form moral judgments but also to have the courage to act upon what one has learned. Moral judgment is only useful if it can be translated into appropriate moral action, or as McIntosh in his 1979 work said, "[t]he morally educated person is expected not only to be able to make moral judgments but act upon them. The moral life necessitates a host of personal dispositions. The moral person must think the issue through to the limits of his capacity but if morally right action is to occur the person must be disposed to act on his moral judgment" (167).[26]

ENVIRONMENT AND ROLE MODELS

Once we have the moral reasoning skills and once we have in place a long-term educational enterprise in which we challenge ourselves through seminars and education, we need to consider the environment in which we reside, both at work and at home.

We are always piqued by individuals who argue that what they do at work does not define who they are as people. How is that? We are who we are, which is our past and present experiences combined. And these combinations of experiences affect our character and our future actions. Our lived environment contains all of our life's experiences from our birth to our present. Our first environmental influence is from our immediate families. We are indirectly educated through our family traditions, family values, religious training, and family history. Our next environment experience comes from school, work, or play. We learn from what our peer group practices, from the values of the group, and from watching what the group does. The environment also instructs us on the greater societal norms, values, and actions. Today our sport influences are highly affected by media presentation, that is, television, Internet, movies, and newsprint. These environmental experiences directly affect what we believe, as well as what we tolerate or do not tolerate. The work environment is who we are—and that environment molds in a great definitive way our character. Hence, it is imperative that the work environment is a place of character and honor. For any less, we will be pulled into the chasm of unethical conduct and immoral behavior.

MODELING

Significant people in our lives serve as role models for us, just as we serve as role models for others. We learn not only by hearing what these important people say, but also through their nonverbal instruction, gestures, facial expressions, and body language. Any person can serve as a role model and can teach others through their actions, words, and behaviors. The character of our role model choice reflects on each of us, and the more powerful job position that individual holds, the more we will be swayed to follow their conduct. Such is the argument for people of character in positions of authority. However, the reality is that all people in role model positions are human and can, do, or will suffer character lapses. The point here is that just because an individual's holding of a position of power does not equate to his or her automatic knowledge of "the right thing to do." And, all individuals in such positions need constant ethical education, reflection, supervision, and challenge from others.

A few years ago, we had a group of football players in a long-term study in moral reasoning. The athletes had numerous classes in moral reasoning and ethics and had scored high on moral reasoning inventories. They "knew" the right and wrong of action on the playing field. Before one of their largest rivalry games, the group was discussing moral action on the field of play. The players made a "covenant" to follow ethical principles: no fights, no dirty play, no taunting during the big game. Saturday the game was televised, and the professor was watching. One of her class leaders made a touchdown and, on television replay, ran down the opponents' sideline, giving them the third-finger salute to celebrate his accomplishment. When the players next met the professor, the professor asked the player what that action was on the sidelines after the touchdown. The player raised his index finger and said, "We're number one!" The professor said, "Chris, I saw the play and I distinctly know the difference between the first finger and the third finger in giving a gesture." The player paused and said, "But doc, it felt so good! I knew better, but it felt so good!"

And that is the crux of doing "good" in ethical conduct—the knowing versus the doing. The environmental forces in sport today do not support ethical action, and thus the challenge will continue to be an uphill battle to combine education with good role models in a supportive ethical environment.

ETHICAL ROLE MODELS, ENVIRONMENT, AND EDUCATION—THE TRUE DILEMMA[27]

Hence the issue is not totally about studying ethical issues or case studies. Rather, the greater dilemma is facing reality: We are mortal and we will fail, unless we understand that an ethical sporting environment—whether it be the sport field, the coach's office, the boardroom, or the president's suite—is dependent upon an ethical vision.

The vision and practice is predicated on the ideals that: (1) moral education, moral discussion, and moral seminars at all levels of business enterprise should be held at the minimum of every other month, including at the NCAA; (2) moral criteria should be a part of every business vision and mission; and (3) moral behavior should be supported, expected, and mandated throughout the community, whether it is in business or athletics.

NOTES

1. Cheating and unethical practice existed at the first Ancient Olympic games. See Gardiner (1978, 1910, and 1925).

2. Research at our Center for ETHICS* has been rather clear. Case studies in and of themselves have little merit in changing moral reasoning or moral development. Rather, intense study in personal morality and development of clear personal goals is imperative, combined with reflection, reading, writing, and further reflection. For further information on this topic, see Lickona (1990); Beller & Stoll (1993, 1994, and 1995); and Shields & Bredemeier (1994).

3. It was a boat race held at a resort, hundreds of miles from either school. The teams were sponsored by a railroad superintendent who saw a good commercial venture. He supplied the teams with free travel on his train to the resort. The teams were there a week ahead of time, in which vast quantities of beer was consumed. When the competition finally occurred, both teams had ringers—boatmen who attended no college. See Smith (1990).

4. See Heschel (1965). Heschel addresses throughout this work the magnitude of "good" intentions that are poorly thought-out and poorly directed.

5. See http://www.usnews.com/usnews/edu/college/sports/rankings/sanctions.htm.

6. Research at our Center for ETHICS* has been rather clear. Case studies in and of themselves have little merit in changing moral reasoning or moral development. Rather, intense study in personal morality and development of clear personal goals is imperative, combined with reflection, reading, writing, and further reflection. For further information on this topic, see Lickona (1990); Beller & Stoll (1993, 1994, and 1995); and Shields & Bredemeier (1994).

7. First rules—meaning more important than any other rules. First rules should govern all ethical decision making. See Fox and DeMarco (1990) and Lumpkin, Stoll, & Beller (2002).

8. See Wooden (1997).

9. Mike Pattison, the father of Mike Pattison Jr., lives in Moscow, Idaho.

10. Bandura (1977) has discussed moral justification in great detail. Bandura's point was about actually physically and emotionally violating others. My example above moral rationalization is about how intellectual people use intellect to convince themselves that what they are doing is really a good thing.

11. "Many people would sooner die than think; In fact, they do," and, "So I had supposed that intellectuals frequently loved truth, but I found here again that not ten percent of them prefer truth." See Russell (1955).

12. Principles predate rules. Principles are written to proscribe personal behavior, and certain first rules should act as guides to behavior. See Lumpkin, Stoll, & Beller (2002).

13. As well as Division II and Division III Manuals.

14. Lickona (1993) does a fine analysis of the three different variables that affect moral development and moral action. He calls them knowing, valuing, and doing. We must know the right, we must value the right, and then we must make a habit of doing the right.

15. Slippery slope means using flawed arguments and more flawed arguments to hold a tenuous position.; or arguing without fact or clear thought to support fallacious reasoning.

16. This is convoluted in the sense of how does one measure harm? William K. Frankena (1973) in his seminal text, *Ethics*, succinctly notes that the problem with utilitarian ethics is deciding how much harm is acceptable. What percentage of harm is acceptable? Is 99% good better than the 1% harm? Or can more than 1% harm be acceptable, that is, 2% or 10% or 20%?

17. Frankena also offers a very good discussion on ethical egoism and hedonism, self-pleasure seeking. Basically, ethical egoism is deciding issues on "what's in it for me," and hedonism is making decisions based on personal pleasure. The chocolate eater is caught up in the pleasure of eating chocolate and attempts to justify breaking promises through the need for self fulfillment.

18. Frankena (1973) discusses the theory of mixed deontic ethics in which principles can function with utilitarian distribution of good. Frankena stresses the importance of principles and how those principles should be applied in a just distribution process.

19. The argument holds that multiculturalism cannot support one standard; therefore, many standards must co-exist, which results in no one standard, which results in cultural relativism as a statement of ethical theory. See Fox & DeMarco (1990).

20. "Foul Shots: Sportswriters on the Basketball Scandals" (2003, March 28).

21. See Suggs (2003, March 28).

22. See schematic attached at end of article.

23. Piper, Gentile, and Parks (1993) describe the difficulties with teaching ethics at a professional school. This an important read for anyone who truly wants to "teach" ethics in the classroom and the barriers that will be met.

24. Socrates is self explanatory in that all Western theory of ethics and reasoning begin in the writings of Socrates. John Goodlad is the educational writer of the current generation who has written often about the importance of thinking and reasoning. He is professor of education and director of the Center for Educational Renewal at the University of Washington in Seattle. Education, according to Goodlad, should cultivate the

sensibilities and the sensitivities of the individual at the highest possible level. That's what it's all about. We want people to be sensitive to the world around them; we want them to have the sensibilities that make it possible for them to recognize the elements of phenomena that need to be dealt with in their lives. We need for them to be sensitive to one another, so they'll have successful relationships with others. It is developing responsible individuals whose individuality is molded in their culture. The school needs to provide that opportunity for interacting. It's entirely a personal thing and an individual thing done in groups.

25. According to Kohlberg (1984), moral education is the encouragement of a capacity for moral judgment.

26. For a fine review of McIntosh and an excellent discussion of sport, ethics, and education, see Arnold (1997).

27. For a more inclusive discussion, see Stoll (2002) and Beller (2002).

REFERENCES

Arnold, P. J. (1997). *Sport, ethics, and education.* London: Cassell.

Bandura, A. (1977). *A social learning theory.* Englewood Cliffs, N.J.: Prentice Hall.

Beller, J. M. (2002, December). "Sport as a positive builder of character." *ERIC Digest.*

Beller, J. M., & Stoll, S. K. (1992, May). "A moral reasoning intervention program for Division-I student athletes." *Athletic Academic Journal,* 43–57.

Beller, J. M., & Stoll, S. K. (1993, August). "Sportsmanship: An antiquated concept?" *Journal of Physical Education, Recreation, and Dance,* 74–79.

Beller, J. M., & Stoll, S. K. (1995, November). "Moral reasoning of high school student athletes and general students: Empirical study versus personal testimony." *Pediatric Exercise Science,* 7(4), 352–63.

Bredemeier, B. J. (1984). "Sport, gender, and moral growth." In J. M. Silva & R. S. Weinberg (Eds.), *Psychological Foundations of Sport.* Champaign, Ill.: Human Kinetics Press.

Bredemeier, B. J., & Shields, D. L. (1986). "Moral growth among athletes and non-athletes: A comparative analysis." *Journal of Genetic Psychology,* 147(1), 718.

Darley, J. M., & Batson, D. (1973). "From Jerusalem to Jericho: A study of situational and dispositional variables in helping behavior." *Journal of Personality and Social Psychology,* 27, 100–08.

"Foul shots: Sportswriters on the basketball scandals." (2003, March 28). [Chronicle Review] *Chronicle of Higher Education,* 49(29), B14.

Fox, J. P., and DeMarco, R. M. (1990). *Moral reasoning: A philosophic approach to applied ethics.* Englewood Cliffs, N.J.: Prentice Hall.

Frankena, W. (1973). *Ethics.* Englewood Cliffs, N.J.: Prentice Hall.

Gardiner, E. N. (1910). *Greek athletic sports and festivals.* London: Macmillan.

Gardiner, E. N. (1925). *Olympia, its history and remains.* Oxford: Clarendon Press.

Gardiner, E. N. (1978). *Athletics of the ancient world.* Chicago: Ares Publishers.

Heschel, A. (1965). *Who is man?* Stanford, Calif.: Stanford University Press.

Kohlberg, L. (1984). *The psychology of moral development: The nature and validity of moral stages.* San Francisco: Harper and Row.

Krause, J. V. & Priest, R. F. (1993). *Sport value choices of United States Military Academy Cadets—A longitudinal study of the class of 1993.* Unpublished research of Office of Institutional Research, United States Military Academy, West Point, N.Y.

Kretchmar, R. S. (1994). *Practical philosophy of sport*. Champaign, Ill.: Human Kinetics.

Lickona, T. (1991). *Educating for character*. New York: Bantam Books.

Lumpkin, A., Stoll, S. K., & Beller, J. M. (2002). *Sport ethics: Applications for fair play*, 3rd ed. St. Louis: McGraw-Hill Higher Education.

McIntosh, P. C. (1979). *Fair play: Ethics in sport and education*. London: Heinemann.

Penny, W. J., & Priest, R. F. (1990). *Deontological sport values choices of United States Academy Cadets and selected other college-aged populations*. Unpublished research, Office of Institutional Research, United States Military Academy, West Point, N.Y.

Piper, T. R., Gentile, M. C., & Parks, S. D. (1993). *Can ethics be taught? Perspectives, challenges, and approaches at the Harvard Business School*. Boston: Harvard Business School.

Priest, R. F., & Krause, J. V. (1999). "Four-year changes in college athletes ethical values choices in sport situations." *Research Quarterly for Exercise & Sport*, 70(2), 170–79.

Russell, B. (1955). *The problems of philosophy*. New York: Capricorn Books.

Shields, D., & Bredemeier, B. J. (1994). *Character development and physical activity*. Champaign, Ill.: Human Kinetics.

Smith, R. A. (1990). *On sports and freedom: The rise of big time college sports*. New York: Oxford University Press.

Stoll, S. (2002). *Can ethics be taught?* Center for ETHICS*, University of Idaho.

Suggs, W. (2003, March 28). "When the president is part of the problem." *Chronicle of Higher Education*, 49(29), A34.

Wooden, J. (1997). *Wooden: A lifetime of observations and reflections on and off the court*. Chicago, Ill.: McGraw Hill, Contemporary Books.

CHAPTER 5

Race in College Sport

Richard E. Lapchick

All across the nation fans cheer for their favorite college teams. Cinderella stories are written, hearts are broken, champions anointed. Yet serious commentators on sport have to focus closely on college sport's lingering problem of the lack of African-American head coaches, especially in football, and poor graduation rates of football and basketball student-athletes, especially African Americans playing those sports.

If you believe in equal job opportunity in sport, then the day in November 2004 that Notre Dame fired head football coach Tyrone Willingham—coming within ten days of Fitz Hill leaving San Jose State and Tony Samuel being fired by New Mexico State—had to be one of the worst moments in the 16-year history of the publication of the *Racial and Gender Report Card.*

The firing left only two African-American head coaches in Division IA football and none in Division IAA. Two coaches was equivalent to only 25 percent of the sport's best mark when eight African Americans led Division IA programs in 1998. Even at that point, only 7 percent of the 117 Division IA coaches were African American. Willingham's dismissal left less than 2 percent when nearly 44 percent of the football student-athletes were African American.

The mercurial and volatile issue of race received a great deal of notice in the days after the firing. It was a low point, but then suddenly West Point, Syracuse, and New Mexico State hired African-American athletics directors within a week, the University of Washington hired Willingham, and Indiana

State hired Lou West as the only African-American head football coach in Division IAA.

I have authored the annual *Racial and Gender Report Card* since the late 1980s. The question we persistently and insistently ask in the *Report Card* is: Can we achieve equal opportunity when it comes to gender and racial equity in the world of college and professional sports?

For 16 years we have documented the gains and losses of women and people of color in the world of sport. What we find is that, over the years, though there is greater opportunity, the world of sport is far from equal. As we saw at the end of 2004, we have gains and losses that can be dramatic. Usually they come one at a time.

I attended the opening games of the college football season in 2003 and 2004. In 2003 it was San Jose State vs. Grambling State in the Literacy Classic. In August 2004, the University of Southern California played Virginia Tech in the Black Coaches Association Classic.

Both games had a notable fact regarding the issue of race. The coaches in the Literacy Classic were Dr. Fitzgerald Hill, then one of four African-American head coaches in Division IA, and Doug Williams, the former Grambling State star who had led the Redskins to the Super Bowl Championship. Up to that point, there had been some 116,000 college football games played. It was only the ninth time in a game between Division I schools in which two African-American head coaches faced each other.

The Black Coaches Association Classic was notable because it marked the eighth game that the association had sponsored. None of the 16 head coaches in those games was a black coach.

In 2004 the hiring of Sylvester Croom as the head football coach at Mississippi State was surely momentous, since Croom was the first African-American head coach in the Southeastern Conference (SEC). Simultaneously, the SEC had its first African-American athletics director, Damon Evans, at Georgia. Those two hirings aside, the positions of head football coach and athletics director remained two of college sports' most segregated positions. Croom was the 19th African-American head coach in the history of Division IA college football. Evans is one of nine African-American athletics directors (ADs) in Division IA. There are three Latino ADs.

As the 2004 season began, none of the five African-American college coaches were at a school listed in the top 25 as rated by ESPN or *Sports Illustrated*. In both polls, Notre Dame was the first to appear, at 38th on ESPN's poll and 41st on *Sports Illustrated's*. UCLA was 53rd and 54th, respectively. No other school with an African-American head coach made the ESPN poll, which included 67 teams that received votes. *Sports Illustrated*, which listed all the schools in Division IA, had Mississippi State 82nd, New Mexico State 99th, and San Jose State 111th out of 117 schools. That made the median rankings of these five schools a dismal 77th.

Of the 19 African-American head coaches, the first breakthrough hire was when Oklahoma hired John Blake in 1996. Three years later Michigan State hired Bobby Williams. Neither lasted more than three seasons. Tyrone Willingham was hired in college football's most storied program at Notre Dame in 2002, and he coached for three seasons. These three men were the exceptions to the prior history of African-American head coaches being hired in losing programs in college football. These are the schools that have hired African-American head coaches: In 1979 Wichita State hired Willie Jeffries. Northwestern and Stanford both hired African-American coaches twice (Dennis Green and Francis Peay at Northwestern; and Dennis Green and Tyrone Willingham at Stanford). Other schools were Ohio University, UNLV, Long Beach State, Wake Forest, Eastern Michigan, Temple, North Texas, Louisville, Oklahoma State, New Mexico State, Louisiana Lafayette, San Jose State, UCLA, and now Mississippi State.

In the new millennium there have been 93 head coaching vacancies at Division IA institutions. Four African Americans have been selected (Willingham was selected twice) to lead those football programs, representing less than 5 percent of the total.

Looking at the previous records of all the schools that have ever hired an African-American coach tells the story. The combined record for those schools in the five years prior to hiring an African American was 528 wins, 736 losses, and 19 ties. The combined record for those schools in the ten years prior to hiring an African-American coach was 1,114 victories, 1,407 losses, and 31 ties. These programs were in deep holes when the African-American coaches took over. Mississippi State was 8-27 in the three years before Croom. Washington was 14-22 in the three years before they hired Willingham and 1-10 in the year before.

In the history of the 117 Division I schools, some of which extends more than a century, there have been 11,754 seasons played. Of those, 85 seasons have been led by an African-American head coach.

Whereas white coaches often bounce from school to school, sometimes fired and other times "moving up," only Dennis Green, Ron Cooper, and Tyrone Willingham have coached at more than one Division IA school. The average tenure of all the African-American head coaches is less than four years. When Willingham was fired at Notre Dame and hired by Washington, he became the first African-American head coach to be hired after being forced out by another institution.

College football can be portrayed as a pyramid:

- At the bottom of the pyramid, 44% of the Division IA football players are African American.
- Looking up the side of the pyramid, as we get closer to the top, 24.4% of the assistant coaches in Division I football are African American. Are

there coaches in the pipeline below Division I? When you combine all three NCAA divisions, only 17% of assistant coaches are African American.

- Approaching the pinnacle, approximately 5% of the coordinator positions, considered to be the most important channels to head coaching positions, are held by African Americans.
- At the top, a narrow 2.6% of all Division IA schools have an African-American head coach. There is one African-American head coach in a Division IAA school.
- White student-athletes were 49.3%, Latinos held 2.2%, American Indian/Alaskan Native held 0.4% and Asian American/Pacific Islander held 1.6% of the football slots in Division I.

I do not think we need to know anything more than the Eddie Robinson story. A news story throughout the three college football seasons prior to publication of this book was whether Bobbie Bowden or Joe Paterno would hold the all-time record for wins in college football. Most seem to have forgotten that Eddie Robinson had 65 victories more than either one of these giants by the end of his incredible career. He sent more athletes to the NFL than any other head coach in the history of college football. His players were good students and good citizens. In spite of this incredible record, Coach Eddie Robinson was not only never hired by a Division IA school, but was never offered an interview. That tells the story even more than the numbers.

WHO COACHES AND PLAYS IN THE OTHER COLLEGE SPORTS

Though media attention has focused primarily on college football, the record for hiring people of color is hardly stellar in any sport except men's basketball.

At the college level, Division I men's basketball set a new high in 2003–04 with 23.2 percent of the head coaching jobs held by African Americans.

In NCAA Division I basketball during the 2002–03 academic year, African Americans made up 57.9 percent of the student-athletes, whites 32.3 percent, Latinos 1.3 percent, "non-resident aliens" 5.3 percent, Native Americans 0.4 percent, and Asian American/Pacific Islanders 0.2 percent, while "others" made up the remaining 2.6 percent. This was the highest percentage for African Americans in more than a decade.

However, the situation in Division I women's basketball programs was very different. At 9.6 percent, the percentage of African-American head coaches was declining just as the percentage of African-American student-athletes was increasing. Another 1.2 percent of the student-athlete slots were held by Asians and Latinos. In fact, there was not a single African-American woman head coach in the 2004 Women's Sweet 16. LSU had Pokey Chatman on an interim basis. She became the head coach after the season ended.

In the 2002–03 Division I women's basketball season, 48.7 percent of the student-athletes were white, 40.9 percent were African American, 1.7 percent were Latina, 0.6 percent were Native American, 1.2 percent were Asian American/Pacific Islanders, non-resident aliens held 4.5 percent, and "others" held 2.4 percent. This was the highest percentage ever for African-American women and made the percentage of African-American women head coaches stand out even more in contrast.

Whereas 100 percent of the head coaches were white in the 2004 Sweet 16, including four white men, 53 percent of the student-athletes on these same teams were students of color. In all of Division I women's basketball, the percent of the head coaching positions held by African Americans is less than half of the rate for men.

We have paid a great deal of attention to the lack of African-American head coaches in Division IA football. The state of women's college basketball may be close behind and could be the next racial frontier to address head-on.

College baseball continued to mirror Major League Baseball with the steep decline of African-American participation as athletes and coaches. There were only two African-American and six Latino head coaches in Division I college baseball in the 2003–04 academic year. During the same year in Division I baseball, African Americans held 6.1 percent (down 0.6 percent), whites held 84.1 percent (up 2.8 percent), Latinos held 5.1 percent (down 0.5 percent), Native Americans held 0.3 percent, Asian American/Pacific Islanders held 1.2 percent, non-resident aliens held 1.2 percent (down 0.9 percent), and "others" held 2.0 percent (down one percent).

The best rate for women of color as head coaches was 20 percent of the women's track/cross country head coaching positions, which was at an all-time high. Ironically, the coach:student-athlete ratio was going in the other direction than that of basketball. Only 23.2 percent of student-athletes on Division I women's cross country and track teams were African American, whereas whites held 65.3 percent of the slots. Latinas held 3.4 percent, Native Americans held 0.4 percent, Asian American/Pacific Islanders held 1.3 percent, non-resident aliens held 3.5 percent, and "others" held 3.0 percent. This was the lowest percentage of African-American women since 1991–92, when they also had 23.2 percent of the positions. Likewise, it was the highest percentage of whites since 1991–92.

As reported in the 2004 *Racial and Gender Report Card* (RGRC), the decade-long decline in the percentage of African-American male college student-athletes stopped. The 24.6 percent of all Division I males student-athletes was up from the 2003 report, which had the lowest percentage since the 1991–92 academic year. Likewise, at 62.6 percent, the decline of white student-athletes was also halted. However, neither African-American nor white student-athletes were near their all-time highs since they have been covered in the RGRC, at 26.2 in 1996–97 and 66.2 percent in 1991–92, respectively.

Participation rates of African-American male Division I college student-athletes continued to be nearly 25 percent, at 24.6 percent, in the 2003–04 year. That was slightly below the all-time high of 26.5 in 1991–92. The rate had been remarkably consistent over the previous 15 years and never varied by more than two percentage points. At 62.6 percent, the participation rates of white student-athletes had also been consistent but was also below its all-time high in the RGRC of 66.2 percent in 1991–92. Latinos, at 3.6 percent, and Asian men at 1.6 percent, had both also been consistent for a decade.

In all Division I women's sports, the percentage of white women was down slightly, to 70.6 percent. It had been between 70–72 percent since the 2000–01 year. It was still far below the 79.8 percent it had been in 1991–92. The percentages of white women was down slightly in basketball and track/cross country, whereas the percentages of African-American women had gone up in basketball and down in track/cross-country. In all sports combined, African Americans had 14.9 percent of the slots, which was their all-time RGRC high. Latinas held 3.3 percent of the female student-athlete positions, which was also their all-time best. Asian women held 2.1 percent, also their highest percent. Native American women had 0.4 of a percent.

For coaches of color, the numbers get even worse when you look at these sports in other divisions. For basketball in all divisions combined, African Americans held 12.3 percent of the head coaching positions. In all divisions combined for football, African Americans held 1.6 percent. In all divisions combined for baseball, African Americans held 0.7 percent and Latinos held only 3.2 percent. Whites, on the other hand, held 86, 97.7, and 96.2 percent of the head positions in basketball, football, and baseball, respectively.

Clearly, we have an even longer way to go in all divisions when you look at both males and females in all sports combined in each division. Whites held 89.5, 90.5, and 93 percent of all head coaching positions in Divisions I, II, and III, respectively. The 2004 *Racial and Gender Report Card* showed, based on NCAA data, that African Americans held only 7.7, 3.4, and 4.1 percent of the men's head coaching positions in the three NCAA divisions, respectively. Latinos held 1.5, 3.4, and 1.5 percent in the respective divisions on men's teams. Asians and Native Americans were barely on the NCAA's radar screen.

In fact, African Americans were so underrepresented as head coaches in Division III that the percentage of women coaching men's teams actually exceeded that of African Americans coaching (4.4 vs. 4.1 percent). In Division II women coaching men's teams almost matched that of African Americans coaching (3.0 vs. 3.4 percent).

More than 30 years since the passing of Title IX, women held just over 41 percent of the head coaching positions of women's college teams in all the NCAA divisions for all sports combined. In all of the other women's sports combined, excluding track/cross-country and basketball, white men continued to hold nearly half of the jobs, at 47.1 percent. Combining male and female head coaches, whites held a dominating 93.6 percent of the head coaching jobs, whereas African Americans held 2.5 percent, Asian men held 0.8 percent, Latino men held 1.2 percent, and "other" men held 0.8 percent of these positions.

Among the women holding the head coaching positions in these women's sports, white women continued to dominate, with nearly 47 percent of these posts, whereas African-American women held just 1 percent. This was a 3.1 percent increase for white women and a 0.5 percent increase for African-American women.

According to the 2004 *Racial and Gender Report Card*, when all the Division I head coaching jobs in all sports were combined, whites held 91.3 percent of the positions on Division I women's teams and African Americans held 5 percent. Women held 41.3 percent (down 1 percent).

The lowest percentage for whites was 90.8 percent in Division II, and the highest was 93 percent in Division III. Women held 35.5 percent of the women's head coaching jobs in Division II.

ASSISTANT COACHES

The position of an assistant coach is obviously a direct pipeline to the coveted head coaching jobs. There is a general belief that African Americans hold a large percentage of the assistant positions on men's teams.

This appears to be true only in Division I basketball and football, where 37 and 24 percent of the jobs were held by African Americans, respectively, in the 2003–04 academic year. The percentage drops to 26 for basketball and 17 percent for football in all divisions combined.

When we look at assistant jobs in all sports combined in each of the divisions, hope for African Americans plummets once again. This is true for both men's and women's teams. On the men's teams, whites held 78, 83, and 89 percent of the assistant positions in the three divisions, respectively. African Americans held 18, 12, and 8.5 percent, respectively. There are more women (8.6 percent) as assistants on Division III on men's teams than African Americans. Women held 8, 7, and 8.6 percent of the assistant men's jobs in Divisions I, II, and III, respectively.

Among the women's teams, whites held 81, 83, and 91 percent of the assistant positions in Divisions I, II, and III, respectively. African Americans had 13, 8, and 7 percent, respectively. As assistants, women held slightly more than half of the jobs on women's teams, with 52 percent in Division I, 50 percent in Division II, and 53 percent in Division III.

THE BLACK COACHES ASSOCIATION

Perhaps the height of the scrutiny on college sports' poor record for hiring people of color came when the Black Coaches Association (BCA) issued its first *Hiring Report Card* in October 2004 to assess how universities handle the process for hiring head football coaches. It evaluated whether the school contacted the BCA for assistance, who was on the search committee, who was interviewed, who was hired, and whether the athletics department followed their school's affirmative action guidelines.

The Black Coaches Association was back in business after struggling since the late 1990s to recover from an erosion of leadership and an embezzlement case involving its former executive director. It is now under Floyd Keith. A former football coach, Keith has restored financial stability while traversing the nation promoting his positive but forthright approach to making things better for coaches and the young people they serve. Long perceived as a vehicle to get jobs for coaches, the BCA spread out its mission to have its coaches embrace youth at risk.

There was once a time when the BCA struck fear in the hearts of athletics directors and the NCAA. Before the BCA mounted boycott and protest efforts in the late 1980s, the issue of race was hardly ever discussed within the NCAA or on individual campuses in athletics departments.

John Thompson's personal boycott after the NCAA passed Proposition 42 in 1989 showed what black coaches had to do to make a point and have it stick. Everything seemed to come to a head in 1994–95, when so many issues mounted up that the BCA threatened an official boycott in the face of reform efforts by the Presidents Commission and the NCAA. The prospect of intervention by the White House and the Department of Justice led to a settlement between the coaches and the presidents. Before Coach Thompson, college officials seemed to think they could ignore race and get away from one of the most tumultuous sport and social issues of our time. The coaches were on the political map with a voice.

Thompson was joined by African-American veteran coaches John Chaney, George Raveling, Nolan Richardson, and other BCA members who fought against the use of standardized tests as part of the admission criteria because they believed such tests were unfair measures of the abilities of children coming from impoverished backgrounds; for more coaching opportunities for people of color; and for expanded access to reach poor African-American children to show them that there was hope for the future.

The BCA definitely had critics who said the coaches merely wanted to admit basketball players who could not be successful students; their interest in more coaching opportunities was self-serving; and they wanted more access to get recruiting advantages.

From my perspective, the BCA brought civil rights into the sports world where it was needed because, like other sectors of our society, people of color rarely get change without raising their voices. I was disheartened when Rudy Washington, the former executive director of the BCA, seemed to lose a sense of purpose and direction for the organization. Coupled with increasing charges that he had improperly used funds, BCA critics had a field day and the elders of the BCA withdrew their support.

I believe there was a correlation between the BCA's subdued or ineffectual voice and the fact that the numbers of African Americans have declined as student-athletes and coaches in all sports except men's basketball, and as athletics directors.

Floyd Keith helped put together a strong board now headed by Eugene Marshall, the Associate Athletics Director at West Point. I joined the board and have been able to watch the rebirth of the BCA from the inside. Not only is it highly organized and financially solvent, but the BCA is once again raising its voice and is being heard. I have no doubt that there is a correlation between that and the breakthroughs in the Division IA athletics directors mentioned below, as well as increases for African-American student-athletes as participants in college sport overall.

Keith stood side-by-side with attorneys Johnny Cochran and Cyrus Mehri when they announced their report on the lack of coaching opportunities for African Americans in the NFL along with the implied threat of lawsuits against the NFL. Lawsuits have been the driving force behind Title IX success stories in the 15 years before publication of this book. Until now, legal action was never publicly mentioned regarding the issue of racial hiring practices.

The BCA holds an annual Summit on Equity in Football Hiring. As mentioned, the first *Football Hiring Report Card* graded each of the 28 Division IA and IAA colleges that hired a head football coach in 2003–04 to see not only who was hired, but whether they worked with the BCA to see its list of "capable" candidates, who was on the selection committee, who was interviewed, how long the search took, and if the process followed the school's Affirmative Action guidelines. The BCA plans to expand the report to cover other sports and college administrators in the future.

The BCA is, once again, striking fear in the hearts of athletics directors. This time, however, the BCA is working closely with NCAA President Myles Brand, who publicly supports the *Report Card* that surely embarrassed some NCAA member institutions.

Though the BCA supports most of the academic reform efforts undertaken by Dr. Brand, the board remains concerned that some pieces of the well-intentioned legislation might have a negative impact on African-American student-athletes, especially those who play basketball where the poor graduation rates have raised the alarm calling for such reform. The Institute for Diversity and Ethics in Sport, which I direct, annually publishes the graduation rates for the Sweet 16 in the men's and women's basketball tournaments. Though we point out that the basketball graduation rates, especially for African Americans, are far too low, that is too simplistic. African-American male basketball players graduate at a rate of 38 percent. That is a huge problem but one not as large as the fact that it is higher than the 34 percent graduation rate for African-American male students who are not athletes and that they are a full 25 percent lower than their white fellow students.

The coaches do not want basketball players used as stereotypes when American higher education has failed to welcome African-American students in general onto our campuses, where less than 10 percent of students, faculty, and administrators are African American. Except for the occasional Martin Luther King Boulevard or a Black Student Union, buildings and streets on campus are all named after white people who have had a long history with the university or are major donors. We must make our campuses more welcoming places for African-American students in general and not merely for athletes.

A flourishing BCA will help alert us to these inequities while fighting for change. Floyd Keith, who for years blew a whistle to help call plays, is now coaching the coaches, helping.them get jobs, to win, and also to be drum majors for justice by standing up for the needs of young people who live in a life-and-death world.

POWER AT THE TOP

These changes will not be an easy task, since the power structure in college sport is so overwhelmingly white. The Institute for Diversity and Ethics in Sport released a 2004 study, *The Buck Stops Here: Race and Gender of Presidents, Athletics Directors, Faculty Athletics Representatives and Conference Commissioners in Division IA* that underlined this fact.

In Division IA, 94.9 percent of the presidents, 92.5 percent of the athletics directors, 91 percent of the faculty athletics reps, and 100 percent of the commissioners were white. Does this have an impact on the hiring of head football coaches and athletics directors? How could it not have an impact?

The old boys network in sport and in society has been in operation for generations. The hiring process in Division IA football is quick, quiet, and exclusive. University affirmative action guidelines are rarely followed. The hiring process is what the Black Coaches Association is trying to address with its *Hiring Report Card*. We know there are many African-American coaches in the wings ready to lead Division IA programs, but when significantly more than 90 percent of our campus leaders are white, chances are they will seek who they know. History shows they will more than likely look like them.

Among the 117 colleges and universities, whites held 334 (93 percent) of the 360 of the campus leadership positions in the 2004–05 academic year. White women held 41 (11 percent) of these positions, and there was only one African-American woman and one Latina out of the 360 people.

The next four sections on conference commissioners, presidents, athletics directors, and faculty athletics representatives will give the specific details.

Conference Commissioners

As will be seen in the discussions later in the book called "The Players," many people now believe that the conference commissioners are the real power brokers and decision-makers in college sport. Jim Delany at the Big 10, Mike Slive with the SEC, Mike Tranghese of the Big East, John Swofford of the Atlantic Coast Conference, Thomas Hansen of the PAC 10, and Kevin Weiberg of the Big 12 are the Bowl Championship Series (BCS) commissioners. They are the elite's elite. However, there are 11 Division IA conferences in total.

All of the 11 Division IA conference commissioners were white men. Only five (12.5 percent) of the 40 listed Division IA associate commissioners were African American, 2.5 percent were Asian, and 2.5 percent Latino. Women held 11 (27.5 percent) of the Division IA associate commissioner posts.

In all of Division I, excluding the historically black conferences, all 31 (100 percent) of Division I conference commissioners were white, with three (9.1 percent) of them being female. Out of 73 listed associate posts in Division I, 88 percent were held by whites, 10 percent by African Americans, 1.4 percent each by Asians and Latinos, and 30 percent by women.

The three female conference commissioners were Linda Bruno of the Atlantic 10, Carolyn Schlie Femovich of the Patriot League, and Patty Viverito of the Gateway Football Conference and the Pioneer Football League.

Presidents

In Division IA, 94.9 percent of university presidents were white, 3.4 percent were African-American men, and 2 percent were Latino. There were no Asian or Native American university presidents. There were 13 females in this position (11.1 percent).

The four African-American presidents were Sidney A. Ribeau (Bowling Green State University), Adam W. Herbert (Indiana University, Bloomington), Sidney McPhee (Middle Tennessee State University), and Roderick McDavis (Ohio University).

The two Latino presidents were Luis Proenza (University of Akron) and Louis Caldera (University of New Mexico).

The 13 women presidents were Carol Garrison (University of Alabama at Birmingham), Jo Ann M. Gora (Ball State University), Nancy L. Zimpher (University of Cincinnati), Carol A. Cartwright (Kent State University), Shirley Raines (University of Memphis), Donna E. Shalala (University of Miami [Florida]), Mary Sue Coleman (University of Michigan), Carol C. Harter (University of Nevada, Las Vegas), Nancy Cantor (Syracuse University), Diana S. Natalicio (University of Texas at El Paso), Judith Bailey (Western Michigan University), Judy Genshaft (University of South Florida), and Karen Holbook (Ohio State University).

Athletics Directors

Division IA had some major breakthroughs for athletics directors. Damone Evans became the first African-American athletics director in the SEC and

Daryl Gross became the first African-American athletics director in the Big East. There was an all-time high of 12 (10.3 percent) athletics directors of color in Division IA.

At the time of publication of the 2004 *Racial and Gender Report Card*, there were nine African-American athletics directors at Division IA institutions. They were Eugene Smith (Arizona State University), Damon Evans (University of Georgia), Herman R. Frazier (University of Hawaii, Manoa), Daryl Gross (Syracuse University), Mike Garrett (University of Southern California), David Williams II (Vanderbilt University), Craig Littlepaige (University of Virginia), Kevin Anderson (West Point), and McKinley Boston (New Mexico State). The three Latino athletic directors at Division IA institutions were Dan Guerrero (University of California, Los Angeles), Rudy Davalos (University of New Mexico), and Barry Alvarez (University of Wisconsin, Madison).

However, people of color and women continued to be vastly underrepresented in this top administrative position in Division I. Whites held 95 percent of the Division I athletics director's jobs. White men held 88.5 percent, and white women were at 6.5 percent. African-American men held 3.4 percent. Latino men held 1.2 percent, and there were no Asian male athletics directors.

Among all the NCAA divisions, women had the fewest opportunities to be athletics directors in Division I, with a mere 7.3 percent. Of these, white women held 6.5 percent, Asian and Native American women held 0.4 percent each. There were no African-American women ADs in Division I when the historically black colleges and universities were excluded.

In Division II, whites held 94.1 percent of the AD jobs, African Americans held 2.2 percent, Latinos held 2.6 percent, Asians held 0.9 percent, and Native Americans held 0.4 percent. Women held 16.2 percent of these posts, with white women holding 14.5 percent. Less than 1 percent of Division II athletics directors were African-American or Asian women.

Whites also dominated AD positions in Division III during the 2003–04 academic year, holding 95.5 percent of these jobs, while African Americans held only 3.2 percent.

Women were strongest in Division III, holding 27.1 percent of the athletics director jobs. Among the female ADs, white women held 26.9 percent while the remaining 0.3 percent were Asian. There were no African-American, Latina, or Native American female ADs.

A rarely mentioned in public but very real reason that more people of color are not hired in the top decision-making positions is that many alumni fear the university or athletics department will be flooded with people of color if a person of color is chosen as president or athletics director. The data from Division IA in *The Buck Stops Here* study showed how wrong this is.

- None of the African-American presidents:
    hired an African-American athletics director
    hired an African-American football coach
    appointed an African-American faculty athletics representative
- Among the Latino presidents, none:
    hired a football coach of color
    appointed a faculty athletics representative of color
    hired a Latino athletics director (Rudy Davalos had been AD before
        his president, Louis Caldera, was appointed)
- Among the African-American athletics directors, none:
    hired an African-American football coach
- Among the Latino athletics directors, Dan Guerrero hired Karl Dorell,
  an African American, as football coach at UCLA.
- Among the 13 women presidents:
    none hired an athletics director of color
    none hired a football coach of color
    none hired a woman as athletics director
    three appointed women as faculty athletics representative
    one appointed a person of color as faculty athletics represen-
        tative

Faculty Athletics Representatives

The faculty athletics representative (FAR) is a key position, especially since the person filling this position is usually appointed by the president of the university. There were 123 FARs in the Institute for Diversity and Ethics in Sport's *The Buck Stops Here* study, since six schools (California, Berkeley; Kent State; Minnesota, Twin Cities; Ohio; Purdue; and Wisconsin, Madison) had two faculty athletics representatives. Among the FARs were:

- 6 (4.9%) African-American men (Michigan; Texas; Alabama, Birmingham;
  Arizona State; Kent State; and California, Berkeley)
- 1 (0.8%) African-American female (Temple)
- 2 (1.6%) Latino men (Rice and Stanford)
- 1 (0.8%) Latina (Nebraska)
- 1 (0.8%) Native American man (Brigham Young University)
- 22 (18%) women

Twenty of the 22 women were white, whereas there was one African American, one Latina, and no Asian or Native American women serving as FAR in Division IA; 91.1 percent (112) of the 123 FARs were white.

In all NCAA colleges, whites filled most of the FAR positions with 92, 92.5, and 95.7 percent in Divisions I, II, and III, respectively.

In Division I, women held 21.9 percent of these posts, whereas people of color held 8.1 percent.

In Division II schools, African Americans held 1.7 percent, Asians held 1.8 percent, and Latinos held 3.6 percent. Women had 22.8 percent of the FAR posts.

In the Division III, whites held 95.7 percent, African Americans held 3.3 percent, and Latinos held 0.8 percent of the FAR appointments. Women held 27.5 percent of the FAR posts in Division III.

People of color cannot gain much optimism when the other professional positions in college sport are examined.

College Associate and Assistant Athletics Directors

At the college level, the next level of senior administrative positions would be the associate and assistant athletics director posts. For the purpose of this chapter, the numbers in these two positions were combined. These are the pipeline positions for the AD positions. The percentages for people of color do not show much promise, with whites holding an overwhelming 89.9 percent in Division I, 89.2 percent in Division II, and 94.4 percent in Division III.

The percent of women associate or assistant ADs in Division I was 30.2 percent, 37.9 percent in Division II, and 44 percent in Division III.

Professional Positions

At NCAA institutions, jobs that fit in this category are academic advisor, counselor, and compliance coordinator; managers for business, equipment, fundraiser/development, facilities, promotions/marketing, and tickets; the sports information director and assistant directors; and strength coaches. These are obviously the training grounds for those who will rise in the professional ranks. In all divisions combined, women held 30.9 percent of these jobs and people of color actually occupied 10.6 percent.

In Division I, 87.9 percent of these jobs categories were filled by whites, 8.2 percent by African Americans, 1.9 percent by Latinos, 0.9 percent by Asians, and 1 percent by other people of color. Women in these positions held 31.5 percent of the Division I professional posts.

In Division II, whites held 89.2 percent of these jobs, African Americans held 5 percent, and all other people of color held 5.7 percent. Women held 37.8 percent.

In Division III, whites held 94.4 percent and African Americans held 4.4 percent. Women occupied 44.5 percent of the Division III professional positions.

NCAA HEADQUARTERS

With 1,028 active member institutions, it is obvious that there are an enormous number of professional positions in the NCAA institutions. There are 117 active member institutions in Division IA, 118 in Division IAA, and 91 in Division IAAA. In Division II there are 281 active member institutions, and in Division III there are 421.

In the NCAA database that we use for this study, there are 14,469 head coaches; 24,229 assistant coaches; 918 athletics directors; 2,390 associate and assistant athletics directors; 836 senior women's administrators; 4,838 academic advisors, compliance coordinators, managers for business development, fundraising, facilities, marketing, ticket sales, and media relations; and an array of assistants and support staff.

Thus, in terms of expanding opportunities for women and people of color, the college level is where the greatest opportunity is in sport. This makes the leadership at the NCAA level critical to influence who is hired into these positions.

Dr. Myles Brand, the president of the NCAA, addressed the issue in his "State of the NCAA" speech at the NCAA Convention in January 2005.

Brand told the attendees:

> The paucity of African-American head football coaches in Division I—as well as in Divisions II and III—and women in high positions from head coaches to athletics directors, is simply appalling. The search process used to identify individuals for high level positions is not universally open and fair.
>
> I can find no moral justification for excluding from serious consideration qualified persons who are not of the over-represented race or gender. While some progress is being made, for example, the increase of African-American males in Division I athletics directorships and men's basketball has achieved a critical mass of head coaches, there is a great deal more that must be accomplished in many areas.

After several years of progress, opportunities for people of color and women in the highest professional positions at the NCAA headquarters declined. By the end of 2004, people of color dropped 6.5 percent and women dropped 6.2 percent at the vice president/chief of staff level. At the chief aides/director level, people of color declined by 2.2 percent, whereas they increased by 1.4 percent at the administrative level. Women increased at the chief aide/director level by 6 percent and remained the same at the administrative level.

At the Indianapolis headquarters of the NCAA, African Americans occupied 12.5 percent of the positions at the vice president/chief of staff level, a 6.5 percent decrease from last year. Whites held the remaining 87.5 percent of the posts, an increase of 6.5 percent since the last report. Women occupied 18.8 percent of these positions, which was a decrease of 6.2 percent since the last RGRC.

The only African-American vice presidents were Bernard Franklin (Vice President for Governance and Membership) and Ronald Stratten (Vice President for Education Services). Charlotte Westerhaus was named Vice President for Diversity and inclusion in the spring of 2005.

Four women were serving as vice presidents, including Westerhaus, Judith Sweet (Vice President for Championships), Elsa Cole (Chief Legal Counsel), and Sue Donohoe (Vice President of Women's Division I Basketball).

At the chief aides/directors level, whites occupied 81.3 percent of the positions (up 2 percent) whereas people of color held the remaining 18.5 percent. This was a 2 percent drop for people of color in the chief aide/director positions. African Americans held 12.5 percent (down 1.5 percent) of the chief aide/director positions, Latinos held 2 percent (down 3 percent), and Asian Americans occupied 4 percent (up 2 percent). Forty-eight percent of theses positions were filled by women, an increase of 6 percent.

At the administration level, people of color occupied 23.4 percent of the positions whereas whites held 76.7 percent (down 1.4 percent). African Americans continued to hold 22.2 percent of the positions, and Asian Americans increased slightly, to 1.2 percent. The percentage of women decreased slightly, to 54.3 percent.

GRADUATION RATES

In spite of the concerns of the Black Coaches Association about stereotyping African-American student-athletes by emphasizing low graduation rates, race remains a persistent academic issue. This is reflected in the continuing gap between graduation rates for white and African-American student-athletes. Although both groups have generally improved over the past decade, the significant gap between the graduation rates for white and African-American football and basketball student-athletes remains.

The Institute for Diversity and Ethics in Sport released three graduation rate studies in the year prior to the writing of this chapter. The first two were on the 2004 men's and women's Sweet 16 basketball teams, and the last was on the 56 bowl-bound teams in 2004–05.

In the latter, the issue of graduation rates clearly remained an area of controversy in college football. In 2004, the NCAA reported that 54 percent of football student-athletes graduated, which was up 3 percent and was among the best football graduation rates in many years. Though that was good news indeed for college sport, among the bowl teams, 51 of 55, or 93 percent, had graduation rates of 40 percent or more for white football student-athletes, whereas only 30 schools, or 60 percent, had graduation rates of at least 40 percent for African-American football student-athletes.

Overall in Division 1A teams, 63 percent of white football student-athletes graduated versus only 47 percent of African Americans.

However, it needs to be noted that both African-American and white football players graduated at a higher rate than their male non-athletics peers in the student body. The graduation rate for African-American male students as a whole was only 40 percent versus the overall rate for male white students, which was 61 percent, making the gap there a scandalous 21 percent. One of the benefits of examining our graduation rates is that they focus light on the fact that too many of our predominantly white campuses are not welcoming places for students of color, whether or not they are athletes.

Among the bowl-bound teams, the following results were found (*note:* Navy does not provide graduation rate information for its student-athletes):

- Of the bowl-bound schools, 16 (29%) had graduation rates of 66% or higher for white football student-athletes, which was more than three times the number of schools with equivalent graduation rates for African-American football student-athletes (5 schools, or 9%).
- Looking at schools with graduation rates of 50% or higher, more than three times as many met this benchmark for white football student-athletes (46 schools, or 84%) than for African-American football student-athletes (16 schools, or 29%).
- More than six times as many schools (26 schools, or 47%) graduated 40% or fewer of their African-American football student-athletes, and four schools graduated 40% or less of their white football student-athletes.
- Eight schools (16%) had graduation rates of 30% or less for their African-American football student-athletes, whereas none of the 55 bowl teams graduated so few white football student-athletes.

In addition:

- Nine schools (16%) had graduation rates for African-American football student-athletes that were at least 30% lower than the rate for white football student-athletes.
- Thirty schools (55%) had graduation rates for African-American football student-athletes that were at least 20% lower than the rate for white football student-athletes.
- Forty-one schools (75%) had graduation rates for African-American football student-athletes that were at least 10% lower than the rate for white football student-athletes.
- Only six schools had graduation rates for African-American football student-athletes that were higher than the rate for white football student-athletes (Cincinnati +19%; Hawaii +12%; Fresno State and UTEP +4%; Southern Mississippi +3%; and Troy +1%).

Though there were teams that scored poorly, some schools were notable for their high football student-athlete graduation rates. Thirteen schools had graduation rates for football players that were better than for overall students, and 10 schools had graduation rates for football players that were better than for overall student-athletes.

If there were a Top Ten ranking for graduation rates among bowl teams, Notre Dame and Boston College would have played for the national championship. Both graduated at least 77 percent of all football student-athletes and at least 74 percent of their African-American football student-athletes. Syracuse (highest for overall football at 78%), Virginia, Southern Mississippi, Purdue, Toledo, Cincinnati, Texas Tech, Virginia Tech, USC, Marshall, and Iowa (the latter four were tied with 58%)—all with football student-athlete graduation rates of 58 percent or higher—would also have made the Top Ten.

NCAA statistics were used in the study. The Institute reviewed 1997–98 graduation (six-year) rates, with a four-class average (freshmen classes of 1994–95, 1995–96, 1996–97, and 1997–98). I believe that the way graduation rates are currently calculated unfairly penalizes a school when a student-athlete transfers in good standing and receives a degree at another institution, and I support the NCAA's current initiative to redefine how graduation rates are calculated.

In March 2004, the Institute released, *Keeping Score When It Counts: Graduation Rates and Diversity in Campus Leadership for 2004 Women's Sweet 16 Teams* as a follow-up to the study on the men's teams released a few days earlier. This report examined graduation rates and the gender and racial breakdown of campus leaders for teams that have reached the Sweet 16 round of the NCAA Women's Basketball Tournament and compared them to the men's record.

The report cited a great record on graduation rates for the 16 college and university teams that had reached the women's tournament's Sweet 16 round. The study compared graduation rates for all student-athletes to basketball student-athletes in general, and for African-American basketball student-athletes in particular. The results for women were in dramatic contrast to the men's teams:

- Five women's teams (Duke; LSU; Notre Dame; Vanderbilt; and California, Santa Barbara) graduated 100% of their African-American student-athletes.
- Nine (75%) of the 12 women's teams whose African-American graduation rates were published graduated at least three-fourths of their African-American student-athletes. Conversely, 9 of the men's teams did not even have their rates published and only 2 of the 16 men's teams graduated 75% of their African-American basketball student-athletes.
- Nine (56%) of the women's teams had a higher basketball graduation rate than Kansas, the men's team with the best graduation rate (73%).*

*"Keeping score when it counts: Graduation rates for 2005 NCAA men's and women's Division I basketball teams," Institute for Diversity and Ethics in Sport, March 2005.

- Seven (44%) of the 16 women's teams had graduation rates for basketball student-athletes that were 80% and higher. No men's team graduated this many players.*
- Stanford topped the women's teams with a 93% graduation rate.
- Eleven (69%) teams had graduation rates for women's basketball student-athletes higher than 70%. Kansas was the only men's team that graduated at this level.*
- Fourteen (88%) of the women's teams had graduation rates for basketball student-athletes of 67% or more. Only 3 men's teams (Kansas, Xavier, and Duke) met that standard.*
- Only 2 women's teams (Louisiana Tech, at 47%, and Purdue, at 43%) graduated fewer than half of their players, whereas among the men only 4 (Kansas, Xavier, Duke, and Vanderbilt) graduated more than 50%.
- Ten women's teams (63%) had basketball graduation rates higher than their school's overall student-athlete graduation rate. Among the men, 64% of the reporting teams had basketball student-athlete graduation rates that were at least 20 to 29 percentage points *lower* than their school's overall student-athlete graduation rate.
- Nine (56%) women's teams had basketball graduation rates higher their school's overall graduation rate, whereas 82% of the reporting men's teams had basketball student-athlete graduation rates that were at least 20 to 29 percentage points *lower* than the school's overall student graduation rate.

It was like two different worlds when you compared the graduation rates of men's and women's college Sweet 16 basketball teams in 2004. It really is sweet in the world of women's basketball, but it is overwhelmingly sour among the men. If you were to combine the two worlds, the two worst women's teams would be among the men's top seven for basketball graduation rates. Nine women's teams had better records than the top men's team. It did not matter if you were white or African American: women's basketball student-athletes got the work done in the classroom while the men lagged far behind.

NCAA statistics were used in the study. The Institute reviewed 1996–97 graduation (six-year) rates, with a four-class average (freshmen classes of 1993–94, 1994–95, 1995–96, and 1996–97).

CONCLUSION

In my chapter on "Race on the College Campus" in *The Rules of the Game* in 1986, I wrote:

> Colleges and universities are supposed to be, along with parents and religious organizations, the guardians of our nation's morals. When

---

*"Keeping score when it counts: Graduation rates for 2005 NCAA men's and women's Division I basketball teams," Institute for Diversity and Ethics in Sport, March 2005.

discrimination is part of the hiring system, when exploitation is part of
the recruiting process, when athletes do not get an education, our nation's
institutions of higher education have forfeited that guardianship.

With all the job opportunities that exist for professionals in college sport
and with all the educational opportunities being afforded to student-athletes
of color, we have a real opportunity to have sport lead the way to progressive
change on racial issues in the years ahead. However, the pace of the incremental progress made since 1986 has to be dramatically hastened to get
people of color to believe that the playing fields, both on and off the court, are
equal. Likewise, there needs to be even more effective academic support
programs at our institutions of higher education to assure all entering
student-athletes—no matter what sport they play or what their economic or
racial background—leave with a meaningful education that will prepare them
for life.

CHAPTER 6

The Impact of Race As It Relates to Employment Opportunities for Collegiate Football Coaches

Fitzgerald Hill University of Central Florida

The current extent to which employment opportunities are limited for African-American football coaches is often underestimated by those associated with intercollegiate athletics. In fact, it is often difficult to convince many university academic leaders, athletic administrators, and influential boosters that current employment patterns of collegiate football coaches do not provide equal opportunities for qualified African-American football coaches.

This misperception occurs largely because many Americans continue to think of racial discrimination in terms of overt and purposeful bigotry. It is, however, normally implemented through subtle and covert tactics that may not appear racially motivated. As a direct result, on many coaching staffs, white administrators and coaches are frequently perceived by African-American coaches as perpetrators of this discreet form of modern-day discrimination. Exacerbating the situation is the fact that most white athletic administrators and coaches do not intentionally attempt to treat African-American coaches any differently than white coaches, yet they fail to understand how their biased attitudes and stereotypical perceptions often create invisible but impenetrable barriers restricting accessibility to equal opportunity.

This chapter has four major goals: (1) provide an analysis of employment barriers restricting employment opportunities for African-American football coaches; (2) examine past and current collegiate football coaching opportunities as they relate to employment equity; (3) review the contrasting employment perceptions between African-American and white football coaches at Division IA institutions; and (4) suggest implications from studies of African-American football coaches employed at predominantly white colleges and universities as well as make recommendations to improve the accessibility of equal opportunity for all coaches regardless of race.

EMPLOYMENT BARRIERS

There are several employment barriers that tend to limit opportunities and hinder advancement for African-American football coaches employed at predominantly white colleges and universities. Employment opportunities for African-American coaches have increased over the past decade. However, in the midst of this good news something is ominous. African-American football coaches seeking employment at NCAA Division IA institutions report feelings of disappointment, dismay, frustration, and anger. They perceive their careers stymied, and they are increasingly disillusioned regarding their chances for professional advancement within the profession (Hill, 1997; Hill, 2002).

Employment barriers for African-American football coaches can be placed into two broad categories: (1) those related to the objective structure of an organization and (2) those inherent in a subjective cognitive process of an organization. Structural barriers are considered to be objective; they include specified rules for advancement and are frequently rooted firmly in the tradition of the profession. Subjective cognitive barriers include personal perception, stereotyping, and labeling. These invisible barriers often operate without any awareness and can be extremely subtle. On many college campuses, white coaches and academic and athletic administrators will usually deny the existence of employment barriers. Consequently, it is difficult for the institution to identify, remedy, or remove restricting barriers (Crocker and Wilson, 1987).

Civil rights legislation and equal opportunity laws removed many of the structural barriers confronting African-American football coaches at NCAA Division IA institutions. Although legislation was designed to diversify the employment arena, the implementation of these laws had little, if any, influence on the social psychology existing in the interracial work setting that African-American coaches face on a day-to-day basis. Employment disadvantages facing African-American coaches at predominantly white institutions cannot be easily remedied by simply requiring a change in formal rules and procedures of organizations. For African-American coaches to gain greater access to employment opportunities it will be necessary to eliminate the negative cognitive barriers that exist in the minds of many white coaches and academic and athletic administrators.

Recent studies have revealed that employment barriers for African-American football coaches are unconsciously constructed based on the following two assumptions: (1) African-American coaches are not capable of doing certain jobs, and (2) permitting African Americans in certain positions would result in social equality (Hill, 1997; Hill, 2002; Ogubu, 1994; McPartland, 1987).

A study by the Pew Research Center for the People and the Press reported that 46 percent of white Americans believe that efforts to promote equal rights for African Americans have gone too far (Vital Signs, 2003/2004). In fact, many white collegiate coaches and leaders remain unconvinced that subtle forms of prejudice and discrimination take place within their institution. In most employment situations, the African-American coaches are the only persons in a position to understand the racial dynamics of what is happening within the work setting. It is unfortunate that white coaches and white academic and athletic administrators have shown a tendency to perceive African-American coaches as touchy and overly sensitive if they speak out regarding employment discrimination or the lack of career opportunities.

COLLEGIATE FOOTBALL COACHING OPPORTUNITIES

Former African-American student-athletes who have found success on the football fields report that opportunities in the coaching profession and athletic administration remain elusive. Most postsecondary institutions embrace the notion that equal opportunity exists for those that are qualified. However, for reasons not fully explored, qualified African-American football coaches have not been given the same career opportunities as their white colleagues. Although affirmative action legislation was designed in an effort to aid African-American football coaches in the employment arena, the implementation of these laws has had little, if any, positive impact in creating employment opportunities and advancement for African-American football coaches. This is evident when considering that in the 21st century there have been 71 head coaching vacancies at NCAA Division IA institutions, but only four (5%) institutions have selected African Americans to lead their football programs.

A closer examination of the employment patterns of collegiate football coaches revealed that between the 1982 and the 2003 football seasons, there had been 381 head coaching vacancies at NCAA Division IA institutions. African-American coaches had been selected for 19 (4%) of the head coaching vacancies, with 15 of the appointments occurring after 1990. In the history of Division IA football, African-American coaches have been selected a total of 21 times to lead as head football coaches.

A historical analysis of African-American head football coaches hired at Division IA institutions revealed that many African-American assistant coaches desiring to be head coaches will be offered the opportunities to take over programs that require a major rebuilding process. The low winning percentages associated with the institutions may negatively influence the perception of the coaching potential of African-American coaches; consequently, many head coaching opportunities at traditional collegiate football powers remain elusive and African-American coaches continue to take jobs that may not look very promising on the surface.

With the exception of Ty Willingham, if an African-American football coach has been relieved of his head coaching duties, he has not been granted another opportunity to lead a Division IA football program. This is vastly different from white counterparts who are frequently recycled and given a second opportunity when African-American coaches often do not even get a first one. These employment practices indicate that African-American coaches are evaluated collectively, whereas white coaches are evaluated individually (Hill, 1997; Hill, 2002; Hill, 2004).

Undoubtedly, the pressure to win at the Division IA level is intense and has greatly increased educational opportunities for African-American student-athletes. African-American males currently make up over 50 percent of all football athletic scholarships awarded at Division IA member colleges and universities. These athletic scholarships (which have been limited in number by the NCAA over the years) are issued on merit, based on the evaluation of athletic ability that coaches believe will give their football teams the best opportunity to compete for a conference and national championship. As a result, it can be safely concluded that few, if any, of these prized scholarships are awarded to student-athletes solely because of the color of their skin. Studies have revealed that when athletic ability and skill are the most important factors in determining the success of athletic football programs, African-Americans have found many doors of opportunities open to them (Hill, 1997; Hill, 2002; Hill, 2004).

In contrast, African-American football coaches have not shared the same opportunities as African-American student-athletes. They have generally been stratified into coaching positions, limiting their possibility for advancement and leadership opportunities. Consequently, African-American coaches are denied equal access to employment opportunities that possess power, prestige, and financial rewards. In the coaching profession, serving as an offensive or defensive coordinator is usually a prerequisite to being a head football coach. Since few African-American coaches are granted the opportunity to be coordinators, they are rarely perceived to possess the necessary qualifications to be considered for the top spot of a collegiate football program.

White academic and athletic administrators and white coaches routinely go on record supporting equal opportunities for African-American football coaches. Also, higher education administrators have shown a tendency to become defensive when it is suggested that their institutions have not provided equal opportunity for all coaches. Statements such as "We want to hire the very best coach, regardless of color" may be used to justify the hiring of a white coach over an African American. It is unfortunate that recent studies have suggested that many white administrators and coaches as well as African-American coaches do not want to accept the fact that competence and leadership traits are often not associated with African Americans. As a result,

African-American coaches may not be perceived as capable of leading a Division IA football program. It will take a conscious effort on the part of white institutional leaders to consider hiring an African American as a head coach, especially when the employment hiring patterns of collegiate coaches have revealed a stratified process along racial lines (Hill, 1997; Hill, 2002; Hill, 2004).

Unfortunately, it appears that collegiate leaders have lost interest in the self-analysis needed to unmask covert forms of employment bias that currently take place within the athletics departments of Division IA colleges and universities. Many institutional leaders and athletics department administrators assume that current hiring practices operate indiscriminately of race and equal opportunities exist for coaches who prepare themselves professionally and academically.

CONTRASTING EMPLOYMENT PERCEPTIONS

The divergent perceptions and life experiences between African-American and white football coaches have resulted in the development of two different definitions of racial and employment discrimination. Perceptions have been described as a fixed tendency to interpret information in a particular way. As a result, what an African-American or white coach perceives to be real is often what is believed to be real.

Studies have revealed that African-American coaches define racism in terms of their personal experiences as well as other African-American coaches' experiences in past and present encounters with white people. Many white coaches, on the other hand, have not personally experienced the feeling of being discriminated against or denied an opportunity because of race. Consequently, white coaches tend to hold a narrow view of discrimination, often to the point of denying its existence (Cose, 1993; Hill, 1997; Hill, 2002).

There are four elements that have been discovered to influence the perceptions of African-American and white football coaches at predominantly white colleges and universities.

Personal wants.   African-American and white football coaches have a tendency to seek fulfillment in regard to their wants and needs relating to personal job satisfaction in the workplace.

Previous employment experience.   Past employment experiences can directly and indirectly affect career aspirations of football coaches. Football coaches who have been passed over for a promotion on several occasions will likely perceive that the opportunity to advance may never come.

Personal motives.   The way African-American and white coaches perceive employment-related issues can be influenced by individual motives. White coaches may fail to recognize the need for diversity and equal opportunity in the profession if it is perceived to be achieved at their expense.

Group affiliation.   Variables such as age, race, sex, educational level, economic level, regional differences, religious background, and personal factors can influence football coaches' perception in the workplace. Historically, African-American football coaches have not been granted equal access at predominantly white colleges and universities. Consequently, African-American coaches may perceive that they will not be granted an employment opportunity based on past hiring practices (Albers, 1974; Hill 1997; Hill, 2002).

A significant disparity remains between African-American and white football coaches regarding what is perceived as racial barriers and employment discrimination. Both racial groups report conflicting perceptions and understanding of racial discrimination because the phenomenon affects each group differently.

An example of this can be found in the results of a recent study examining the differing perceptions of nearly 300 African-American and white Division IA football coaches. This study revealed a wide gap in perceptions between African-American and white coaches. Some key findings were:

- Seventy-five percent of African-American coaches compared to 23% of white coaches agree that negative stereotypes held by white administrators and coaches hinder opportunities for African-American coaches despite their professional competencies and accomplishments.
- Twelve percent of white coaches compared to 78% of African-American coaches agree that African-American football coaches' intellectual understanding of football strategy is often questioned by white colleagues and African-American coaches do not receive the same respect as that of their white peers.
- Eighty-two percent of African-American coaches agree that there is a strong indication that African-American coaches are not hired for their strategic understanding of the game, but rather for recruiting and monitoring African-American student-athletes. Thirty-one percent of white coaches agree.
- When a white football coach departs a coaching staff, 88% of African-American football coaches compared to 29% of white coaches believe the vacancy will most likely be replaced with another white coach.
- Seventy-one percent of African-American coaches compared to 38% of white coaches agree that African-American coaches who cannot recruit successfully in African-American communities face an increased chance of termination.
- Twenty percent of African-American coaches compared to 62% of white coaches agree that access to equal opportunities is available to all regardless of race.
- Eighty-seven percent of white coaches perceive that African-American coaches have been accepted as equals in the coaching profession.

Twenty-one percent of African-American coaches share the same employment perspective.

• A diversity plan to increase the hiring of African-American coaches to eliminate subjective hiring practices is felt necessary by 84% of African-American coaches compared to 25% of white coaches. (Hill, 2002)

Other findings suggest that African-American coaches do perceive employment biases and do not feel they share the same opportunities in the coaching profession. African-American coaches report that they have been racially stratified into coaching certain positions, limiting their chances for career advancement. Studies also revealed that white coaches do not perceive that these employment biases hindering the advancement of their African-American peers exist (Hill, 1997; Hill, 2002).

The following comments are from white coaches and offer a stark contrast to those of African-American coaches.

A white coach from the Big East Conference between the ages of 35 and 39 wrote:

I have personally been excluded from a job due to affirmative action. A job should be filled with the most qualified individual, excluding no one, on the bases of color, race, or nationality.

An older white coach (55–59) of the Big East Conference wrote:

It seems that this study infers that African-American coaches are discriminated against in the hiring process. It is my opinion that the opposite is occurring. White coaches are finding it more difficult to find jobs. I know of jobs that are targeted specifically for African-American coaches and white coaches are not even considered.

A white assistant coach from the Mid-American Conference stated:

I have been on three college staffs and race has never been a problem. One for all—all for one has been the motto.

A white coach affiliated with Conference USA wrote:

White coaches and African-American coaches have no problem. (Hill, 2002)

If is often difficult for white coaches to understand the general discontent shared by African-American coaches regarding their chances for career advancement. Exacerbating the situation is that many white coaches appear tired of hearing African-American coaches complain about the lack of coaching opportunities. But as the literature suggests, how coaches—white or

African-American—perceive a particular employment situation is usually reflected by how that individual is affected by the situation. However, data supports the fact that race has dramatically affected the careers of African-American football coaches (Hill, 1997; Hill, 2002; Hill, 2004).

The following comments are from African-American coaches.

An African-American assistant coach employed in the Pacific-10 Conference expressed his views on employment issues facing African-American coaches:

> The bottom line is that racism exists in all areas of life and football is no exception. Administrators hire white head coaches because the vast majority of them are white. In turn, white head coaches hire mostly white staffs because they want to work with people that they are familiar with. In most cases that person is someone of their own race. The African-American coach is then hired to fill a quota, recruit the African-American athlete and become their mentor.

Another African-American football coach from the Big West Conference wrote:

> There seems to be a mentality that two African-American coaches are basically enough. If you have two, then you're okay. I've been here going on four years and we've had no more than two coaches of color during that time. The head coach didn't know either of us before we were hired. There also is a perception amongst the white assistants that we have it made, because of our color. What they don't realize is that we are competing for those two spots out of the nine assistant jobs, while they are competing for the other seven. Also the "good" African-American coach gets over it. Any straying from that gets you labeled as a troublemaker, malcontent and subversive.

An African-American coach from the Big East perceived himself as an "expert" in regard to issues dealing with African-American recruits and their families.

> I am perceived as the resident "expert" on all minority affairs. African-American players come to me for social, personal and academic problems. That does not set well with others on the staff. Recruiting weekends regardless if I have a recruit or parents in, I host the African-American parents. I have developed great relationships with parents and players. Often other coaches come to me to find out about "their" recruits or personal problem. (Hill, 2002)

Studies suggest that the percentage of collegiate football coaches is not reflective of the number of African-American football coaches with qualifications to do the job. However, caution must be used when applying statistics to show underrepresentation. Nevertheless, Dr. Terry Don Phillips, a licensed attorney and director of athletics at Clemson University, believes that qualified coaches should come primarily from those who actually participated in athletics (Shropshire, 1996; NCAA News, 1997).

CONCLUSIONS AND IMPLICATIONS

It is important to note that much progress has been made in the world of sports since Jackie Robinson integrated Major League Baseball in 1947. However, over a half-century later, studies indicate that race continues to have a dramatic influence on the employment opportunities for African-American football coaches at predominantly white colleges and universities. Blalock (1967) discovered during the civil rights era that sports created educational and economic opportunities by making skill the most important determinant for success. It is unfortunate that white administrators and coaches seldom judge African Americans solely on the basis of character and merit. To say that society is color blind and that equal opportunity exists for everyone is aversion and neglect of the real problems and issues of race (Anderson and South, 1993; West, 1994).

Ron Brown was employed as an assistant football coach at the University of Nebraska for more than 15 years. He possessed an impressive résumé with impeccable credentials. When his alma mater, Brown University of the Ivy League, began their search for a new head football coach, Brown was contacted and asked to interview for the position. During the process of the interview, Brown was told that there were individuals who had reservations about hiring an African-American head football coach. According to Brown:

> The athletic director told me just prior to the interview, "Some alums are not happy because you're African-American." They said, "we don't want to play that experiment here." It really bothers me. I played there. You get all the pats on the back while you're playing. All of a sudden, there's a drawn line. (Maisel, 1992, p. 28A)

Recent hirings of head football coaches at Division IA colleges and universities indicate that college presidents and athletics directors are seeking individuals who are diverse and well perceived by the institution's constituents. Institutional leaders must seek potential coaches who possess talents and characteristics that give their institution the best chance of achieving success. White collegiate administrators often become appalled at being labeled racist for the lack of African-American coaches hired at their institutions. The truth is that there is a demand for coaches who are articulate and well dressed, and those qualities are not frequently associated with African-American coaches. Consequently, in many hiring situations, the thought of selecting an African-American head football coach rarely crosses the mind of a white college president or athletics director (Rosellini, 1987).

White administrators and coaches are on record supporting equal opportunity for African-American coaches. Yet, when it appears that white Americans will be cast into the status of a numerical minority on a Division IA football staff, an attempt to promote equal opportunities for African-American coaches has a tendency to evaporate. Social scientists suggest that a large number of African-Americans on a coaching staff at a predominantly white institution can significantly affect the character of intergroup relations between African-American and white coaches. Consequently, the larger the number of African-American coaches, the more likely whites will perceive them as threatening and deny them access to the decision-making process. For this reason, the number of African-American football coaches hired at postsecondary institutions is frequently limited (Smith, 1987; Boyer, 1986; Feagin & Sikes, 1994; Hill, 1997; Hill, 2002).

Many African-American and white coaches alike will not openly discuss their true feelings concerning race-related issues because of fear of possible reprisals or harm to their career. The lack of genuine, open, and honest dialogue regarding personal feelings toward equal employment between African-American and whites coaches contributes to a stale and stagnant employment situation. As a result, recent studies of African-American football coaches have discovered the following:

- African-American football coaches often lower their expectations, do not expect any more out of the profession, and tend to become complacent with just being employed. The literature refers to this as the "shattered dreams syndrome."
- African-American coaches may find themselves the recipients of faint praise at the expense of degrading the rest of the African-American race.
- African-American coaches often see white coaches with the same or lesser qualifications advancing and assume that skin color is the explanation.
- African-American coaches develop what is defined as coping fatigue as they perceive that white coaches do not acknowledge their competence or knowledge of the game.
- The current hiring trend continues to stratify African-American football coaches into positions that tend not to lead to head coaching positions.
- To advance careers, African-American football coaches may perceive it is necessary to deny their culture for acceptance. This can lead to an identity crisis.
- African-American coaches perceive they cannot voice true feelings regarding perceived employment barriers for fear of damaging career opportunities. The result of this is defined as self-censorship. (Cose, 1993; Hill, 1997; Hill, 2002)

The current hiring patterns of African-American football coaches may possibly explain why a significant majority of African-American coaches surveyed agree that a "diversity plan to increase the number of African-American coaches is necessary." However, it is possible that many white coaches may perceive that implementing institutional hiring practices based on goals of achieving diversity or equal opportunity for qualified African-American coaches actually promotes reverse discrimination.

It is astounding that African-American football coaches often seem content to complain loudly to everyone except their institutional leaders who possess the authority to change the unjust hiring practices. In addition, many African-American coaches have concluded that there is a more efficient way to succeed within the profession at predominantly white collegiate institutions: Rather than challenge the obvious bias that confronts them on a daily basis, they instead utilize short-term manipulations of the system so they can continue to remain employed (Graham, 1995; Bell, 1994). But if meaningful changes are going to occur, African-American coaches must join together and voice their opinions regarding employment perceptions and actual treatment. However, to avoid alienating collegiate academic and athletic administrators, African-American coaches must also take a sensitive approach when addressing these issues. The words *racism* and *discrimination* can provoke a defensive posture on the part of many white academic and athletic administrators.

The lack of mutual understanding and open and honest dialogue regarding equal opportunity between African-American and white football coaches and the athletic administration contributes to the disparity of employment perceptions within the coaching profession. Many college and university academic and athletic administrators will definitely refute any biased hiring practices occurring at their institution. However, it is difficult to comprehend why, of the 381 Division IA head coaching vacancies since 1982, only 19 African-American football coaches have been deemed qualified to lead a football program.

For genuine equality to occur within the coaching profession, white collegiate administrators and coaches must come to terms with the fact that they are a product of a racially biased society that unconsciously can negatively affect their perceptions of African Americans. Recent studies and content analysis of Division IA football media guides indicate that past employment patterns as well as current hiring trends indicate a definite need to seek measures that will genuinely promote equal opportunity for all coaches within the coaching profession.

RECOMMENDATIONS

To provide this opportunity, the following recommendations are offered.

Address the problem.   The first step to improving access to equal employment opportunities for African-American coaches is for institutions to admit there is a serious problem within the current system used to select and hire football coaches at postsecondary colleges and universities. It is not enough to merely discuss the issues in regard to past and current hiring practices; specific goals are needed to address the core problems. Unfortunately, many well-meaning academic and athletic administrators refuse to admit that race may still be a major factor in the employment of African-Americans as head football coaches. The identification of education regarding employment barriers is necessary to create access to equal opportunity within the coaching profession. Justice Harry African-Americanmun, dissenting in an Affirmative Action Case (*Regents of the University of California v. Bakke*) stated:

> In order to get beyond racism, we must first take account of race. There is
> no other way. And in order to treat some persons equally, we must treat
> them differently. (Shropshire, 1996, p. 62)

Although the data speaks loud and clear, there are many white coaches that believe that race is not an issue. Denial of the problem also contributes to the frustrations of African-American football coaches in regard to employment opportunity. But barriers are hard to remove when there are coaches that have not come to grip with the reality of the problems.

Specific hiring criteria needed.   The informal nature of hiring practices in the selection of intercollegiate football coaches denies African-Americans opportunities to lead programs. Most postsecondary institutions do not have specific hiring criteria and qualifications from which they select coaches. Defining the term *qualified* is the first place to start. Without clear criteria, African-American coaches are often confused and placed at a disadvantage regarding what is needed to become "qualified."

On college campuses, many athletics directors can often hire a head football coach without regard to specific criteria or clearly stated qualifications. Unfortunately, athletic administrators have shown a tendency to use extremely subjective criteria to evaluate potential coaching candidates. Surprisingly, more academic preparation is required to coach at the high school level than is necessary to be employed as a coach at a Division IA institution. This point was underscored by an African-American assistant football coach employed in the Mid-American Conference who stated:

> I do not believe, or I would like to think, the administrators (presidents,
> athletic directors, head coaches) are not outwardly racist. Unfortunately,
> in this profession employment is generally based on who you know. I
> sincerely wish résumés were taken a lot more seriously in our profession so
> a person can get hired/interviews on his credentials and accomplishments.

Identify and address racial barriers.   The identification of and education regarding restricting employment barriers is another positive step to creating employment equity among African-American and white football coaches. But identifying employment barriers in the workplace can be tough for African-American football coaches to do. It is very difficult for African-American coaches to take employment issues regarding equal opportunity to head coaches and athletic administrators. African-American coaches tend not to speak out about inequity and unfairness at predominantly white colleges and universities. African-American coaches are uncomfortable addressing employment issues and feel they will not be perceived as a team player among white colleagues if they complain. However, Elsie Y. Cross, a Philadelphia diversity consultant, notes that ignoring unfairness and employment barriers lets them grow. She suggests that African-Americans have to be willing to speak up and point out the problems experienced and be courageous enough to risk their careers (Lancaster, 1997).

Manage perceptions.   How institutional leaders perceive African-American football coaches can play a major role in minorities being pigeonholed in staff assignments with no potential for professional growth. African-American coaches must face the fact that some of their white colleagues will assume that the only reason that African-American coaches attain employment is directly related to the color of their skin. African-American coaches must ignore this fact and stay focused on getting the job done. African-American coaches can even use this to their advantage. On many predominantly white coaching staffs, African Americans can erase negative stereotypes and perceptions by seeking professional development and increasing their knowledge regarding the X's and O's of the game. According to Coach Bill Walsh, former head coach of the Super Bowl Champion San Francisco 49ers:

> African-American football coaches should prepare themselves. It's critical
> they cast off that defeatist feeling, because you have to produce when you
> get the chance. (Smith, 1994; Blauvelt, 1992, p. 2C)

It is unfortunate that the success or failure of one African-American coach can directly or indirectly affect the perception and job opportunities of other African-American coaches. Nevertheless, even when there is no hope or perceived opportunity for advancement, African-American coaches must work relentlessly, waiting for the opportunity to show coaching potential and skills. Unlike white coaches, it takes only one "goof up" for African-American coaches to be labeled unqualified for the task they were hired to do. In fact, past employment trends of African Americans being hired as head football coaches revealed that if an African-American coach is terminated from a head coaching position, that individual is extremely unlikely to be rehired as a head football coach at a Division IA institution. Ty Willingham became the first African-American head coach who was fired to be rehired when he took the position at the University of Washington for the 2005 season.

Honesty and frankness. Using tactful and strategic planning, African-American coaches must be honest and frank and continue to educate those they come in contact with as well as institutional leaders who possess the authority to change the unjust hiring practices. The reluctance of African-American football coaches to speak openly about their perceived inequities regarding employment opportunities should not be confused with complacency. According to Alvin Poussaint, associate professor of psychiatry at Harvard Medical School, African-American coaches may self-censor themselves as a simple means of survival. Dr. Poussaint points out that it could be very risky for an African-American coach employed at a predominantly white institution to express individual anger in regard to issues of race (Cose, 1993).

Thanks in part to the ill-advised comments of individuals such as the late Jimmy "The Greek" Snyder, the public has been exposed to stereotypical perceptions regarding the ability of African-American coaches. Snyder, a colorful and often-quoted CBS sports commentator, was fired from the network after making racial remarks regarding African-American athletes and African-American coaches. He was quoted as saying that if African-Americans "take over the coaching jobs like everybody wants them to, there's not to be anything left for the white people" (Jimmy "The Greek," 1996, p. 1C).

The studies that I have written about African-American football coaches employed at predominantly white colleges and universities were an attempt neither to spark nor agitate African-American football coaches to speak out about employment inequities. Furthermore, there was no intent to alienate or provoke reprisals from the many white athletic administrators and coaches who have been instrumental in increasing opportunities for African-American coaches. The rationale for the studies was simply a means to provide an in-depth analysis and explanation of how race affects and impacts the careers of African-American football coaches at Division IA colleges and universities. Like this chapter, I wrote these to illuminate the actual situation, to illustrate the divergent perceptions of both African Americans and whites regarding African-American coaches, and to provide proposed solutions to increase real opportunities for African-American coaches.

REFERENCES

Albers, H. H. (1974). *Principles of management: A modern approach* (4th ed.). New York: John Wiley & Sons.

Anderson, A., & South, D. (1993). Racial differences in collegiate recruiting, retention, and graduation rates. In D. Brooks & Althouse (eds.), *Racism in college athletics: The African-American athlete's experience* (pp. 79–99). Morgantown, W.V.: Fitness Information Technology, Inc.

Bell, D. (1994). *Confronting authority, reflections of an ardent protester*. Boston: Beacon Press.

Blalock, H. M. (1967). *Toward a theory of minority group relations*. New York: John Wiley and Sons.

Blauvelt, H. (1992, November 25). Temple takes new direction for football. *USA Today*, 1C, 2C.

Boyer, J. B. (1986). Developing a mentality of equity: Expanding academic and corporate leadership challenges. *Journal of Educational Equity and Leadership, 6*(2), 139–51.

Cose, E. (1993). *The rage of a privileged class*. New York: HarperCollins.

Crocker, J., & Wilson, M. (1984). Summary and conclusions. *American Behavioral Scientist, 27*(3), 403–7.

Feagin, J. R., & Sikes, M. D. (1994). *Living with racism*. Boston: Beacon Press.

Graham, L. O. (1995). *Member of the club*. New York: HarperCollins.

Hill, O. F. (1997). *Examining the barriers restricting employment opportunities relative to the perceptions of African-American football coaches at NCAA Division IA colleges and universities* (doctoral dissertation, University of Arkansas, 1997).

Hill, O. F. (2002). *Contrasting perceptions of employment opportunities among collegiate football coaches: "The truth and the consequences."* Unpublished manuscript, San Jose State University.

Hill, O. F. (2004, February). *Employment patterns of African-American head football coaches at NCAA Division IA colleges and universities*. Paper presented at the meeting of the American Association for Higher Education for African-American Caucus, Greensboro, N.C.

Jimmy "The Greek." (1996, April 22). *Arkansas Democrat Gazette*, 1C.

Lancaster, H. (1997, March 4). Managing your career. *Wall Street Journal*, B1.

Maisel, I. (1992, May 31). African-American coaches sidelined. *Dallas Morning News*, 1, 2.

NCAA News (1997, June 16).

Ogbu, J. U. (1994). Racial stratification and education in the United States: Why inequality persists. *Teacher College Record, 96*(2), 265–91.

Rosellini, L. (1987, July). Strike one and you're out (racism in sports). *U.S. News and World Report*, 52–57.

Shropshire, K. L. (1996). *In African-American and white*. New York and London: New York University Press.

Smith, A. W. (1987). Racial trend and countertrends in American organizational behavior. *Journal of Social Issues, 43*(1), 93–94.

Smith, E. (1994). *37 more things every African-American man needs to know*. Valencia, Calif.: St. Clair Rene Publishing.

Vital signs: Statistics that measure the state of racial inequality. *Journal of African-Americans in Higher Education*, (2003/2004, Winter).

West, C. (1994). *Race matters*. New York: Vintage Books.

CHAPTER 7

Gender and Sport

Donna A. Lopiano Women's Sports Foundation

HISTORY AND CONTEXT

Title IX

When Title IX of the Education Amendments of 1972 was adopted by Congress, no one realized that one sentence would change sports and society in America forever: *"No person in the United States shall, on the basis of sex, be excluded from participation in, be denied the benefits of, or be subjected to discrimination under any educational program or activity receiving Federal financial assistance."*[1] Male-dominated education programs from business, medical, and law schools to varsity athletics were required to open their doors to women and treat them as equals to men.

Few remember that in 1972 boys were enrolled in wood shop and auto repair and girls in sewing and home economics. In colleges and universities there were admissions quotas preventing women from accessing graduate professional school programs that led to the highest paying jobs such as in science, engineering, law, medicine, and architecture. Women were relegated to the professional schools leading to "caretaking" professions with the lowest salaries: teacher, librarian, social worker, and nurse. There were few women in the front lines of the military, police, or fire departments. Women were secretaries, and men were managers. If a woman wanted a credit card, her husband, brother, or father had to sign the application, even if he was unemployed. For the most part, prior to Title IX and the women's movement of the

1970s, society dictated and women accepted their roles as caretakers, sex objects, and/or decorative objects.

Title IX was not a law that targeted athletics. Rather, it was an omnibus education act that applied to all educational programs and activities, including extracurricular activities. When Title IX was adopted, few knew about the law and what it meant until two things happened: (1) a sports television spectacular captured the attention of the American public, and (2) the National Collegiate Athletic Association (NCAA) and the American Football Coaches Association responded negatively to Title IX, creating a media and congressional debate about the application of Title IX to athletics.

The Battle of the Sexes

In 1973, when Billie Jean King played Bobby Riggs in *The Battle of the Sexes*, it was more than a tennis match between the best female tennis player in the world and a former top-ranked professional male player. The match was much more than sport. It was a cultural phenomenon played on the national television stage, an event that would decide once and for all whether the female stereotypes of the day were right or wrong. Billie Jean's decisive win before a huge television audience and the largest in-arena crowd ever to watch a tennis match shattered many of the physical and psychological myths that had prevented women from aspiring to participate in the world as equals to men.

Billie Jean is a physically strong and competent woman who used her body to do powerful things. Intellectually, she demonstrated her ability to intelligently communicate a strong message about women's rights and aggressively and directly challenged cultural myths about the place and abilities of women. Most important, she demonstrated that women would not fall apart—physically or mentally—under the pressure of national television, the psychological challenges of competition, and the harassing and demeaning attacks of an outspoken male chauvinist who echoed in stereo the national male view of females and female athletes.

Bobby Riggs was the symbol of male dominance of women in the workplace and every life arena. Billie Jean King was the embodiment of a woman with strength of spirit, skilled competence, confident demeanor, and a strong voice that spoke for all women. She was the counterpoint of media-manufactured images of women; she was real. Using a national media platform, she chastised those who would discriminate on the basis of sex. She literally and figuratively vanquished the myth of male dominance. She made it possible for all women and girls to think differently of themselves, to elevate their expectations, and to identify and defy the strong and covert barriers characteristic of gender discrimination. Billie Jean King gave women permission to speak out and demand equal treatment.

Title IX and Billie Jean King also gave men permission to acknowledge women as equals and to encourage, teach, play, and share sports with their daughters and other women in their lives. In fact, fathers have been a strong force in the Title IX sports movement over the last three decades. Most mothers had little or no sports experience or passion for sport because they had never had the chance to play. When dads were given the green light to encourage their daughters, a generation of girls became surrogate sons as they were taught to play and love sports. These fathers were the first to protest or go to court when their daughters were not treated equally in high school or college.

Protest of the Athletics Establishment

The objection of the college athletic and football establishment, namely the NCAA and the American Football Coaches Association, to Title IX had the unanticipated consequence of educating the American public about the benefits of sports for girls. In the 1970s the NCAA governed collegiate men's athletics only. The Association for Intercollegiate Athletics for Women (AIAW) governed collegiate women's athletics. Faced with having to support women's sports, including a huge athletic scholarship price tag, men's athletics described the impact of Title IX as a "zero sum" game. They were fearful that if women were given an equal opportunity to play sports, men's sports would lose because resources would be redirected to new women's sports teams. They contended that successful football programs resulted in increased general alumni fundraising benefiting the financial health of universities, that the revenues that were generated by football supported other sports, and that both alumni fundraising and the overall financial health of athletic programs would be diminished if athletics departments had to fund women's sports. They also contended that women were simply not interested in playing at the college varsity level. These organizations led failed congressional efforts to amend Title IX to exclude football and men's basketball. More important, they created media debate about whether equal opportunity for women in sports mattered.

Media Education of the Public

The controversy generated by the objection of the athletic establishment coupled with the spectacle of *The Battle of the Sexes* forced the media to tell both sides of the story. NCAA data revealed that few football or basketball programs generated revenues that exceeded their own expenses, countering the myth of these sports supporting other sports. Even in Division IA, the NCAA's top revenue-producing division, over half of the 100 football programs were in deficit spending in 2000. The average annual deficit for those in the red was $3.3 million, which was up from $2.8 million in 1997.[2] These deficits in all subsections of Divisions I and II have been steadily increasing over the past decade—from 22 percent making profits in 1993 to 15 percent in 1999, and 78 percent running deficits in 1993 to 85 percent in 1999.[3]

Despite running huge deficits, NCAA data showed the continued explosive growth of football programs with regard to team size and expenditures and undermined the football death prophecy. United States General Accounting Office[4] and NCAA data[5] showed that the elimination of men's minor sports was either about institutional decisions to fuel football and basketball rather than support wrestling or men's gymnastics or about choices related to supporting the growth of more popular men's sports such as soccer and baseball. These data showed that the richest athletic programs were cutting men's minor sports while Division II and III programs were successfully adding women's sports programs while maintaining existing men's sports offerings.

Ellen Staurowsky's review of research through 2002[6] exploded the myth that successful athletic teams aided non-athletics fundraising. She showed that no empirical data supported the athletics fueling alumni general giving relationship. In fact, the majority of alumni givers favored de-emphasis of athletics and athletes themselves did not participate in supporting their institutions as actively as other students. In fact, when limited financial resources existed, athletics fundraising competed with other academic priorities.

Benefits of Participation

Even more important than myth-busting, the media informed the public why sports participation was as important for girls as it was for boys. Public controversy over Title IX created an enormously effective communications platform for advocates of girls' and women's sports. The current widespread American support for equal treatment of males and females in sports is directly related to the fact that the public now understands that sports and physical activity are not just about fun and games. A 2004 compilation of research on the relationship of girls' and women's health by the Women's Sports Foundation summarized these benefits.[7] Regular participation in physical activity during childhood and adolescence promotes the development of positive body image,[8] confidence,[9] and self-esteem.[10] Girls who participate in sports and physical activity are academically more successful,[11] more likely to graduate from high school,[12] and more likely to matriculate in college,[13] and they experience greater career success.[14] Participation in sports and other physical activities can help reduce a girl's health risk for obesity,[15] diabetes,[16] heart disease,[17] osteoporosis,[18] breast cancer,[19] depression,[20] unintended teen pregnancy,[21] anxiety, and lack of self-esteem,[22] among others.

These health benefits are important if society wants to change these startling statistics:

- One in every 6 girls is obese or overweight[23] and, as women, are 60% more likely to die from breast cancer.[24]
- One in 3 teens get pregnant by the age of 20.[25]

- One in 3 girls in grades 9–12 currently smoke;[26] lung cancer is the leading cause of cancer deaths among women.[27]
- One in 3 adolescent girls will experience depression,[28] anxiety, or eating disorders.[29]
- Girls ages 4–19 have significantly higher "bad" cholesterol levels than boys; heart disease is the #1 cause of death among American women.[30]

The public understands that girls are at greater risk for inactivity in our society than boys, especially girls from underserved and lower socioeconomic populations. By the time a girl is 17 years old she has seen 250,000 television commercials focusing on her looks—not her health or physical abilities.[31] Forty-two percent of girls in grades one through three want to be thinner,[32] 51 percent of 9- to 10-year-old girls feel better about themselves when dieting,[33] and 53 percent of 13-year-old girls are unhappy with their bodies, increasing to 78 percent at age 17.[34] The media has convinced girls that "big" is unattractive and they must achieve an unattainable body type, even though big girls can be fit and healthy. One in 6 girls is now obese or overweight, contrasted to 1 in 21 in 1970.[35] Black girls are twice as likely to be overweight as white girls.[36]

If a girl does not participate in sports by the time she is 10 years old, there is only a 10 percent chance she will participate when she reaches the age of 25.[37] Between middle school and high school, girls drop out of sport at a rate that is double that of boys.[38] By the age of 16 or 17 only one in seven girls attends physical education class daily and 15–30 percent report no regular physical activity at all.[39] High school boys receive 40 percent more chances to play varsity sports than girls with similar statistics in college.[40]

CONTINUED PRESSURE FOR COLLEGES AND UNIVERSITIES TO PROVIDE MORE OPPORTUNITIES FOR WOMEN TO PLAY VARSITY SPORTS

This historical context and these health statistics are essential to understanding the context of gender and sport in higher education. As much as alumni and the public are fanatically in love with their college football and men's basketball programs, they are unwilling to say that the quest for a winning football or basketball team gives license for violating federal laws prohibiting sex discrimination. The American public believes that sports participation is just as important for our daughters as it is for our sons. In a 2001 USA Today/CNN/Gallup Poll, 70 percent of Americans who knew about the law supported Title IX in its current form—across both political party affiliation and gender lines.[41] According to the Center for the Advancement of Women, 38 percent of women consider increasing the number of girls who participate in organized sports a top priority for a new women's movement.[42] Parents are encouraging their daughters to be active, and almost any kind of encouragement on the part of parents is effective in increasing their daughter's physical activity. A national survey of preadolescent and adolescent girls shows that girls who are most active report being encouraged by their parents. The survey also reported that girls who were active at the highest levels also had parents who were currently physically active and/or shared an interest in their daughter's sport.[43] The pressure to provide equal opportunity for women in sport has deep roots with regard to public support.

Thus, there will be no rollback of laws prohibiting sex discrimination, just as there will be no rollback of laws prohibiting race discrimination or discrimination against the differently abled. The public knows that females are still underserved in sport and in great need of equal opportunities to participate in physical activity because their lives depend on it from a health perspective and sex discrimination is simply not acceptable.

GENDER DISCRIMINATION CONTINUES IN SPORTS PARTICIPATION

There is no dearth of girls interested, ready, and willing to participate in college sports and benefit from over $450 million in college athletic scholarships.[44] Girls' high school sports participation grew by 847 percent from 1972 to 2001.[45] Boys' high school sports participation has remained at about 47 percent, one out of every two boys, for more than 10 years, while the rate for girls has been rising slowly to about 33 percent, or one out of three, in 2002.[46] Throughout the 1980s, 35 percent of all high school athletes were girls; in 2001 that percentage only increased to 41.5 percent, still well short of the 49 percent female high school student population.[47] But, progress has been made. High school girls' athletics participation numbers were at an all-time high of 2,856,358 for the 2002–03 school year. High school boys' participation numbers also increased to 3,988,738. Participation in high school athletics for both boys and girls for the 2002–03 school year rose by 77,581 students, to a record 6,845,096.[48]

Contrary to popular thought, the increase of participation opportunities for girls has not resulted in a decline of opportunities for boys at the high school level. While the number of female athletes increased 40 percent on high school varsity teams in the 1990s, boys' participation increased 12.5 percent during the same time.[49] Yet, over three decades after Title IX, girls still are not getting their fair share of high school sports opportunities. In 1997, the Office of Civil Rights (OCR) received 83 complaints under Title IX relating to sports programs at elementary and secondary schools, the most received in a single year since the agency began collecting data.[50] Pressure continues at the high school level to provide equal opportunity for girls in varsity sports, and this pressure will exert itself upwards as the 2.8 million girls vie for less than 200,000 college sports opportunities.

In 2001–02, females comprised 56 percent of the college student population[51] but only received 42 percent of all college athletic participation opportunities.[52] In that same school year, college female athletes received $1.05 billion or 79 percent fewer sport operating budget dollars than college male athletes.[53] Again, like high school sports, contrary to popular thought, men's college sports participation has not declined as a result of women's sports participation. In the last 23 years (1981–2004), overall women's participation in collegiate athletics has increased 136 percent across all three divisions from 68,062 to 160,650. Men's participation grew from 156,131 to 216,991, an increase of 39 percent.[54] From 1988–89 to 2001–02, NCAA member institutions added 1,938 sports for men while dropping 1,890 men's sports, for a net gain of 48; during that same time period, 3,127 women's sports were added and 1,275 sports for women were dropped, for a net gain of 1,852.[55]

The gender equity gap continues because colleges and universities are engaged in an arms race in men's basketball and football, two sports that consume 74 percent of the total men's athletic budgets in Division IA.[56] Division I schools still binge on men's sports: Division I colleges can give out 85 football scholarships, and 75 Division I schools pay their men's basketball coaches more than $1 million a year.[57] The average NCAA football roster has increased over the past 20 years, from 82 to 94 players.[58] While the average athletic budget in leagues with Division IAA football has climbed from $3.2 million to $5.4 million over the last decade, the norm for conferences with Division IA football has risen to about $20 million, with the Universities of Texas and Michigan having passed the $50 million mark.[59] Only 15 NCAA Division I schools spend more on all women's sports combined than on football.[60] In the past five years, for every new dollar going into athletics at the Division I and II levels, male sports receive 65 cents and female sports receive 35 cents.[61]

GENDER DISCRIMINATION IN EMPLOYMENT

Though Title IX has resulted in the dramatic expansion of participation opportunities for women in sport, the same has not been true of employment opportunities. In our colleges and universities, women are not even close to participating in their fair share of jobs as coaches and administrators and participating in positions of power in governing structures for college sports.

In 2004 women held 41.0 percent of all administrative jobs within all divisions of the NCAA; but of all administrative jobs, women hold 18.5 percent of head administrator/athletics director jobs.[62] There are more female college presidents of Division IA schools than there are female athletics directors in Division IA programs. The total of 187 female athletics directors of women's programs in 2004 was 11 women more than in 2002.[63] Division I had the lowest percentage of female athletics directors at 8.7 percent, up from 8.4 percent in 2002.[64] Division II had 16.9 percent of female athletics directors, up from 16.1 percent in 2002. Division III had the highest percentage of female athletics directors at 27.5 percent, slightly down from 27.6 percent in 2002.[65] In 2004, 17.8 percent of NCAA women's athletic programs did not have a woman anywhere in the administrative structure; this is an improvement from 2002, when 18.8 percent of women's programs had no women involved.[66]

In 2003, six of the 20 NCAA Executive Committee members were women.[67] In 2001, 26.7 percent of senior-level positions at the NCAA headquarters were filled by women. Seven out of 23 association-wide committees were chaired by women. Lenti Ponsetto is the first woman to head the championships/competition cabinet, and Elsa Cole is the NCAA's lead attorney.[68] In 2001, the nine-member NCAA infractions committee included two women, the NCAA minimum. The championship and academic eligibility compliance committees combined have 83 members, and 32 of the members are women, the NCAA minimum.[69]

In 2004, 44.1 percent of the coaches of women's intercollegiate teams (all divisions) were female, slightly up from 44.0 percent in 2002, which was down from 47.4 percent in 1998. The current percentage is close to the lowest representation of females as head coaches of women's teams in history; 25 years ago, more than 90 percent of women's teams were coached by women. The percentage of females among the coaching ranks of men's athletics remains under 2 percent, as it has been for at least the past three decades. In 2004 the percentages of NCAA female coaches by division were: Division I (44.9%), Division II (39.4%), Division III (46.0%). Between 2000 and 2002, women were hired for less than 1 out of 10 of the new head coaching jobs in women's athletics and 1 out of every 50 of the new head coaching jobs in men's athletics.[70]

The gender of the athletics director among NCAA institutions has a strong impact on the gender of the coaching staff within women's athletics. When the athletics director is a woman, the percentage of female head coaches at Division I NCAA schools is 49.4 percent, compared to 44.5 percent if the athletics director is a male.[71]

The average salary for coaches of women's NCAA Division I teams in 2000 was $38,191, whereas coaches of men's teams earned an average of $61,534. Assistant coaches of women's teams earned on average $18,623, while their counterparts on men's teams earned $30,584.[72] In 2001–02, NCAA Division I coaches of women's teams made about $3,500 more than they did the year before, but coaches of men's teams received an average raise of $9,300.[73] In 2001–02, in Division IA, the average amount of money allocated for all men's head coaches' salaries increased by more than $258,000, to more than $1 million. The average amount spent in Division IA for all women's head coaches' salaries increased by an average of $97,000 to $577,000. However, the proportion of head coaches' salaries spent on women's teams decreased by 2 percent in Division IA to 36 percent.[74]

The situation is no different in other athletics department positions. In 2004, only 12.2 percent of the full-time college sports information directors were females. The highest percentage of female sports information directors was 14.5 percent, found in NCAA Division III. Similarly, in 2004, only 30.0 percent of full-time college head athletic trainers were females.[75] Of the 31,000 active members of the National Athletic Trainers' Association (NATA), 48 percent are women, and 26 percent hold key leadership positions in the NATA.[76]

RACE AND GENDER: DOUBLE JEOPARDY

Between 1971 and 2000, female college athletes of color realized a dramatic increase (955%) in NCAA sports participation opportunities. Women athletes of color received approximately $82 million in college scholarship assistance in 1999, compared to less than $100,000 in 1971.[77] Black female student-athletes in NCAA Division I schools currently graduate at a far higher rate (60%) than black females in the general student body (45%).[78]

That's the good news. Sex discrimination impacts all female athletes, but female athletes of color are in double jeopardy. Compared with the percentage of women of color enrolled at NCAA institutions in 2000 (24.9% of female students), female athletes of color were proportionally underrepresented (14.8% of female students). A similar pattern of disproportionate representation existed for all female athletes in that year (54.7% of all students enrolled, but only 42.1% of athletes were women). Unlike female athletes of color in 2000, male athletes of color in NCAA varsity sports (22.1% of male athletes) were proportionally represented compared to their presence in the student body (22% of male students).

The overrepresentation of male athletes of color in basketball and football, sports with high participation numbers, disguises a pattern of racial inequality in many other men's NCAA sports. There is a pattern of racial inequality in most NCAA sports that appears to be related to continuing racism and the disparate impacts of economic inequality on populations of color. Analysis uncovered an overall pattern of underrepresentation of males of color in 14 of 25 intercollegiate sports and females of color in 20 of 25 intercollegiate sports in 2001.[79]

In 1999, male and female athletes of color were overrepresented among scholarship recipients and received a larger proportion of the scholarship dollars than would be expected considering their proportion in the total athlete populations. However, female athletes of color in 1999 were underrepresented in comparison to their proportion in the overall student body. Both white female scholarship athletes and female athletes of color who were on scholarship graduated at higher rates than their respective counterparts in the general student population in 2000. White male scholarship athletes and male athletes of color who were on scholarship graduated at about the same rate as their respective general student counterparts. It should also be noted that the graduation rates of both female and male students of color were significantly lower than the corresponding rates for white students.[80] According to NCAA statistics on scholarship athletes, 1.8 percent of female athletes were Asian, 3 percent were Hispanic, and 7 percent were from other countries. The proportions of American Indian, Hispanic, Asian, and foreign athletes have grown while the proportion of black women has remained the same since 1990.[81]

Nearly a third of women playing basketball on scholarship and a quarter of track athletes on scholarship in Division I schools are black. Only 2.7 percent of the women receiving scholarships to play all other sports are black (excluding historically black colleges).[82] Black female student-athletes had a graduation rate of 62 percent, compared to only 46 percent of black females in the general student body. White female student-athletes had a graduation rate of 72 percent, compared to 64 percent of white females in the general student body.[83]

Women of color are also in double jeopardy when it comes to employment. Between 1995 and 1996, the percentage of black senior woman administrators in NCAA Division I was 2.4 percent; this number increased to 7 percent in 2001. Among top-level administrators in all divisions, any increases in the percentage of blacks seem to be the result of increased hiring of black women. The most popular positions for black females at NCAA member institutions are academic advisor (10%) and administrative assistant (10%).[84] Twenty-nine percent of assistant and associate athletics directors at Division I schools are women. Ninety percent of women in these positions are white.[85]

African-American women comprise 12 percent of all women's sports head coaches and 10.2 percent of all women's sports assistant coaches in the NCAA.[86] The percentage of black coaches of Division I women's teams increased from 9.7 percent in 1995 to 11.4 percent in 2001. In all divisions the percentage went from 7.5 percent to 8.5 percent. The percentage of black assistant coaches for women's teams in Division I rose from 14.9 percent in 1995 to 17.7 percent in 2001.[87]

There are only three African-American female athletics directors and only 165 black women who are head coaches at non-historically black colleges and universities.[88] Only 10.5 percent of administrators at NCAA Division I institutions are members of minority groups and fewer than 38 percent of them are women.[89]

DISCRIMINATION AGAINST DIFFERENTLY ABLED FEMALE ATHLETES

Virtually no varsity athletic opportunities are offered to male or female athletes with disabilities, despite the fact that more than 10 percent of the college student population have disabilities.[90] Women made up only 25 percent of the athletes competing in the 2000 summer Paralympics and 21 percent in the 2002 winter Paralympics. Women in Paralympic sports report social factors, shortened sport careers, definitions of elitism, cultural implications of both gender and disability, and limited "grass roots" opportunities as factors limiting their participation in sport.[91] It is clear that opportunities for the differently abled at the collegiate varsity level require leaders to champion the cause and a strategic plan to make steady progress toward providing participation opportunities proportional to the differently abled population attending colleges and universities.

FINANCIAL CHALLENGES TO THE ACHIEVEMENT OF GENDER EQUALITY

Though there is no permissible economic excuse for failing to comply with federal law, many institutions maintain that they do not have the financial resources necessary to comply. When resources are limited, schools have several options: (1) reduce the funding of all existing sports (e.g., 10% across-the-board cuts in every sport budget) and use the financial savings to fund new women's sports; (2) maintain funding of the most important men's sports, discontinue minor men's sports, and use those savings to fund new women's sports; or (3) create a tiered structure where an equal number of participation opportunities for male and female athletes are funded at a very high level (e.g., high salary coaches, national schedules, maximum scholarship numbers, etc.), a second tier where equal numbers of male and female athletes are treated in a less expensive way (e.g., regionally limited competition, 50% of maximum scholarship limits, etc.), and a third tier where equal numbers of male and female athletes are treated in an even lower cost way (e.g., part-time coaches only, no scholarships). Any of these institutional choices can produce Title IX compliance, with options 1 and 3 maintaining opportunities for male athletes while increasing opportunities for female athletes and option 2 resulting in a loss of opportunities for male athletes.

While tiered athletic programs will not meet the philosophy of athletic programs desiring to treat all sports equally, such tiering is consistent with how all universities prioritize their academic programs. Just as an institution may choose to be among the top 10 medical or engineering schools and provide for a minimal program in social work, an athletic program can choose to make similar decisions. Connee Zotos has an excellent publication addressing how an institution can achieve tiered programs in athletics without running afoul of Title IX requirements.[92]

A 2001 United States General Accounting Office Report reported on three methods used by schools that added opportunities for female athletes without cutting men's teams: obtaining funding from non-school sources, finding ways to contain costs, and/or reallocating existing revenues. Obtaining additional revenues and reallocating existing revenues rather than containing costs were more frequently used strategies among the 693 schools that added one or more intercollegiate athletic teams over the 1992–93 to 1999–2000 period without discontinuing a team. Sources of funds varied with the size of the intercollegiate athletic program. Schools with smaller programs (NCAA

Division III and NAIA) were more likely to use additional funds from the institution's general fund and/or reallocate savings from budget cuts across all sports. Larger schools (NCAA Division I and II) were more likely to rely on increased donations from individuals and businesses and charging rental fees for the use of athletic facilities to outside entities.

Cost containment efforts among all institutions examined included:

- Recruiting most prospective student-athletes via telephone rather than in person
- Denying requests for some teams to be elevated from club to varsity status
- Replacing a retiring full-time faculty member with a coach who also assumed other administrative duties
- Limiting the size of the football team roster
- Trimming administrative costs
- Not awarding the maximum number of scholarships allowed
- Limiting team travel outside the region to one trip every two to three years to minimize travel expenses[93]

Because intercollegiate athletics is an interinstitutional activity, administrators believe that it is impossible for individual institutions to unilaterally disarm without reducing competitiveness against institutions that do not make similar cutbacks. Thus, national or conference-level legislation to reduce costs and free up funds for gender equity becomes a critical strategy. The Coalition for Girls and Women in Education advanced the following suggested conference or national organization legislation:

1. *Contract Limitations.* Approve national legislation to create one-year, renewable contracts for all coaches and staff in order to eliminate such practices as "buy-outs" and "golden parachutes."
2. *Debt Service and Capital Expenditures.* Require the approval of the faculty senate for major renovation or the building of new athletic facilities.
3. *Recruiting Reform.* Reform the current recruiting system. Consider allowing campus tryouts for prospective student-athletes (as is done in Division II) and other ways to restrict the excessive costs of off-campus recruiting.
4. *Size of Coaching Staffs.* Reduce coaching staffs and base the number on a reasonable coach:student-athlete ratio.
5. *Size of Non-Coaching Staffs.* Limit the number of non-coaching personnel to a figure based on the number of student-athletes in the athletics department (e.g., employees in the areas of sports information, marketing and promotions, administration, secretarial support, etc.).
6. *Size of Administrative Staffs.* Eliminate administrative assistants in specific sports.

7. *Excessive and Unnecessary Expenditures.* Prohibit football and men's basketball practices such as staying in hotels before home games, non-player travel parties to bowl and championship games, entertainment, and other non-essential expenditures during pre-season training periods, etc.

8. *Scholarships.* For example, change "head count" scholarships to "equivalency based" scholarships and reassess scholarship limits in all sports to conform to commonly accepted team size. If football scholarships in Division IA were reduced from 85 to 65, using the 1999 average scholarship costs and applying a formula of 30% in-state student-athletes and 70% out-of-state student-athletes, there would be a savings of almost $300,000 each year.

9. *Travel Expenses.* Streamline all travel parties during the regular season by establishing maximum travel-party limitations.

10. *Number of Competitions.* Reduce the length of seasons in appropriate sports, curtail the excessive number of competitions in some sports (e.g., softball and baseball), and consider reducing or eliminating institution-sponsored practice and competition in the off-season.

11. *Sport Budget Limits.* Establish legislation to limit overall maximum expenditures (all-inclusive) on a per-sport basis, with differences in travel budgets based on geographical factors.

12. *Roster Limits.* Establish roster limits in every sport based on numbers of athletes required to practice and compete.

13. *Anti-trust Exemption.* Some have suggested that Congress should give schools a limited exemption from anti-trust laws in order to tie the total recompense for head and assistant coaches to the top five full professors at the institutional or conference level or other justifiable salary levels.[94]

Though all of these suggestions are viable alternatives, there appears to be little inclination to cap expenditures on men's sports as a solution to help achieve gender equity.

Laws cannot prevent unethical behavior by individuals or institutions; they can only penalize them. When the penalty for violating the law is non-existent or minimal, the law does not act as a deterrent. Institutions continue to ignore Title IX because there is no penalty for doing so. If the Office of Civil Rights or courts find institutions guilty of non-compliance, they order the institution to come into compliance immediately, with no penalty for years of non-compliance. Thus, many institutions wait until they must comply rather than doing so voluntarily. This absence of moral obligation coupled with weak or non-existent enforcement efforts by the Office for Civil Rights and the high cost of individuals bringing lawsuits against educational institutions has resulted in the snail's pace progress toward gender equality. Three decades following the passage of Title IX, the majority of athletic programs are still not close to offering equal opportunity and treatment for their female athletes.

ADDRESSING GENDER DISCRIMINATION IN EMPLOYMENT

There is almost always a way to get around the letter of the law, and nowhere is that more true than in the area of employment, covered by Title VII and numerous other laws. Over the past 30 years, it appears that anti-discrimination laws have driven discriminatory treatment, policies, and practices underground as opposed to eliminating such conduct. Discriminatory employment practices have become more artful, more deceiving, more difficult to uncover and combat. It is essential that administrators recognize and understand these new, subtle forms of discrimination.

First, there has been a gradual extinction of advocates of women in sport. There were more advocates of gender equity within athletics in the 1960s and early 1970s than there are now. Women held 90 percent of the coaching and athletics director positions in women's sports.[95] They were leaders. They ran their own sports programs. In the name of Title IX compliance and financial savings, most of the high school and collegiate men's and women's athletic programs in the country were merged under single administrative structures, with the director of the men's program taking the top administrative position. Women administrators lost decision-making power, control of the employee acquisition and retention process, and responsibility for the development of women's programs.

This change in who hired coaches and other employees coupled with increased funds for women's sports proved significant. When Title IX mandated that more money be spent on women's programs, paid coaching and administrative positions in women's sports became lucrative and attractive to men. Where once 90 percent of all coaches of women's college teams were women, that figure in 2003 was down to 44 percent.[96]

The women who were once able to promote the development of women's athletic programs and uncover and publicly expose program inequities have either disappeared or are now working under male athletics directors. Many of these female coaches and assistant and associate directors are fearful of being fired if they play the role of a whistle-blower or push too hard for more resources to be devoted to the development of women's athletics. When women are hired, strong and outspoken candidates are rejected in favor of inexperienced or passive women.

Some athletics directors maintain that women are simply not applying for coaching and administrative positions. However, a close look at NCAA Division I women's programs not affiliated with men's programs and governed by women athletics directors or at those programs having organizational structures where there was equal authority of men's and women's athletics directors reveals a very different picture. Sanders reported that among 14 of 17 such institutions responding (82%), only 29 of 102 (28%) of head coaching positions of women's teams were occupied by males—almost half the national average.[97]

When searching for coaches of women's teams, the athletics director may only look at formal written applications and make a "paper hire." When looking for coaches of men's teams, the athletics director may spend days on the telephone hunting for the best candidates and hire good coaches away from other programs whether or not they apply for the position. Administrators cannot underestimate the impact of not "hiring women away" from their current positions. Progress in breaking gender discrimination barriers (or race discrimination, for that matter) occurs one person at a time. When an organization hires a woman and has a successful experience with her, it is more likely to hire a woman again. If women are not moving within the marketplace, even laterally, employment possibilities soon stagnate. It is as important to go to the marketplace to hire proven female coaches and administrators as it is to hire male coaches and administrators.

Women coaches and administrators also confront a very common and insidious underground campaign that stems from the lesbian or unfeminine stereotype applied to women who engage in sport or wish to gain access to previously all-male professions (e.g., construction, police, military, etc.). It is not unusual, when an athletics director is checking on the credentials or references of female coaching candidates, to hear concerns that the applicant may have homosexual inclinations or references to her physical attractiveness as being more masculine than feminine. Homophobia is an equal opportunity employment issue that is a lot like communism. It is talked about behind the backs of applicants and almost impossible to combat.

In many cases, this discriminatory treatment is not intentional. It happens because people are not educated in the importance of ethnic, cultural, and gender diversity and simply do the easiest and most comfortable thing: hire people they are comfortable with, know, and associate with—people just like them. It is easy not to be sensitive. It is easy to believe in stereotypes. It is hard for those in the majority to understand how hurtful these stereotypes are to minority groups.

Another factor is that there is little effort on the part of many athletics departments to develop women's sports into major revenue producers. All of the extraordinary perquisites—huge salaries, multiyear contracts, extensive media coverage, complimentary cars and country club memberships—go to coaches and administrators responsible for revenue-producing sports. If women's sports are not allowed to become revenue producers, we will continue to see the following:

- Depressed salaries of coaches because revenue production will continue to be used as justification for salary differences
- Lack of attention by the media because no one goes to women's sporting events that are not receiving any promotional effort
- Denial of access to major sponsors, contributors, and supporters
- Lack of power connections that can help remedy discrimination simply by their ability to influence those in control of athletic programs

It is economically irresponsible for institutions not to make every effort to ensure that all men's and women's sports are doing all they can to produce any revenues that can contribute to defraying program expenses. Moreover, the lack of effort to make women's sports revenue producers is directly related to discriminatory treatment. Undervaluing and treating the women's sports product as inferior has a substantial impact on athletics department promotional priorities. When a product is presented to the public as inferior, a person's decision to pursue coaching women's sports may also be affected.

The impact of discrimination gone underground cannot be underestimated. Such discrimination has produced a generation of coaches of women's teams who are angry, and rightfully so, at how difficult it is to pursue their chosen profession and be compensated as well as coaches of men's teams. We have produced male and female coaches of women's teams who are angry at salary and employment inequities that are present simply because they coach women, are frustrated at how their players are treated, and are angry over their players receiving less. This anger and frustration can have tremendous impact on female athletes who are not being encouraged by what they see and experience to consider athletics as a profession.

PROPOSALS FOR CHANGE

Significant progress in dealing with gender discrimination in employment can be made. Following are suggestions regarding what should be done:

1. Directly and immediately confront discriminatory practices. Doing this demands constant vigilance and perseverance.
2. Make every effort to educate those overseeing the conduct of athletic programs—members of faculty athletics councils, college presidents and vice presidents, athletics directors—to the new forms of subtle discrimination that are undermining the ability of higher education to create an open, fair, and supportive employment environment for women in sports-related careers. Every coaching association and national sport governing body (NGB) convention program could have a session on recognizing subtle discrimination and the behaviors and responses that keep women and other minorities out of the coaching profession.
3. Work against any effort to reduce participation opportunities for women, even in bad economic times. Equality of participation opportunity and treatment of women athletes affects how coaches feel about their profession and how athletes feel about moving into coaching and other sports careers after their participation days are over.
4. Develop women's sports as revenue producers. There has been considerable debate as to whether women's athletics will ever be able to pay for itself. The real point is whether institutions are making every

effort to ensure that men's and women's sports are doing all they can to produce any revenues that can contribute to defraying program expenses and eliminating unnecessary expenses. A strong economic environment for sports programs will contribute to better paid coaches and better treatment of professionals, and will increase the attractiveness of the coaching profession to young people.

5. Promote coaching as a profession to all current athletes—men and women. Each NGB, coaches association, the USOC or the NCAA, NAIA, or NJCAA could produce an attractive "We Want You" brochure that presents male and female role model coaches talking positively about their professional and volunteer activities. The seeds of coaching as a career possibility must be planted in the minds of female athletes. Along with encouraging our athletes to consider a career in sport is the need to educate current coaches about how they affect the decisions of their athletes to pursue coaching. Coaches who complain that they are overworked, underappreciated, underpaid, or angry about their profession affect the career choices of athletes. Though players should understand the realities of coaching, both good and bad, they should see a balance between the positive and rewarding and the challenges of coaching careers.

6. Insist on open and fair employment practices. Administrators need to act affirmatively to redistribute coaching opportunities fairly among women and minority groups. We cannot continue to permit athletics to operate as a "closed shop." Leaders need to speak out about the importance of affirmative action and a commitment to remedying past discrimination every time there is a position opening. Those who care must find out who is on the search committee, give them the data, and encourage them to act affirmatively. Laws do not prevent discrimination in employment or participation opportunities— people do. Athletes, parents, other relatives, and fans can make a difference. One voice can produce change, and we cannot think that the voice is going to be that of someone else. Educational leaders need to advocate to athletics department employers that individual responsibility is key to the success of remedying discrimination against women and minorities.

7. Colleges and universities need to maintain data on numbers of coaches, administrators, and other professional positions by gender, race, and ethnic group and show comparative salaries and positions. That data can then be assembled, published, and reviewed each year. These organizational report cards send an important message about the importance of diversity and encourage accountability.

8. Tenured faculty have the power to speak without concern for retribution and it is critical that they step forward to help women in the athletics trenches who have no such job security.

9. Administrators who are doing the hiring have to be educated on the importance of marketplace hiring and how this practice actually increases the salary and pool of qualified candidates over the long term.

10. Coaches and administrators have to establish new networks for minority and female recruiting, because existing networks are predominantly white-male. Employers should never accept the "no women applied" or "no minorities applied" excuse. See what happens when the higher education administrator over the athletics department sends the message that "no money is available for a position unless you can find a minority and you can justify this hire under affirmative action." Acceptable candidates will suddenly materialize.

11. Recognize the importance of and implement new employee orientation, support, and mentoring to ensure the retention of minority employees—be they women or racial minorities. Insecurity and discomfort in the work environment produces defense mechanisms in minority employees and reduces retention rates. Every intern or new woman or minority employee should have an assigned mentor who knows that it is his or her responsibility to educate and help assimilate the new employee into the organization. The head of the athletics department has to make clear how important this responsibility is. It is too expensive to recruit employees from limited minority pools and then lose them and have to start over again.

12. Internships should be used to create test positions, especially in a bad economy. Undergraduate coaching internships will play a vastly more important role given NCAA limitations on numbers of coaches. Every organization should have at least one if not two or three internship positions designated for women and minorities.

13. Coaches need to be educated about the fact that what they say and do in front of their student-athletes influences their decisions about whether to make sport a career.

14. Make scholarships in fee-charging junior programs or summer camps conducted by athletics departments a rule rather than the exception. Sport opportunity cannot be available only to youth who can afford it. Minorities are overrepresented in lower socioeconomic groups. Coaches are going to come from our participant pools, so we must ensure that those pools have enough women and minorities. Insist that every youth sport program charging fees offer scholarships to boys and girls from lower socioeconomic groups.

15. Advocate for certification of coaches. Certification goes a long way toward preventing employment discrimination because it mandates objective criteria for weighing the basic qualifications of applicants. Administrators still maintain that women coaches are less qualified and less experienced than their male counterparts despite the fact that research shows that just the opposite is the case.[98] Certification requirements also initially reduce the supply of coaches, which increases demand and therefore increases salaries—both of which increase the attractiveness of the coaching profession.

16. Recommend qualified women for positions. Males seldom criticize another male when it comes to whether that man is qualified for a job, and females must do the same.

17. Female professionals must recognize that employment longevity is power. The longer a woman stays in her position, the more contacts she has and the greater support she develops. Doing good deeds in the community also generates power by providing a power base of appreciative citizens outside of the institution.
18. Speaking out against wrong is powerful and important. It is each individual's obligation to speak out against wrong if we want our educational institutions and athletic programs to exhibit integrity.

HOMOPHOBIA AND SEXUAL HARASSMENT

Historically, women have been deterred from sports participation by myths and stereotypes ranging from excessive exertion causes damage to reproductive organs, to female athletes have large and unattractive muscles, to the smaller lungs and circulatory capacities of females do not allow them to run long distance races without adverse physiological effects. Fortunately, each of these myths and stereotypes has been dispelled over time. Unfortunately, there is one remaining stereotype that is still being used to diminish the experience of women in sports: the use of society's fear of homosexuality. There are those who feel threatened by women participating as equals in sports, who are labeling women who participate in sport as lesbians, hoping to deter many from participating. Some coaches use negative recruiting tactics, implying to a recruit that a rival college or university's coach is gay, or that an opposing team is "full of lesbians," in an effort to prey on unsubstantiated fears that a gay coach or gay players might influence a recruit's sexual orientation.

The presence or absence of gays and lesbians is not the issue. There are lesbians and gays in men's and women's sports. Any label applied to an entire group wrongly stereotypes every member of the group and is patently unethical. All football players are not dumb. All female athletes are not lesbians. All male dancers, artists, and designers are not gay. The bottom line is that educated people must understand how homophobia is "used" by those who would like to destroy the reputation of a program or school or coach or to remove the opportunity to play or work. The use of homophobia is unethical and patently wrong. Educators are morally obligated to be honest and to create safe learning environments that respect the rights and treatment of all students.

It is also important to distinguish between homophobia and sexual harassment. We cannot and should not discriminate on the basis of sexual preference in the provision of any educational program or activity. Conversely, we need to punish sexual harassment at all times. Any male or female student, whether they participate in athletics or not, should not be subject to unwanted sexual advances from members of either sex. In fact, the possibility of being propositioned by a lesbian student-athlete is not the only uncomfortable situation that a heterosexual female student-athlete may face. Sexual harassment by male students or male student-athletes are situations that occur much more frequently to female students. Sexual harassment or even sexual assault by male coaches of female student-athletes is a significant problem in school and open amateur sport settings across the country that often goes unreported.

Rather than focus on the presence or absence of lesbians, parents and coaches should focus on helping young women student-athletes know that they can turn down any unwanted advances and should not put up with sexual harassment from any source—male or female.

Athletics administrators can and should establish clear policies and positions on these issues. With regard to dealing with issues related to sexual orientation:

- No athletics department or sport organization employee or volunteer, athlete, parent, or fan should harass, threaten, slander (e.g., anti-gay slurs, pushing or shoving, property damage, graffiti directed at a particular person or group) a coach or athlete (or any person, for that matter) on the basis of sexual orientation.
- A coach or athlete's sexual orientation should not be a factor in determining his or her eligibility for teams, scholarships, coaching positions, or athletic or academic honors or awards.
- Coaches, athletes, other athletics department personnel, or students who participate in the harassment of lesbian or bisexual athletes or who contribute to a hostile environment for these athletes and coaches should be appropriately disciplined.
- Lesbian and bisexual coaches and athletes should be able to participate on a team or in an athletics department or sport setting that is free of hostility.
- The provisions of all policies prohibiting sexual harassment and sexual relations between coaches and athletes should be applicable to all coaches and athletes without regard to the sexual orientation of athletics department/sport organization personnel.
- Lesbian and bisexual athletes and coaches should be able to identify themselves if they choose to without fear of negative consequences (e.g., loss of job, scholarship, or starting position; negative performance evaluation; dropped from team).
- Administrators should support coaches and athletes in addressing anti-gay incidents.[99]

Similarly, policies on sexual harassment or appropriate coach/athlete relationships or relationships with other professionals who work with athletes such as athletic trainers, sports psychologists, officials, and sports information personnel should be in place. Sexual harassment is a violation of Title IX and impairs girls' and women's access to educational resources. Romantic and/or sexual relationships between coaches or other athletics professionals and athletes are regarded as an abuse of professional status and power.

Sexual harassment consists of unwelcome sexual advances, requests for sexual favors, and other verbal or physical conduct of a sexual nature when:

> (a) Submission to such conduct or communication is made either explicitly or implicitly a term or condition of an individual's employment or status in a course, program, or activity; (b) Submission to or rejection of that conduct by an individual is used as a factor in decisions affecting that individual; or (c) Such sexual conduct has the purpose or effect of unreasonably interfering with an individual's work, educational, or athletic performance, or of creating an intimidating, hostile, or offensive environment for working, learning, or the development of athletic skills.[100]

Romantic and/or sexual relationships between coaches and athletes compromise the professional integrity of the coach and educational mission of athletics. Coaches exercise power over athletes, whether in giving them praise or criticism, evaluating them, making recommendations that further their athletic goals, or conferring any other benefits on them. Romantic and/or sexual relationships between coaches and athletes are wrong when the coach has professional responsibility for the athlete. Such situations greatly increase the opportunities for a coach to abuse his or her power and sexually exploit the athlete. Voluntary consent by the athlete in such a relationship is suspect, given the fundamentally unequal nature of the relationship. Moreover, other athletes and coaches may be affected by such unprofessional behavior because it places the coach in a position to favor or advance one athlete's interest at the expense of others and implicitly makes obtaining benefits contingent on romantic and/or sexual favors.

Officials who are responsible for the administration and oversight of coaches and athletic programs should:

1. Formulate a written policy that details appropriate and inappropriate behavior. The policy should clearly explain the sanctions for sexual harassment. Job descriptions for coaching staff and volunteers should address the issues of sexual abuse and sexual contact.
2. Develop and distribute clear rules that prohibit coach/athlete dating and/or sexual relationships. These rules should specify the length of time that should pass after the cessation of a coach/athlete relationship before dating might occur. (The length of time specified should fit the age and/or social-psychological characteristics of athletes in the administrative setting, e.g., interscholastic athletes, college athletes, elite athletes, or professional athletes.)
3. Provide coaches with information, training, and continuing education about how power, dependence, "love," and sexual attraction can influence coach/athlete relationships. Upper-level administrators need to take responsibility for organizing educational and training sessions for coaches and staff.

4. Develop a complaint procedure for reporting sexual harassment. Athletes should be given multiple opportunities to report cases of sexual harassment to neutral persons, that is, officials from outside the athletics department (e.g., guidance counselors, school psychologists, or school nurses might be identified as referral agents). Procedural guidelines should also recognize that, in addition to needing direction and assistance in order to process the complaint itself, victims may benefit from personal counseling.

5. Ensure that procedures for reporting sexual harassment protect the privacy of any athlete or coach involved as much as possible. It is helpful to distinguish between informal and formal procedures for reporting sexual harassment. Informal procedures may involve initial discussion of alleged incidents with athletes, clarification of circumstances and perceptions, and counseling. Strict confidentiality should be maintained during informal reporting. Formal procedures incur the filing of an official complaint against the alleged perpetrator. Both athlete and coach need to be advised of their rights at this time, and limitations on confidentiality must be explained.

6. Safeguard that procedures for determining whether sexual harassment has occurred protect the legal rights of coaches until litigation or administrative hearings have been completed.

7. Develop an appeals procedure in the event that the accused harasser or alleged victim is dissatisfied with the outcome of a hearing. Coaches or athletes should not be expected to waive their right to pursue legal redress in a court of law. Administrators need to inform those involved about statutes of limitations.

8. Draft policy guidelines to protect coaches and athletes from retaliation during and after a hearing or appeals process.

9. Respond quickly to allegations of harassment. Take immediate action to ensure that the environment is free of sexual harassment. Ensure that an investigation proceeds in a timely manner.

10. Prepare a press statement that specifies your organization's sexual harassment policy. This statement should be posted in prominent places and distributed to new staff.

11. Screen all applicants for coaching staff and volunteer positions. The policy on sexual harassment and consensual relations between coaches and athletes should be explained in all pre-employment interviews with all prospective staff or volunteers.[101]

SUMMARY

Discrimination on the basis of gender still exists in intercollegiate athletics with regard to both employment and participation opportunities and treatment. The requirements of Title IX, the federal law prohibiting sex discrimination in education programs and activities receiving federal funds, are being ignored by many institutions that are moving at a snail's pace in fulfilling their compliance obligations. Females of color are in double jeopardy with regard to participation and employment discrimination. Additional issues negatively impacting the participation of women in sport and sport-related careers are the failure to adequately address limitations in financial resources with systemic policy and rule changes that would control or more equitably distribute athletics department expenditures; the use of homophobia to deter participation, reduce employment opportunities, and negatively recruit; and sexual harassment. These challenges and issues related to gender and sport require the immediate attention of educational leaders and outspoken criticism by sports professionals. There is much to be done to create a safe, equitable, respectful, and rewarding collegiate sports culture for female athletes and career professionals.

NOTES

1. Education Amendments of 1972, P. L. 92-318, Title IX-Prohibition of Sex Discrimination, July 1, 1972 (now codified as 20 U.S.C. § 1681(a)).

2. Fulks, D. L. (2000). *Revenues and Expenses of Divisions I and II Intercollegiate Athletics Programs—Financial Trends and Relationships—1999.* Michael V. Earle, ed. Indianapolis, Ind.: National Collegiate Athletic Association

3. Fulks, D. L. (1994). Revenues and Expenses of Divisions I and II Intercollegiate Athletics Programs—Financial Trends and Relationships—1993. Indianapolis, Ind.: National Collegiate Athletic Assocation.

4. U.S. General Accounting Office. (2001). *Intercollegiate Athletics: Four-Year Colleges' Experiences Adding and Discontinuing Teams.* Washington, D.C.: National Federation of State High School Association (NFHS). The report made participation comparisons based on NAIA and NCAA data from 1981–82 to 1998–99. Athletics director survey data also compared the experience of adding and discontinuing teams from 1992–93 to 1999–2000. A full copy of this report is available at http://www .gao.gov. Search GAO Reports by date: March 8, 2001.

5. National Collegiate Athletic Association. (2003). *NCAA Sports Sponsorship, 2001–2002.* A full copy of this report can be obtained at http://www.ncaa.org.

6. Staurowsky, E. (2003). *The Relationship Between Athletics and Higher Education Fund Raising: The Myths Far Outweigh the Facts.* Unpublished manuscript, Department of Sport Studies, Ithaca College, Ithaca, N.Y.

7. Sabo, D., Miller, K. E., Melnick, M. J., & Heywood, L. (2004). *Her Life Depends On It: Sport, Physical Activity, and the Health and Well-Being of American Girls.* East Meadow, N.Y.: Women's Sports Foundation.

8. Women's Sports Foundation. (2001); President's Council on Physical Fitness and Sport. (1997). *Physical Activity & Sport in the Lives of Girls,* Spring 1997, published by the President's Council on Physical Fitness and Sports, Washington, D.C.: U.S. Department of Health and Human Services; Colton, M., and Gore, S. (1991). *Risk, Resiliency, and Resistance: Current Research on Adolescent Girls.* Bethesda, Md.: Ms. Foundation; Available from the Women's Sports Foundation, East Meadow, NY (1985).

9. President's Council on Physical Fitness and Sport. (1997). *Physical Activity & Sport in the Lives of Girls.* Bethesda, Md.: Ms. Foundation; Women's Sports Foundation. "Miller Lite Report on Women in Sports." 1985; Melpomene Institute, 1995.

10. Fox, K. R. (1988). "The self-esteem complex and youth fitness." *Quest,* 40: 230–246; Fox, K. R. (2000). "Self-esteem, self-perceptions and exercise." *International*

Journal of Sport Psychology, 31:228–240; Guinn, B., Semper, T., and Jorgensen, L. (1997). "Mexican American female adolescent self-esteem: The effect of body image, exercise behavior, and body fatness." *Hispanic Journal of Behavioral Sciences*, 19:517–526; Palmer, L. K. (1995). "Effects of a walking program on attributional style, depression, and self-esteem in women." *Perceptual and Motor Skills*, 81:891–898; Sonstroem, R. J. (1984). Exercise and self-esteem. In G. L. Terguny (Ed.), *Exercise and sport science review* (pp. 123–155). Lexington, Mass.: The Collmore Press; Sonstroem, R. J. (1997). Physical activity and self-esteem. In W. P. Morgan (Ed.), *Physical Activity and Mental Health* (pp. 127–143). Washington, D.C.: Taylor and Francis.

11. Sabo, D., Melnick, M., and Vanfossen, B. (1989). *The Women's Sports Foundation Report: Minorities in Sports*. East Meadow, N.Y.: Women's Sports Foundation.

12. Sabo, D., Melnick, M., and Vanfossen, B. (1989). *The Women's Sports Foundation Report: Minorities in Sports*. East Meadow, N.Y.: Women's Sports Foundation.

13. Marsh, H.W., and Kleitman, S. (2003). "School athletic participation: Mostly gain with little pain." *Journal of Sport and Exercise Psychology*, 25:205–228.

14. Bunker, L. K. "Life-long benefits of youth sport participation for girls and women." Presented at the Sport Psychology Conference, University of Virginia, Charlottesville, June 22, 1988; "From the locker room to the boardroom: A survey on sports in the lives of women business executives," *Game Face*, Feb. 2002.

15. U.S. Department of Health and Human Services. (1996). *Physical Activity and Health: A Report of the Surgeon General*. Atlanta, Ga.: U.S. Department of Health and Human Resources; Colditz, G. A. (1999). "Economic costs of obesity and inactivity. (Physical activity in the prevention and treatment of obesity and its comorbidities)." *Medicine and Science in Sports and Exercise*, 31:5663–5668; Ward, D., Trost, S., Felton, G., Saunders, R., Parsons, M., Dowda, M., and Pate, R. (1997). "Physical activity and physical fitness in African-American girls with and without obesity." *Obesity Research*, 5:572–577.

16. Associated Press. (2003). "Diabetes in children set to soar." MSNBC. June 16, 2003; Colditz, G. A. (1999). "Economic costs of obesity and inactivity. (Physical activity in the prevention and treatment of obesity and its comorbidities)." *Medicine and Science in Sports and Exercise*, 31:5663–5668.

17. Centers for Disease Control and Prevention. (1995). *National Health and Nutrition Examination Survey III 1994*. Hyattsville, Md.: U.S. Department of Health and Human Services Center for Disease Control and Prevention; National Center for Chronic Disease Prevention and Health Promotion. (1996). *Physical Activity and Health, A Report of the Surgeon General*, (S/N 017-023-00196-5). Washington, D.C.: U.S. Department of Health and Human Services; Haddock, B. L., et al. (1998). "Cardiorespiratory fitness and cardiovascular disease risk factors in postmenopausal women." *Medical Science and Sport Exercise*, 30:893–898; Kendig, S., and Sanford, D. (1998). *Midlife and menopause: Celebrating women's health. AWHONN Symposia Series*. Washington, D.C.: AWHONN.

18. Kannus, P. (1999). "Preventing osteoporosis, falls, and fractures among elderly people." *British Medical Journal*, 318:205–206; D. Teegarden, et al. (1996). "Previous physical activity relates to bone mineral measures in young women." *Medicine and Science in Sports and Exercise*, 28(1):105–113; Bonaiuti, D., et al. (2002). "Exercise for preventing and treating osteoporosis in postmenopausal women (Cochrane Review)." *Cochrane Library*, 3.

19. Bernstein, L., Henderson, B., Hanisch, R., Sullivan-Halley, J., and Ross, R. (1994). "Physical exercise and reduced risk of breast cancer in young women." *Journal of the National Cancer Institute*, 86:1403–1408; Thune, I., et al. (1997). "Physical activity and the risk of breast cancer." *New England Journal of Medicine*, 18:1269–1275; A. McTiernan, et al. (2003). "Recreational physical activity and the risk of breast cancer in postmenopausal women: The women's health initiative cohort study." *Journal of the American Medical Association*, 290(10):1331–1336; Patel, D. R., et al. (2003). "Recreational physical activity and risk of postmenopausal breast concern in a large cohort of U.S. women." *Cancer Causes Control*, 6:519–529.

20. Dunn, A. L., Trivedi, M. H., and O'Neal, H. A. (2001). "Physical activity dose-response effects on outcomes of depression and anxiety." *Medicine and Science in Sports and Exercise*, 33(6):S587–S597; Dimeo, F., Bauer, M., Varahram, I., Proest, G., and Halter, U. (2001). "Benefits from aerobic exercise in patients with major depression: A pilot study." *British Journal of Sports Medicine*, 35:114–117; Page, R. M., and Tucker, R. A. (1994). "Psychosocial discomfort and exercise frequency: An epidemiological study of adolescents." *Adolescence*, 29(113):183–191; Nicoloff, G., and Schwenk, T. S. (1995). "Using exercise to ward off depression." *Physician and Sportsmedicine*, 23(9):44–58; Ahmadi, J., et al. (2002). "Various Types of exercise and scores on the Beck Depression Inventory." *Psychological Reports*, 90(3):821–822; Sanders, C. E., et al. (2000)."Moderate involvement in sports is related to lower depression levels in adolescents." *Adolescence*, 35(140):793–797.

21. Dodge, T., and Jaccard, J. (2002). "Participation in athletics and female sexual risk behavior: The evaluation of four causal structures." *Journal of Adolescent Research*, 17:42–67; Miller, K. E., et al. (1999). "Sports, sexual activity, contraceptive use, and pregnancy among female and male high school students: Testing cultural resource theory." *Sociology of Sport Journal*, 16:366–387; Page, R. M., et al. (1998). "Is school sports participation a protective factor against adolescent health risk behaviors?" *Journal of Health Education*, 29(3):186–192; Rome, E. S., Rybicki, L. A., and Durant, R. H. (1998). "Pregnancy and other risk behaviours among adolescent girls in Ohio." *Journal of Adolescent Health*, 22:50–55; Sabo, D., et al. (1998). *The Women's Sports Foundation Report: Sport and Teen Pregnancy*. East Meadow, N.Y.: Women's Sports Foundation.

22. Artal, M., and Sherman, C. (1998). "Exercise against depression." *Physician and Sportsmedicine*, 26(10). Available at http://www.physsportsmed.com/issues/1998/10Oct/artal.htm.

23. National Center for Health Statistics. (2002). *Health, United States, 2002*. Hyattsville, Md.: U.S. Department of Health and Human Services Center for Disease Control and Prevention.

24. Calle, E., et al. (2003). "Overweight, obesity, and mortality from cancer in a prospectively studied cohort of U.S. adults." *New England Journal of Medicine*, 348(17):1625–1638.

25. Henshaw, S. K. (2003). *U.S. teenage pregnancy statistics with comparative statistics for women aged 20–24*. New York: Alan Guttmacher Institute; National Campaign to Prevent Teen Pregnancy. (2002). *Not just another single issue: Teen pregnancy prevention's link to other critical social issues*. Washington, D.C.: Author.

26. Centers for Disease Control and Prevention. (2002). "Annual smoking-attributable mortality, years of potential life lost, and economic costs—United States, 1995–1999." *Morbidity and Mortality Weekly Report*, 51:300–303.

27. U.S. Department of Health and Human Services. (2001). *Women and smoking: A report of the surgeon general*. Rockville, Md.: U.S. Department of Health and Human Services.

28. The Commonwealth Fund. (1997). "Survey finds missed opportunities to improve girls' health." *Commonwealth Fund Quarterly*, 3(3). Available at http://www.cmwf.org/publist/quarterly/fas97qrt.asp?link=6.

29. Schreiber, G. B., et al. (1996). "Weight modification efforts reported by black and white preadolescent girls: National Heart, Lung, and Blood Institute growth and health study." *Pediatrics*, 98(1):63–70.

30. American Heart Association and American Stroke Association. (2003). *Heart Disease and Stroke Statistics, 2003 Update*. Dallas, TX: American Heart Association and American Stroke Association; Centers for Disease Control and Prevention. (1995). *National Health and Nutrition Examination Survey III 1994*. Hyattsville, MD: U.S. Department of Health and Human Services Center for Disease Control and Prevention.

31. Mediascope. (2003). *Body Image and Advertising*. Available at http://www.mediascope.org/pubs/ibriefs/bia.htm.

32. Colton, M., and Core, S. (1991). *Risk, Resiliency, and Resistance: Current Research on Adolescent Girls*. Bethesda, Md.: Ms. Foundation.

33. McNutt, S., Hu, Y., Schreiber, G. B., Crawford, P., Obarzanek, E., and Mellin, L. (1999). "A longitudinal study of dietary practices of black and white girls 9 and 10 years old at enrollment: The NHLBI growth and health study." *Journal of Adolescent Health*, 20(1):27–37.

34. Brumberg, J. (1998). *The Body Project: An Intimate History of American Girls*. New York: Vintage.

35. National Center for Health Statistics. (2002). *Health, United States, 2002*. Hyattsville, Md.: U.S. Department of Health and Human Services Center for Disease Control and Prevention.

36. Centers for Disease Control and Prevention. (1999–2000). *National Health and Nutrition Examination Survey, 1999–2000*. Hyattsville, MD: U.S. Department of Health and Human Services Center for Disease Control and Prevention.

37. Bunker, L. (1988). "Lifelong benefits of sports participation for girls and women." Presented at the Sport Psychology Conference, University of Virginia, Charlottesville, June 22.

38. U.S. Secretary of Health and Human Services and U.S. Secretary of Education. (2000). *Healthy People 2000*. Hyattsville, MD: U.S. Department of Health and Human Services—Health and Fitness

39. Centers for Disease Control and Prevention. (2002). "Surveillance summaries." *Morbidity and Mortality Weekly Report*, Vol. No. 51(SS-4): pp. 300–303.

40. National Federation of State High School Associations. (2003). *NFHS Handbook 2003–2004*. Indianapolis, Ind.: National Federation of State High School Associations; National Collegiate Athletic Association. (2001). *Participation Statistics 2001–2002*. Available at http://www.ncaa.org.

41. NBC News/*Wall Street Journal* poll, January 2003, and *USA Today*/CNN/Gallup Poll, as reported in *USA Today*, Jan. 7, 2003.

42. *Progress and Perils: How Gender Issues Unite and Divide Women Part II*, published by the Center for the Advancement of Women, New York, April 7, 2003, p. 4

43. "Mothers' and Fathers' Encouragement of Daughters' Physical Activity," *Melpomene Journal*, Spring 2000, 19(1).

44. National Collegiate Athletic Association. (2003). *NCAA Gender Equity Study, 2001–2002*. Available at http://www.ncaa.org.

45. National Federation of State High School Associations. (2002). *Participation Surveys 1972–2001*. Indianapolis, Ind.: National Collegiate Athletic Association.

46. National Federation of State High School Associations. (2003). *2003 Participation Survey*. Indianapolis, Ind.: National Collegiate Athletic Association.

47. National Federation of State High School Associations. (2003). *2003 Participation Survey*. Indianapolis, Ind.: National Collegiate Athletic Association.

48. National Federation of State High School Associations. (2003). *2003 Participation Survey*. Indianapolis, Ind.: National Collegiate Athletic Association.

49. Sporting Goods Manufacturers Association. (2000). *Gaining Ground*. Washington, DC: SGMA International.

50. Sommerfeld, M. (Nov. 1998). "What's Compliance According to the Office for Civil Rights," *The School Administrator*, 55(1), 34.

51. National Center for Educational Statistics. (2001). *2000–2001 National Center for Educational Statistics*. Available at http://nces.ed.gov/.

52. National Collegiate Athletic Association. (2002). *Participation Statistics, 2001–2002*. Available at http://www.ncaa.org.

53. National Collegiate Athletic Association. (2003). *NCAA Gender Equity Study, 2001–2002*. Available at http://www.ncaa.org.

54. National Collegiate Athletic Association. (2004). *Participation Statistics, 2002–2003*. Available at http://www.ncaa.org.

55. National Collegiate Athletic Association. (2002). *Sports Sponsorship, 2001–2002*. Available at http://www.ncaa.org.

56. General Accounting Office. (2001). *Four-Year Colleges' Experiences Adding and Discontinuing Teams*. Washington, DC: National Federation of High Schools Association.

57. *ESPN The Magazine*, June 24, 2002.

58. *ESPN The Magazine*, June 24, 2002.

59. *The Post Courier* (Charleston, S.C.), Sept. 2, 2002.

60. *ESPN The Magazine*, June 24, 2002.

61. National Collegiate Athletic Association. (1997). *1995–1996 Gender Equity Report*. Indianapolis, Ind.: National Collegiate Athletic Association; National Collegiate Athletic Association. (2001). *1999–2000 Gender Equity Report*. Indianapolis, Ind.: National Collegiate Athletic Association.

62. Acosta, R. V., and Carpenter, L. J. (2004). *Women in Intercollegiate Sport: A Longitudinal Study—Twenty-Seven Year Update, 1977–2004*. Unpublished manuscript, Brooklyn College.

63. Acosta, R. V., and Carpenter, L. J. (2004). *Women in Intercollegiate Sport: A Longitudinal Study—Twenty-Seven Year Update, 1977–2004*. Unpublished manuscript, Brooklyn College.

64. Acosta, R. V., and Carpenter, L. J. (2004). *Women in Intercollegiate Sport: A Longitudinal Study—Twenty-Seven Year Update, 1977–2004*. Unpublished manuscript, Brooklyn College.

65. Acosta, R. V., and Carpenter, L. J. (2004). *Women in Intercollegiate Sport: A Longitudinal Study—Twenty-Seven Year Update, 1977–2004*. Unpublished manuscript, Brooklyn College.

66. Acosta, R. V., and Carpenter, L. J. (2004). *Women in Intercollegiate Sport: A Longitudinal Study—Twenty-Seven Year Update, 1977–2004*. Unpublished manuscript, Brooklyn College.

67. National Collegiate Athletic Association. (2003). *2003 NCAA Manual*. Indianapolis, Ind.: National Collegiate Athletic Association.

68. *USA Today*, Sept. 27, 2001.

69. *USA Today*, Sept. 27, 2001.

70. Acosta, R. V., and Carpenter, L. J. (2002). *Women in Intercollegiate Sport: A Longitudinal Study—Twenty-Five Year Update, 1977–2002*. Unpublished manuscript, Brooklyn College.

71. Acosta, R. V., and Carpenter, L. J. (2004). *Women in Intercollegiate Sport: A Longitudinal Study—Twenty-Seven Year Update, 1977–2004*. Unpublished manuscript, Brooklyn College.

72. *Chronicle of Higher Education*, June 8, 2001.

73. *Chronicle of Higher Education*, July 21, 2003.

74. *NCAA News*, Jan. 5, 2004.

75. Acosta, R. V., and Carpenter, L. J. (2004). *Women in Intercollegiate Sport: A Longitudinal Study—Twenty-Seven Year Update, 1977–2004*. Unpublished manuscript, Brooklyn College.

76. National Athletic Trainers Association. (2003). Dallas, Tx.: personal communication with Sandy Ward, Director of Membership at the NATA, March 5, 2003.

77. Butler, J., and D. Lopiano. (2003). *Women's Sports Foundation Research Report: Title IX and Race in Intercollegiate Athletics*. East Meadow, N.Y.: Women's Sports Foundation.

78. National Collegiate Athletic Association. (2003). *2002 Graduation-Rates Report for NCAA Division I Schools*. Indianapolis, Ind.: National Collegiate Athletic Association.

79. Butler, J., and D. Lopiano. (2003). *Women's Sports Foundation Research Report: Title IX and Race in Intercollegiate Athletics*. East Meadow, N.Y.: Women's Sports Foundation.

80. Butler, J., and D. Lopiano. (2003). *Women's Sports Foundation Research Report: Title IX and Race in Intercollegiate Athletics*. East Meadow, N.Y.: Women's Sports Foundation.

81. *Chronicle of Higher Education*, Nov. 26, 2001.

82. Lapchick, R. (2001). *Racial and Gender Report Card*. Boston, Mass.: Center for the Study of Sport in Society.

83. *NCAA News*, Sept. 1, 2003.

84. *NCAA News*, Oct. 14, 2002.

85. Lapchick, R. (2001). *Racial and Gender Report Card*. Boston, Mass.: Center for the Study of Sport in Society.

86. Lapchick, R. (2001). *Racial and Gender Report Card*. Boston, Mass.: Center for the Study of Sport in Society.

87. *NCAA News*, Oct. 14, 2002.

88. *NCAA News*, July 7, 2003.

89. Lapchick, R. (1999). *Racial and Gender Report Card*. Boston, Mass.: Center for the Study of Sport in Society.

90. Association for the Disabled, 1992. Personal communication with the communications officer of the association in 1992.

91. International Paralympic Committee. (2001). "Women and Sport Progress Report." *Paralympian Newsletter*, Oct. 31, 2001, pp. 1–4.

92. Zotos, C. (2004). *Constructing a Tiered Sports Program for College Athletics: A Cost-Effective Approach to Meet Equity Standards and Preserve Participation Opportunities.* Unpublished manuscript, Drew University, Madison, N.J.

93. United States General Accounting Office. (2001). *Intercollegiate Athletics: Four-Year Colleges' Experiences Adding and Discontinuing Teams.* Washington, D.C.: National Federated State High Schools Association. The report made participation comparisons based on NAIA and NCAA data from 1981–82 to 1998–99. A full copy of this report can be obtained at http://www.gao.gov. Search GAO Reports by date: March 8, 2001.

94. Coalition for Women and Girls in Education. (2002). *Title IX Athletics Policies: Issues and Data for Education Decision Makers.* Unpublished manuscript, National Coalition for Women and Girls in Education, Washington, D.C.

95. Uhlir, G. A. (1987). "Athletics and the university: The post-woman's era." *Academe*, 73(4):25–29.

96. Acosta, R. V., and Carpenter, L. J. (2004). *Women in Intercollegiate Sport: A Longitudinal Study—Twenty-Seven Year Update, 1977–2004.* Unpublished manuscript, Brooklyn College.

97. Sanders, M. T. (1985). *Comparison of various operation procedures in division I women's athletics.* Unpublished manuscript, University of Tennessee.

98. Uhlir, G. A. (1987). "Athletics and the university: The post-woman's era." *Academe*, 73(4):25–29.

99. Griffin, P. (1998). *Strong Women, Deep Closets: Lesbians and Homophobia in Sport.* Champaign, Ill.: Human Kinetics; Griffin, P. (1993). "Homophobia in women's sports: The fear that divides us." In G. L. Cohen (ed.). *Women in sport: Issues and controversies.* Newbury Park, Calif.: Sage Publications, 193–203.

100. Women's Sports Foundation. (2000). *Position Paper: Addressing the Issue of Sexual Harassment and Sexual Relationships Between Coaches and Athletes.* East Meadow, N.Y.: Women's Sports Foundation.

101. Women's Sports Foundation. (2000). *Position Paper: Addressing the Issue of Sexual Harassment and Sexual Relationships Between Coaches and Athletes.* East Meadow, N.Y.: Women's Sports Foundation.

CHATER

National Collegiate Athletic Association and the Issue of Sports Wagering

Bill Saum NCAA

INTRODUCTION

The National Collegiate Athletic Association (NCAA) is a voluntary association of 1,273 colleges, universities, athletics conferences, and related organizations. The NCAA's primary purpose is to regulate and promote intercollegiate athletics for male and female student-athletes, in a manner that fully integrates athletic programs with the academic mission of higher education and student-athletes within the student body. Participation in intercollegiate athletics provides a path to earning a degree, and it also promotes the learning of the teamwork, competitive spirit, character-building, and self-esteem inherent in college sports. The NCAA also educates student-athletes about health, safety, sportsmanship, and ethical conduct, including education about the risks associated with gambling, particularly sports wagering.

Like many other sports organizations, the NCAA has a clear and direct policy regarding sports wagering. The NCAA prohibits participation in any form of legal or illegal sports wagering because of its potential to undermine the integrity of sports contests and jeopardize the welfare of the student-athlete and the intercollegiate athletics community. Sports wagering demeans the competition and competitors alike by a message that is contrary to the purposes and meaning of "sport." Sports competition should be appreciated for the inherent benefits related to participation of student-athletes, coaches, and institutions in fair contests, not for the amount of money wagered on the outcome of the competition.

The issue of gambling, especially sports wagering, has been of significant importance to the NCAA membership throughout the existence of the association. Wagering-related scandals, unfortunately, have been a part of the athletics landscape since the days of the "Black Sox" incident. Sports-wagering scandals have not been seen solely in the professional ranks. Intercollegiate football and basketball have both been marred by wagering-related incidents over the past half-century. These incidents threaten to undermine the integrity of all sports and cannot be tolerated by those entrusted with protecting the good of the game.

For these reasons, the NCAA membership adopted NCAA Bylaw 10.3 prohibiting athletics department staff members, staff members from a member conference, staff members from the national office, and student-athletes from engaging in gambling activities as they relate to intercollegiate or professional sporting events. NCAA Bylaw 10.3 stipulates that staff members of the athletics department of a member institution, conference office, or national office and student-athletes shall not knowingly:

- Provide information to individuals involved in organized gambling activities concerning intercollegiate athletics competition;
- Solicit a bet on any intercollegiate team;
- Accept a bet on any team representing the institution;
- Solicit or accept a bet on any intercollegiate competition for any item (e.g., cash, shirt, dinner) that has tangible value; or
- Participate in any gambling activity that involves intercollegiate athletics or professional athletics through a bookmaker, a parlay card or any other method employed by organized gambling.

The following are sanctions for violations of Bylaw 10.3 that are referenced in the NCAA legislation as Bylaw 10.3.1:

A student-athlete who engages in activities designed to influence the outcome of an intercollegiate contest or in an effort to affect win-loss margins (i.e., "point shaving") or who solicits or accepts a bet or participates in any gambling activity through a bookmaker, a parley card, or any other method employed by organized gambling that involves wagering on the student-athlete's institution shall permanently lose all remaining regular-season and postseason eligibility in all sports.

A student-athlete who solicits or accepts a bet or participates in any gambling activity that involves intercollegiate athletics or professional athletics—through a bookmaker, a parlay card, or any other method employed by organized gambling—shall be ineligible for all regular-season and postseason competition for a minimum period of one year from the date of the institution's determination that a violation has occurred and shall be charged with the loss of a minimum of one season of competition. A request for reinstatement may be submitted on behalf of a student-athlete who has participated in such activity only upon fulfillment of the minimum condition indicated above. If the student-athlete is determined to have been involved in a subsequent violation of any portion of Bylaw 10.3, the student-athlete shall permanently lose all remaining regular-season and postseason eligibility in all sports.

GROWTH OF SPORTS WAGERING

The explosive growth of gambling has caused a noticeable increase in the number of sports wagering–related cases processed by the NCAA and it threatens the integrity of college sports.

Big money attracts organized crime, and illegal sports wagering is big money. Money skimmed from sports-wagering schemes is used to fund a host of illegal activities including the sale of narcotics and loan sharking. These activities are rarely evident to the casual bettor but are not lost on the law enforcement community.

Student-athletes are viewed by organized crime and organized gambling as easy marks. When student-athletes place bets with a bookie, they have jeopardized their eligibility and have broken the law. The bookie now is in control. If a student-athlete is sufficiently indebted or addicted, point shaving often is introduced as a way out. In addition, bookies use students as "runners" to collect debts and parlay sheets for which the bookie pays a commission. Gamblers also pay a commission for information related to sports teams (e.g., injury reports, morale, game plans, and discipline issues).

EVIDENCE OF ILLEGAL SPORTS WAGERING AND ITS EFFECTS

As a sports organization, the NCAA is well aware of the direct threat sports wagering poses to the integrity of each intercollegiate contest. In the early 1950s, the academic community and the public were shocked to learn that a well-known men's basketball team was involved in a point-shaving scandal. In the decade before publication of this book, two major point-shaving scandals in men's basketball and football occurred on two prominent campuses. The importance and seriousness of these cases and other sports-wagering incidents should not be underestimated.

In 1996 former NCAA president Cedric Dempsey created an entirely new department within the enforcement branch of the NCAA. The department was created to deal with three specific areas: agent issues, gambling, and amateurism activities. The staff at the time that the department was developed consisted of two people, one director and one staff assistant. In 2004 the staff included one director, one associate and one assistant director, and two additional staff members.

The Nevada Gaming Control Board reported that in 2003, 1.864 billion dollars was wagered on all sports, mostly comprising college and professional football, basketball, and baseball. The sum of $825.9 million was wagered on college and professional football, $489.1 million on college and professional basketball, and $378.5 million on college and professional baseball.

College sports are by no means immune. The NCAA Division I Men's Basketball Championship has more money wagered on its game than on the Super Bowl in the same year. Today, evidence of gambling's harmful influence is all too common and on the rise.

In 1995, four University of Maryland (College Park) football student-athletes and one men's basketball student-athlete were found to have bet on college games. In 1996, 13 football student-athletes at Boston College were involved in sports gambling and 4 admitted to betting against their own team. In 1997, a men's basketball student-athlete at California State University at Fullerton was offered $1,000 per game by another student to shave points. In 1997, two Arizona State University men's basketball student-athletes were charged and indicted for their part in a point-shaving scheme with a student bookie on campus. According to federal law enforcement officials, more money was wagered in the Arizona State case than on any point-shaving scam in the history of intercollegiate athletics. It is important to note that over $1 million was wagered legally in Nevada casinos in the Arizona State case.

In that same year, another point-shaving scandal rocked the world of intercollegiate athletics when news broke that members of the Northwestern University men's basketball team were also involved in a point-shaving case with a bookie. Likewise, in the Northwestern case, wagers were placed legally in Nevada casinos. In 1998, law enforcement officials dismantled a large sports-wagering ring operating, in part, out of a Columbia University fraternity house.

In 2003 a football student-athlete from the University of Massachusetts engaged in Internet gambling on intercollegiate and professional basketball contests. The student-athlete was suspended from all regular-season and postseason competition for a minimum period of one year. Also in 2003, a men's track and field student-athlete from the University of Buffalo solicited bets on professional and collegiate contests. The student-athlete was dismissed from the track team and the institution revoked his athletics scholarship.

CONTRIBUTING FACTORS ASSOCIATED WITH GROWTH OF COLLEGIATE SPORTS WAGERING

Several key trends are fueling the expansion of sports wagering among college students:

Increased acceptance of gambling.   Many experts believe the proliferation of legalized gambling nationwide has cultivated an environment more accepting of illegal betting. With the poker boom that has enamored millions across the country and glamorized the game with popular shows like the *World Series of*

Poker and *Celebrity Poker Showdown*, millions are learning at an early age that gambling is an acceptable way to try to make money and that gambling is a harmless way to socialize. Rev. Edward A. Malloy, president of the University of Notre Dame, stated: "the surge of interest in poker, particularly among male college students, and the way it is fostered by television may just be a fad, but it is a troublesome fad. It creates a climate in which a lot of people are gambling perhaps for small stakes, but it has relevance since we're dealing with student-athletes who are living and functioning in the same environment."

This newfound tolerance has also led to a rage of riverboat gambling and on-land casinos. Many state and local governments are looking to the gambling arena as a way to help with decreasing state and local budgets. In 2004, the city of Indianapolis announced plans to use slot machines as a way to finance the building of a new sports arena for its National Football League team, the Indianapolis Colts. Over the past decade, 21 states have legalized commercial casinos.

Access to point spreads and sports handicappers.   Today, there are over 1,500 different services selling sports-wagering tips. Advertisements for sports touts, as they are known, appear in almost every major newspaper. Syndicated television and radio shows across the country feature sports touts promoting their services. Additionally, virtually every major newspaper in the country (the *Washington Post* is a notable exception) routinely publishes point spreads for college and professional games. As former University of North Carolina coach Dean Smith observed, "The media publication of point spreads gives the public a false sense of acceptability about college sports betting and promotes an activity that is not only harmful to college sport but largely illegal."

Internet gambling.   A *Sports Illustrated* cover story outlined the rapid growth of Internet gambling. According to experts quoted in the article, "what was a $60 million business in 1996 will handle $600 million in bets in 1998, with another tenfold increase likely by 2001." The number of online sites that handle sports bets has grown from two in 1996 to several thousand today. Internet gambling plays an important role in the growth of sports gambling on college campuses across the country. College students have ready access to computers, most have credit cards, and the Internet lets them place wagers from the privacy of their campus residences in virtual anonymity. The NCAA in 2000, due to concern about this phenomenon, held an educational seminar for its membership at regional rules conferences that specifically discussed this issue.

2003 NATIONAL STUDY OF COLLEGIATE SPORTS WAGERING AND ASSOCIATED HEALTH RISKS

The NCAA's 2003 *National Study on Collegiate Sports Wagering and Associated Health Risks* is the most comprehensive of its kind to measure the

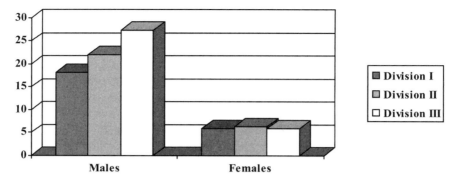

Figure 8.1. Proportion of Students who Reported Wagering on Sports, by Division

preponderance of wagering among student-athletes. It encompasses responses from approximately 21,000 male and female student-athletes at NCAA member institutions across all three NCAA divisions. A total of 2,003 individual sports teams at 1,032 NCAA member institutions participated in the study.

The NCAA conducted this study with the hope of providing a baseline of information related to the level of gambling behavior within the student-athlete population. Additionally, it is hoped that this study will help member institutions identify and alter problem behavior in this area. It is important to note that it is intended that there will be periodic replications of this study so that the membership of the NCAA can monitor changes in the behavior and the effectiveness of programs designed to minimize the amount of gambling among collegiate student-athletes. "By commissioning this study, the largest examination ever of sports wagering by student-athletes, the NCAA is taking a leadership role at the national level to address this problem among student-athletes before it reaches crisis proportions," NCAA president Myles Brand said.

The major goal of this study was to quantify the levels of various wagering activities among the population of student-athletes at NCAA member institutions. Student-athletes were asked a multitude of questions about sports-wagering behaviors and associated health risks, such as alcohol and drug use. The questionnaire was developed with the assistance of Dr. Durand Jacobs, a noted national researcher in the field of youth gambling.

Brand stated after the study was complete that "[t]he scope of sports wagering among intercollegiate student-athletes is startling and disturbing; sports wagering is a double threat because it harms the well-being of student-athletes and the integrity of college sports."

The study's key findings indicated that male student-athletes are engaged in gambling or sports wagering at rates much higher than are female

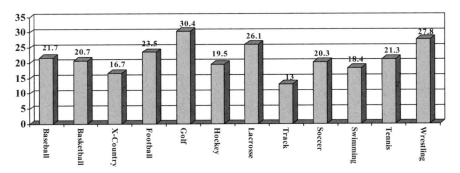

Figure 8.2. Proportion of Male Students Who Reported Wagering on Collegiate Sports, by Sport

student-athletes. Specifically, the data shows that almost 35 percent of male student-athletes have engaged in some type of sports-wagering behavior in the past year, compared to only 10 percent of female student-athletes.

According to the study, the highest percentages of male student-athletes involved in wagering on collegiate sports are in men's golf, wrestling, lacrosse, and football. For female student-athletes wagering on collegiate sports, the sports with the highest involvement are golf, lacrosse, basketball, and field hockey.

The survey also shows that Division III student-athletes are the most likely to engage in gambling or sports wagering, followed by Division II student-athletes, whereas Division I student-athletes were the least likely.

Though many believe student-athletes to be competitive individuals who sometimes engage in risky behaviors, the study found that the top three reasons student-athletes gambled was for fun, excitement, and to win money.

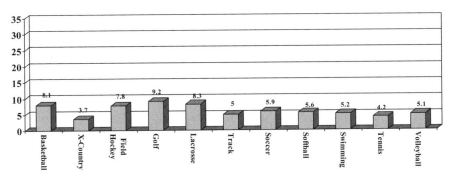

Figure 8.3. Proportion of Female Students Who Reported Wagering on Collegiate Sports, by Sport

Table 8.1. Reasons Student-Athletes Gamble

Reasons to gamble	Male			Female		
	Division I Percent	Division II Percent	Division III Percent	Division I Percent	Division II Percent	Division III Percent
For relaxation	6.4	6.1	6.9	5.6	4.5	6.6
For fun	34.2	33.7	34.3	38.6	37.4	38.2
For excitement	21.1	20.5	22.0	21.7	21.2	21.6
To win money	24.3	25.0	23.4	23.4	25.0	22.5
To escape from stress	0.8	0.8	0.5	0.2	0.6	0.8
To be popular w/friends	0.7	0.7	0.6	0.2	0.3	0.8
To feel less shy	0.3	0.2	0.2	0.1	0.1	0.3
To feel in control	0.6	0.8	0.8	0.2	0.4	0.1
To forget about problems	0.6	0.7	0.5	0.4	0.5	0.4
I am bored	4.9	5.6	5.0	6.4	6.2	4.9
I am lonely	0.3	0.4	0.3	0.0	0.2	—
I am sad/ depressed	0.3	0.4	0.2	—	0.1	0.1
I am good at it	4.3	3.7	3.6	1.5	1.7	1.6
Everyone does it	1.4	1.4	1.7	1.7	1.8	2.1

Other key findings show that football student-athletes reported taking part in significant infractions of NCAA gambling bylaws at rates slightly higher than men's basketball student-athletes. Specifically, 1.1 percent of football student-athletes reported taking money for playing poorly in a game. A total

Table 8.2. Men's Basketball and Football Student-Athletes Involved in Infractions of NCAA Gambling Bylaws

Action	Men's Basketball Proportion ($N = 388$)	Football Proportion ($N = 2,132$)
Taken money for playing poorly in a game	0.5%	1.1%
Known of a teammate who took money for playing poorly	1.5%	1.6%
Been threatened or harmed because of sports wagering	1.2%	1.1%
Been contacted by an outside source to share inside information	1.2%	2.0%
Actually provided inside information about a game	1.2%	2.8%

Table 8.3. Actions by Male Basketball and Football Student-Athletes Resulting from Gambling Indebtedness

Action "Because of Gambling Debt I've ..."	Men's Basketball Proportion (N = 388)	Football Proportion (N = 2,132)
Been asked to affect the outcome of a game	2.1%	2.3%
Actually affected the outcome of a game	1.0%	1.4%
Involved a teammate in affecting the outcome	1.0%	1.3%
Known of a teammate who has been asked to affect outcome of a game	2.1%	1.3%
Had a teammate who affected the outcome of a game	1.0%	1.3%
Been asked by a teammate for help in affecting the outcome of a game	1.2%	1.0%

of 17 individuals (4.4%) in basketball and 102 individuals (4.8%) in football reported at least one of these extreme behaviors (including those on the following chart).

A total of 2.3 percent of football student-athletes admitted they had been asked to affect the outcome of a game because of gambling debts. Additionally, 1.4 percent of football student-athletes admitted having affected the outcome of a game because of gambling debts.

In addition to determining the type and extent of wagering activities engaged in by NCAA student-athletes, this study examined whether these wagering activities were associated with other problematic behaviors (e.g., alcohol and drug use, criminal activity). Student-athletes categorized as frequent or potential problem gamblers were more likely to report risk-taking and impulsive behaviors such as:

- committing traffic violations
- making impulsive purchases
- spending time with family and friends who gamble
- using and abusing various substances
- stealing
- having sex with multiple partners and engaging in risky sexual behaviors
- developing different post-college goals than non-gamblers

SPORTS WAGERING TASK FORCE

In 2004, in response to the findings of the NCAA's 2003 *National Study on Collegiate Sports Wagering and Associated Health Risks*, President Myles Brand announced the formation of a national task force to further analyze the study's results and recommend strategies to counteract sports wagering among student-athletes. University of Notre Dame president, Rev. Edward A. Malloy, served as task force chair. Grant Teaff, executive director of the American Football Coaches Association, served as vice chairman.

The task force was appointed by Dr. Brand and was composed of member institutions' athletics directors, men's and women's basketball coaches' association representatives, gambling/sports-wagering researchers and experts, faculty athletics representatives, law enforcement officials, and student-athletes.

Dr. Brand said the task force's charge was to develop recommendations with a dual focus of ensuring the well-being of student-athletes as well as ensuring the integrity of intercollegiate athletics. The recommendations could include expanding education efforts, proposed NCAA legislation, and suggestions for legislation at the state and federal levels, Brand said.

"When we started our work on the task force, I was overwhelmed because of the magnitude of the problem in this country based on the cultural environment in which we live. Gambling in many parts of our culture is second nature," said Grant Teaff.

The final report of the task force focused on three main areas: compliance and policy, education, and law enforcement/coalition building. Initiatives have been formulated to help educate the NCAA member institutions and student-athletes of the effects that sports wagering can have not only on their campuses but on student-athletes' lives. The task force proposed actions, including expanding background check programs for Division I officials in basketball, men's ice hockey, and baseball, all of which currently have betting lines in Las Vegas. A "best practices" document was also created to advise institutions on how they should try to combat the problem on each of their campuses.

The bulk of the action steps, however, occur in the educational area. This area proves to be an important part of deterring student-athletes from avoiding sports wagering based on the results of the study, educating them on how sports wagering can negatively affect their careers and lives. Bill Saum, NCAA director of agent, gambling, and amateurism activities, stated: "The study shows that the grass-roots education effort, particularly in basketball, has been successful. We believe in that grass-roots approach, and we try to educate at every level within the athletics world. The study shows us, though, that we have a campus-wide problem, and the task force has encouraged us to broaden our impact to groups outside of athletics."

The third area that the task force focused on was law enforcement and coalition building, with the primary emphasis being building relationships to foster awareness of this issue. An example and important recommendation is to work with the National Federation of State High School Associations to educate high school student-athletes as well as parent organizations.

Malloy believes that the task force's work focused more on the student-athlete and the athletics world rather than trying to combat the entire culture of gambling. "The fact that we did not try to take on the world and attempt to address questions about the trends in the way the culture is headed, or the role and function of gambling in general, freed us up to focus on the two things we said mattered most: the health and well-being of the athlete and the integrity of the game," Malloy said. "We had to be aware of the cultural context within which student-athletes and athletics in general is going to be seen, but we were able to separate out the two issues effectively."

CONCLUSION

Sports wagering continues to be an important issue that requires the NCAA and its membership's special attention. The nation's college and university system is one of our greatest assets. The United States offers the world the model for postsecondary education. Betting on the outcome of college sporting events tarnishes the integrity of sport and diminishes the esteem in which we and the rest of the world hold U.S. colleges and universities. The NCAA's goal is to protect and educate the student-athletes and remove the unseemly influences of sports wagering from our amateur athletes and the games they play.

REFERENCES

Brown, Gary T., "Wagering War On Gambling," *NCAA News*, December 6, 2004.

Brown, Gary T., "Task Force Betting on Education As Most Effective Weapon," *NCAA News*, December 6, 2004.

Christianson, Erik, "NCAA Study Finds Sports Wagering a Problem among Student-Athletes," *NCAA News*, May 12, 2004.

Copeland, Jack., "Sports Wagering Survey Focuses Attention on High Rates of Misbehavior in Division II, III," *NCAA News*, December 6, 2004.

NCAA, *National Study on Collegiate Sports Wagering and Associated Health Risks*, Indianapolis, Ind.: NCAA, 2003.

CHAPTER 9

Performance Enhancing Drugs: The Wounds Behind the Glory

Yun-Oh Whang Kansas State

When a student-athlete contemplates the idea of using a performance enhancing drug (PED), the answer seems quite obvious. Taking a PED is cheating and does involve health risks. Unfortunately, this simple logic fails to register for more than a few student-athletes. Tests conducted by the National Center for Drug Free Sport, which has administered National Collegiate Athletic Association (NCAA) drug testing since 1999, found about 2 percent of student-athletes tested positive for PEDs annually for the last few years, mostly due to nutritional supplements.[1] It translates to a disturbing number of more than 7,000 student-athletes among 360,000 college athletes of all divisions and sports combined.[2]

The NCAA has been testing student-athletes for illegal substances year-round since 1990 while simultaneously expanding the subject pool and banned substance list. However, we have not seen any significant progress toward drug-free college sports. Why? The discussion on PED usage by student-athletes often focuses on the athlete himself/herself making a wrong choice, and it often overlooks the roles of many entities other than the athletes. This chapter places the entities involved in the PED issue in college athletics into four categories—the users, the suppliers/distributors, the influencers, and the regulators—and examines the overall structure of the problem and possible solutions.

THE NATURE OF PED

Various types of PEDs are widely used by athletes at every level of athletics. Stimulants such as amphetamines and caffeine are used to increase motor activity, while steroids, testosterone, human growth hormone (HGH), androstenedione, and dehydroepiandrosterone (DHEA) are commonly used for muscle growth. Erythropoetin (EPO) is known to increase endurance, ephedra is often used to delay fatigue, and creatine is said to improve performance in brief, high-intensity exercises.[3] These effects clearly provide advantages to athletes who take PEDs, mostly by providing extra power, speed, and endurance. Adding to this temptation, a new PED called tetrahydrogestrinone (THG), an anabolic steroid developed and cloaked to avoid detection by doping tests, has shaken the sport world by sidelining big name athletes.

Unfortunately these advantages do come with a price. All these PEDs have short-term and long-term side effects, some of which are irreversible. These PEDs can cause heart and liver problems, male and female trait reversal, unbalanced bone growth, hyperextension, dehydration, and muscle cramping and tearing. For example, it is reported that 10 people died and 13 are permanently disabled after taking ephedra between 1997 and 1999.[4] Even though there is no scientific proof, the drastic rise in the frequency of certain injuries could be another example of side effects due to long-term PED use. According to USA Today's analysis of its database covering 1992 to 2001, injuries to large joints increased by 58 percent in Major League Baseball, compared to an increase of all other injuries of only 5 percent. Injuries that can be categorized as tendon or ligament injuries skyrocketed 224 percent in baseball during the same time period.[5] It is suspected that these particular injuries result from stress on tendons caused by overdeveloped muscles.

In addition to physical health, mental health is also in danger when PEDs are used. Steroids are known to cause drastic mood swings, emotional disturbances, and what the National Institute on Drug Abuse calls "homicidal rage, mania and delusion." "Roid rage" is another common term used among athletes when they see someone quickly gaining rock solid muscle and becoming overly aggressive at the same time.[6] Donald Hooton, the father of Taylor Hooton, who killed himself at his Plano, Texas, home, believes that "anabolic steroids played a significant role in causing the severe depression that resulted in his suicide." Taylor was a baseball player who wanted to get bigger even though he was 6 feet 3 inches and weighed 175 pounds at age 16.[7]

These physical and mental health risks are difficult to study, because the side effects may not be detectable for a long period of time and the physician may not be able to identify PED as the cause when the symptoms become observable. Combined with the fact that users tend to hide their history of PED use, doing research on this use and providing more concrete evidence for its negative consequences become a challenge. To make the matter worse, student-athletes often feel nothing wrong physically and mentally after ex-

perimenting with a PED and rarely personally witness its negative consequences. These factors make it difficult to educate athletes that PEDs do
damage their mind and body, and with new undetectable drugs, testing has a
limited role as a deterrent.

This is why we need to take a look at a more fundamental structure of the
PED issue in college athletics and tackle the problem by focusing not only on
the student-athletes, but also on everyone involved. The collective effort by
everyone involved is the only way to keep college sports clean and safe.

THE INVOLVED ENTITIES IN PED USE IN COLLEGE ATHLETICS

Everyone involved in college sports has a certain role in the PED issue and
has to share the responsibility. Of course, the student-athletes themselves are
at the center of the issue, but they are not the only ones who should contribute to the task of cleaning up college sports.

(1) The User

The users are not limited to male athletes in major sports. Rifle, lacrosse,
wrestling, water polo, and golf are reported to show a higher-than-average
usage rate of at least one of the three most popular PEDs (amphetamines,
anabolic steroids, and ephedrine). The data in women's sports is even more
disturbing. Even though anabolic steroid use is below 1 percent in most of the
sports women play, amphetamine and ephedrine usage is higher among females than in their male counterpart, and ephedrine use has skyrocketed
since 1997, up to 11.8 percent in female ice hockey and 8.3 percent in female
gymnastics based on a 2001 NCAA survey. In this survey, the motivation
behind PED use by student-athletes included performance enhancement, injury recovery, and appearance improvement, and the major reason for not
using a PED was "no desire to get the effect."[8]

Even more disconcerting than the number of users is the perception of
PEDs among student-athletes. The survey shows that there are many potential
PED users among the non-users who would pick up use if they had the "desire
to get the effect." In other words, the choice is based on the benefits of PEDs,
not the health risks involved. With this kind of perception, the scare tactics
emphasizing health risks often employed by educators to prevent PED use
would not work. This perception has to be changed and health concerns need
to be more emphasized as the focal point of PED-use prevention programs.

(2) The Supplier/Distributor

The manufacturer.   The key supplier/distributor of PEDs is the drug manufacturers. The PED market is huge, and the manufacturers have strong
incentives to promote their products as safe. One of the common tactics used

by the manufacturers is to promote their products as "natural." It is a common myth among users that "natural" means no health risk. Considering the fact that nicotine, cocaine, and heroin are all extracted from plants, that myth cannot be any further from the truth.

For example, University of Alabama defensive end Todd Bates tested positive after taking Ripped Fuel, a dietary supplement promoted as a fat burner, and was suspended for a year. He had checked the label before he bought it and did not find any banned substances in the ingredients listed. But what he did not know was that ma huang—an herb listed as an ingredient on the label—contained ephedra.[9] The NCAA banned substance list has contained ma huang in its drug testing guidelines since 2002–03, but there are still many ways for manufacturers to avoid listing banned substances on the label. The International Olympic Committee (IOC) surveyed 624 dietary supplements and found that 41 percent of the products from American companies contained a steroid precursor or banned substance not disclosed on the label.[10]

The distributors.   Many NCAA-banned substances are sold over the counter, but not all PEDs are available without a prescription. Anabolic steroids require a prescription, but athletes can easily find a backdoor to get them. There are retailers south of the border shipping steroids to the United States, and many steroid precursors are sold on the Internet. Spam emails are sent out to millions of people every day with links to websites where steroids are sold, and they never ask visitors to provide a prescription or warn them of the health risks involved.

A more disheartening fact regarding the distributors of PEDs is that they often are the ones who are in the best position to educate athletes about the risk of PED use. A recent NCAA survey shows that among the continuous users of anabolic steroids in colleges, 17 percent said their coach/trainer/team physician provided the drugs for them. "Friend" or "relative" ranked high on the list as well, which means that most of the PED distribution is going through unofficial routes without a prescription.[11]

Perhaps these distributors are unaware of the health risks involved in PED use. They might think that they are actually helping the student-athlete improve his or her athletic performance by providing PEDs. Therefore, educating the student-athletes themselves would not be sufficient to clean up college sports, and everyone around the athlete with any level of interaction with them should be on the same page. Taking the drugs out of the reach of the athletes would be a much more effective way of solving the PED use problem than asking the athletes to think about health and testing when they already have the drugs in their hands.

(3) The Influencers

The third category—the influencers—involves all constituents of college sport including family, peers, athletics department (director, coaches), school administration (boards, committees), fans, alumni, corporate America, and the media. In addition, college athletes' K–12 experience and their idols in professional sport both have impact on their perception on PEDs and willingness to use them. Please note that all these influencers can provide either positive or negative impact on the user on PED-related issues. Therefore, the influencer category is a key group that can make a significant difference in solving the problem.

I do not claim that the entities discussed below are mostly a negative influence. We all agree that the majority of these influencers are doing a terrific job of keeping college sport clean and educating the athletes. However, their role is so important that even small cases of negative influence should be brought to our attention. One student-athlete who uses PEDs because of a negative influence by someone around him is one too many.

Parents/guardians.   Parents/guardians are the first line of defense against the use of PEDs. It is recommended that parents have frequent conversations with their kids about all forms of drugs, as these conversations seem to help reduce the desire by the kids to try them. PED use should be a part of these dialogues and they have to start early, because the average age of first PED use is getting younger every year. Unfortunately, a survey conducted by Blue Cross Blue Shield shows that about 9 percent of PED users of ages 12 to 17 said they were influenced to use them by their parents.[12] Charles Yesalis, professor of exercise and sport medicine at Penn State, shares the even more horrifying story that he sometimes receives calls from parents who want his blessing to their use of growth hormone or anabolic steroids on their child.[13]

This happens partially because of ignorance. The lack of knowledge, combined with the desire to create a star athlete, tricks the parents/guardians to encourage the use of PEDs, and it is often disguised as wanting only the best for the child. It is a good example that shows educating athletes would not be enough to eliminate PED usage. The parents/guardians should have a thorough understanding of PEDs to protect their child against their dangers.

The peers.   As the age of learning of and using PEDs for the first time is getting younger, the influence by peers on student-athletes is becoming critical. Sometimes peers can be the ones who introduce PEDs to the others, encourage them to try PEDs,[14] or even serve as a dealer.[15] We have to understand that however small the number there is, the mere existence of PED users among college athletes makes it difficult for the others to escape the idea of using them. Losing to a better athlete or team is one thing, but losing because the opponent(s) was on steroids is another issue. When steroids are suspected to be in play, the non-users might consider taking them themselves to be able to compete. In other words, a chain reaction of PED use can result unless no one, absolutely no one, uses them.

On the other hand, a "clean" athlete can be a tremendous influence to the others by promoting fair play and protecting the integrity of sport. The clean athletes need to speak up. It is not difficult to tell if a teammate is using PEDs because student-athletes train together. Some student-athletes believe PED use is a matter of choice and look the other way even when they witness a user. This is dangerous. Athletes should understand that even one teammate's use of PEDs hurts the integrity of the team, the sport, and the school. Athletes should assume an active role as advocates of clean college athletics.

Professional athletes. The impact of professional athletes on student-athletes is enormous. They are the idols and role models, and student-athletes watch them closely to learn not only from their game, but also from their lives. Unfortunately, the controversy over PED use in professional sport is well documented and is believed to have a strong influence on the PED issues around college athletics. What would student-athletes learn from watching the recent investigation into BALCO, a Northern California nutritional supplement company, for allegedly distributing illegal steroids to Olympic and professional athletes? Major League Baseball has been struggling to implement a testing policy for illegal substances due to the resistance from the players' union. Listening to the arguments presented by the players' union on the PED testing issue, student-athletes find multiple reasons why they should not submit to drug tests.

For example, when Fordham University implemented its first internal drug testing policy for student-athletes in 1999, some student-athletes raised issues of privacy rights and unfairness in opposition to the new policy. They argued that "athletes who have not been caught with drugs should not be subject to testing."[16] These arguments sound very similar to the those presented by professional athletes whenever a new mandatory drug testing policy is proposed. It is difficult to deny that college athletes are influenced by the justifications often used by professional athletes for not being tested.

The inconsistent standard for punishing illegal drug use in professional sports raises yet another concern. The Major League Baseball (MLB) commissioner's office recently decided not to penalize Yankees star Gary Sheffield after his admission of unknowingly using a cream that contained illegal steroids for his injured right knee a couple of years ago.[17] The decision was based on the fact that the steroid use happened outside of the 12-month limit MLB and the players' union agreed on. As mentioned earlier, a student-athlete who took Ripped Fuel not knowing that it contained ephedra was suspended for one full year. If a superstar like Gary Sheffield can get away with unknowingly using steroids simply because it happened a couple of years ago, why does the student-athlete have to be suspended when he, like Sheffield, unknowingly used an illegal substance?

Even if Sheffield's steroid use had been found within the 12-month window, the penalty would not have included any suspension or fine. MLB's drug policy at that time stated that first offenders only had to go through mandatory treatment. A second violation resulted in a 15-day suspension with fine, and a player had to test positive five times to receive a one-year suspension. These weak penalties finally got toughened after strong criticism by the public and the Congress. Effective with the 2006 season, there will be a 50 game suspension for a first offense, 100 games for a second offense, and a lifetime ban with possible reinstatement for a third.[18] The other professional sport leagues are not any tougher in terms of their drug policies. The penalty for a first violation is a four-game suspension in the NFL, and a five-game suspension in the NBA. A third violation results in a minimum one-year suspension in the NFL, but only a 25-game suspension in the NBA. The NHL currently does not test the players for drug use.

With these previously light penalties across major professional sports, it was difficult to convince student-athletes that using PEDs is wrong and dangerous. The NCAA imposes a much tougher penalty—a one-year suspension with the first positive test—but the penalty can serve its purpose only when it teaches the violator and many others that PED use is wrong. When the violator watches his favorite NBA player coming back from a short 10-game suspension after failing the drug test twice, it would be difficult for him to learn that lesson.

K–12 athletes.   Some of K–12 athletes go on to become college and professional athletes. Therefore, examining the PED use of these young athletes provides us with some insights on the future problems in college athletics. Unfortunately, pre-collegiate student-athletes are equally exposed to the danger of PEDs. A study by University of Michigan in 2003 found that 3.5 percent of American high school students had used illegal steroids at least once. The same study showed that only 45 percent of all 12th-graders were aware of the potential health risk of steroids.[19] Another study of high school seniors estimated that 4 percent were using steroids in 2002, a significant increase from the 2.5 percent reported in 2000.[20] These studies translate to about 500,000 to 600,000 kids in the United States having used steroids at some point.[21]

The age of first PED use is getting lower as well. A survey conducted by the NCAA in 2001 reports that 41.8 percent of the PED users in college first picked it up in high school, a substantial increase from 25 percent reported in a 1997 survey.[22] The pediatric medical literature also reports that anabolic androgenic steroids are used by athletes as young as middle school age, and a study shows that 2.6 percent of both male and female athletes as young as 5th grade have used steroids.[23]

These staggering reports paint a discouraging picture for future college athletics. Why is PED use among young athletes growing so fast? First, the young athletes often do not fully understand the risks involved in PED use, as mentioned earlier. They are also at the age where they believe they are invincible. These two factors collectively make it very hard to convince a young athlete that PEDs harm both body and mind. The serious side effects do not come immediately, so they believe nothing is wrong. Second, pre-college athletic programs rarely have a structured education program on PEDs. Every level in education aggressively tackles the problems of recreational drugs such as marijuana and cocaine, but education on PEDs receives relatively less attention. Coaches are not always well informed about PEDs and related health risks, and schools lack the resources to provide helpful guidance to student-athletes about PED use. Third, there is no systematic testing program in high school athletics compared to what the NCAA does for college sport. It means that there is no deterrent device in place to discourage young athletes from experimenting with PEDs. Fourth, these young athletes and their institutions are not getting much help. Colleges and professional teams maintain close relationships with high school athletic programs for recruiting purposes, but they do not always involve information sharing and support for PED education programs. Higher education and professional leagues have to understand that K–12 education is the place where the seeds are planted. To avoid their future PED problems, it would be smart to start with the root.

In short, K–12 athletics need more aggressive education programs starting in elementary school, and some degree of testing program should be implemented. Colleges, the NCAA, and professional leagues have to be involved in this effort to help pre-college institutions keep their athletic programs clean and safe. The role of individual colleges and the NCAA is especially important because their expertise and experience can be of tremendous value to high schools. For example, colleges can help by setting up PED education programs in the high schools from which they recruit, and the NCAA can lend support on designing and implementing a drug testing program. College sports need to remember that they are bound to inherit the problems of high school sports, and drug-free high school athletics means less problems for colleges and the NCAA.

The school.   Every layer—coaches, team doctors, athletics department, and school administration—in the organizational structure of a school has to be on the same page when it comes to PED use. When a student-athlete tests positive for PEDs, the blame often lands only on the shoulder of the athlete himself/ herself. However, the school is equally responsible for educating the athletes and providing the environment where student-athletes understand that PED use is not an option. Many schools do a great job in all layers of the system to educate the student-athletes about PEDs and prevent their use by implementing independent tests outside of NCAA testing.

On the other hand, the nature of college athletics as a business makes it difficult for universities to do their job preventing PED use. Coaches are paid to win, and they rely on the performance of student-athletes for their job security. Athletics departments need superstars who can sell tickets and help them promote their programs. The success of athletics allows the school administration to effectively solicit donations to build classrooms and fund research. With the amount of money involved in college sports today, some school officials even go one step further and directly promote the use of PEDs.

For example, a Vanderbilt University weight coach along with a pharmacist and the pharmacist's former aide were indicted in 1985 on charges of illegally dispensing more than 97,000 doses of muscle-building steroids and other prescription drugs to athletes at Vanderbilt, Clemson, and Colgate.[24] In 1989, four former South Carolina assistant football coaches were indicted for illegal use and distribution of anabolic steroids.[25] It was reported in 2003 that a physician for the University of Washington's athletic program illegally pre-scribed steroids and other drugs to student-athletes over many years.[26] This kind of practice is not limited to colleges. Three percent of teens (ages 12–17) surveyed by Blue Cross Blue Shield in 2001 said they knew a coach who en-couraged or even pressured athletes to use PEDs.[27]

Coaches and team physicians do not have to be directly involved in the use and/or distribution of PEDs to be guilty. When a coach tells an athlete that he needs to gain 20 pounds to start, the message suggests an extreme measure, which is anabolic steroid. When a coach yells at an athlete for being too slow, the quickest solution for the athlete is ephedrine. It is ironic that coaches are the ones with the responsibility to educate the athletes on PED use. A coach's job is to bring the best performance out of athletes, but coaches have to make it clear that using a PED is not an option.

To help coaches and team doctors to communicate this message, the ath-letics department and school administration have to show their commitment to keep the athletic programs clean. The "win or get fired" approach by the school puts the coaches in a difficult position to do their job protecting athletes from the temptation of PEDs. School administration also has to provide active ed-ucation programs for both coaches and athletes. Coaches are often not knowledgeable enough to guide the athletes on PED issues, and they need updates on new drugs and their risks. Since very little education on PED use is provided to athletes before the college level, it is critical that school admin-istration does the job right. It is reported that 45 percent of teens (ages 12–17) had never received any information about the risk of using PEDs or sport supplements from their school, and 72 percent had not received any infor-mation from their sports teams when participating in organized sport. This lack of education has probably contributed to the decline in the risk perception of PED use by teens over the last several years. Seventy-three percent thought PED use posed serious health risk in 1999, but only 58 percent thought sim-ilarly in 2001.[28] When these athletes come to college and face the challenge of intense competition, the temptation of PEDs is obviously there, and athletics departments and school administrations have to make sure the athletes un-derstand the issues of PEDs as soon as they step on the campus.

Fans/alumni.   Since college sports have grown into some of the major spec-tator events in the United States, the role of fans/alumni cannot be ignored in the discussion of PED use in college athletics. Sue Estler, associate professor of higher education at the University of Maine, said, "we are the only country in the world that has spectator sports tied to higher education. Universities in the U.S. use name recognition to build pride in the institution and for development and enrollment."[29] In other words, college sports has become a major vehicle for building a better institution, and the fans/alumni play an important role by paying for the tickets to the game and supporting the athletic programs through contributions, sponsorships, and volunteer work.

This role of fans/alumni grants them a strong influence to the school and athletics department. Frank Solich led the University of Nebraska football program to a 58-19 record over six seasons with one Big 12 championship and an appearance at the national championship game at the Rose Bowl after the 2001 season. Athletics director Steve Pederson dismissed Solich after going 9-3 in his final regular season. There is no doubt that the disappointment by the fans and alumni played a part in this decision, and their reaction puts enormous pressure not only on the coaches and players, but on the whole school. It is unfortunate that this pressure sometimes translates to a "winning at all cost" mentality and the integrity of the game gets pushed aside. It trickles down to the coaches and the athletes, and it certainly has a strong impact on PED use among student-athletes. When a heroic performance by an athlete paints the front page while a failed drug test gets two sentences buried in the corner, some athletes would take a chance on PEDs to be on the front page.

Again, the responsibility to communicate with the fans/alumni the school's commitment to a clean athletic program falls on the shoulders of the athletics department and school administration. The job cannot be done solely by educating the insiders (e.g., coaches and athletes). The fans and alumni also need to learn about the issues related to PEDs and serve as watchdogs in the community to keep the program clean. It is critical that the athletics department and school administration communicate with their fans/alumni that protecting the athletes, preserving the integrity of sports, and upholding the reputation of the school are more important than winning.

Media.   As an integral part of college sports, the media has an important role in battling the PED issues in college athletics. In his testimony during a Senate hearing in 2002, Dr. Bernard Greisemer, a pediatrician and sports medicine specialist, warned that the frequency of questions on PED surge with each new media exposure of its use by professional athletes.[30] Looking back on the media coverage for Mark McGwire's admission to using androstenedione in 1998, most of the articles and news coverage mentioned the benefits of it (e.g., muscle growth) but did not spend much space and time to explain the potential side effects, whose long list includes liver and heart damage, acne, mood changes, emotional disturbances, male pattern baldness, and feminization of males. From the coverage, it was clear why an athlete would want to use androstenedione—to grow muscle and gain strength, speed, and endurance. In contrast, the frequently mentioned reason why an athlete would not want to use it is that it is illegal. When a student-athlete reads and watches the coverage, it is not difficult to imagine what kind of impact it would have. As a result, the sales of androstenedione increased by 1,000 percent after 1998,[31] and its success led to the heavy marketing campaign of other steroid precursors such as 19-noradnrostenedione.[32]

Dr. Greisemer also said that "the media and the aggressive marketing campaigns used by manufacturers all identify these products as being 'used by the pros.'"[33] In other words, a report on PEDs actually encourages young people, including student-athletes, to consider PEDs rather than educating the readers/viewers about the dangers of PEDs. Combined with the heavy marketing effort through mass media by manufacturers, it is clear that the media industry can and should do a lot more to support the battle against PED use. For example, 25 percent of teens (ages 12–17) found out about PEDs through advertising in 2001 that was not strictly regulated by the government or the media themselves.[34]

Corporate America.   Corporate America's involvement in college sports has grown into a multi-billion-dollar business. With this heavy involvement as sponsor, advertiser, and licensee comes the power to influence various other entities in college sport. This power also comes with the responsibility to protect the integrity of the sport. Many companies sponsor the drug education programs on college campuses and put pressure on school administrations to keep the athletic program clean to preserve their marketability. However, a 2001 survey by Blue Cross Blue Shield showed that most adults wanted companies to take a more active role against sports supplements and PEDs. Ninety-three percent agreed that marketing of sport supplements to kids under 18 should be banned, 84 percent agreed that companies should not sponsor athletic teams or competitions when it is known that athletes on the team or in the competition are using PEDs, and 82 percent believed that sport sponsors should become more involved in reforming the sports that they sponsor.[35]

(4) The Regulators

The fourth category of the constituents of college athletics is the regulators who have the authority to regulate the student body with incentives and punishments. This group includes athletics departments, school administration, the NCAA, and federal/local governments. The NCAA is in the center of this category, but the roles of the other entities should not be discounted.

The school.   The regulating of PED use starts with the student-athlete himself/herself making the choice, but the immediate parties with control over the decision are the coach and team physician. They have the responsibility to monitor and regulate PED use among student-athletes. To do this job, they have to be well informed and provided with proper incentives for keeping the program clean and safe, as mentioned earlier in the section on influencers. They are in the best position to identify any student-athlete using PEDs, and taking an immediate action against this use can prevent further damage to the athlete's health, to the integrity of the program, and to the school's reputation.

It is comforting to know many schools have an internal testing policy, including Fordham University mentioned earlier. Some schools, such as Monroe College, have a strict measure where urinalysis accompanies all physical examinations.[36] Other schools have an internal random testing program. For example, the College of the Holy Cross tests about 25 randomly selected football and track athletes either quarterly or bi-annually.[37] As of 2001, 93 percent of colleges and universities had their own drug-testing program, but with a wide variance in the intensity of the testing program. "Some conduct hundreds to thousands of tests every year, and others just do a few," says Frank Uryasz, director of the National Center for Drug Free Sport.[38] It raises a question on the effectiveness of the internal testing programs. Charles Yesalis, professor of exercise and sport medicine at Penn State, is even more pessimistic about the internal testing programs. He suspects that the true motivation behind internal testing is "to catch the problems in-house," not to keep the athletes clean and safe.[39] Another discouraging fact of internal drug testing is the lack of attention given to PEDs relative to recreational drugs such as cocaine and marijuana. Only 64 percent of colleges and universities include anabolic steroids in their testing program.[40]

Another critical issue is the increased use among student-athletes of creatine, which is known to improve quickness. It has already established itself as the favorite PED among teens (ages 12–17). Fifty-eight percent of teen PED users reported that they used creatine compared to 30 percent using steroids.[41] Another study by Cornell Medical College and Mount Sinai Medical Center found that 5.6 percent of middle and high school respondents have used creatine, a significantly higher figure than the steroid use by the same age bracket.[42] The fuel for this popularity is the fact that it is not on the banned list by the NCAA and its potential health risks are relatively unknown. However, it is reported that creatine can cause diarrhea, dehydration, and muscle cramping and tearing.[43] If schools wait until its side effects are scientifically proven, it would be long after the health of many athletes had already been damaged. Therefore, it calls for a proactive testing policy, and colleges and universities should start testing for creatine right away. The testing by itself sends a clear message to student-athletes that creatine is a health risk even without severe punishment such as suspension. The identification of the athletes taking creatine, combined with their physical examination records, will enable researchers to have access to a reliable data set to study its health risks. The findings from this research will allow the NCAA to take proper action against creatine, and it will be able to save many student-athletes from its potential side effects.

In short, we have come a long way in internally regulating PED use by student-athletes, but we still have our work cut out for us. More active information sharing among schools would improve the testing programs by learning from each other's experience. More aggressive and proactive testing procedures for a comprehensive set of drugs—including all banned PEDs and the ones that are not banned but under suspicion—would be necessary to serve its true purpose as a deterrent.

NCAA. The NCAA has done a great job in a short period of time fighting against PED use in college athletics. It started with the NCAA Council forming the Drug Education Committee in 1970. After a series of studies on PED use in college athletics that clearly indicated that it was a serious problem, the NCAA began making major progress when it started an official drug testing program in 1986. This was expanded to year-round random testing in 1990. The testing procedure has been outsourced to the National Center for Drug-Free Sport since 1999.[44] The banned list has been constantly expanded to include all dangerous PEDs, such as ephedrine added in 2002 and tetrahydrogestrinone (THG), a designer drug undetectable by common doping tests, added in 2004.

One-year suspension is mandatory for a drug test failure, and this stiff penalty has been an effective deterrent. Testing is only a part of the NCAA's program. It offers various services to educate athletes and help them make the right choices. For example, the Dietary Supplement Resource Exchange Center was founded to provide answers to student-athletes who are confused by the smart marketing claims of these drugs being "natural" and "legal." The National Center for Drug-Free Sport, the official testing agency for the NCAA, also provides education programs for school officials, coaches, and athletes.

Despite the success of the NCAA's effort over the last couple of decades to clean up college athletics, we have to recognize the limitations of the NCAA's role in achieving drug-free college athletics. There is no doubt that the NCAA testing policy has had a positive impact, but it has been limited at most. The first limitation is that it is impossible to cover the majority of student-athletes in year-round testing due to budget and time constraints. In a Senate hearing, an anonymous former college football player testified that it is not impossible to get around the NCAA random drug testing. He said that "the policy is weak and fairly predictable, with the drug tests falling in roughly the same period of time every year."[45] The subject pool for year-round testing has been expanding to include various sports and different division levels, but it still leaves many areas uncovered.

Where do we go from here? First, we have to realize that the NCAA has limited resources to effectively regulate PED use in college athletics. Individual schools need to work closely with the NCAA by securing the credibility of their own internal testing policy and actively sharing information among them and with the NCAA. The NCAA needs to improve the effectiveness of its

year-round testing procedure by making it less predictable and provide incentives to schools that accomplish drug-free athletic programs across all
sports.

One more issue that needs attention is the recipient of punishment upon
positive test. Under the current system, the athlete is the only one who gets
punished unless there is evidence of deliberate effort by others including the
coaches who might aid the athlete's acquisition and/or use of the drug. As
discussed throughout this chapter, the athlete should not be the sole person to
take responsibility for his or her PED use. Imposing penalties on the school,
coaches, and team physicians to some degree would encourage them to actively prevent PED use among athletes and provide some level of accountability for the problem. When a student-athlete takes steroids because he is
asked by his coach to gain 20 pounds to keep his starter status, it seems unfair
that the athlete is the only one who has to suffer from the consequences. Even
though the coach does not have anything to do with the athlete's PED use in
any way, he or she should have known the athlete was using something by
recognizing abnormal changes in the athlete's body and behavior. College
coaches have to understand that they are teachers and mentors as well as
being a coach in college athletics. Athletics departments and school administrations need to take responsibility by providing the coaches with the support and tools they need to do the job. This is why all levels of college
athletics, not just the athletes themselves, need to be held accountable when
an athlete gets caught using a PED.

Government.   The government has been an active regulator of PED use at every
level of sports. Whereas regulation by the NCAA focuses on the user's side of the
picture, the regulation by the government mainly deals with the supplier side.
For example, the Senate passed a revised bill that outlawed the non-prescription
sale of many PEDs on October 6, 2004. The designer steroid tetrahydrogestrinone (THG) and andros (e.g., androstenedione) are in the banned list, and
the bill includes an education component that allows the Secretary of Health and
Human Services to award grants to educate schoolchildren about the risks of
anabolic steroids.[46]

Despite the active role of the government to effectively regulate the PED
market, many problems in battling PEDs are related to the Dietary Supplement Health and Education Act passed by the U.S. Congress in 1994. The act
states that dietary supplement products must be proven to be a health hazard
to be removed from the marketplace, though no pre-market clearance to test
the product is required by law before its distribution. In other words, it is not
the manufacturer's responsibility to test its product before shipping it to the
stores, which is completely different from what the Food and Drug Administration (FDA) requires for other drugs. Since the manufacturers are not
obligated to test their products, the product is not regulated at all unless
consumers come up with scientific evidence that proves the product to be a

health hazard. This is the main reason dietary supplements are flooding the market.

The government needs to take more proactive action on dietary supplements, which often contain illegal substance precursors. Tougher regulations in testing, promoting, and distributing these products need to be in place as well as an updated list of banned substances. If the government had a grip on the supply side by eliminating the products that contain banned substances from the stores, and the NCAA and the schools had good control over the demand side with education and testing, it would be much easier for everyone to handle the PED issues around college athletics. Without the commitment of both the government and NCAA members, though, the battle against PEDs will be extremely tough.

Finally, more funding should be available for research on PEDs, and extensive consumer education on PED use needs more attention.

CONCLUSION: WINNING IS NOT EVERYTHING...

We have discussed the constituents of college athletics and their roles in PED problems in the categories of (1) users, (2) suppliers/distributors, (3) influencers, and (4) regulators. It is clear that everyone involved has the power and responsibility to make a difference, but it is also evident that each constituent is part of the problem as well. Therefore, a simple conclusion is that everyone needs to take responsibility and work together to solve the problem. However, this is much easier said than done. Only a fully collective effort can effectively solve the problem and achieve safe and clean college athletics.

The question, then, is: How can we integrate our efforts? To answer this question, we need to look at the most fundamental questions. First, we need to start with the acknowledgment that PEDs work. They do enhance performance, which obviously motivates student-athletes to consider using them. Testing is a reactive measure that tries to prevent PED use with punishments but fails to attack the motivation behind it, which limits its effectiveness. We have lowered the number of positive test results to 2 percent without being able to further reduce it for the last several years. This illustrates that 2 percent might be the lowest we can achieve with our current approach to the problem. It is time to implement more proactive measures that attack the heart of the problem—the motivation to use PEDs.

Being proactive means that every constituent needs to work on eliminating the motivation by student-athletes to use PEDs. The users have to learn that PEDs not only hurt their body and mind, but also hurt the ultimate goals of playing sport—fair play, integrity, and sportsmanship. The influencers need to take responsibility for educating the users about these noble goals of athletics and provide the environment to promote them. The suppliers/distributors have to develop and market supplements that are truly clean and safe and try to appeal to the majority of users who have no intention to cheat. Finally, the regulators have to make sure all the violators, including everyone who is responsible, get punished. They also need to provide clear principles and guidelines for the athletes to follow.

We also have to understand that there is an even more fundamental issue related to PED use in college athletics, which is winning. As soon as one or more constituents in college athletics start putting winning ahead of the health of student-athletes and the true spirit of the game, it is difficult to ignore PEDs as an option to achieve that goal—because they work. Every example presented in the previous section where an athlete was encouraged or pressured to use PEDs had "trying/wanting/needing to win" as the underlying premise. Without attacking this premise, it looks like eliminating the 2 percent who continue to use PEDs could be a tough challenge.

It is not difficult to find the cases where mixed messages are communicated among the constituents. For example, the NCAA puts in so much effort and resources in its drug testing program but, at the same time, heavily rewards the winners of major college sports financially. Bowl Championship Series participants receive more than a $10 million payout, whereas a small bowl participant receives $600,000. We all understand that the NCAA has done a great job promoting college sport and securing financial rewards for its members. The question relates to the concentration of the award, which is in huge favor of the winners. This "winner takes all" system puts enormous pressure on athletics departments, coaches, and everyone involved in college athletics to win. There is no doubt it has a huge impact on the athletes, and this pressure sometimes leads to the wrong choice of taking a shortcut with PEDs.

Even without the pressure to win, student-athletes are constantly under pressure to perform. Competition is everywhere, starting from getting attention from the scouts, making the team, earning the scholarship, winning the starting position, and keeping the position. As a student-athlete, it never ends. We are witnessing the same trend in middle and high school athletics, where our future student-athletes are relying more and more on PEDs to stay ahead of competition. The competition has become more intense than ever, and it has probably contributed to the sharp increase in PED use among pre-collegiate student-athletes.

As the pressure to win is intensifying even more every day, I ponder if we will ever see the decline of PED use among student-athletes. A lot of resources have been spent and are devoted to prevent PED use, and it would be disheartening to see the rate turning upward after all the efforts. It seems that we are at the critical juncture where we can turn toward either the right direction or the wrong one. If we value winning as we do now and transform college athletics into even more of a business, it is likely that we will turn in the wrong direction in the battle against PEDs. If we start putting more emphasis on pride and integrity over winning and celebrate the fun and excitement of the game rather than the outcome, I believe it is possible to move in the right direction and reduce the number of PED users down to just a few helpless and hopeless people.

NOTES

1. Toland, Jennifer (2004), "Test finds cheaters among college athletes," *Sunday Telegram*, Mar. 28, p. 1A.

2. NCAA (2004), *Guide for the college-bound student-athlete*, p. 5.

3. Manning, Anita (2002), "Steroids can build muscles, shrink careers," *USA Today*, July 8.

4. Chyka, Peter A. (2003), "Health risks of selected performance enhancing drugs," *Journal of Pharmacy Practice*, 16(1), pp. 37–44.

5. Manning, Anita (2002), "Kids, steroids don't mix," *USA Today*, July 9.

6. Manning, Anita (2002), "Steroids can build muscles, shrink careers," *USA Today*, July 8.

7. Hooton, Donald (2004), Testimony Before Senate Caucus on International Narcotics Control, July 13.

8. NCAA (2001), *NCAA Study of Substance Use Habits of College Student-Athletes*.

9. Sacrbinsky, Kevin (2004), "Special report: Illegal supplements testing is an effective deterrent since 1989," *Birmingham News*, Aug. 29.

10. Shorter, Frank (2002), Testimony Before Senate Subcommittee on Consumer Affairs, Foreign Commerce and Tourism, June 18.

11. NCAA (2001), *NCAA Study of Substance Use Habits of College Student-Athletes*.

12. Blue Cross Blue Shield, *National Performance-Enhancing Drug Study* (2001), Aug.

13. Manning, Anita (2002), "Kids, steroids don't mix," *USA Today*, July 9.

14. NCAA (2001), *NCAA Study of Substance Use Habits of College Student-Athletes*.

15. Anonymous (2004), Testimony before Senate Caucus on International Narcotics Control, July 13.

16. Aldax, Mike (1999), "New Fordham drug policy raises issues for athletes," *Norwood News*, 12(21), Nov. 4–17.

17. SI.com (2005), "Sheffield won't be penalized for steroid use," Oct. 5.

18. ESPN.com (2005), "Steroid penalties much tougher with agreement," Nov. 15.

19. Hennessey, Kathleen (2004), "Senate panel focuses on athletes, steroids," *Los Angeles Times*, July 14, p. 5D.

20. Anonymous (2003), "Ramifications on . . . ," *St. Petersburg Times* (Florida), Nov. 30, p. 10C.

21. Manning, Anita (2002), "Kids, steroids don't mix," *USA Today*, July 9.

22. NCAA (2001), *NCAA Study of Substance Use Habits of College Student-Athletes*.

23. Greisemer, Bernard (2002), Testimony Before Senate Subcommittee on Consumer Affairs, Foreign Commerce and Tourism, June 18.

24. Anonymous (1985), "Three men indicted for illegally dispensing steroids to college athletes," *Los Angeles Times*, Apr. 20, p. 5.

25. Anonymous (1989), "Four coaches at S. Carolina indicted in steroid case," *Los Angeles Times*, Apr. 19, p. 8.

26. Silver, Beth, and Craig Hill (2004), "State alleges UW steroid abuse," *News Tribune*, Jan. 30.

27. Blue Cross Blue Shield (2001), *National Performance-Enhancing Drug Study*, Aug.

28. *Ibid.*

29. Lauzon, Jerry (2002), "Agree with it or not, college athletics held to a higher standard," *Portland Press Herald*, Dec. 22, p. 5D.

30. Greisemer, Bernard (2002), Testimony Before Senate Subcommittee on Consumer Affairs, Foreign Commerce and Tourism, June 18.

31. Manning, Anita (2002), "Kids, steroids don't mix," *USA Today*, July 9.

32. Shorter, Frank (2002), Testimony Before Senate Subcommittee on Consumer Affairs, Foreign Commerce and Tourism, June 18.

33. Greisemer, Bernard (2002), Testimony Before Senate Subcommittee on Consumer Affairs, Foreign Commerce and Tourism, June 18.

34. Blue Cross Blue Shield (2001), *National Performance-Enhancing Drug Study*, Aug.

35. *Ibid.*

36. Aldax, Mike (1999), "New Fordham drug policy raises issues for athletes," *Norwood News*, 12(21), Nov. 4–17.

37. Toland, Jennifer (2004), "Test finds cheaters among college athletes," *Sunday Telegram*, Mar. 28, p. 1A.

38. Bruscas, Angelo (2003), "UW scandal stuns NCAA's expert," *Seattle Post-Intelligencer*, Oct. 24, p. 1A.

39. *Ibid.*

40. *Ibid.*

41. Blue Cross Blue Shield (2001), *National Performance-Enhancing Drug Study*, Aug.

42. CNNfyi.com (2001), "Teen athletes: Study says save creatine for later," Aug. 7.

43. Manning, Anita (2002), "Steroids can build muscles, shrink careers," *USA Today*, July 8.

44. Copeland, Jack L. (2002), "Withstanding the test of time," *NCAA News*, Sep. 30.

45. Anonymous (2004), Testimony Before Senate Caucus on International Narcotics Control, July 13.

46. Anonymous (2004), "Senate committee approves steroid act," *NCAA News*, Oct. 1.

CHAPTER

Agents on Campus

Fritz G. Polite University of Central Florida

The sport world in which we are living has changed drastically. The increase in player's salaries, expanded media coverage, and the globalization of sport have had a profound effect on the status of amateur, professional, and intercollegiate sports. One challenge has been the issue of agents. The commercialism of sport creates complex issues regarding accountability and preventative mechanisms for administrators in addressing the problem of agents on our college campuses. Increasingly the problem goes back to agents contacting high school students. The traditional path for all students-athletes is from high school to college. The National Collegiate Athletic Association (NCAA) is the main governing body for college sports.[1] There are other agencies that also govern or participate in the regulating of college sports, including the National Association of Intercollegiate Athletes (NAIA). The NCAA is not a single organization that rules or governs what takes place in collegiate sports but is composed of over 1,000 member institutions.[2] This chapter will focus on the issue of agents on campus, the role of the NCAA, historical evolution of agents, high school student-athlete impact, university legal issues, recommendations, and future implications.

HISTORICAL COLLEGE ISSUES

Over the past several years, the number of high school graduates and college underclassmen applying for early entry into the various professional sport leagues has risen dramatically. Any discussion into the issue of agents on campus has to relate to significant antitrust laws. This is important because they provide the legal access by student-athletes to the various professional leagues, sometimes bypassing college. The Sherman Antitrust Act provides a blanket restriction against every contract, combination, or conspiracy in restraint of trade.[3] The rule of reason is a flexible method of antitrust analysis that weighs an activity's benefit to competition against its injury to competition.[4] This rule of reason has played a significant factor in young student-athletes' capacity to jump directly from high school or college to the professional ranks.

The other important factor in discussing agents on college campuses is the role of the NCAA in regulating intercollegiate athletics. During the latter part of the 19th century, premier student-athletes were heavily recruited by rowing teams. It was reported that students received exclusive rooms, food, cash, and paid vacations to participate with the top Yale or Harvard teams.[5] These teams were usually sponsored by powerful corporations, including railroad companies and local banks. University presidents had little control over the sponsors or the students running the varsity programs. Recognizing the need to oversee intercollegiate athletics at the institutional level, whether through faculty or student governance, was a positive turning point. The creation of conferences further contributed to the regulation and control of athletics.

PAST HISTORY AND DEFINITION OF AGENTS

It is important that we gain an understanding of the historical significance of agents to better comprehend the problem of agents on campuses. In the past, the focus has been on college campuses. High schools had traditionally been the major feeding system for the next level of competition (college). That feeder system has been altered by the insurgence of agents and the lure of professional sports. Now students are being contacted not only at the university level, but also in high school.

The business of sport agency has taken a life of its own, with dramatically increased financial stakes. Signing bonuses of $10 million are common practice and long-term megadeals are the norm for emerging stars with great potential. The definition of the term *agent* describes a relationship in which two parties agree that one will act on behalf of the other.[6] To add clarity and provide a legal framework, the law of agency imposes certain duties that the principle and agent owe to each other.[7] Sport agencies have formed large multiservice firms that incorporate marketing, event management, financial investments, insurance, taxes, trusts, wills, endorsements, and television/radio appearances, thus becoming quite complex in the nature of their functions, responsibilities, and duties.

Historically, agents evolved out of necessity. C. C. "Cash and Carry" Pyle is often referred to as a pioneer in the sport agency field. C. C. Pyle facilitated a contract with George Halas, the founder and owner of the Chicago Bears, for Red Grange (1925). The terms of that agreement stipulated that Grange earn $3,000 per game and it included endorsements of an additional $300,000.[8] There were several significant cases that accelerated the growth and involvement in player-agent relationships. Commissioners as well as team owners controlled the limited movement of players. In 1966, a lawyer for the United Steel Workers of America sought to represent baseball players on the importance of organizing themselves and the strength of solidarity.[9] Marvin Miller became the driving force for the players, with the formulation of the Major League Baseball Players Association in 1966. Miller was instrumental in negotiating the first collective bargaining agreement in professional sports (1983). After the 1974 season, Oakland A's pitcher Catfish Hunter claimed A's owner Charles O. Finley had breached a part of his contract. An arbitrator agreed and based on the ruling, invalidated the rest of the provisions of the contract.[10]

One of the most important cases in professional sport was the case of Flood versus Kuhn. Kurt Flood was a player for the St. Louis Cardinals, and Bowie Kuhn was the Commissioner of Major League Baseball. This case was significant in that it challenged the legality of baseball's claim to the right to continually renew players' contracts that essentially lock each player to one organization with no opportunity to move. Three years after the Flood case, Andy Messersmith and Dave McNally challenged the reserve clause by filing a suit against the league, where it was heard and reviewed by an independent arbitrator. The reserve clause in a player's contract gave teams the option to renew players for the following season,[11] and the reserve list was a list sent to each team in the league. League rules entitled each team to place its reserved players on the list, and the management of the teams within the league agreed not to offer contracts to any of the other team's players.[12] In 1975 the players won the right to free agency, which changed the protocol for player movement and started the immediate rise in players' salaries.

One of the most important labor-management issues in professional sports is free agency because it allows players the opportunity to openly sell their services to other teams. The National Football League (NFL) exercised a form of limited free agency dictated by its commissioner. This was known as the Rozelle Rule on free agency, which allowed NFL Commissioner Peter Rozelle to award compensation (players, draft choices, money) to a player's former team when he signed a contract with a new team.[13] The federal courts ruled that the Rozelle Rule was an unreasonable restraint of trade under the Sherman Antitrust Act of 1890 because it acted as a deterrent to player movement in the NFL.[14]

Prior to 1971, the NBA By-Laws had prohibited the drafting of an athlete until four years after his high school graduation.[15] Spencer Haywood took advantage of this rule and signed a contract with the Denver Nuggets of the American Basketball Association (ABA). The court found the National

Basketball Association's (NBA) four-year rule to be a per se violation of the antitrust laws and allowed Haywood to play in the NBA.[16] A similar case involving professional hockey's minimal age requirements took place shortly after the Haywood case. Ken Linseman, a 19-year-old Canadian junior hockey player, challenged the World Hockey Association's rule that prohibited persons under the age of 20 from playing in the league. The court held that the "20-year-old rule" constituted a group boycott and thus was a violation of the Sherman Act.[17] The court found the case indistinguishable from that of the Denver Rockets and referred to it in its ruling. The National Hockey League adopted the 19-year-old draft rule, though any player turning 18 by September 15 of the draft year or 19 between September 16 and December 31 after the draft who petitioned the league for entry could be selected. This rule is included in the league's present collective bargaining agreement.[18]

These cases have created a chain reaction among agents, athletes, and sporting organizations that deal with the issue of rising salaries and young athletes. The number of agents has significantly increased. As of June 12, 2002, the National Football League Players Association (NFLPA) reported that there were 1,104 certified agents, of which 625 had no clients (NFLPA, 2003). The Major League Baseball Players Association (MLBPA) has over 300 certified agents on record. The data tend to indicate that there is an oversaturation of agents.[19]

Understanding the history of agents will provide a conceptual framework for many of the negative factors associated with agents. What follows is a brief overview on the high school level and then college.

High School

The escalated signing of high school athletes to professional contracts has created a dilemma among high school administrators as well as professional organizations while creating a domino effect at the university level. More high school student-athletes are attempting to join the ranks of Kobe Bryant, Tracy McGrady, LeBron James, and Kevin Garnett as the new-age millionaires that have made the successful jump directly from high school programs to the NBA.

There are athletes in other sports who are considering turning professional while still in high school. Ty Tyron became the youngest player to earn his Professional Golf Association (PGA) Tour card (2001) at the ripe age of 17. The PGA Tour policy board passed a rule that players must be 18 to become a member.[20] Tyron was allowed to play seven tournaments under a sponsor's exemption until he turned 18. Michelle Wie was 13 years old when she received a sponsor's exemption to play in the Chick-Fil-A Charity Championship in Atlanta in April, 2003. She was in the 8th grade and was not eligible for the school's varsity team yet. Wie became the youngest player to win an adult U.S. Golf Association tournament at the 2003 U.S. Women's Amateur Public Links Championship at Ocean Hammock, Palm Coast,

Florida.[21] Swimming champion Michael Phelps was 17 years old when he signed a multi-million-dollar contract with Speedo and was a world record holder at age 15. He signed several megadeals shortly after his 17th birthday. With the blessings of his parents, he acquired a Cadillac Escalade, valued at $49,000.[22]

The LeBron James phenomenon has further highlighted the issue of high school sports and agents. James, a 6-foot, 8-inch senior, was the number one pick of the Cleveland Cavaliers in the 2003 NBA draft. His high school in Akron, Ohio, received an unprecedented amount of media coverage. The Yankees Entertainment & Sports Network broadcast a basketball tournament featuring 12 of the top 16 teams in the nation. The ESPN2 network telecast a game that generated a 2.0 cable rating, the highest for the network since its coverage of NASCAR driver Dale Earnhardt's death, which had produced a 2.2 rating in 2001.[23] In James's final state tournament (2003), the crowd was a sellout at 18,409. Tickets were reportedly scalped for hundreds of dollars. The local newspaper estimated that the school would gross close to $1 million in ticket sales to boys' basketball games.[24]

During his senior year in high school, James came under investigation for the purchase of an Hummer2 valued at over $50,000. The vehicle was equipped with three televisions, a DVD player, a video game system, and elaborate rims. He was later suspended for receiving retro sports gear that was determined to be a violation of high school rules and regulations. After his senior season, James signed a $90-million apparel contract with Nike. Several companies including Reebok, And1, and Adidas were jockeying for his services. These negotiations took place while James was officially a high school student.

Where will it end? What are the governing bodies doing to prevent these types of activities? Where does the term "amateur" stop and "professional" begin? These are all relevant questions that have to be answered in order to successfully address the issue of agents in dealing with high school and collegiate athletes. According to Ohio State High School Athletic Association Commissioner Clair Muscaro, as long as James satisfied the school's residency requirements, did not turn 19 or attend more than eight semesters of school, and had passing grades (he surpassed a 3.0 grade-point average and made the merit roll), James could accept perks that were not tied to a specific game or tournament and still maintain his athletic eligibility.[25] Muscaro later recanted his statement under great media scrutiny and stated that "this is all such an unprecedented phenomenon that I do not have all the answers to many of your questions."

Was James being represented by an agent? What or how much contact took place with that agent while James was competing as a high school athlete? What provisions are in place to eliminate the gray areas of contact between student-athletes and agents? These are all relevant questions yet to be clearly answered.

Agents have moved from college campuses to high school campuses. The selling of sponsorships, athletic apparel, endorsements, television rights, tickets, and corporate suites are all fallouts from hundreds of millions of dollars and revenues generated from big-time sport programs.[26] Many of these student-athletes are from lower socioeconomic backgrounds with little or no financial security. Agents approach family members and offer large amounts of money, access to loans, and offers of homes, cars, and expensive jewelry in exchange for a promise of the opportunity to represent the athlete. Economists refer to such actions as "opportunism."[27] The self-interest of sports agents is the right to receive 2 to 5 percent of multimillion-dollar contracts. This does not include the additional money that can be generated from endorsements that can run as high as 30 percent of the agreed-upon contract. The motive is clear: A chance to cash in on one prospective student-athlete is so large that agents have taken on the task of searching out, pursuing, and landing top athletes at all levels. But high school and college student-athletes are not supposed to be receiving payment for services.

Colleges

The college student-athlete has taken on new dimensions in the world of sport. Coaches and agents deliver visions of grandeur to student-athletes, with promises of megapro contracts. For every student-athlete that is successful in his or her professional career, hundreds will never play professionally. For example, an African-American high school football player has a 1 in 43 chance of playing for a Division I college football team.[28] The chances of playing in the NFL are 6,318 to 1. The chances of a high school basketball player getting a scholarship to a Division I basketball team are 130 to 1 and the odds are 10,345 to 1 against his playing in the NBA.[29]

The issue is whether colleges are providing a safe haven for students participating in college athletics to successfully compete as well as complete their academic degrees without interference from agents on their campuses. Also, is the NCAA providing the guidance and protection for student-athletes against the forces of agents on campuses? With the present graduation rates for all student-athletes having entered the class of 1994 at 58 percent,[30] there are legitimate grounds for questioning the role of the NCAA and whether it is fulfilling the mission of the organization. Special attention should be given to student-athletes of African-American descent due to their lower graduation rate of 41 percent.[31] One must take into account that these statistics reflect those students who have transferred or left early for professional careers. Due to the inclusion of these students, the statistical significance is lower, thus reflecting a lower percentage in posted graduation rates. The NCAA counts early departures against the graduation rate percentage.

Agents can make substantial amounts of money by acquiring an athlete who is drafted in the early rounds. As an example, the average salary for a first-round pick NBA player will be approximately $11.92 million over three years. The agent's share would be around $158,990 for the length of the contract.[32] Once the player reaches free agency status, the pot gets even larger and the chances for profit increase. Scot Boras represented Alex Rodriguez in negotiations that led to an astronomical 10-year, $252-million-dollar contract. The agent's fees will come to approximately $12.6 million over the life of the contract. Again, this does not include any endorsements. Thus, the push to acquire young star athletes is tremendous. Generally, athletes tend to stay with a selected agent for the duration of their playing days. So, to acquire an athlete at 18 years of age and to negotiate contracts for their entire career at great profit can lead some agents to want to actively engage young talented student-athletes at the collegiate and high school level.

COLLEGE LEGAL ISSUES

One of the prevailing challenges of addressing the issue of agents on campuses is the lack of past legislation governing the actions of agents. The rise in agent activity has created a frenzy of contact with student-athletes. These contacts have raised alarms for the NCAA in focusing on events involving these students. Although the NCAA is explicit in the wording that a student-athlete may lose his or her eligibility by dealing directly with an agent, it does not preclude them from receiving advice and or guidance in proposals.[33]

Under NCAA By-Law 12.3, a student-athlete (any individual who currently participates in or who may be eligible in the future to participate in intercollegiate sport) may not agree verbally or in writing to be represented by an athlete agent in the present or in the future for the purpose of marketing the student-athlete's ability or reputation.[34]

Several cases have involved student-athletes and contact with agents. When the University of Michigan was one of the premier basketball programs in the country, they were named the Fab Five. This was a collection of top players including Jalen Rose and Chris Webber. Agent Eddie Martin became a fixture at games and was involved in a sports scandal that rocked the University of Michigan program. Martin was indicted on charges of running an illegal gambling operation and laundering some of the profits by loaning more than $600,000 to four University of Michigan players. Martin allegedly gave Webber $280,000 from 1988 to 1993. The indictment alleges that former University of Michigan player Robert "Tractor" Traylor received loans of about $160,000 from September 1993 through September 1998.[35]

Marcus Camby, while at the University of Massachusetts, was involved in a bizarre case involving agent Wesley Spears. Spears acknowledged that he gave financial assistance to Camby while he was playing at the University of Massachusetts. Camby admitted that he took valuables from Spears and agent John Lounsbury and the NCAA stripped the school of its 1996 regional championship and ordered it to return the money it had earned by reaching the Final Four.[36]

Jason Terry, a former University of Arizona basketball player (1995–99), disclosed that he received benefits from agents in violation of NCAA rules. The violations occurred after the end of Terry's junior season. Terry claimed he received approximately $4,500 in cash, checks, and wire transfers from New York sports agent Larry Fox. Terry also stated that he received approximately $7,000 from San Francisco agent Ndidi Opia during his senior season. He claimed Opia had provided free legal advice and had assisted in arranging catastrophic injury insurance, both of which constitute benefits from prospective agents and preferential treatment, which amount to additional violations.[37]

In August 2000, the National Conference of Commissioners on Uniform State Law (NCCUSL) convened to establish criteria for the purpose of protecting the interests of student-athletes and academic institutions by regulating the activities of agents. This process was a three-year endeavor that involved athlete agents, coaches, administrators, and player representatives from all of the major sport entities. The NCAA was also very involved in the discussions. These discussions resulted in the enactment of the Uniform Athlete Agents Act (UAAA, 2000). This act assisted in developing a code of uniformity and addressed a form of reciprocity in existing statutes.[38] The UAAA also required the registration of all agents in their respective states and established guidelines for educational institutions to have civil remedies against either an agent or a former student-athlete for damages caused by violations. Agents are now required to provide security ranging from $10,000 to $100,000 in case of violations and to ensure a protective blanket for individual states.[39] Although it is still a work in progress, it is one of the first major legislative acts to address the issues of conformity in dealing with agents on a national level.

Another group that has taken a proactive stance in addressing agents on college campuses is the National Association of Basketball Coaches (NABC). A major topic of discussion is the issue of how to effectively confront the issue of agents on campuses. The fact that coaches are being held responsible for contact between agents and student-athletes, including the imposition of violations and fines on their programs, has further heightened coaches' concerns for effective measures to attempt to formalize concrete ways to address the notion of agents.

Recommendations

With the recent signing of Freddy Adu, a 13-year-old soccer phenomenon, to a multimillion-dollar endorsement deal with Nike, the plot continues to thicken. The future of amateur sport has changed. The solicitation of young student-athletes has reached alarming proportions. At some point society and particularly administrative leaders have to take a more proactive approach toward protecting the status of amateurs while developing agendas to address the issue of agents on campuses. There are several reasons that a prospective student-athlete may feel the need to advance to the professional level. The key point is almost invariably the financial needs of many of these students. The capacity to provide economic security to one's family is a driving force behind why some student-athletes are forgoing college. There were nine high school entries in the 2004 NBA draft.[40] Eight out of the nine were selected in the first round. This included the number-one pick, Dwight Howard (SW Atlanta Christian Academy), who was selected by the Orlando Magic. The draft positions ranged from number one to nineteen and it marked the 4th consecutive year that a non-college player went as the number-one pick. In the 2002 draft, Amare Stoudemire was the only high school player taken. There were also four high school players who withdrew from the 2004 draft.[41]

For every LeBron James success story, there is a Lenny Cooke shattered dream. Lenny Cooke attended Northern Valley Regional High School in New York City. He was regarded as one of the top NBA prospects in the country. His senior year an agent arranged a considerable line of credit for him. Cooke had several unspectacular workouts and was not drafted. By having had contact with agents and having received financial support and gifts, he had violated the NCAA amateurism rules and was ruled ineligible to participate in collegiate basketball.

There were 35 players listed as NFL 2004 draft early entries.[42] Fifteen were selected in the first round. Is it wrong for student-athletes to make the jump to the professional ranks because they may get paid an enormous amount of money by participating in a sport they love? Vast amounts of financial profit are made off of the talent of many of the premier amateur superstars, whether in high school or at the college level. The NCAA must not get caught up in the circle of profit, endorsements, and television ratings. This inevitably may fuel the environment that agents operate in. Who can these athletes turn to for advice and answers? The greed of capitalism may be driving us into a realm of no return. Where will it end? The future of sport as we know it is changing at such blinding speed, administrators have not quite figured out a concise plan to deal with the issue of agents and amateur athletes. Only the future will tell us what lies at the end of the tunnel. In 10 years, look back in retrospect and again ask the questions: Where are we going? What have we done to deal with the issue of agents on our campuses?

Sports can be a vehicle that can significantly raise the educational attainment of many student-athletes from lower socioeconomic conditions. The commercialization of sport has strongly influenced the minds of many of our leaders as well as youth, and it has artificially divided the amateur, collegiate, and professional ranks. Educators, parents, coaches, and administrators need to confront many of the broader societal issues concerning the exploitation and manipulation of our young athletes. If we continue to ignore the present conditions that we are confronted with, we may be forever doomed to a sports world consisting of a lack of moral conscience and ethical principles. It is creating a vacuum in which potential students become victims of a system that engulfs their vision and thoughts. The notion of amateur sports is under attack, and the very nature of competition as well as the educational process is threatened. Steps need to be immediately taken to protect these students as well as their institutions. I recommend the following steps be taken:

1. Establish a formal national body or group that would include administrators, coaches, student-athletes, and state and local governments to openly discuss the issue of agents.
2. Formulate programs to support and promote student-athletes' continued participation in collegiate athletics. Examples would be: (1) more focused programs geared toward meeting graduation requirements, (2) seminars and training workshops focusing on long-range career goals, and (3) mentoring programs with former student-athletes who graduated and have successful careers.
3. Create strict and uniform guidelines for agents, boosters, and alumni concerning contact with student-athletes. The current policies are vague and not vigorously enforced, and penalties are minimal and do not protect the interests of the student or the educational institutions.
4. Require agents to compensate universities for student-athletes who leave early and declare agents as their representatives. This may involve legal implications, but it is a needed remedy.
5. Address the issue of various forms of security within the university system that would encourage athletes to continue participating in collegiate sport. This could include health insurance, opportunities for graduate/advanced degree completion, job training, and professional development programs.
6. Provide quality services to the student-athlete that foster a holistic approach to the continued development of the individual. Rather than have the student seeking advice from outside sources (agents), provide a foundation of support for the student within the university. This could include financial, medical, educational, and legal advice.

FUTURE IMPLICATIONS

One of the most recent legislative acts relating to the issue of agents on college campuses is the Sports Agent Responsibility and Trust Act, which was signed into law by President Bush on September 24, 2004. This act designates certain conduct by sports agents relating to the signing of contracts with student-athletes as unfair and deceptive acts or practices to be regulated by the Federal Trade Commission.[43] This act is historically unprecedented. Section 3 (H.R.361-2) states that it is unlawful for an agent to: directly or indirectly recruit or solicit a student-athlete to enter into agency by giving false or misleading information, provide anything of value to a student-athlete or anyone associated with the student-athlete before the student enters into an agency agreement, enter into an agency contract with a student athlete without providing the student-athlete with the proper disclosure documents, and predate or postdate an agency contract. A violation of this act shall be treated as a violation of a rule defining an unfair or deceptive act or practice prescribed under section 18(a)(1)(B) of the Federal Trade Commission Act.[44] This sends a strong message to agents that the continued engagement of student-athletes by unethical methods will now fall under the auspice of the Federal Trade Commission. This is one of the first legislative acts to target the issue of agents and contact with student-athletes.

Isolating the student-athlete from the mainstream of university life can create the opening of channels for communication and contact with agents. A change in the attitudes, perceptions, and thought processes of our young student-athletes will require a strong, concerted effort from our leaders. There must be continued progress toward developing mechanisms within the legal system and educational institutions that hold the amateur sports world accountable. The relationships between the university and the student-athlete must be concerted. The physical, social, and intellectual development of our student-athletes is critical if we are to produce responsible citizens. We have the power and influence to make a difference. The steps that will be taken in the coming years will not define sport, but they will define and lay the foundation of sport as a continued positive and integral component of our society. Sport is often viewed as a precious commodity full of important values and principles. University presidents, athletic directors, coaches, professors, parents, and student-athletes must act with integrity, honor, and character to reduce or eliminate the influence of agents on campuses.

NOTES

1. Masteralexis, P. L., Barr, C. A., and Humms, M. A. (1998). Excerpts from *Principles and Practice of Sport Management*. Gaithersberg, MD: Aspen Publishers.

2. Shropshire, K. L., and Davis, T. (2003). *The Business of Sports Agents*. Philadelphia: University of Pennsylvania Press.

3. Rosner, S. R. (1998). "Must Kobe Come Out and Play? An Analysis of the Legality of Preventing High School Athletes and College Underclassmen from Entering Professional Sport Drafts." *Seton Hall Journal of Sport Law*, 8(8), 539–553.

4. Rosner, S. R. (1998). "Must Kobe Come Out and Play? An Analysis of the Legality of Preventing High School Athletes and College Underclassmen from Entering Professional Sport Drafts." *Seton Hall Journal of Sport Law*, 8(8), 539–553.

5. Rosner, S. R., Shropshire, K. L. (2004). *The Business of Sports*. Jones and Bartlett Publishers, Sudbury, MA.

6. Berry, R. C., Gould, W. B., and Staudohar, P. D. (1986). *Labor Relations in Professional Sports*. Dover, Mass.: Auburn House Publishing.

7. Ruxin, R. (1993). *An Athlete's Guide to Agents (3rd ed.)*. Boston: Jones & Bartlett Publishers.

8. Berry, R. C., Gould, W. B., and Staudohar, P. D. (1986). *Labor Relations in Professional Sports*. Dover, Mass.: Auburn House Publishing.

9. Shropshire, K. L., and Davis, T. (2003). *The Business of Sports Agents*. Philadelphia: University of Pennsylvania Press.

10. Lowitt, B. (1999). "Free Agency Era Opens in Baseball." *St. Petersburg Times*, Online Sports (10/22/99) http://www.sptimes.com/news/1022/99/sports/Free section.

11. Blum, R. (2000). "25 Years later, Free Agency Rules Sports." *South Coast Today* 7/21/00.

12. Masteralexis, P. L., Barr, C. A., and Humms, M. A. (1998). Excerpts from *Principles and Practice of Sport Management*. Gaithersberg, MD: Aspen Publishers.

13. Rosner, S. R. (1998). "Must Kobe Come Out and Play? An Analysis of the Legality of Preventing High School Athletes and College Underclassmen from Entering Professional Sport Drafts." *Seton Hall Journal of Sport Law*, 8(8), 539–553.

14. Rosner, S. R. (1998). "Must Kobe Come Out and Play? An Analysis of the Legality of Preventing High School Athletes and College Underclassmen from Entering Professional Sport Drafts." *Seton Hall Journal of Sport Law*, 8(8), 539–553.

15. Rosner, S. R. (1998). "Must Kobe Come Out and Play? An Analysis of the Legality of Preventing High School Athletes and College Underclassmen from Entering Professional Sport Drafts." *Seton Hall Journal of Sport Law*, 8(8), 539–553.

16. Rosner, S. R. (1998). "Must Kobe Come Out and Play? An Analysis of the Legality of Preventing High School Athletes and College Underclassmen from Entering Professional Sport Drafts." *Seton Hall Journal of Sport Law*, 8(8), 539–553.

17. Masteralexis, L. P., Barr, C. A., and Humms, M. A. (1998). Excerpts from *Principles and Practice of Sport Management*. Gaithersberg, MD: Aspen Publishers.

18. Shropshire, K. L., and Davis, T. (2003). *The Business of Sports Agents*. Philadelphia: University of Pennsylvania Press.

19. Major League Baseball. (2003). Available at http://bigleaguers.yahoo.com/mlbpa/faq.

20. PGA Tour. (2001). Available at http://www.pgatour.com/u/ce/multi/0.

21. LPGA Newsline. (2001). Available at http://LPGA.com/Newsline/Tour.

22. Michaelis, V. (2002), "Phelps Just Normal High Schooler with Pro Contract." *USA Today*, 8/13/02.

23. Staff writer. "More TV Time for LeBron James." *Orlando Sentinel*, December 17, 2002.

24. ESPN.Com, March 8, 2003. LeBron James is an "unprecedented phenomenon."

25. ESPN.Com, March 8, 2003. LeBron James is an "unprecedented phenomenon."

26. Coakley, J. (2001). *Sport in Society*. New York: McGraw Hill.

27. Shropshire, K. L., and Davis, T. (2003). *The Business of Sports Agents*. Philadelphia: University of Pennsylvania Press.

28. Lapchick, R. L. (1999). *Smashing Barriers: Race and Sport in the New Millennium*. Lanham, Md.: Madison Books.

29. Lapchick, R. L. (1999). *Smashing Barriers: Race and Sport in the New Millennium*. Lanham, Md.: Madison Books.

30. NCAA. (2002). *NCAA Graduation Rates Report*. Available at http://www.ncaa.org/rates/2002.

31. NCAA. (2002). *NCAA Graduation Rates Report*. Available at http://www.ncaa.org/rates/2002.

32. Shropshire, K. L., and Davis, T. (2003). *The Business of Sports Agents*. Philadelphia: University of Pennsylvania Press.

33. NCAA. (2003). Available at http://www.ncaa.org/releases/infractions/2003050801in.htm.

34. NCAA. (2003). Available at http://www.ncaa.org/releases/infractions/2003050801in.htm.

35. Mullin, L. (2003). "Sleaze Factor Off the Charts." *Sports Business Journal*, January 23.

36. Wise, M. (1996). "Camby Embroiled in Uproar on Gifts." *New York Times*, June 5.

37. NCAA. (2003). Available at http:www.ncaa.org/releases/infractions/2003050801in.htm.

38. Shropshire, K. L., and Davis, T. (2003). *The Business of Sports Agents*. Philadelphia: University of Pennsylvania Press.

39. NCAA. (2003). Available at http//:www.ncaa.org/membership/enforcement/agents/uaaa/index.

40. NBADraft.net. *Early Entries 2004*. Available at http://nbadraft.net/early.htm.

41. NBADraft.net. *Early Entries 2004*. Available at http://nbadraft.net/early.htm.

42. ESPN.com. (2004). Available at http://espn.go.com/ncf/s/2003/0110/1490310.html.

43. *The Sports Lawyers Agent Responsibility Act*. (2004). Available at http://Lawyers.findlaw.com.

44. *The Sports Lawyers Agent Responsibility Act*. (2004). Available at http://Lawyers.findlaw.com.

CHAPTER 11

"Show Me the Money" Created a College Sportocracy: The Influence of the Media

Charles S. Farrell Sports Perspectives International

Mike Wilbon, sports columnist for the *Washington Post* and one-half of ESPN's *Pardon the Interruption*, remembers vividly the day the University of Maryland signed veteran coach Bobby Ross to be head football coach. It was supposed to signal a new era of respectability for Terrapins football.

Ross was at Georgia Tech and had been an assistant on a Super Bowl team and was highly coveted as a coach. "I remember it well," Wilbon recalled. "It was the winter of '81 and I asked him how much he made. Forty-four grand! That was it! Oh, and use of a house."[1]

Now, $44,000 won't pay for a good assistant coach at a top school, in either football or basketball, where coaches at even mid-majors make $1 million or more. "Money changed everything," Wilbon says.

Now, college sports are covered more and covered differently. People didn't take a critical look at college sports back then. It was very rah, rah, very chummy. The Big East had just formed, but basketball teams were still playing on their campuses before 5,000 if they were lucky.

The Atlantic Coast Conference was the only tournament; there were fewer big time teams. But then the money started changing. The NCAA basketball tournament went from 32 to 64 teams. Schools started paying for people, for coaches. And, they said, if you are going to make that much money, expectations are up. It is not $44,000 we are giving you; it is $440,000. Shoe companies got into the act. Everybody at the school got sneaks and $250,000 to run a camp.

Alums who raised the money to hire the coaches, they also had expectations, so they started lobbying newspapers, television, trying to get their teams on TV, so the media became more important. The 64 teams in the NCAA tournament all get payouts in March Madness. Everybody has a chance, so it is all about the money. If they just cared about winning, there wouldn't be a tournament.

And media coverage has become 24/7, with both national cable, like ESPN, and local, like Jefferson Pilot. "Logic is," Wilbon asserts, "if you are seen more, you can recruit more ... you are a bigger brand and can fill your stadium as well. There is really no such thing as truly local; everything is national. I can watch Santa Clara as much as St. John's or Georgetown."

But with the yearly March Madness and bowl frenzy that accompanies college sports is also overexposure and a twisted perspective, Wilbon says.

We get recruiting information on rising 8th-graders; I heard of Sebastian Telfir (New York high school star and current NBA rookie who jumped right from high school) when he was in junior high. It is like kiddie porn; I loathe it but can't turn the clock back now.

College sports are overexposed and interest is declining. College basketball is not as good as it used to be. With some of the best jumping to the pros from high school or after a year or two in college, a lot of people don't want to watch it because they are not seeing the best product.

There is nothing you can't know. Every bit of information is at your fingertips. Athletes have their own websites, you can get the latest recruiting gossip, and everything is available.

And, as *everything* is available, it means that athletes, and the colleges they play for, no longer have the luxury—or even the ability—to protect themselves against what is increasingly negative publicity. Years ago, when a coach had a drinking problem or an athlete smacked his girlfriend around, "[t]hat stuff was covered up," Wilbon reminds us, "or it wasn't covered critically. Years ago, writers traveled with the team. Personal life stayed out of it—like politics, it was not fair game."

But in the new age of college sports, with the money and prestige that is readily available, there is also a new age of journalism, according to Wilbon. "You are fair game," he says. "With the money, with the exposure, there is no off season, no off time. If you are getting paid millions, or go to tournaments and bowl games worth millions, it is not just what you do athletically any more. At this point, you are a small corporation. You are paid for your image, for being able to communicate, for being the franchise. Athletic ability is not worth that much anymore; image is worth more because nobody is beaming your image around the world every five seconds like ESPN."

It is ESPN, and its imitators, who have helped hype college sports and the money that has come to both support and represent the college sports scene.

"I think ESPN, like other television entities, has absolutely changed the way in which sports are viewed, analyzed, and interpreted by sports fans," offers David Aldridge, former basketball reporter for the all-sports network. "TV changed everything," he says. "It heralded an era where money has become the dominant force in sports.

"With television, there was more interest, which generated ratings, which generated more ad dollars, which drew more people, which created higher salaries, continuing a circle that gets larger and larger."[2]

As a result, coverage of college sports has changed, Aldridge says. "It is no longer enough to just write what you see," he states. "You now have to know beyond that because of TV. Because of TV, everybody knows what the score is well before it gets into the papers. The Internet has had an impact on that as well, so you have to go beyond traditional coverage of an event."

And that means trying to get additional insight, inside information, things that fans cannot get simply from picking up the morning paper, Aldridge says.

> Television has made it difficult for print writers to do their job because there is so much pressure to be first on everything. The workday has been compressed and there is now a 24-hour news cycle.
>
> Reporters are under incredible pressure to come up with something different. It creates situations where they need more and more access to athletes at a time when athletes, because of media scrutiny, are trying to get away from the media.

Aldridge believes this has created both good and bad. "I don't think we need to lionize athletes the way we did in the '20s and '30s, making Babe Ruths into larger-than-life figures. On the other hand, we do go a little too far in terms of competitive nature and the explosion of the number of media and the desire for everyone to get a piece of the pie, the pressure to produce something that is noteworthy—and normally, that can be a more trivial matter that is made into something noteworthy."

But should college sports, which are amateur in concept at the very least, receive the same media scrutiny as their professional counterparts? And, by default, should college athletes be immune from scrutiny of their personal lives?

"There are different schools of thought," Aldridge explains. "You shouldn't criticize people who aren't paid, leaving aside the question whether college athletes are being paid. I don't think the scrutiny is quite as harsh and searing on college athletes as it is on pro athletes. There are a certain number of transactions that get scrutiny, but not a lot nationally. But they may be big stories in that town where the college is. That is just the nature of the beast."

And, Aldridge believes that networks that cover sports are not as aggressive on "bad stories" as they are on good, because it would give the appearance of biting the hand that feeds them. "Many don't come down that hard at what happens negatively."

Steve Weiberg, who has covered college sports for *USA Today* for 20 years, agrees with both Wilbon and Aldridge that money and TV have been factors in the way the media currently covers college sports. But for many college programs, he believes, the pressure is on not the money they make but more on the money they want to make.

"There is more pressure for top football schools to be self-supporting," Weiberg says, "and not only self-supporting, but in a lot of cases, football subsidizes other sports."[3]

He uses the University of Oklahoma as an example, saying that football had been foundering there a few years ago until they got the right coach in Bob Stoops, who produced a national championship, "and everything is beautiful there. They are sinking money into other sports and they are prospering. What there really was is pressure to make the money work. So, you have this whole pressure dynamic going on, as well as a big business."

USA Today, other newspapers, and television play a role in that dynamic, Weiberg asserts.

> We are another media entity out there. Schools are aware of that, and schools like to have their names in a positive light, because it is a national newspaper.
>
> But I don't think we, the *LA Times*, the *New York Post*, or anything outside of *Sports Illustrated* has had the impact that ESPN has had and that is because of the immediacy of it and popularity of it. How many people, young people, are tuning into *Sports Center*?
>
> And it is not just *Sports Center*, but the other media outlets on ESPN as well. *Pardon the Interruption* is hugely popular among the college crowd. You can't underplay the impact of ESPN. We are not setting starting times (of games). We are not moving basketball games to midnight. We are not moving college football to Thursday and Friday night. That is a college thing to get more media attention. Some say that is good and bad.

In general, media exposure is good for college sports, Weiberg claims. "Schools love the exposure, just at what cost? That cost could be the public view of selling out by moving games. The high school football people are not happy. Schools that have to tip off late at night and play into the wee hours of the morning are not happy."

But, for the most part, people like to get as much information as possible, says Weiberg, particularly when there are classic matches. "The Texas-Oklahoma [football] game—I wrote stories going into that game," he recalls, "which people want, and I wrote a story out of the game. I was not a public relations firm beating the drum for the game; I was presenting information they wanted to read. Does that build the hype? Certainly, but I am not going into it with the idea of beefing up the crowd. My job was to give information they want to read, and in the process that hypes the game."

Weiberg believes journalists do not have to sacrifice impartiality to cover a sporting event, which is a news event just like a war or a fire or anything else with news value. And, according to Weiberg, it is that impartiality that permits the same sports journalist to write about harder edge stories, such as personal scandal or a National Collegiate Athletic Association (NCAA) investigation.

Weiberg recalls that in the early 1980s, when academic reform was being debated in the NCAA and Proposition 48 resulted, it was no accident that the Southwestern Conference was beset with scandal after scandal.

> Southern Methodist University was not playing football because of scandal. People were realizing how important a scandal could impact on a school. Now, we had these new sets of academic rules that required a certain number of freshman athletes to sit out of competition—that's a big deal if it is the wrong players.
>
> If my favorite football players are not going to play, that is a big deal to me as a fan. I do think this might be the place where *USA Today* had an impact. We immediately jumped on that coverage. We did hit Prop 48 hard, and then the mainstream media started paying attention to it.
>
> Also, the NCAA began compiling graduation rates. That was a yardstick to measure how well a school was adhering to its academic calling, and that was something that was national publicity. It was local also. Every school had athletes' graduation rates, and it mushroomed from there. Only a handful of publications carry issues on a national basis, but every local paper looks at things in its area.

It also meant that the media scrutinized a lot more than graduation rates, Weiberg says. "We are long gone from the era where the media rode the train with the teams and played cards from city to city," he explains.

> That doesn't happen any more. The media has become more aggressive, and for me, uncomfortably so. I am uncomfortable doing a stakeout in the front yards of media suspects.
>
> This is the era of Scott Peterson, of O.J., you name the story, and there are so many more media than there used to be. There is the rise of broadcast media and beaming pictures nationally and across the world. And, somewhat uncomfortably so, it naturally extended into sports, and without a doubt, there are times when the media is sensationalist. A 90-yard touchdown is news, and so is the star running back that ended up on the police blotter. The networks discovered that this is news as well.

Talk radio and the Internet also fueled the flames, according to Weiberg. "But where is it going? I do see a trend for the media to become more sensationalists. They are tripping all over themselves and overdoing things. Now, I don't think they can go back to covering the game and writing puff pieces and going home and having dinner."

He reflects that the media has done a lot of good, going beyond the game, because without the media scrutiny of graduation rates, many schools would not even make the effort to improve graduation rates, which many have. Those who do not still must face the scrutiny—and often the embarrassment that a low graduation rates brings.

And, he concedes, when the media camps at the door step of a college sports program, it is sometimes warranted.

He uses as an example the scandal at Baylor a couple of years ago, where a star player disappeared and later turned up murdered, and the accused killer was a teammate. Later, the coach of the team was forced to resign after he made up a story that the murdered player was a drug pusher. "Here was a story that played out the way it should have," Weiberg concludes.

But what about other stories, where coaches lie about their résumé or players make accusations about under-the-table payments that often cannot be proved, but are media fodder? "Some should have suffered consequences, yes, but I am not sure if their career should have ended," Weiberg said. "Some didn't get certain jobs, but their career didn't end. It shouldn't haunt them for the rest of their lives."

And, he adds, college athletes—just because they are college athletes— should not be immune. "I don't think you ignore transgressions because of youth," Weiberg says, "if they are serious transgressions." Look at the University of Colorado, he suggests, where several athletes were accused of sexual misconduct. It garnered national attention and led to reforms, not only at Colorado but also at other schools that wanted to avoid similar disgrace.

"You can argue over the scope of coverage at Colorado, but national reforms are in place because of that," Weinberg asserts.

> We should be aware that we are dealing with people in terms of them still doing silly things. It is not national news if a kid has too many parking tickets, and, it is a stupid thing to park in handicapped spaces. It is the kind of things college kids do. It is wrong, yes, but is it a federal offense? No.
>
> At Baylor, there were serious transgressions. You have to use common sense, which the media doesn't always use as we trip over each other to get the sensational.

And, the media can also expose other wrongs, Weiberg says, as it has in recent years, with coverage on the lack of diversity and equity in college sports—particularly in the poor graduation rates of black athletes and the lack of minority hiring.

> I do think the media is more sensitive to those issues, but we also have more watchdog groups out there like Rainbow/PUSH and the Black Coaches Association.
>
> We are in an era now where congressmen, at the drop of a hat, are holding congressional hearings about colleges and the lack of minority hiring. This makes more sense than a whole lot of issues they have held hearings on. This is a good part of media attention. For the most part, the media serves an extremely valuable purpose, but sometimes we cross the line and sensationalism takes over, and I am not sure what purpose that serves than to lower the common denominator.

That the media is taking a bigger interest in diversity in sports, or the lack thereof, is one positive of a sports reporter's job not ending on the field of competition, claims Floyd Keith, executive director of the Black Coaches Association. "If we can get scrutiny about the lack of blacks as athletics directors, as coaches, we are accomplishing our objective," Keith says.[4]

> One of our whole approaches to this is awareness and knowledge. That is crucial, because a lot of people just don't know and it is up to the media to educate the public. For years, the sports media ignored that.
>
> Now, it is easier to get the message out, and it is even more important to the media if it is a high-profile position, like the job at Notre Dame when Ty Willingham was hired [he has subsequently been fired].
>
> Across the board, unfortunately, there is also a gender issue. The media doesn't really jump up and down about women's basketball, and that has had an effect. We have probably gotten better in 15 years, but there is still something that needs to be done. The media, in a lot of cases, determine who is a capable candidate for a job. Local coverage is important, because if local people don't feel sensitivity, then it doesn't matter what national-level institutions do in hiring.

Keith adds:

> I understand the media game and that it is all about business and they print what people want to read. If it is not controversial, it isn't front and center. The media does affect names and does affect hiring, even though it is often not that obvious to them.
>
> The media creates conscientiousness and a credible need to be aware of positions when job openings occur and what names to promote. The media needs to be diverse in promoting and in being concerned about what they put out there. It shouldn't all be magnifications of job changes, or jumping the gun on coaches who are struggling to build programs.

"Sometimes that has nothing to do with race," Keith states, "but the impact it can have on minorities is something the media has to be mindful of as part of its responsibilities. It is no longer just who won the game."

NOTES

1. Interview with Mike Wilbon, September 2004.
2. Interview with David Aldridge, October 2004.
3. Interview with Steve Weiberg, September 2004.
4. Interview with Floyd Keith, October 2004.

PART II

The Players

CHAPTER 12

Presidents' Forum

John DiBiaggio Tufts University
Joe Crowley University of Nevada
John C. Hitt University of Central Florida
W. Roger Webb University of Central Oklahoma

IMPORTANT ISSUES IN ACADEMICS AND ATHLETICS

RL: Many academic advisors told me that their job was to keep student-athletes eligible rather than leading them towards academic success. Do you think that is a general problem on campuses? If so, what can be done to help the academic services staff?

RW: I think it is true. The fact is that many of the coaches and athletic administrators believe that it is their responsibility, which obviously results from the pressure of winning. The pressure is to win and increase revenues. Totally decent human beings get caught up in that competitive pressure and do things outside of their normal personality. It happens every day with coaches and athletic administrators who try to get the edge, get players into school, stay eligible, and to stay in school. We don't do enough as presidents to bring the athletic directors into the mainstream of the academic program. I have been experimenting here with making our athletics director part of my executive team so he can truly understand the mission, goals, and objectives of the university. He can then share that with his coaches and have a much better understanding of what we stand for as a university. To some extent, it also helps take the pressure off the coaches to bend the rules.

JC: When we created the academic support staff at the University of Nevada, we put it under the academic vice president. I discovered that it was bifurcated when I came to San Jose State. There were some staff under the provost and some under athletics. We moved all the academic support staff to the provost's office, where it belonged. While it does not ensure that coaches won't put some pressure on the staff, it certainly gives the staffers a kind of protection that they wouldn't have if they are housed in athletics.

JD: You may recall that the Knight Commission's one in the one plus three model was presidential control and engagement. There are a number of presidents in the country, and you're talking to some of them, who have made an effort to be well advised as to what is happening within their athletic departments. However, there are others who really have not done so, or have not been very much engaged in decision-making at the NCAA level. I was disappointed myself, after we had gone through the Knight Commission exercise and after the NCAA had reorganized itself, that there were still presidents who were not really deeply involved. That is unfortunate because institutional integrity and leadership is really what the issue is all about. The NCAA can't address these issues alone. They have to be addressed at the local level.

COMMERCIALIZATION OF COLLEGE SPORT

JC: The challenge that concerns me the most is the ever-increasing commercialism of college sports, one consequence of which is the growing set of differences between the haves and have-nots. It is changing the landscape in a way that we can't fully appreciate. But soon enough, we will know that it has changed quite dramatically from what it was once envisioned to be. I think money is just driving the engine in a way that is hard for me to defend. It seems the logic of the process is to continue to increase commercialization, increase spending, and further widen the gap in Division IA. At this point, I don't see any way of doing enough to inhibit that logic from playing itself out to an unhappy ending. But we shouldn't stop trying.

JD: Intercollegiate athletics is looking more and more like professional sports. It forces people into a circumstance where they cut corners academically, continuously erect new facilities, and enhance salaries being paid to coaches. Recently a basketball coach received a $500,000 increase in base salary, and that did not include what he received from outside sources. These things just keep ratcheting up. Unless we find some way to control it, we're not going to be able to handle all the other fundamental issues of our institutions.

JH: Now there is the challenge that Tulane President Scott Cowen has made to the BCS.[1] Some are looking at that and wondering how it will go. What he is responding to is the cartel-like behavior of the BCS conferences, who have locked up an enormous cash flow machine and determine who can participate in this revenue stream. It doesn't really matter if Tulane is 11-0, because they are not going to be able to be a part of it. The major bowl games are locked up. There are that fortunate group of 30 to 50 institutions that are pretty well taken care of in that process, and then there is a much larger group who are struggling because they are locked out. In moments of candor, folks from BCS schools say they are not going to let happen to football what happened with the basketball tournament when the NCAA took it over and the revenue was shared with everybody. Commercialism is alive and well and seems to be becoming even stronger in the whole process.

Even if you are blessed to be at a very wealthy institution, there are always more demands on those funds than there really are funds to meet them. However, if you are in a BCS athletic conference, then there is serious revenue potential. If your budget is $30 million a year for athletics, you have the resources to bring to bear on some of these questions that others simply do not have. It's a little less challenging in some ways if you can throw a good bit of money at a problem like this for staff and facilities than if you have to really scramble for funding.

RL: Do you see ways to contain costs of these large athletics programs at this point?

JH: It is difficult to see how to contain costs without in some ways doing more harm than good. I don't know if President Cowen has the right idea or not. Based on my experience, I am certainly reluctant to suggest that the Congress ought to step in and do something. When we ask the government to get involved in something, we often get a different solution than we hoped for. Even though we can certainly criticize the basketball championship, we do find little-known schools that have a fine year and manage to spring upsets. There may even be a way of handling football so that it's more equitable.

JD: I am not sure you can achieve this through legislation because, frankly, there is always going to be the potential of a restraint of trade court challenge. I think it is a moral responsibility on the part of institutions to recognize that there is something wrong with all of this. This is not acceptable behavior. A corollary can be drawn to affirmative action. When the California resolution was passed eliminating affirmative action, our faculty asked what that would mean to us. I said "not a thing," because we believe diversity is being morally right, educationally sound, and pragmatically necessary. I didn't care at all what the California legislation said. We were still going to stay committed to a program where we would actively recruit underrepresented groups who were qualified for admittance and employment. We would serve the society in the way for which we were created. The reality is that cost containment is not something that the NCAA can address. This has to come from the institutions themselves. When will people finally stand up? After the debacle with the ACC taking in Miami and Virginia Tech, there were then reports of behavior which was not acceptable. You would think there would have been a huge outcry and people would have said, "ok, it's time we do something about this."

I think the institutions could control it if they really wished to. If they believed in the spirit of fair play, all institutions would have the same opportunity to participate in any kind of postseason experience. Apparently this is not occurring.

JC: It's an interesting point that you make because, as you recall, it was a fairly widespread scandal that gave birth to the reform movement in the '80s. In one conference (and maybe more than one), most member schools had major, highly publicized violations. Student-athletes who had gone through four years were coming forward to capture the public's attention when they said they didn't know how to read after playing four years. That sort of thing helped get the reform movement started, the Knight Commission going, and produced some useful results. But we were not focused on financial integrity. One of the Knight Commission's recommendations was in that area. The NCAA never had much success at cost control, though that was not for a lack of trying. There must have been three or four committees charged with looking at that. There was a lot of hard work done but with few substantial changes.

I don't think cost control is a way of getting after this problem. We should be concerned that we let this happen to intercollegiate athletics. We have BCS bowl games with a payout of $13.5 million. I believe that sums like that are very hard to defend in the realm of higher education. I know I cannot defend them. Similarly, coaches' contracts are in the millions. It may be okay for the pros, for Hollywood, for the entertainment business in general, but I think it's a big problem for higher education. Maybe some moral fervor on the part of campuses, the faculties, the media, and the public could help affect some change here. Right now, I just don't see the likelihood of that change occurring absent a major scandal or some kind of catastrophe.

JD: However, you would think that the Baylor situation, which is so outrageous, would have influenced a number of people to say that things are out of hand. Hopefully, it still will. With the ACC, the embarrassing thing was that the only reason they were talking about incorporating other institutions was in order to have a playoff to generate more income. That is a terrible reason. If they have good academic or geographic reasons for making an argument for expansion, then perhaps their case would have been valid, but that wasn't the case at all.

JH: But look at the conference they raided. Dave Gavitt put the Big East together based on television. It was kind of funny how it all came apart, but if you go back to its premise, it was that there was a great market for basketball in those cities. We can all find things to criticize with the NCAA basketball tournament, but if you look at the commercialism of it, it is still probably a lot more open and fair than anything in the current bowl system.

JD: It's a bit easier to do because in basketball you can play two times a week. You cannot possibly do that in football. Yet Division III has structured a playoff system where the teams that reach the championship would be playing

14 games. That is almost as many as the pros, and I feel that is outrageous in Division III.

COST CONTAINMENT

JC: If you are looking at significant issues over the next 5 to 10 years, then obviously the acceleration of costs and the need for cost containment would be one of them. Next there is the proliferation of the number of games. With the saturation of games, we bump the season up in football to before Labor Day, and it continues into January. With 50 to 70 baseball games that are being played, it is difficult for a student in the spring semester to play the sport and meet the academic demands. We see this saturation on television as well. On Saturdays, we have games (in the Western time zone) that can run from 9 a.m. to 11 p.m., which then absolutely floods the market and has had a really serious impact in Division IAA, II, and III schools, which do not have much access to football television. Go back to when college football was regulated by the NCAA. In the 1970s and '80s, say, you got up on a Saturday morning, looked at the sports pages and found that maybe one regional game and one national game would be aired that day. Now you have 12 to 14 games, and people don't have to drive long distances to see top football. I imagine this has impacted small-college America in terms of game attendance.

JD: There is the fundamental economic principle that your expenses rise to meet your income. However, in athletics the expenses exceed income almost annually at most institutions. The idea that we're generating money in order to enhance the institution financially is not true. If you include the cost of facilities, the reality is that virtually none of the athletics programs are making money. You ask yourself: What is the driving force that compels these institutions to spend more and more? What happens is that lots of compromises are made, and some of those involve student-athletes and their academic performance. In some cases, we ask for outrageous time commitments on the part of the athletes.

We interviewed a youngster from Auburn at a Knight Commission meeting. I asked him how many hours he spent at football weekly. He said the NCAA has a requirement that you can only spend 20 hours. I again said, "How many hours do you actually spend?" He said he spent time in the weight room, although that's not part of the official program. He finally said that altogether he spent maybe 35 hours. I asked if he could do without the weight room. He said if you do you won't play, because the coaches observe time lifting. The reality is that here was a youngster, who might have come in marginally prepared academically, who had to spend 35 hours a week with his sport between practice, travel, playing, and outside-of-practice preparation. How can you anticipate that such a student can legitimately perform in the classroom? It's unreasonable, and it is not just 35 hours a week during the school year but it's now year-round.

That's definitely unfair to the youngster and that is why I, unsuccessfully, argued for freshman ineligibility at the Knight Commission. While I was concerned about student-athletes in some sports, like swimming, who have to be involved year-round if they are going to compete in the Olympics, I think it would help many if they had a least a year to prepare themselves and to develop study skills needed to succeed.

JH: The fact that we are really not making any money is starting to be better understood. However, there is still a widespread assumption among the general public that we're doing all of this for money. In our case, we are not making money from football, basketball, or any other intercollegiate sport. Why do we do it? In part it is because it is one of the things you do in the Southeast culture if you want to be taken seriously as a major university. Emory is probably the only really good southeastern university that isn't in big-time athletics. Maybe I'm overlooking somebody, but it is just the way the world is wired in the Southeast.

JC: I think we're talking about religion when we are in the Southeast and places like Texas, but John, you probably experienced it at Michigan State. There is this mystical tie in the public mind between the quality of an institution and the success of its athletic program. I guess it is what keeps us in the business.

JD: That's not reality, because there have been a number of studies that indicate that winning teams do not result in greater contributions to the institution, other than to athletics. Winning teams don't seem to impact the quality of the students an institution attracts, either. There have been a number of institutions that, after remarkable seasons saw an increase in the numbers of students applying, the quality of those students stayed consistent. The reality is that outside of getting increased press, a winning team doesn't necessarily translate into more money for the institution, particularly for its academic programs.

JC: I agree. I am talking about something else that I don't know exactly how to explain. However, for a significant part of the public, somehow having a Division IA athletic program translates into your institution being a better institution.

JH: We all say we know that's not the case, but I would agree that, at least in some parts of the country, to be taken seriously as a major university you must have a successful Division IA program. I'm not saying that's true, but that's how the public perception runs.

JD: You know a component of an institution where this can easily occur is athletics. There is also the perception that if mischief is occurring within athletics, then perhaps it's happening throughout the institution. That's a danger. If there is a lack of integrity in one part of the institution, perhaps it exists throughout the entire institution.

RELATIONSHIP BETWEEN PRESIDENTS
AND ATHLETICS DIRECTORS

RL: What has been the relationship between you and your AD [athletics director]?

JH: Our AD is part of the president's advisory staff. We have two groups who meet separately, the VPs and a somewhat larger group of university administrators who meet every other week. Bringing the AD in on part of that is a good thing. It certainly helps the AD understand the larger university issues. It also has given the AD a chance to share what the athletics department is trying to accomplish with a group of key people in the university. Beyond that, I have had a very close working relationship with all three ADs at the University of Central Florida and at the University of Maine when I was interim president. I have really enjoyed the relationship we've had at UCF. At the same time, I have a sense that athletics, while it has so many good aspects, has a tremendous potential to go wrong for you. So if you do not spend some time with your AD learning about what he or she is doing and trying to make sure that he or she is informed about what your own standards are, you are courting disaster.

RL: Did boosters cause problems?

JH: We have not had any serious problems. We had people who had good intentions but wanted to do things that would violate NCAA rules. If the AD had people who were deliberately trying to do things that were unethical or improper, then I do not know about them. I do not want to be so arrogant as to say that something like that has not occurred, but I am not aware of it if it did. We had people who wanted to extend courtesies to families of players or to players that in the opinion of the AD and myself would have violated NCAA rules. We were able to head those off. We have not found anything serious like paying players. I am confident that has not happened.

RL: Are you knowledgeable about individual coaches' contracts?

JH: In the major sports, yes. I am aware of what we are paying and what the perks are for basketball, baseball, and football. I must confess that I typically do not pay much attention to what we do in Olympic sports. We do not pay large salaries, and there are not a whole lot of perks in these sports. I pay attention to the NCAA rules and to athletics-related income and expenses in all sports.

RL: Do you have information on academics issues?

JH: There has never been an issue of not being able to get information if I wanted. Steve Orisini, our current AD, was never a coach and has always been involved in administration of both professional or collegiate sports. He has a more organized system of getting me information, but I have always been able to get all of the information I wanted in a timely and complete manner.

JD: I was at the University of Connecticut when John Toner was AD. He was also president of the NCAA at that time. He really educated me about the NCAA and was the one who got me involved with the NCAA, which I have always appreciated. He was a man of enormous integrity, and I trusted him completely. He kept me very well informed about his activities and had the right attitude about intercollegiate athletics, particularly at the Division I level. He monitored academic performance and kept me informed as to how the student-athletes were doing. It was a plus, but it turned out to be a negative. I went to Michigan State with that kind of confidence and trust in an AD. I believed I would be well informed about everything and behaved accordingly. I developed what I thought was a good relationship with the AD but then discovered there was a lot that I was not being told. Indeed there was something happening in the department that I should have been advised of because we were together regularly. I even had a very good relationship with the coaches and went into locker rooms of both men's and women's teams to talk to players. I traveled with the teams often and thought I had a very good relationship with everyone. Then our football coach decided that after the AD stepped aside, he should be both AD and coach. (All of this was prearranged with the outgoing AD.) I did not think that was rational, but the coach worked behind my back with trustees. Despite the fact that under their own by-laws they could not make an appointment that I had not endorsed, he got appointed to both positions without my recommendation. It turned out to be a very difficult situation. Unfortunately, I had trust in the integrity of people in those roles. Even reports on what the coaches were really generating in income from various sources were not totally accurate.

When I went to Tufts, a Division III school, we had a wonderful AD who was involved with the NCAA and was a man with tremendous integrity. He rekindled my faith in the system. So, you cannot make a blanket condemnation of ADs. Perhaps it was the pressure to succeed at MSU, or a culture that had developed in which the AD did not feel a responsibility to keep the administration well informed as to what was happening. I do not make the assumption that this is the case at every institution, but it certainly has been the case in at least a few where national reports indicate the ADs have not been monitoring their programs as closely as they might have.

At that time, there were also issues with boosters. There were one or two boosters who we had to take action against, after an NCAA investigation. Before I arrived, there was a rather serious case of that kind and there was a major investigation at Michigan State. I read the outcome, but I do not know if the NCAA was well informed as to what went on. The president at the time took very aggressive action to address the issue. Again, it just shows that presidents can be doing their job and doing it well without being fully aware of what is happening within the athletic enterprise. If you look at the budget of a university, athletics is a relatively small fraction. The president has lots of other things to oversee. You cannot spend all of your time on athletics, because you have to address other issues.

In a Big 10 university, it is astonishing how many people have their hands in athletics. I am not just talking about trustees, but also governors and members of the legislature. It is not just boosters. Boosters did not give me a big problem. They knew that I liked athletics and was a supporter, and they did not intrude on our efforts. They did ask me a question when I was on the Knight Commission. "If you do what you are suggesting in the Knight Commission report, what will that do to our athletics program?" My answer was if we are playing an arch rival like Notre Dame or Michigan and all of our players on the field have "B" averages, do you think there will be fewer people in the stands? If all of the players are equivalent, it will be equally competitive and interesting, and that should make us feel good about who we are. That seemed to address the issue as far as they were concerned. The trustees were my problem. So were people in government, rather than boosters at Michigan State. People who supported athletics supported me.

RW: In my experience with two universities over the past 24 years, I have worked closely with four ADs. As I think back, the relationship has evolved from the traditionally distant and hands off in the '70s and '80s to one that is very close. Awareness of what is going on throughout the university extends to a much greater extent to the ADs that I have worked with in the past. Administrators and faculty have a greater understanding of the issues and problems surrounding the program itself because of this relationship. The profile of the AD has changed as well as this relationship. An old-style AD saw his responsibility as being sure the lights got turned off at the field or the gym officials got paid. The AD today is much more professional, with a business background or experience in public relations, marketing, or as an entrepreneur. The AD is a spokesperson for the university as well as the athletics program. My relationship, and my understanding of the role of the presidents as it relates to athletics, has also changed and matured. The job of the AD and relationship to the university is much more involved in a positive way.

JC: I had two ADs at Nevada. I inherited one and appointed the other. The one I appointed served 18 years and has just left the job to return to coaching. When I became president, the university was in the middle of a messy athletics violation situation that had gone to court. There was a recruiting problem. According to the NCAA, a player had been improperly recruited because he was not eligible. The university was ordered not to allow him to play, but the athlete sued, went to court, and got to play. At that time, the AD did not report to the president. I changed that right away, but I never had the AD as a member of the central staff that met regularly. I met with him regularly and assured him he would meet with VPs on a regular basis as well. The AD I inherited was an old-school guy. He was a former player, coach, and general university good guy who kept the place in good working order. He left after a few years, and then we hired our football coach as our AD. He was an enormously successful coach. I had some concerns about the transition to the AD position, which was then in the early stages of moving to the business model that others have described. The AD and I met before I appointed him, to reach an agreement. He knew I would expect that the job required an understanding that athletics was increasingly a business, an understanding that entrepreneurial capabilities would be required, an understanding of the need to work with the academic side of the house, and that we had as a priority doing the proper job with gender issues. Some time on my part was required to working with him on these matters in the transition. He became a very good and successful AD. In my 23 years as president in Nevada, we did not have a major NCAA violation. We did make progress in all of the areas. I met with him frequently. We had a very candid relationship with each other in terms of subjects that we talked about, and he kept me fully informed.

We were the only game in town, so athletics was extremely visible in the local media. I got acquainted with that right away. On one occasion, early on, we had to appoint a new basketball coach and a new academic vice president at almost the same time. The appointment of the basketball coach was a media magnet. Reporters practically parked on my doorstep and called me regularly. So the press conference, by Reno's standards, was huge. A couple of weeks later we appointed the academic vice president. There was no press conference. We were able to get a story in the second section of the paper on page 12, or thereabouts, and it was one paragraph long. It gave a sense, not that I needed it, of how the public weighs the importance of athletics versus academics. I learned from those early experiences that I had to keep in close touch with athletics and have the right person in the AD job. In looking at the whole experience, I would say it has worked out pretty well.

JD: When I arrived at Michigan State, the AD reported to the vice president for administration and finance. That was true for some time and was a very comfortable arrangement for the AD. I ultimately had the AD report to the provost to make it clear that academic performance of the athletes was important.

JH: At UCF the AD reports directly to the president. The academic support area for athletics reports to the provost office.

JD: That was difficult to do at Michigan State because of its size. At least we sent some kind of message when we had athletics report to the provost.

HIRING COACHES

JC: At the Division IA level, it is important for the president to be involved in hiring of coaches in the major sports, where there is potential for things to go astray. In this era we see embarrassing instances that come as no surprise because we have created a situation where coaches in Division IA often become "princes of the realm," with huge salaries, compensation packages, and sometimes an outsized sense of their importance in the scheme of things. If you have that kind of standing and salary, some people think that they can do whatever they want because they are now, indeed, princely people. Even good, solid people can surrender to the temptations. The one thing that can be done is for presidents to be involved in the appointment process, be clear about their expectations generally, and be very clear about the expectations with regard to coaches' behavior.

JD: The basketball coaches addressed this because they have people in their own ranks whose behavior has been less than ideal. In the Big 10, we discussed this issue at great lengths, because we had some coaches whose behavior was embarrassing to the conference and should have been equally embarrassing to their universities. We really did not have the authority to do much about it except to suspend a coach for a game or two. Even when we did, our authority to do so was challenged by the university, or the state that they represented, because the majority were state institutions. In a few of the cases the behavior was so outrageous you would have thought there would have been a huge public outcry over it. Rather than that, the coach was defended against any president who tried to take actions to change the situation.

Myles could not fire Bobby Knight until his behavior became so outrageous that the board of trustees and the chairperson were compelled to support him. When Ohio State fired Woody Hayes, after that incredible incident when he hit an opposing player on the sidelines on television, the president was condemned by many of the people in Ohio. Some coaches become bigger than life.

JH: We play at a lower level than the Big 10. We had to release a football coach when he got involved in a cover-up of a relatively small problem that ended up in the courts. There are still some friends who hold that against me because they think I should have found some way to keep him as a football coach even though he was adjudicated as a felon in a federal court on a plea deal. They believe the only thing that he did wrong was to get caught. That is just how society is these days. Even at our level of playing competition, people develop strong values with regard to how we treat our coaches.

JH: If you were to give a paper and pencil test on morality and ethics, you'd find that most people know what is right and what is wrong. In abstract or objective situations, they will not have a problem telling you what is unethical or improper. But when they are immersed in a real situation, they may lose their moral compass. Yet in that more abstract or impersonal realm, they would have been able to tell you that the behavior that got them into trouble was improper, immoral, or unethical.

JD: The reality is we know what is right and wrong, and ADs know what is right and wrong. We all have a moral compass. There is no question when they do something inappropriate that they know it is inappropriate and it should not be done. It is like the Supreme Court justice who said, "I cannot define pornography, but I know it when I see it." You might not be able to clearly define what you mean by ethics, but when there is a violation of ethics, you know it is there. It would not hurt to have such a course, but I do not think it would do any good.

RL: Would you consider coaches who had problems at other universities?

JH: You would like to think that there is a possibility that people will learn from their mistakes, and we would all like to believe that there is redemption. It would be pretty hard for me to appoint, or allow to be appointed, someone who had been involved in a serious ethical problem, because the programs are so prominent. We try so hard to get the people to know that we want to do the right thing the right way. But you always at least want to give someone the chance to explain why this could be a good idea.

JD: It would depend on the seriousness of the issues and whether it was something that resulted from a misunderstanding or was because of personal behavior. I was interviewed by a reporter about Bobby Knight when he was being appointed at Texas Tech. I knew him and had contact with him in the Big 10. I was asked would I hire Knight if I was president at Texas Tech. My response was that Bobby is a very good coach. He is also very serious about having his students perform acceptably in the classroom, but his behavior and comments are often outrageous. Further, his complete lack of respect for authority made it impossible for anyone to work with him. My answer was I doubt I would hire him, but if I were to, I would need the equivalent of a prenuptial agreement, so that if his previous misbehavior continued, I would have the right to dismiss him.

RL: How much do you weigh the role of a coach as an educator?

JH: You must ask if the welfare of the development of student-athletes is a real issue for you. Are you the kind of coach or athletic administrator who looks only to win and see student-athletes as instrumental in that, or do you care enough about them to help them get an education and develop as young men and women? You have to try to ascertain that and come up with people who are really committed to those values. At the Division IA level, you hope for that, but they also have to win. You are looking for the person who has those values but also can win for you. We have an incentive that we need to expand on and do better with. It is not so much in the individual coach's contracts at this point, but it needs to be in the future. We give modest bonuses to the coach whose team has the highest GPA and highest graduation rate. As we do new contracts in the future, we need to include such incentives for football and basketball coaches. There are very few Division IA schools where the basketball or football program is going to beat out women's track or swimming to have the best GPA or graduation rate. It might happen, but it will be rare.

JC: Before the era of published graduation rates, we were hiring a basketball coach who was a good, ethical fellow. I was also interested in how he saw his role as an educator. I asked how well student-athletes did in the classroom in his previous coaching assignments. His response was "every student-athlete that I ever recruited and who played for me graduated, except for one." I was most impressed with that, because he struck me as a sincere guy. I later discovered that maybe what he meant to say was that "every student-athlete that I ever recruited and who played for me *did not* graduate, except for one." He did not make that a high priority. He felt student-athletes benefited by simply being part of a higher education institution, and it did not matter all that much if they graduated.

These days you have to think of better ways to ask questions. You now have access to information that you did not have access to years ago. You have to make a judgment based on that information and also ask yourself, "what is your gut feeling about this person," assuming that part of what you are interested in is having a coach who is going to understand the importance of the academic side, of the "student" component of the student-athlete equation. You have to be clear with him or her that the expectation is simply one for the entire department and university. Everyone expects the AD to pursue that with the coaches. But even then there is no guarantee. Even those with incentives in contracts to assure performance, if you have someone who is winning a lot of basketball games but whose players are not graduating, you find yourself in the same kind of spot that John DiBiaggio found himself in with his football coach. Those decisions are sometimes made for you outside of your office.

JD: There is one thing you can give coaches, not that they always honor them. Long-term contracts remove some pressure and reduce the temptation to violate in order to win. It also depends on how you define winning. I gave all of the major coaches at Michigan State long-term contracts. I told them they would not lose their jobs while I was there because of their won/lost records, but they would if I found that they were seriously violating academic standards or breaking NCAA rules. That does not mean that I did not expect us to be competitive, but I felt we did not have to win the conference or be national champions every year. As long as we were interesting, I promised to defend them. I did on occasion defend coaches when I thought they were doing the right thing with the team. The president can set the tone.

RW: That philosophy is the exception and not the rule. College coaches in America feel the pressure to win from the alumni, media, and often from the president more often than they feel pressure to improve graduation rates.

JD: They put that pressure on themselves for their own national visibility and to attract income from other sources. Sometimes their loyalty does not rest with the institution, but rather with their own reputations. I can say that about faculty as well.

RW: Faculty are not paid $2.4 million annually, like the head coach of University of Oklahoma.

JD: If you assume that every coach you hire is going to take you to the national championship, that is like assuming every faculty member you hire is going to be a Nobel Prize recipient.

NOTE

1. The Bowl Championship Series (BCS) was formed to determine the national champion for college football while maintaining the current bowl system that is nearly 100 years old. The BCS consists of the Rose Bowl, Nokia Sugar Bowl, FedEx Orange Bowl, and the Tostitos Fiesta Bowl. Those bowls joined with the ACC, Big East, Big 12, Big 10, Pac-10, and SEC conferences and the University of Notre Dame to form the BCS.

CHAPTER 13

Conference Commissioners' Forum

Jim Delany Big Ten
Mike Slive SEC
Patty Viverito Gateway Football
Chris Monasch America East
Kevin L. Weiberg Big Twelve

GRADUATION RATES: INCENTIVES/DISINCENTIVES

RL: Myles Brand has proposed incentives and disincentives for graduation rates. These are the first major sanctions in the area of academics and athletics. What would be the most effective forms of incentives and disincentives?

JD: I think that it is a novel and creative response to some of the problems that we have. Historically, we have tried to address the academic challenges on the front end either by initial eligibility rules or continuing eligibility rules, and those are probably worthwhile approaches. But I think the incentive/disincentive approach gives us a more focused way of addressing underperformance and, in cases where you have excellence, rewarding that. It also is precise in that it focuses on teams. A lot of the criticism of the NCAA has been by the media and the public regarding teams doing really well in tournaments and bowls and other championships but not having good graduation rates. Incentives/disincentives is really meant to focus primarily on those who I would describe as "habitual underperformers," where there appears to be almost no support for the academic goals of student-athletes. I think that we will work through the problems that we have, have standards, and have notice with incremental penalties. I welcome it.

PV: I support the idea. I hope that we avoid using dollars as the big carrot or big stick in incentives or disincentives. I think there are other means, including postseason access, scholarships, or recruiting restrictions. It seems when we use the dollar to reward or punish, the system is impacted in negative ways.

MS: The one area that creates some discomfort is the question of incentives. Disincentives are clear but there are some, myself included, who wonder whether there ought to be any incentives at all. How do you measure the incentives? Do we need to be rewarded for doing good?

JD: There is very little support within the working committee which I serve on either with the respect of the use of dollars for incentives or disincentives, except to the extent that dollars might be tied to championship access. A restriction with respect to the postseason play obviously carries a financial penalty. In regard to Mike's comments, we wouldn't be at the table except for bad performance. If we had exceptional performance, they would never have created our committee.

It has been interesting how much effort there has been to gain some level of symmetry between the incentive and disincentive. That has mostly come from presidents. I think that their notion is they don't want to make this too draconian or give a sense that we are only concerned about the underachievers. The committee struggled with that. It will have something positive to say about overperformers but not spend as much time on that side as the disincentive side.

CM: This is really about the decisions people make on which student-athletes they choose to recruit and which they choose not to recruit. We have debated eligibility standards for many years. There has always been much discussion on how those standards impact on the African-American athletes. I do not hear that discussion regarding the incentives/disincentives issue. Depending on where the standards we set fall and how high the expectation is for graduation rates, it has the potential to impact the demographic makeup of our student-athlete population.

JD: That is a good point. It is hard to have a discussion about football and basketball recruitment and academic standards without the race issue rising. I think one of the reasons it hasn't arisen is almost everybody who is involved understands that you can provide an opportunity but you can't guarantee an outcome. Once there has been an effort to provide academic support, the outcome is really between the individual, the institution, and the institution's relationship to the larger community. If the system is focused on the habitual offender—which is defined as a school which graduates no one or at such a low rate that it is an embarrassment to the program, the institution, and the NCAA—then I really think race is irrelevant. There would have been a failure in the identification of qualified student-athletes, a failure by the student-athlete, and a failure by the institution. If you understand that the filters are intended to identify the habitual offenders, I don't think that race ought to be the question. The question ought to be: How has the institution gone about identifying people who have a reasonable chance of graduating?

MAJOR ISSUES FACING COLLEGE ATHLETICS

RL: What do you think the most significant issues are or will be in college athletics in the next 5 to 10 years?

MS: Some of these issues are universal and not necessarily simply athletic issues. In the NCAA's strategic planning exercise that is ongoing now, some of the more global aspects of the 5- to 10-year future have been identified. One is demographics. We have a changing demographic and ethnic mix in the athletic world. Obviously, we have a situation where we may have more women than men in a college education because the female population has risen significantly. What will the effect be of our aging population as it impacts interest, enrollments, and funding issues? Then there is, of course, the business and economic climate and the role that plays. It is hard to predict what that climate will look like in 5 to 10 years.

What role will the government play? For example, right now we have a crisis in state funding. That had an impact not just on athletics but on the funding of higher education as a whole. Will there be an increase in legislative and regulatory control by government? If you track the NCAA's history, you see early success almost without exception of using common law in the courts. You see an age of regulation and regulatory reinforcement, and then the litigation history begins to shift as we get more and more legislative and regulatory interest in what we are doing. What will be the political and social values we place on collegiate athletics and higher education? What will the public perception of those values be like? Will they continue to be accepted? I am always struck by the fact that in collegiate athletics we have a unique experience in this country, where we decided that athletic competition would take place in a context of higher education. Otherwise, we are professional. Can we maintain those values and balance with the commercial pressures that are on us? I think that all of these issues in one form or another will impact us as we move ahead. There are lots of details within each one of those, but I think that is a start.

KW: We are dealing with growing cynicism about the role of intercollegiate sports. The misconduct of some coaches has been in the news. There is a growing distrust in how we conduct our business. Finding ways to deal with that is challenging. The cynicism that is certainly there on the media side is growing among the public.

JD: I would focus in on the financing of intercollegiate athletics, especially at the Division I level, and maybe even at the Division IA level. There are 30 to 60 athletics departments which have successfully operated their programs without receiving much, if any, subsidy from the institution. They are not competing for institutional dollars with the classroom teacher or the lab. I think the questions for those schools is: Can they continue to operate in that fashion without institutional help and still sponsor broad-based programs? Then there are Division IA schools where there is major institutional subsidy occurring. Those institutions often do not have the public support or support within their own states or regions to raise the revenue. Yet the subsidy has continued to grow.

As Mike mentioned, the funding for higher education is a challenge right now in most states. Thus the funding of intercollegiate athletics raises a lot of questions. Can the subsidized schools continue to operate at a fairly high level with growing subsidies? For the others who are not subsidized, can they continue to operate their programs without subsidy? What will schools do if they are challenged economically? Will they shrink their programs and, if so, how will they do that? Over the next 10 years I think even if the economy turns (and I expect that it will), the fact of it is we are going to see tuition rise probably at double the rate of inflation. The effect that has on broad-based programs is very significant. I would focus in on that because the cost of the enterprise and the pressures to continue to pay for the ongoing enterprise create other pressures for managers, administrators, coaches, and presidents.

CM: I think we could have had this conversation 10 years ago and probably many similar comments would have been made. If we have this conversation 10 years from now, similar comments will be made. The issue of integrity in intercollegiate athletics and the public perception is critical. We have to keep in perspective that there are always going to be some journalists that wake up and proclaim that college athletics has become a big business. It has had a business element to it in the years I have been in the industry, and probably for 50 years before that. We have made more progress than taken steps back in the 20 years I have been in college athletics. We need to keep that in perspective.

PV: I think there are two other critical issues. Gambling has a big potential influence on college athletics; that is especially true with the proliferation of Internet gambling. It is a potential huge influencer here, like a house of cards that could come tumbling down with the wrong set of circumstances. The second is the entitlement issues related to student-athletes' rights. This could take us in a really unknown direction. And I think that those are two influences that need to be realistically considered.

CM: Those are two great examples where you can look back at history and see similar issues. Gambling scandals in basketball go back to the early 1950s, and there were students' rights issues back in the 1970s. I work with the NCAA Student Athlete Advisory Committee. While they have concerns about issues of entitlement, there is very much a conservative element within the group that is quite satisfied with their current status. There is a vocal minority pushing certain issues. Also, the perspective on many issues is vastly different with football and basketball student-athletes, who are just a very small percentage of all of the athletes.

JD: Historically we have run up against these issues over time, but I do think that we now are confronted in a different time with the 24/7 news cycle. Perception is reality in politics, education, and entertainment. Whether or not it is reality is one thing. Cynicism can cascade out of control. It can force policy-makers to arrive at conclusions that might not necessarily be the best way to approach a problem.

The judiciary is an example. These are people who are in their late 40s, 50s, and 60s. I see them reacting to the NCAA regulatory system in a very different way than they did 20 years ago. The problems may be the same, the challenges may be the same, the legal defenses may be the same, but I see a great deal more vulnerability for conference and NCAA regulatory systems because I think the cynicism has eroded the "benefit of doubt" that higher education gets when they attempt to defend a regulation. We are seen much more as being involved in a business process than an educational process. I think that perception and that cynicism, whether it is a fair characterization or not, tends to affect people in national and state government.

Things that used to be local became regional events. What was a regional event became a national event. Everybody aspires to be exceptional on the national level. The 24/7 news cycle and the effort to nationalize everything really creates a situation where every weakness, every strength, every fault, every asset is seen as part of the national quilt. For example, what happened this summer with the ACC and the Big East affected everyone. It was in the news 24/7 for almost 60 days. What happened at Baylor wasn't a local or regional situation. It was a national situation. It was in front of us and is still in front of us, not unlike the O.J. Simpson trial which became a 24/7 drama.

You get a certain critical mass of information. Stories build on stories. It all has a tendency to erode and debase higher education and the institutions that sponsor us. The cumulative effect on the public makes it more difficult and more challenging for ADs, commissioners, coaches, presidents, or young student-athletes who make a mistake. That, in itself, is qualitatively different than what we experienced in 1960, 1980, or even 1990.

PV: I would concentrate on academic integrity issues and think that we have made good strides in that direction. I would focus on amateurism and play-for-pay issues and address those directly. I also think that we need to deal with the legislative process and the unintended consequences of the disenfranchisement of a vast majority of stakeholders in the NCAA process. I think that there is going to be a growing cynicism within our ranks if we don't find a way to more effectively involve all of our presidents in Division I, not just the IA presidents, as well as faculty reps and administrators within the structure. We have to talk about what we do in the area of expenses without bringing down the wrath of the antitrust lawyers.

KW: One of the most difficult things that the NCAA has on its plate is dealing with its diverse nature of its member institutions. That is one point. The other point is I think it is important to constantly remember what the NCAA should be doing and think critically about what it might try to do that it really shouldn't do.

JD: You had serious gender problems and the NCAA has addressed them constructively over the last 10 years. They have helped in that. We have had tremendous racial issues in terms of the hiring of head coaches. They have been able to provide some leadership there. But at the bottom line, while the conference commissioners and the NCAA can help, those decisions have to be made at the local level.

TITLE IX

RL: Do you see a model for a university in which they can be totally compliant with Title IX and not negatively affect other programs on campus?

CM: I believe that the current Title IX process works. I think the strain comes when you mix in the free-market economy and its impact on spending in basketball and football. Men's basketball and football put great stress financially on all the programs. If the spending in these areas is controlled, there is enough money to have equitable programs. I don't know how you solve the stress the open-market causes. You can't do it legally. How do you balance spending to support and be competitive in those two expensive programs and also create as many opportunities for all student-athletes? The money in the industry has increased enough over time so that schools should be able to reach equity within their programs. In some cases, schools have not been responsible. Assuming that the economy and financial resources will expand, I think there needs to be some vision to create equitable programs and still be competitive in football and basketball. I do think it is possible.

KW: I think that the funding issue is really, over the long run, probably the critical issue where we need to make progress. It is hard to see how it could be achieved if there was a regulatory push to proportionalize those funding levels without impacting in some way opportunities in the broader sense on the spending side. Those challenges are still there. I don't know whether they will rise to the surface in the short run.

PV: I think the peer-review portion of NCAA certification has helped. It has caused our athletic programs to look beyond their walls to the entire university community to try to find the right place for their athletics program and how gender equity plays out within that model. I would agree with Chris that achieving that model is certainly more challenging when football is part of the equation, but I see evidence of that happening also. I think, historically, the biggest challenge to Title IX was that attitudes needed to change, and I have seen huge progress over the last 30 years. I see very few people who doubt the value and necessity of providing gender-equitable programs now. Now the biggest challenge is what everybody has identified so far: How do you find the money to achieve it? I think the attitudinal change was a necessary precursor, and I think that has happened.

RACIAL HIRING PRACTICES

RL: This issue of African-American coaches in college football, as well as athletics directors in particular, has been one that has been discussed for quite some time. What do you think will affect changes in the future, or will it remain the same?

KW: I am optimistic about it, despite the fact that the numbers speak for themselves relative to the number of head coaches in Division I football and IAA football, as well as in leadership positions in general. But I do believe that more attention is being focused on the issue. There are more systematic efforts in place to identify qualified candidates. There are several for head-coaching positions right now. You need real effort to make sure that institutions do the right thing by identifying diverse candidates, including them in the interview process, and giving them serious consideration. One problem is that some institutions are not willing to take a chance on individuals who, because only a few Division I coaches are top college assistants or are from the professional sports ranks, to give them the opportunity to demonstrate what they can do.

Because of previous mistakes in hiring coaches with long-term contracts, presidents, chancellors, or athletic directors sometimes find it is a difficult leap of faith to get leaders to hire men without head-coaching experience in Division I. However, I do think that there is more of a systematic effort today to try to break down some of these barriers perhaps than there was five years ago. We have made significant progress in the sport of men's basketball. There are some differences in the sport. It is more of an urban game. You have different dimensions to it in terms of the way it is structured, but I do think that progress can be made in the sport of football. I hope that as individuals are brought into these positions and demonstrate success, that it will lead to much greater numbers of African-American football coaches.

MS: I think of the things that have happened to put the spotlight on this issue, which is healthy. It keeps it at the top of the priority list for all of us, and our institutions as well. As a result of that in part, in addition to the good-faith efforts of many people, the lines of communication have opened dramatically. For example, at the Collegiate Commissions Association meeting this past summer, we invited Floyd Keith, the head of the Black Coaches Association, to come sit with us. We had a very candid discussion about this issue and got acquainted on a personal level. We want to find ways to increase minority initiatives in all of our conferences. Many of us had different ideas, which we shared from our bully pulpits. We can continue to try to make this issue a priority for all of our institutions when opportunities arise.

RL: Mike, can you elaborate on some of the initiatives that there are on the conference level on the issue of diversity that you are talking about?

MS: The SEC issues a huge notebook, which is a database of minority coaches including every coach in IA and in the NFL who is a minority coach. We issued that last fall, and we will issue it again to all of our athletic directors, presidents, and chancellors. We started a minority internship program here, and we are working very hard in our recent hires to look at diversity at the conference level. We can set an example. I know that Tom Hansen of the PAC-10 has developed a dinner that takes places between athletic directors and minority coaches in his conference. We will do the same. I know that all of us on the phone have our own initiatives, but I think that this is at the top of all of our lists in terms of how we try to do what we can to at least create the kind of atmosphere that provides guidance, help, and support for our institutions as they make these difficult decisions.

It is important to note that in the academic year that followed this forum, Mississippi State hired Sylvester Croom as the SEC's first African-American head coach and Georgia hired Damon Evans as the SEC's first African-American athletics director.

KW: I think also we tried to focus some attention on making sure that our current head coaches understand the important role they have to play in mentoring and developing future head coaches. There is now much more time with the head coach to grow future head coaches by leadership opportunities, by training, and [by] mentoring of our assistant coaches. Our head coaches are committed to that.

JD: I think the Big 10 is far from perfect, but for a variety of reasons its ability to attract and provide opportunity goes back further than most. We had integrated teams in the 1920s. We have had some success at some times in attracting African Americans and women to leadership positions at the level of president, athletics director, basketball coach, football coach, and in conference administration. I don't think anybody in our conference would say that we are where we want to be or that all of those hires have been successful.

We have had three athletics directors since I have been in the conference at Michigan, Michigan State, and Minnesota. We have had men's basketball head coaches at Ohio State, Minnesota, and Penn State and head coaches in football at Michigan State and Northwestern. Some of them have been more successful than others. Some have been successful immediately, and others have not. We also had athletics directors of majority race that have not been successful at all. The challenge is, especially in football and basketball, is how to reduce the risks associated with failure. You cannot have a risk-free decision. What I am looking for is a 2-in-3 or 3-in-4 chance that the individual that I am hiring can compete in the Big 10 and at the very highest level nationally. The best indicator of that is a person who previously has been a head coach and has demonstrated success over a period of time. While we might look at a coordinator, or we might look at an assistant coach, we have collectively come to a decision that we can best reduce our risk in most cases.

There is a larger pool in basketball than in football because you are dealing with 300 head coaches who could have demonstrated success. And my athletics directors are open to the nontraditional career. Meritt Norvell was not an athletics director before. He was a former athlete who was successful in the private sector.

Our problem in football and in basketball is that we are operating at the highest level. We are not likely to hire someone from the NFL who hasn't had a college leadership position either as a head coach or as a coordinator, or hiring someone who hasn't won big. I think that you can look at Division II or III. But at a minimum you are looking for coordinators and head coaches. Bo Ryan, who has been the coach of the year the last two years in the Big 10, won four national championships in Division III. Tressel won four championships at IAA. The difficulty for the minority coach or the majority coach at this juncture is that no school with the stakes and the financial involvement where they are will hire someone based on a good personality or good recommendation unless there is a demonstrated area of success. If you haven't had leadership experience, whether you are white or you are black, I think that your chances of getting up in into this level are going to be challenging in the future.

KW: Yet in the Big 12 we have had four head coaching positions in the last seven or eight years that have gone to white head coaches who were coordinators.

JD: I would put coordinators in the category of a leadership position because they are responsible for half the team. They have demonstrated leadership and overall responsibility. That's the pool from which both blacks and whites are being pulled.

MS: The spotlight is on IA because there are only four minority head coaches in all of IA, and one in IAA.

PV: Interestingly, we have this incredible pool of qualified candidates in the historically black conferences, and no one outside of those conferences has tapped them.

JD: I think basketball has really suffered by eliminating the graduate assistants. For kids that want to get in—white or black—at 22 years old, they are not ready for a $50,000-a-year third assistant's position. That is going to a person that is 40 or 50. That kind of close-ends it. I think talking to Mike and Kevin at least at the commissioners' level, what you are going to see in the future is more small gatherings, more dinners with assistants. We don't know assistant coaches, white or black. What we are going to try to do is get some of our senior coaches and commissioners to direct us to the young people (and not so young people) who they feel are ready. Then we can sit down and get to know them so that when we get called by our ADs and presidents, the pool is established. Then we will be not talking about a name, but a person.

KW: We have also seen the growing influence of professional search firms involved in the hiring process for head coaches and athletic directors. It is important those firms understand we want a diverse pool of candidates. We need to be sure that the firm is plugged in to those people.

ACADEMIC ADVISORS

RL: Many academic advisors feel that their role is to keep athletes eligible instead of ensuring their academic success. Are there things being done at the conference level to address that feeling among your own advisors at your member schools?

JD: Our presidents last year advocated for giving these athletic support systems to a direct reporting line to the academic provost. We are concerned about the diminishing understanding of what the advisors' own work is.

Plagiarism is a big issue, with having people write papers and the use of the Internet. We are trying to get a greater integration of the writing centers, a better understanding of what is expected in terms of writing, and being responsible for your own work product. We are concerned. We had a terrible situation at Minnesota. There have been allegations at Ohio State. We understand that in the last 10 to 15 years so much effort has gone to support athletes who are perhaps not ready to do the work or, in some cases, not interested in doing the work. Some athletes are overwhelmed by the work as well as the athletics. The amount of resources is greater than it has ever been. Additional oversight is necessary, as well as additional support for the people leading those academic advisement programs. There is no question that they are under pressure with respect to eligibility.

KW: I think as we increase the standards, particularly the continuing progress standards, we further increase the pressure on expediting the services in the academic support area. And I think that it is going to be increasingly important as we go forward to provide independence in reporting lines.

MS: In the SEC, we have a summer compliance workshop with about 150 people attending a very intensive workshop. It involves the directors of financial aid, athletic people, counselors, and people from the registrar and academic services and concerns.

They get a chance to interact and we go through a whole litany of things, and I think that this is very helpful to get people on campuses to interact with all of the components of compliance.

PV: I think the institutions in my league and our level are in different circumstances because we haven't had the luxury of elaborate support systems. We haven't had the finances to support them historically. We have worked really hard over the last decade or two to improve our support services. Obviously, as we have put those in place, we have also created systems with greater opportunity for abuse. I am hoping that our administrators are learning from the problems that have become public.

JD: In the late 1990s there was more NCAA attention on our programs. It had increased over what we have had in previous years. We have started institutional visits. Our compliance director and I are going to each campus. We spend a couple of days on campus with the president, boards of control, [and] head and assistant coaches. We also spend two to three hours with the academic support services people. There is no question they are under pressure. They feel it. The new rules have put them under additional pressure.

KW: There also continues to be too much willingness on the part of some institutions to provide a highly successful coach with a lot of control with sort of a separate or direct administrative line to their own academic support structure.

COST CONTAINMENT

RL: I would like to discuss the costs of college sports, especially at the Division I level, in the current state of the economy as well as the competition for the entertainment dollar. How can we contain these costs?

JD: There is no way that you can effectively argue that there is not an arms race. There are two areas where the arms race is active and, well, one is with regard to coaches' salaries and one is with respect to facilities. Intuitively everybody knows that, yet the NCAA study of the economics of college sport excludes those two points. How can it draw any conclusion with respect to an arms race? Institutions have grown, and our budgets have grown.

MS: I think they were careful to say that the study didn't find evidence of an arms race as defined by increased operating expenses.

KW: I think the intended message was increased spending did not necessarily result in increased winning. There is no question in the Big 12 that this rapid escalation of costs hasn't always resulted in increased winning.

JD: No one ever argued that there was a major arms race in operational costs. Coaches at one time were making $80,000, then $350,000, then $500,000, then $1,000,000. Some of them make $1.5 to $2 million. That is what it is. We are all chasing it, and we are all having to respond to it. With facilities, we are responding to that too.

KW: I have tried to defend the growth of spending in those two areas. I have tried to make the argument that there isn't a linkage between the "go-go" mentality in this area, and some of the integrity problems that we increasingly see. Now I think that is an argument that I am going to have a harder time making.

CONFERENCES

RL: I would appreciate knowing how the ACC's expansion and the public's view of it affected you as conference commissioners. Has it affected your own work in your conferences and in dealings with your presidents and ADs?

MS: To paraphrase the great Winston Churchill, this summer was not collegiate athletics' finest hour. It took the focus away from some of the good things that we are all trying to do. It was difficult to cut through all of the cynicism to get the message across about some of the other things that we are trying to accomplish.

PV: I think sadly it reinforced the notion that college sports is about money and only about money. I thought that was bad and not necessarily true.

JD: It was different. We've had expansion in one form or another for a long time. So the first big one I remember was when Arizona and Arizona State moved from the WAC to the PAC-10. Arizona and Arizona State were the two strongest members of WAC. At that time, the WAC champion was playing in the Fiesta Bowl. That was probably the most similar to expansion. When the ACC expanded with Florida State, there were very few dominos that fell. When the Big East expanded with Miami, it was the same. Likewise, when the Big 10 expanded with Penn State, while it affected the Atlantic 10, there were no dominos in a major way. In the case of the merger of the Southwest and the Big 8, there were a lot of politics. But the Southwest conference, with eight schools in one state, they knew that it was going be hard for themselves to sustain. I think it was much more consensual. In the other case of the Big East, it was a firmly established viable working entity. The dominos, the effect on that conference and that region, and historic collegiality between the two conferences made it appear as fairly aggressive relative to the other expansions.

PV: It was certainly no more aggressive than past realignment at the mid-major level, but the Big East/ACC played out in the media 24/7 environment.

JD: I think the reason why schools have gotten out of their geographic footprint is because there has been a lot of concern about the BCS. It used to be people shifted and changed for automatic bids in basketball. Now they shift and change for marketing reasons and football TV. It's more transparent. In some cases, there is not the great institutional similarity but more of a sense of the business purpose.

CM: Part of my reaction is that this is not new and should not be read as an indicator or where college athletics has evolved to. There are a lot of different angles to this that are unique. The Big East has such a range of diverse schools, from small, private, Catholic to large state institutions. While there is a business aspect to this—which, by the way, is not new—schools make decisions on conference alignment for many different reasons.

JD: It is interesting that this expansion stimulated the attorneys general, private litigators, and governors to involve themselves. I think that is an unhealthy trend. It is indicative of some of the problems that I was trying to express earlier in the area of compensation. When you have a successful program and a successful coach, the people get involved and when the people get involved, there is a sense of ownership of the university. Then the program's ability to make rational and solid decisions long-term sometimes gets narrowed or actually frozen. What happened in this case was the ACC chose the institutions involved in the Big East. Those schools' ability to act became frozen and narrowed by the effect of these actions on the people in these locations, resulting in reactions of the representatives of the people who were either governors or attorneys general.

MS: In most of the historic expansions, the decisions were made, announced, and were not so much in the public eye. This one was done in public, and you had people who felt jilted at the altar.

RL: Has everything that happened this summer changed the way you are perceived by your publics in your conferences?

JD: I think that we are all touched, and that is the nature of the system. What happens at Minnesota touches everybody. What happens at Texas Tech or the ACC, not to equate those issues, are just high-profile examples of what can go wrong. One is a governance issue, and two are NCAA issues. One is a criminal investigation. But whatever happens to each of us in intercollegiate athletics can affect us all.

MS: The ACC, head-coaching issues, and other issues get the media talking about the landscape of college football and the landscape of intercollegiate athletics. There is a tendency on the part of the media and the public to talk about what is wrong and how do you fix it.

JD: There are two ways that we look at the issues. First, everybody is trying to make it better, most of the coaches are good, and most of the student-athletes are good. Yet others would say we've got these 12 incidents which have occurred in the last four months, so it must be bad.

CM: Sometimes I wonder if we wouldn't be better off defending the image by saying, "You know what? This has happened in the past, and we can pretty much guarantee that it is going to happen in the future." It is no different than any other industry in our society. We are a reflection of what happens throughout our culture. These individual incidents cannot be avoided by setting NCAA rules or mandates from governing bodies.

MS: We operate in the context of higher education. We hold ourselves to a higher standard. The public has a right to hold us to a higher standard. To say that it happens in other industries is not acceptable to our critics. We are in this very unique, contentious situation.

CM: We also operate in a free and open market. A great segment of the public does not care whether students graduate. It is source of entertainment for them. That does not mean, though, that we should not help student-athletes graduate.

MEDIA COVERAGE OF COLLEGE SPORT

RL: Almost all of you have referred to the media. Overall, do you think the media treats college sport fairly?

JD: What is "fair"? Is CNN fair? Fox Network? They have orientations and perspectives. Are most writers realists? are cynics? are skeptics? What are they? We put ourselves out there, and they seem to have the right and the obligation to do what they do. What we are doing in a large part is defensible, although there are extreme aspects of it which we all have a hard time getting our arms around. I feel like generally we are dealt with fairly. I think that what has changed is we have gone from two newspapers in a town to one. But we also have gone from 3 networks to 6, and 7 channels to 500. With the talk radio, there are so many different levels of media coverage. Some are more responsible than others.

I don't think that you could ever characterize it as unfair. It is simply pervasive, with lots and lots of layers. People who I talk to always seem fair to me, the quotes always seem to be accurate, and the coverage is extensive. You like some of the people better than others. In general, I don't think it is unfair. I think that it has become less supportive or as it was 50 years ago. I don't think that there is anything about the media that is supportive. But that is probably not their role.

KW: I think that it is a reflection of our enterprise. As the broadcast side has grown and the issue of sport news has developed more fully with talk radio and broadcast companies like ESPN, I do think the trend of the last 10 years is a transition of the sports writer who covers the team into that of an entertainer in a more direct way than I think we have seen. Maybe it is more similar to what existed in some respects back in the '20s and '30s, where the people covering the sports events became personalities in and of themselves. We are even seeing it in markets that are not necessarily the national sports markets—like Kansas City, where there are now two full-time sports talk-radio stations. Writers are prominent personalities in key time slots. It leads to a different mentality about coverage and events. That calls into question their role as journalist or entertainer. Which side of the equation are they really on?

PV: I think that we might all wish that the coverage were generally more positive or broader, to include more sports and more programs. But I think that complaint is typical of news coverage in general.

MS: I think that in my experience here in one year that I would categorize the coverage as pervasive, intense, 24/7, but, on balance, fair and consistent. To some extent, by virtue of putting the spotlight on certain issues that are important for us to address on a constant basis, the media has actually been helpful.

JD: I would point out one thing that I think that is bothersome to me as an individual. I don't really know if it comes under the category of unfair. It bothers me that in some parts of the media it becomes personal between a writer and the person they cover. If you are a journalist and you have to hold someone accountable, then hold them accountable. But in some forms of the news media, it seems to me that there is a personal level where there is an effort to personalize the objection that they are writing about. It doesn't contribute much to the substance of anything.

CM: Any observations we make about the media can be made about the coverage the media give to every other topic in the country. Whether it is war, politics, the economy, entertainment, it is really the same thing. If we were in those industries, we would have very similar reactions to the accuracy of the coverage. Their job is to sell newspapers and write things that sell them. If you open any newspaper and read columns, editorial pages, op-ed pages, a majority of the things written are critical.

SPORTSMANSHIP

RL: What do you think conferences can do to promote sportsmanship on the field?

MS: In February, we put together a sportsmanship summit that attracted about 150 people of different walks of life relating to sportsmanship, fan behavior, and coaches' behavior. We had athletics administrators, psychologists, event managers, presidents, ADs, and commissioners. It was a unique get-together and was well attended. As a result of that, a document is now being distributed. The NCAA was very helpful in joining in this enterprise. The document has some best practices and identifies some of the problems. I think that most of the conferences this year spent some time at their spring meetings dealing with these issues, looking at recommendations, and taking a very hard look at how we manage our events, how we deal with our fans, how our fans deal with our student-athletes, and how our coaches deal with student-athletes and fans. I think that at least raised the national consciousness amongst our fans about their need to conduct themselves in a civilized way around and during our events. Hopefully, this effort will result in a raised awareness about the practices that our institutions should employ.

JD: We came out of the Dallas summit meeting energized. We have had significant discussion on some initiatives with our coaches involved. We met with all the ESPN talent and brought them up-to-date on what they can expect. I read in the paper this morning there is going to be more aggressive controlling of alcohol laws in and around Ohio State. We are going to have heightened security for our teams as they come in and come out of town for football and basketball games. We have asked the university to set up a student section in basketball. If they go after the coach or the official, we don't have a problem. But if there is an orchestrated, two-hour outing of a player for personal reasons, we are going to ask them desist. If they continue, we are going to publicly embarrass the school. We are going to simply say that they do not have control of their student section and if it continues the following year we will ask them to break up the student section. They can sit them wherever they want to sit them but not together, because we have had some really ugly incidents. We have also moved bands, and we have taken the video replay off the big board on officiating flaws. If you want to see officiating flaws on replay, you have to stay home and watch them. And we have had a very, very tight reign on player conduct in football and in basketball. That is not our problem. Our problem is from the outside in, rather than from the inside out.

MS: We issued a press release on all the various steps that we have taken with our athletics directors to deal with these issues. We are more focused on this issue than we have been in a decade.

KW: The meeting was particularly helpful in allowing us at the conference level to be more active in terms of insisting upon certain guidelines relative to game management practices. We have been able to get in place some conferencewide standards that did not exist prior to this past year.

JD: We want students to be exuberant, but we do not want them talking about the fact that the mother of one of the players went to jail 20 years ago for two hours. We want bands, but we don't want them positioned in a way that they make the visiting team not think. We know we want people to scream and holler, but we want the visiting team to be treated with respect. There are coaches that are going to be real helpful and make PSAs for both TV and for the big screen. The presidents do not want things out of control. We did not get here overnight. I know in Chicago, we have had people come out to the fields and attack a coach, attack a player, throw cell phones, and hit a player in the face.

PV: There is sort of a pendulum that swings. Administrations were once turning a blind eye to a lot of things that were going on that would not normally be considered acceptable under anybody's standards. I think that what that sportsmanship summit did was help swing the pendulum back to encourage our administrators to recognize that they have an equal responsibility for ensuring safety and fairness. We undertook a pretty comprehensive survey and audit of game management and sportsmanship issues in the off-season with the help of our officiating referees. We made a comprehensive list of problems and potential problems. Every one of our institutions have stressed their willingness and enthusiasm to address those issues using the best practices that were circulated via the NCAA document. We have seen real, positive change.

JD: I think that the leadership from conferences on this was really helpful. Schools that had serious problems, like Ohio State and Michigan State in terms of riot control, sent their people forward because they have been dealing with it on their own. I think that raising it to a national level was helpful for all of us.

CHAPTER

Athletics Directors' Forum

Clarence Underwood Michigan State University
Don DiJulia St. Joseph's University
Dan Guerrero UCLA
Bill Byrne Texas A&M University

GRADUATION RATES: INCENTIVES/DISINCENTIVES

RL: The first question is about Myles Brand's incentives/disincentives proposal. What do you think would be the most effective forms of incentives/disincentives from your points of view as athletics directors?

DJ: It is unfortunate that we have to look at the concept of incentives/disincentives as it relates to academic success. Nevertheless, we have come to the point that it is important that we do this. The path that the NCAA has taken relates specifically to the awarding of additional scholarships for those who perform well and the reduction of scholarships for those who don't. Conceptually, that is a good place to start. Certainly the economic variable is an incentive for all of our institutions, and that's why I think that the NCAA is going in that direction.

CU: I would say that this is going in the wrong direction. We need to look initially inside of our institutions at several components. The first thing you look at is your admissions policies. You must tighten up your admissions policies to reduce the number of at-risk student-athletes that come into your institutions. Not everybody that enrolls is going to graduate or even have the desire to graduate. Some don't have the qualities or the discipline to graduate. So if you crucify coaches by reducing the number of scholarships in their programs because somebody did not graduate, you are putting it all on the coach's back. Just by putting in incentives/disincentives to a program will not solve this complex problem.

DJ: Whatever we are reporting to be good or bad numbers, we must be in agreement about what we are going to count as a graduate. It is about graduation rates. We do have athletic departments, and we receive fault or praise. The more other people are involved, I think the better it is going to be.

CU: There is another issue related to this. Institutions are raising their admissions standards because they are so competitive now. They have many students enrolled already, and there are more students qualified out of high school that are enrolling annually. I feel they are raising their standards every year, and then two to three years later the NCAA raises its eligibility standards. Student-athletes still don't catch up, and this creates an educational lag. Therefore, there always will be at-risk student-athletes. The other issue is: Are coaches and academic counselors forming good partnerships and doing their jobs? This is a big issue. You can't just put in incentives/disincentives and walk away and say that it is going to work. That is too simplistic.

PRESSING ISSUES IN COLLEGE SPORT

RL: What do you think are the five most important issues that the NCAA is going to have to tackle in the next 10 years?

CU: The first thing would be ethical issues. There is now a flurry of unethical conduct issues in athletics. We have not found a way to reduce the number of violations in athletics. I think there are 30 institutions that are on probation for the 2003 school year. That's a lot. And that number is consistent from year to year. All those institutions have major violations and yet, everyday in the paper, we see more athletic unethical conduct issues. We haven't found a way to address those issues that have been ongoing for years.

The second is finance. There is a tremendous gap between the haves and have-nots in collegiate athletics. We have schools that are in the second tier of Division IA that are struggling financially. Some are playing most of their games on the road at major institutions in order to earn enough money so that they can pay their bills. That is a major problem. How we are going to bring equity and give teams at those institutions a chance to fare well financially is a major issue.

The third thing that has to be done in the future is a downsizing of the athletics programs financially. These major institutions cannot continue to have the number of scholarships they have now. Inflation has set in with the down economy, and finding new revenues continues to get worse at the collegiate level. There has to be a national agreement among people in athletics that they have to come to some reasonable number of sports that a school can carry per year with aid.

DJ: I'll add deregulation or decentralizing. The NCAA continues trying to add rules to solve issues. Put some things back on the conferences and get away from the NCAA having to solve everything.

DG: A fifth issue addresses the overarching theme of student-athlete welfare. Today's student-athletes are voicing their concerns about their role on our campuses and in the association to a degree never before seen. The willingness of the administrative leadership on our campuses to foster dialogue and to reach compromise or consensus on issues relating to student-athlete welfare is critical. While the NCAA has looked at avenues to address student-athlete concerns through the National Student-Athlete Advisory Committee, the Leadership Forum, and by including them as members of selected association committees, a continuing focus at the conference and campus levels will be necessary to identify and address their concerns. Contrary to popular belief, not all of their issues have a financial price tag attached to them. Those that have financial implications, however, will force some schools to examine the "cost" of doing business differently. Spiraling costs in our programs, in general, create a huge strain on our programs, and we are all working hard to balance our budgets. But some issues raised by student-athletes must be addressed and funded. We have seen this occur with the enactment of recent legislation.

TITLE IX

RL: I think most people in your positions agree that complying with Title IX has been one of the most difficult tasks in college athletics. Is there a model in which a university can be compliant with Title IX and not negatively impact any other programs on campus in the department?

DG: Last year I had the opportunity to personally visit with a staff member of Secretary Page's office right before the Title IX Commission released its report. Of major concern to me and for many of my colleagues was to understand the definition of "compliance" in clear, unambiguous terms. This has not been an easy thing for universities to grasp. Prong one, proportionality, is one that most universities understand. However, the other two prongs have been moving targets, or so it seems. It was disconcerting for me to find out that different regional offices across the country had varying interpretations of compliance for the various prongs. This cannot be the case.

DJ: If there is a model, let's get it in the mail quickly to everybody. If complying means being compliant with Items II or III, then it is easy. But the perception is that, under proportionality, it might be nearly impossible to obtain compliance.

RACIAL HIRING PRACTICES

RL: It is obvious that when we do the Racial and Gender Report Card every year we see the challenges that college athletics face in terms of the number of people of color hired as head coaches and athletics directors. This seems to be particularly true in the sport of football. I would like to ask you what you have individually been able to do in your own experiences as ADs about the small number of head coaches who are people of color.

CU: This issue has been quite sensitive to me. At Michigan State University, we have had a number of student-athletes who were minority who had performed well in their sport and graduated. Some made All-American, played pro, and some were successful in coaching. Yet when we had openings in the major sports, we never hired and seldom interviewed any minority candidate. I was very proactive in making sure the university's athletics committees looked for minority candidates in their searches. They would put one or two on the list and invite one in for an interview. Even though few were hired, there were two occasions where I thought we had very qualified candidates who should have been considered to be hired for a position.

The other thing I think that schools, ADs, and the committees could do is to make sure that at least there are a number of minority candidates in the search conducted. They are out there. They played for us or they played for somebody else. You just have to search for them. The idea that we cannot find them is not really accurate. I know even in swimming there are a few minority coaching candidates available. We just have to be more proactive in trying to identify a larger pool that represents our communities and our nation as it is.

I had a seminar at Michigan State that I conducted two years ago in the spring on this very issue. I wanted to bring in athletics directors and sit down for a day and talk about the issues, the barriers, the social problems, and the training problems that we are facing—about why we think we can't find minority candidates. The discussion at the seminar made people aware of the issues and that we can do more than what we are currently doing.

RL: In his chapter, Fitz Hill talked about the unique issues in football that have kept the number of African-American head coaches so small. In fact, it is at the lowest point in the last decade. Do you agree that there are unique factors, and if you do, what can be done to change the situation in football?

DG: I look at this issue as a matter of personal responsibility. I need to do what I can to educate our membership about the merits of diversity in our department and coaching staffs. The decision-makers have to understand that looking at a broad base of diverse candidates is good business. The first football coach that I had the opportunity to hire happened to be an African American, with no previous head-coaching experience, but with a profile—including a strong coaching background and a core value philosophy—that I feel will result in long-term success for this university.

All of us have a personal perspective about what makes our program successful. If that perspective, or philosophy, is such that diversity is important to you, then seeking a broad base of candidates is a given. For the past two years, Pac-10 athletics directors have invited minority football coaches from across the conference to a dinner prior to conference meetings. We did that so all athletics directors had the opportunity to familiarize themselves and to begin to formulate relationships with the minority coaches on our respective campuses. By getting to know these individuals better, we begin to develop a pool of prospective candidates down the road. We intend to continue this practice every year.

RL: What do you do when you have a senior administrative position open to identify a pool of candidates for it?

DJ: Telling colleagues and peers would probably be the most common and most effective way of identifying the good people out there who might make sense for our fit. That's why we tell people who know about us, the area, and what kind of school we are. Often they would have candidates to recommend, especially diversity candidates. More often than not, if we're going to get diverse candidates in the pool, that is the vehicle.

RL: I've heard a number of coaches looking for assistant coaches as well as a number of athletics directors saying that it is difficult to find a diverse pool of candidates. Have any of you experienced that?

BB: Absolutely.

RL: What would have helped you in that regard that doesn't exist now?

DJ: We need to know who is out there. We just did a search for an assistant sports marketing director. You advertise, follow the affirmative action guidelines, and get your hundred responses. Then you put the word out that you would like some diverse candidates. Without that, it won't go anywhere.

CU: Since I know many minority people in athletics who are assistant ADs or who work in the compliance office or the academic office, I would get names of candidates from them for people they felt were qualified for the jobs I had available at Michigan State. When information was circulated around, that got me other names. In the end, I had many names to go through, with a large pool of diverse candidates. I could choose from those minority recommendations at each position and interview them for jobs. I wasn't playing games and was not just having the pool to satisfy affirmative action. When we thought they were qualified for that position, we brought some of them to campus to see if they were the kind of persons we wanted. That is how I did it.

DG: There is real value in serving on our NCAA committees, committees of national governing boards, etc. The ability to network and to meet prospective candidates—both up-and-coming ones and those who are established—is much greater when you have those opportunities. It is also advantageous to recognize those colleagues who have a great track record in developing strong talent pools or recommending prospective candidates. They can contribute a great deal in establishing a strong pool of candidates for your search.

CU: Each year at Michigan State we brought in four or five minority interns. We found them, for example, at the historically black colleges in the south, or from other institutions after they graduated. We would be proactive in recruitment. They would work in various areas in the department of athletics. When they finished their one-year internship, we would hire them if we had openings that they qualified for. If we didn't, we would help them get jobs someplace else. I don't know anybody who did not leave there with a job. We have had this internship program for at least four or five years.

RL: Have any of your departments done diversity management training for the staff and, if so, what were the results?

CU: We did at Michigan State. There was some grumbling, but overall it was successful. There was a variety of subjects, university-sponsored and university-mandated for every department including athletics. We had our entire staff there for a day. Sometimes the coaches wanted to get out of there and start practicing with their squads. The morning was very good, but once it got to 1 p.m., people started complaining to get out of there.

BB: We had an annual process that we had to go through for the university. All of the managers and staff members who were in hiring positions had to go through our diversity training. We had a variety of things that we had to deal with, from race to gender to sexual orientation. I have coaches who so disliked the subject they turned all the away around in their chairs!

ACADEMIC ADVISORS

RL: I have spoken at the National Association of Academic Athletic Advisors (NAAAA) conference a few times. People come up to say that they entered the profession because of its idealistic framework. However, they now feel that their job is really to keep athletes eligible instead of helping them achieve academic success. Is this a problem, and, if so, what possibly could be done about it?

BB: Those students that come here just wanting to major in eligibility can't do that any longer with the NCAA rules on the 40-60-80, and the conference rules where you must pass six hours of "C" every semester or be ineligible the next semester. I think that we've gotten their attention here. There are some, particularly the really elite athletes, who have been pampered coming out of high school who expect us to take care of them. I talked to some of the families of these student-athletes who can't understand why their youngster is expected to have to do all this stuff and is not able to spend all his time practicing. It is really disconcerting to see some of the family pressures that these kids are under to go out and make the family millions. We had a youngster here who said in the newspaper that he wouldn't flunk out because he was too valuable to the program. He was gone at the end of the semester. So there are kids who come here with the wrong attitude, and they don't last very long.

DG: With the academic reform movement under way, more and more institutions will realize that making investments in their academic support programs is smart business. Academic performance has always been the prerequisite to athletic performance, but the new standards will force schools to pay much more attention to their respective student-athlete populations. This will cause more schools to raise the bar in the types of services they provide for student-athletes and the quality of student that is both recruited and admitted to the institution. While the new satisfactory progress requirements, especially degree progress, are designed to enhance the graduation rate of student-athletes, academic advisors will still feel the pressure to keep them eligible. This dilemma is remedied in part by assuring that your coaches recruit student-athletes to your program that are capable of graduating from your institution. As obvious as this solution may sound, it may not always be the practice.

CU: I think that sometimes we have forgotten that the NAAAA has done a great job of refining its mission and developing concepts of what their membership stands for. However, the primary reason people were hired to counsel athletes in the first place was to keep athletes eligible. There was no other way you could justify hiring those persons. When you talked about graduation, that was too far away. When we started integrating athletics with black athletes in the early 1970s, we needed academic advisors to come in to keep these students in school and keep them eligible. It wasn't all about black athletes, but that is when the proliferation of hiring athletic counselors started. The coach still sees it as "I need to have eligible athletes." The first thing you need to have before graduation is to remain eligible. I think sometimes we want to make the job loftier than it is, but the fundamental purpose is eligibility. If you keep an athlete eligible four years, then that athlete has a good chance to graduate provided the athlete has made progress towards his/her degree by taking the proper courses. They should be in striking distance of graduating.

ADMISSIONS AND RECRUITING

RL: What impact will the new eligibility standards have on who you are trying to recruit? Have you seen much of a change in the freshman class that you have got coming in terms of SAT scores or grade-point averages? If so, is it different in football and basketball?

DJ: I think students are generally becoming more prepared, not just because of the NCAA and the academic reforms. It is being force-fed to the high schools and the junior high schools. Fewer seem to be on the bubble as nonqualifiers that we're seeing anyway. I think, with the new standards, we will see more of the same thing over time.

RL: Might part of that reflect that more are going the two-year college route?

DJ: We haven't seen it yet here in the East at the private-college level. Perhaps we're going to see it, maybe not in the sports of football and basketball. It may be in the other sports, where there might not be as much aid available. The affordability might have high-level athletes go the community college routes. They may even be qualifiers who will not go to four-year schools because of the academics but because of the affordability.

BB: We have a 10-percent rule in Texas (the top 10 percent of the class). We do have some marginal students here, that is, outside the 10 percent. But by and large, our students are coming in pretty well prepared. We have some that come in that think that because they are a superstar that they don't have to care about college, that they'll be taken care of, but they quickly learn the error of their ways there. Most of them get good grades and good test scores.

DG: At UCLA the academic profile of the average admit is off the charts. Student-athlete recruits at our institution must be able to compete in the classroom with the regular student. Therefore, our coaches must be very cognizant about recruiting the right type of student for this campus. If they don't succeed academically, everyone loses. Certainly a coach wants to minimize the heartache and disappointment for themselves and for the student.

CU: Each year there have been appreciable differences in the initial eligibility standards accepted by the institutions for incoming student-athletes. We're seeing, for example, better grade-point averages and test scores, but it's all relative because the institutions also are increasing their overall standards for admissions. The admissions academic competition is still strong among institutions. The academic support programs we put in place for at-risk student-athletes to survive in school and, hopefully, graduate, are increasingly important.

COST CONTAINMENT

RL: I would like to discuss the costs of college sports, especially at the Division I level in the current state of the economy, as well as the competition for the entertainment dollar. How can we contain these costs? John Gerdy argues that, as college sport has become modeled after the professional level, the only way to really reform and make costs contained is by eliminating athletic scholarships altogether and going to a needs-based scholarship model.

BB: At Texas A&M, our grant and aid budget is 7 percent of our total. Our salaries are 20 percent of our total. Like many states, Texas is cutting back on financing higher education. Our tuition and fees are going up substantially this spring semester. As universities look at scarce resources, they are looking at athletic programs. We are an auxiliary enterprise on our campus. We pay by a factor of about three times for services from the university than what the English department pays. We are looked upon as a cash cow by the parking department to increase the rates on game-day weekends to help pay for garages and help keep the rates for students and faculty low by increasing the expense to our fans.

The other issue we are facing is our aging infrastructure. We have an issue right now with our press box. Texas has declared it a high-rise, at eleven stories off the ground. We have to add sprinklers to it for fire protection and update the elevators before 2005. It was built in 1969 and also has asbestos in it. We don't know what that's going to cost. The initial estimate is $13 million, and that's all our cost. So, as we do our budget forecasting, just to fix fields or repair stadiums that were built so long ago, our aging infrastructures is the most expensive entry that we have.

If they want to put the students on need-based aid, we're going to be competing with the rest of the student body, taking money away that we would have been awarded for scholarships. Many of our young people would qualify for need-based aid right now. What would be the unintended consequences of putting our student-athletes—because many of them come from very poor backgrounds—on need-based aid rather than grant aid?

RL: Where do you see the biggest pressures being put on your departments to contain those costs?

DG: Any cost containment decision must be well conceived. The association has learned the unintended consequences of attempting to save dollars by establishing legislation for restricted-earnings coaches a few years ago. The cost to the association and to member institutions was significant. On the campus level, however, every institution is autonomous relative to the management of their budgets. Many of us are self-sufficient, with no financial support from the institution of any kind. Revenues must offset expenses. At some levels the institution will support the program with such forms of assistance as student-fee funding or various forms of institutional or government subsidy. Generally this type of assistance is found at the Division I (I-AA and AAAs) and at the Divisions II and III levels.

CU: We have a current need of trying to grow athletically to create more revenue for the NCAA programs. It may be growing in fundraising, winning success, or postseason events. All those growth opportunities are reduced when you talk about cost containment. You can't have both. Either you are going to grow, and raise new revenues to meet your growth goals, or you are going to downsize or stay as you are. In athletics, at least for now, we are in a growth period. We've got to think about growing. We must be cautious and prudent to not be excessive in our spending, but I still think it's a growth period.

DG: The ability to generate revenues is limited. Revenues are generated from gate receipts, donations, corporate sponsorships, television/radio, and some ancillary sources, such as royalties. By and large, if these areas are not yielding the types of numbers you require in order to meet your budget, you have to suppress your costs.

CONFERENCES AND THEIR COMMISSIONERS

RL: What do you see as the current and future role of conferences in college sports?

DJ: The NCAA, in putting together a long-range strategic plan, has as one of its key questions, "Does sports need to be more regionalized?" But with this conference concept, as we're seeing with the BCS, will all of this lead to less equal opportunities? Maybe things might be more regionalized. In 10 years, will the conference configuration be the same, or will they be competing in the same way? Likely not, but I don't know what the options are.

CU: Part of the answer would be, how did the public view the ACC expansion? The people I talked with saw it as alliances to get bigger and to become the most powerful conference in the nation. The public thinks it's just the beginning of what's going to happen in major college athletics in the future. There will be more strategic alliances between conferences as well as for certain individual institutions going to other high-profile conferences.

RL: Has there been any ripple effect in your own conferences?

DG: There hasn't been on the West Coast. Certainly, everyone needs to be vigilant and stay abreast of the movement occurring across the country in other conferences.

BB: I've been through two conference expansions with the old PAC-8 to the PAC-10 and the Big 8 to the Big 12. I have never seen anything as hostile as what went on with the ACC and the Big East. It appeared that both sides had attorneys involved very early, and public relations firms were printing out news releases that were not very complimentary to either side. I hope we've all learned a lesson from that. Perhaps we should try to do these in smoke-filled rooms rather than in the media.

RL: In all the years that you've each spent in college sport, how would you describe the shift in power of conference commissioners over the last 10 or 15 years?

BB: I think they've really filled a void. When Dick Schultz, the strong NCAA executive director, was forced out, the presidents tried to take over more of the policy. I think the commissioners moved in to work with the presidents and to set the tone themselves. The presidents, except for a few, don't really have a lot of interest or want to be bothered by what's going on in college athletics unless there is a scandal. I think the commissioners have filled that void. I'm not saying that it's for the better, but I think it's certainly what has happened. I serve on these NCAA committees, and they run legislation past the Collegiate Commissioners Association.

DG: They are a major player now. I don't think it's going to lessen, either.

DJ: I think this development is a plus. Just having executives doing business on behalf of so many makes the process better. Most of the commissioners look forward to the change. They all came through the athletic culture, the athletic experience, and I think that's a positive. A lot of the things have happened in the last 10 years with the presidents. Some of these commissioners and presidents are going to have to build a better bridge so the athletic community and the nonathletic community are not adversaries.

CU: In the Big 10 Conference, I do see a stronger bridge being built in terms of the leadership of the commissioner and the information flow going to the university presidents and conference representatives generally. It's a good thing.

DG: I would concur. As presidents become more involved, which they will be, intrinsically linked to the issues of their programs, the role of their commissioner will be more significant.

THE NCAA AND CONFERENCES IN THE FUTURE

RL: Do you see a difference for the existence of the NCAA and different roles that it plays now than it did 15 years ago, and what would you say would be its most important role today?

CU: That's a tough question. I think the role of the NCAA today is miniscule in athletics, other than in certain postseason events, limited infractions cases, the enforcement staff, minicommittee meetings, and discussions. Broad issues never come to fruition. I really question the usefulness of the NCAA in a broad sense. However, I think there is a gap in some conferences which are not strong in the compliance areas. Such weakness preserves the necessity for the NCAA. If the conferences were adequately prepared to perform major infraction cases, then I don't really see the need for the NCAA in its current form.

DG: There is a greater demand for accountability on our college campuses, in a general sense, and a greater demand for accountability from the NCAA. The by-product is legislative reform that demands more from our member institutions and our conference offices. The NCAA, under the leadership of Myles Brand, has articulated a desire to be more accountable to student-athlete concerns. This theme will continue to be a driving force when it comes to decision-making on all fronts, such as television, championships, academics, and eligibility.

BB: It used to be that the NCAA was a great gathering place to meet your colleagues and potential new employees. At least for Division I, that has gone away. NACDA (National Association of Collegiate Directors of Athletics) has become the place where we go to meet potential new employees and meet with our colleagues. I think that NCAA does a good job in championships, and it did a nice job with negotiating the television agreement. But in talking to collegiate IA colleges across the country, we feel that we've lost ownership of the legislative process. We don't have a voice any longer, and I think that's unfortunate.

DL: The biggest example I can think of for the role of conference commissioners has been through the changes in Division IA football. We remember there used to be a CFA, and there used to be a national television agreement with the NCAA. When those two things disappeared, all of a sudden we had six conferences with six effective leaders command of a lot of what happens. It is not just perceptual. There is a strong command and presence by the conferences and the leaders today that grew ever since the CFA dissolved.

PRESIDENTS

RL: What is your relationship with the president at your institution? Do you directly report to the president, or is there an intermediary? Should it be different from what it is now for you?

BB: My president is the former director of the CIA. I do report directly to him. He doesn't know a whole lot about athletics and admits it. He wants me to run the program. When there are problems, he doesn't like to be surprised. He has a five-member cabinet, and I'm on that. We meet every Monday morning, and he takes my advice on NCAA legislation. I enjoy the relationship very much. He's a fine man, sees the big picture very quickly, but he doesn't have a lot of interest in athletes. We have very few presidents who are actively involved in the Big 12 athletics.

The president does review coaches' contracts. I have to justify that what we're doing is in the market. I have to justify that we've gone out and tried to gather a good pool, but the call on who to hire and fire is mine. He told me he doesn't intend to be there on television when we announce the hiring or firing.

DG: I report to the administrative vice chancellor at UCLA, but I have access to our chancellor 24/7 and interact with him on a very regular basis. We went through two significant hires during my first year on campus. I was in contact with him throughout the entire process, and he was very engaged and very supportive of the eventual hires. I was encouraged to see the level of participation from the CEOs in our conference. The presidents and chancellors are very involved and make every effort to attend council meetings.

DJ: I think presidents and athletic people need to have direct access to one another as the ideal. The athletics programs at an institution as relatively small as ours can be the plus a university has. Yet we can also be the biggest Achilles heel. That is why I think that the communication has to be direct. We used to report directly to the president. Our president needed more time off campus and wasn't going to keep eight direct reports. We had it streamlined, and it's a dotted lined now. I report directly to a vice president for operations. The president is more involved with policy, but because of the visible nature of athletics, he wants and needs to have an idea of what's coming. People are asking him every day in the street, "What's going on in athletics?"

CU: At MSU, we reported to the vice president, who in turn reported to the president. But we had access to the president to talk about issues at the university. The president was interested in the details of what was going on in the department.

If the president did not get information from the VP, he called the AD for detailed information. The president met with the AD and the VP to discuss issues and get all the facts involved and then shared that information with the board of trustees. He was intimately involved with athletics.

COACHING ETHICS

RL: Obviously some of the bad news that has gotten coverage were cases of individual coaches over the past year. How do you feel about hiring a coach who has had a notable track record at a university with major violations? Do you feel that that person should be given some time off, should not be hired again, or just give them another chance right away?

CU: If I were in a position to hire a coach who had a track record of major violations or of conduct that was unethical, I would not hire the coach, period. However, I wouldn't suggest what other institutions should do or not do.

DG: It gets back to your core philosophy. If integrity is the cornerstone of that philosophy, one might think twice about bringing in someone with a record that is not glowing in that regard.

DJ: The athletic people are more visible than the typical figures on the campus. They are going to be held to a higher standard, and the image and the reputation are at serious stake here. Can we afford to take risks when there are so many capable people that don't have image or reputation issues?

BB: I think part of it depends on how long ago it has been. I think of what happened to my friend, Rich Brooks. He was my head coach at the University of Oregon and left there to become the coach of the Rams, and then the defensive coordinator of the Falcons. Back in 1979, they had an NCAA violation at Oregon involving an assistant coach who paid for a parent to come out and see a game. They fired the coach. Rich was recently named head coach of Kentucky, and the Lexington newspaper did a great big story on an incident that had happened 25 years before. The school had checked it out and David Price called Rich one of the most honorable men he had ever met. But the newspaper really tried to crucify him. They investigated him when he was in high school, found out that he had had a child out of wedlock, and printed that in the paper. When you do things that happened 25 plus years ago, are you still held responsible? I think the time factor has to be weighed here. Other than that, I agree with what you're saying. You don't want to import more bad guys to your campus. Where you see the real problems is like what happened at Georgia, where the president overruled the AD on the basketball coach. I think every case is unique.

RL: That brings up a good point, Bill. There were several instances this year where presidents were involved with the ethical dilemmas at Fresno State, Georgia, and St. Bonaventure. Do you think that is going to make presidents stand back more or get more directly involved in athletics in the future, or do you think it won't change?

CU: The difference today, over even just 10 years ago, is the media. I think the media is spotlighting the presidents, knowing they're currently in charge, knowing they've been officially in charge since about 1989, through legislation. I think that when something major happens on a campus, the media are going straight to the president for the answer or response. I think that is why we have recently seen action being taken at major universities fairly quickly. Ten years ago, those issues would have certainly not arisen to the level they did. And I doubt if some of those coaches would have been dismissed from their institutions. But today the bottom line is on the president because of the media and NCAA legislation.

RL: In his chapter, the NCAA's Bill Saum talks about gambling being one of the greatest threats to college sports. Is that something you worry about at your institutions?

DJ: I think it is a great threat. In planning for this year's life skills program for student- athletes in gambling, it is a concern not only for men's basketball. There is gambling on women's basketball and a little bit elsewhere. Gambling on college campuses is still pretty prevalent. We could have baseball players and tennis players betting real money on NFL games throughout the year, and they could get themselves into big trouble. We have situations with student-athletes who had to be counseled for it. It's still a big issue, and we need to keep in the forefront, keep educating people, and create fear factors/ consequences to keep it in the limelight.

DG: It is a very important issue. I would also throw agents and their "runners" into the mix as well. We must be constantly vigilant in all of these areas.

CU: And a third concern related to those two would be drugs, whether they are using or selling. That's always a temptation among young people to personally use drugs or to sell them. That's another major issue.

COLLEGE SPORT AS A CHANGE AGENT

RL: What has been the best thing that has happened to help you in your work since you have been in the business of college sport to make sport live up to its ideals?

DJ: I think it really is the people inside and outside the industry who keep the issues on the table. They are having us set high standards for ourselves and others. I think that creating awareness of issues and helping students develop and grow as real people and keeping the focus on that are among the best things that have happened.

CU: I agree that's number one. The second would be the development of women's athletics. That was something that was so needed. It has really grown and developed and given women opportunities to compete comparable to men in so many ways.

BB: I agree with both issues, particularly the one on women. I'm quite moved here. I was asked, "What was your favorite sporting event you've ever seen?" I told them a Nebraska/Penn State volleyball game. It was one of the most amazing spectator events I have ever been a part of. I'm just very proud for what we've done for several generations of young women that would never have had that opportunity. I've been in this a long time. I think that inter-collegiate athletics have also helped the integration of our nation. I think we've brought many young minority people into our colleges who would never have had a chance before. Besides all the work that we still have to do, we've done some good things.

CHAPTER 15

Faculty Forum

Percy Bates University of Michigan
Murray Sperber Indiana University
Earl Smith Wake Forest University
Keith Harrison Arizona State University
Ellen Staurowsky Ithaca College

RL: What should constitute the faculty's authority relative to athletics in higher education? Where would that authority come from?

PB: The faculty authority relative to athletics in higher education should be the central authority, but I do believe that the source of that authority probably should come from the presidents. Some faculty members were a little reluctant because they felt that athletes would get out of hand. I don't think anybody saw where it was headed. We have gone from the time that you had to get faculty permission to compete, to where we are today. In many instances faculty members are simply not involved at all or in some cases only peripherally.

MS: I think one positive aspect of faculty control is that, most often at an institution, faculty have more at stake than do presidents. I mean in my own years at Indiana since 1971 I have seen quite a number of presidents come and go. According to the *Chronicle of Higher Education*, the average president now serves at a major university less than five years, while faculty are there much longer. Faculty move around more than ever before in American higher education history, but their professional identities are very much tied to the institution. I mean, you say "Percy Bates," I say "Michigan." For faculty to abrogate their power over athletics to the presidents seems to me wrong.

The original name of the Big 10 is the Intercollegiate Conference of Faculty Repersentatives, and that was its name for 100 years.

The idea was essentially that the faculty committee had the power over athletics at each Big 10 school, and then there was a conference committee of faculty representatives for the conference. The history of the Big 10 is a much cleaner history. While there have been lots of abuses if you compare the history of the Big 10 with faculty control to, say, the history of the SEC, without much faculty control and not a lot of presidential control the history of the SEC was a much more sordid one.

PB: Murray, I agree with you in terms of the Big 10 history. When I came into it, it was a lot different than it is today. But at some point, either the presidents and/or the governing boards of Big 10 universities decided that it probably shouldn't be controlled by faculty but should have faculty in an advisory role.

MS: You are absolutely correct. Where we are disagreeing is, I say faculty should take back the power. Whether or not they are in a position to take it back, I think, is a different issue.

ESm: Faculty may have the power to do many things. The question becomes whether or not they can exercise it. Institutions that allow athletic departments to run rampant deserve whatever they get. I would argue that faculty is in control of their institution. We teach the classes. The primary mission is still the education of young men and women. If we sit back and allow athletics to dictate scheduling and all the other kinds of things student-athletes do, then I argue that we weaken our control. Faculty must realize that we don't have to give up anything in these instances just because our school has a good team. If faculty allow boards of the athletic department to take over, then I lay the blame with the faculties.

KH: What type of policy needs to be implemented so faculty clearly know that our roles shouldn't be any different with student-athletes than other students? Athletics is a major monster in American higher education. Too often faculty members are fearful of athletics. What we should be doing with athletics is unclear. We need a policy either in each conference or nationally.

MS: At many schools in the Big 10, including Indiana, the faculty athletic committee—or "the board," as it is called at other schools—is appointed by and reports to the faculty senate. That is a very standard model. However, at many schools the president appoints the faculty athletic committee, sometimes in consultation with the athletic director.

MS: That question goes to the heart of the whole matter when presidents want faculty input when it is positive or advisory, but they certainly don't want faculty input when it is critical. Faculty have the most at stake. If you read about these various academic scandals that have taken place in the Big 10 at Minnesota and, of course, what's happening at Ohio State right now, faculty create and teach these courses and look stupid when it hits the media. It seems important to have power in these areas.

PB: There has been an evolution since athletics became a much bigger business. Now there seems to be a view that we make a business side of athletics and an academic side of athletics. The faculty maintains the control in relation to the academic parts, including anything related to eligibility or progress toward a degree. But it seems to me there is a clear notion that when it comes to the financial part and involves money, the faculty should not necessarily be in control.

MS: This is in an age where business schools are so important and so powerful. There are many faculty in business schools who could understand the finances of the athletics department. One faculty member of a business school said to me, "This is the most dysfunctional business in America! If a regular business ran the way the athletics department does, they would be out of business in a month." Michigan, which has lost so much money in recent years, defies the imagination with its 106,000-seat stadium filled. They should have faculty who are objective and have some background in finance or accounting look at athletics.

PB: As I participate around the country with various groups, the question is being raised once again about the role of the faculty. There is certainly some belief that it ought to be a lot stronger than it is at the present time.

RL: Should the oversight for the faculty's involvement with athletics issues emanate from the faculty athletics representative or an academic oversight group such as the AAUP or the institutional accrediting body rather than the NCAA?

ESt: I perceive faculty athletics committees and faculty athletics reps, to some degree, may play a public relations role rather than a substantive governance role. I don't know if that perception is valid. What I can tell you (because I think I am the only one on the call who's from a Division III institution) is that many of my Division III colleagues don't know what it means when I ask who their faculty athletics rep is. I am just wondering if faculty athletics control really needs to be located solidly in some kind of academic accrediting body.

The Drake Group[1] was at the University of Tennessee two years ago. We attended a faculty meeting while we were there. During that meeting, several faculty members indicated they were baffled about NCAA rules. I think it was the provost who said she was very grateful to the athletics director for his help in educating her about the NCAA. She was head of the faculty athletics committee, but she had the athletics director interpreting the rules.

ESm: In the institutions where I have worked, the athletics director and the faculty rep were side-by-side. Whatever the decision, the athletics rep underscored it. I have never been in an institution where the faculty rep was an independent voice for that institution. The president or athletics director can't appoint the faculty rep. In the constitution at Wake Forest, the faculty rep is voted for and appointed by the faculty. It has to be an independent voice.

PB: We are dealing with very different issues on different campuses. The Faculty Athletics Representatives Association has never been successful in trying to come up with a universal set of responsibilities that everybody could be comfortable with.

PB: My experience has been that the faculty athletics rep is someone who is appointed by the president, independently of the faculty senate. That person essentially represents the university and is not necessarily the same faculty member who represents the broader faculty on campuses. I think there is a lack of clarity as to which faculty actually represent the broader faculty on campus.

ESt: On one hand, we faculty go along to get along. Yet at the same time, we're attempting to critique the things we need to critique in order to do our jobs appropriately. As long as faculty athletics reps are defined by the NCAA rather than being defined by an independent entity like the AAUP, I would argue faculty are not really contributing to the dialogue about athletics in its relationship to higher education. My impression is that the vast majority of faculty say nothing about athletics and don't care a great deal about athletics because they don't think it really has anything to do with them.

MS: There is concrete proof that you are right about the co-optation. Many members of faculty boards and faculty committees get skybox seats or fifty-yard-line seats or mid-court seats. When their school goes to a bowl or tournament, they are on the gravy train. It's all free, and it's all glorious. These are the people who are supposed to have some oversight over the athletics department. At many schools, that includes financial oversight. Yet they have just been on this trip to a bowl game where the school got a payout of millions but it spent more, in part by taking them and their significant others to the bowl game. If it was clearly stated that members of faculty boards and faculty athletic committees could not take these perks, we would have a lot less faculty applying. Too many faculty apply to be on these boards because they want the mid-court seats. So if you said no more perks, you would immediately weed out a whole raft of faculty who shouldn't be on athletic committees.

MS: Many faculty won't speak up because they know the consequences. College sports doesn't exist in a vacuum. At Division I schools and Big 10 schools, there's a huge number of fans who are boosters, with no other connection to the college or university other than their love for its athletic teams.

I know during the firing of Bob Knight, I felt their wrath. It doesn't take a mid-court seat to keep a lot of faculty silent. Then there's the large number of faculty who are genuinely not interested in sports. In fact, part of the reason some became academics is they don't like that part of American culture. To find faculty who know about sports and are not willing to be co-opted is slightly difficult, but they do exist.

PB: We have to deal with the question about what the relationship really ought to be in order to make it work. In so many cases that I know of, there is no relationship between the faculty and athletics. Then it is hard for the faculty to get any information about what is really going on. We need at least some reasonable relationship so we are not fighting all the time. Yet at the same time, we need to be able to reasonably provide some oversight and to feel free to speak.

In most cases that I know, faculty reps serve that position. They are supposed to have the right and the authority to go to the president when things are not going the way he or she thinks they ought to be. Somehow you have to create a situation where you get close enough to the inside that you know what is going on and can influence it rather than putting on the boxing gloves from day one and saying, "I'm here to really pick a fight with you." I don't know how you can have an outside agency provide the oversight. How will it be able to know on a day-to-day basis what's going on to be able to provide the oversight?

RL: Murray, if I understood you correctly, you are clearly saying you think faculty do risk job security if they deal directly with the shortcomings of intercollegiate athletics. You raised questions about faculty members demanding enhanced transcripts or speaking out when they see "Mickey Mouse" courses that some athletes take in departments. If you or a faculty member does this, do you think you have serious risk to your job security?

MS: I agree with Percy that the financial side has gotten shifted away to the detriment of the institution. However, on this academic side it is absolutely clear that the faculty is in charge of courses. There is not a faculty senate in the country that does not have to approve courses or take courses off the books and all of this. We as faculty are at fault when it is revealed that athletes such as those at Georgia where Harrick's son were given all A's in his Mickey Mouse course.

It seems to me one of the things that faculty committees could do and should do is look at the academic careers of the athletes. Now, they do to a certain extent, but I know the Drake Group has long pushed for transparent transcripts. Certainly these enhanced transcripts are very revealing, where they tell how many people in the course got A's. They can give you an idea of what kind of course it was. Just in a simple, practical way, I think faculty should get involved with these academic things. They always say, "yes, we are in charge of the academic side," but certainly that faculty athletics committee at Georgia wasn't looking too deeply. Now, I know that it brings up questions of the Buckley Amendment and students' privacy. But there are many university committees that look at transcripts and all kinds of things, and it stays in the room. A faculty committee looking at an athlete's transcripts stays in the room.

And we also should be much more concerned about the cohort of athletes. Are 50 percent of the players on the football teams taking a ridiculous course of studies or major?

PS: If it is just one or two faculty on campus versus a large group, those persons are very vulnerable. I don't see a groundswell of faculty on campuses coming over to say, "Listen, I support you on this."

PB: The whistle blower is vulnerable until we can get the faculty to rise up. A member of the Knight Commission asked, "Why aren't the faculty outraged?" I ask that question all the time. I don't hear any answers coming back, because I don't see the outrage.

ESm: I would be absolutely opposed to having faculty poking in and out of student's transcripts and other professors' grading practices. It is a matter of academic freedom. When we hire faculty, we should be sure that they are of the highest integrity and ability. When you find that your colleague had 30 students in a class and 25 of them were athletes and there were 28 A's, I think that it is the collegiate nature of that particular department unit to police its own. As a dean and a department chair, I can tell you we do that in places that I work. I worry about exposing these student-athletes to the admissions or joint athletics admissions committee. Murray said "it stays in the room," but I have never known those discussions to stay in the room.

I am also concerned that this particular issue starts to intersect with issues of race and ethnicity. It is easy to go into the faculty lounge and hear people talk about "why does this university let people in from Compton or some other place?" If student-athletes want to major in recreation land management, or whatever, that's their prerogative, just the same as for other students who want to major in math or music. It is up to them and their parents. I think that the only thing we as faculty have to do is to make sure what we do in our classroom is of the highest integrity.

MS: I would like to reply briefly to what you said. I agree that faculty should act with the highest integrity, but unfortunately some don't always do. What Percy said about whistle blowers is important because the question becomes: How do you institutionalize this process? To whom do the whistle blowers go? Hopefully the faculty athletic committee has faculty who are objective and knowledgeable about college sports. Whistle blowers can go with their concerns, and this committee can do something about it.

I do feel that it should be proactive and should look at enhanced transcripts. You know Phi Beta Kappa societies use enhanced transcripts. This is the day of grade inflation with so many A's. There was a time when you just needed a straight-A average to make Phi Beta. Well, that day is long past. If the faculty members who are on the Phi Beta Kappa committee to choose students can do it, why can't the faculty athletic committee do it? I agree it brings up privacy issues. But I am much more interested in faculty athletic committees looking at the whole cohort. Look at the women's crew and the men's basketball team and not at individual athletes. Now I agree that it should stay in the room and sometimes it doesn't. But there are ways of impressing upon faculty that they are violating the Buckley Amendment at their own risk and peril of their own career. You are not going to get a handle on the whole academic side of athletics until you do something like this.

ESt: The organizational structure that comes to mind is something along the lines of an office of internal affairs for athletics. No matter how many rules are formulated, some schools get around the spirit of the rules. I think that is what the dilemma is. My Drake Group colleagues know that I have not felt comfortable sacrificing an athlete and putting them out in public view in order to achieve a goal. That is deeply problematic to me. On the other hand, even at this level our coaches here play a huge role in academic advisement to the point where things are, sometimes, out of our hands because we have an online registration process. Coaches do suggest what courses a student should take or greatly affect the registration process by setting the parameters for when students can take classes (not after 2 p.m., even if practice does not start until 4 p.m.). They have access to academic records. When a student enrolls and is confronted with the paperwork to sign which waives their Buckley Amendment rights, they often agree to allow athletic personnel to review their academic records without knowing the rights they are giving up. The game has shifted considerably. Some kind of internal affairs mechanism is missing.

ACADEMIC ATHLETIC ADVISORS

ESt: The Drake Group was visiting a Big 12 school. We met with several staff, including the head of their athletic academic unit. Very matter of factly she indicated that they had a list of preferred faculty to whom they referred athletes. They were faculty members favorably disposed to athletics. This is an affront to academic freedom as well. It does happen.

MS: I addressed the national meeting of the academic athletic advisors. There is no question they are making up the schedules for the athletes. In fact, one of the reforms that Myles Brand called for is to move academic advising out of the athletic department and into the main academic advising.

KH: I am always curious why we have academic support in athletics and general academic advising in whatever their major. Yet we don't have athletic support within the academic institution to deal with the culture of athletics. Isn't that what the purpose of the academic support in athletics is? I support moving academic support out of athletics. Why don't we have a support system for the athletic culture in academics? It would come from an academic pedagogy. When we all intervene to deal with this, we often don't have enough time. They are sometimes channeled in the other areas beyond intellectual pursuit. We need a complete staff in academics that just deals with that infrastructure, just like athletics has an infrastructure called academic services.

ESt: I like that very much, Keith. Educators, if they are doing their job, are supposed to be sensitive to the needs of their students. And we have all types of students who are working, who have time conflicts and pressures in their lives. Some of them have families that have financial concerns. The list goes on and on. I think it really does beg the question of: How did higher education arrive at the point where "special" areas for athletics academic advisement are routinely offered? Doesn't that say something about the failure of the institution to serve these students, period?

MS: The problem with academic support people is that their bosses are the coaches and the ADs, and they have a very clear issue with academics and athletics and it's called keeping the student eligible. Above all, that is the number one priority. Yes, they would also love the athlete to get a good education. The better the education, the better they feel, but they realize this is the real world and they have got to keep the students eligible. That often works against the athlete's education. I have known too many cases where athletes wanted to be pre-med and were channeled into leisure therapy. These advisors are very well meaning. I have been very impressed by them over the years. They are truly sincere about wanting to help the athlete get a good education, but they are also aware that they have to be able to buy groceries, and their paycheck is signed essentially by the coaches and the athletics director. They have got to do what they are told. Keith's ideas about moving them out of the athletics department and making them more academic strikes me as a very positive step.

THE EFFECT OF TRAVEL SCHEDULES

RL: Could you address the issue of faculty response to the pressure in terms of missing classes and travel and what effect that has on the academic performance and potential of student-athletes?

ESm: This is an area where the faculty has been hoodwinked from day one and has no control about how it works. We get a letter saying the golf team can't play at these expensive golf courses on the weekend, therefore their travel is during the week.

KH: One of my frustrations as a university faculty member has been it doesn't go both ways. They dictate to us almost when they are going to come to class or when they are going to take our exams, etc. I can't go down on the field at Florida State and say, "Hey, Bobby Bowden, it is the fourth quarter, but I need two of your linebackers. We are finishing up a million-dollar grant for NIH and they are going to be absent the fourth quarter."

ESt: Last semester I got this idea that we reword the letters sent by the athletics department to faculty about students missing class time from a faculty perspective. I asked athletes in my classes what their experience would be like if they brought this note saying please excuse "so and so" from practice or a game because they are attending class. There is just such an assumption that the academic side will yield, and there is no counterbalance to that. The reworded letter got an interesting conversation going.

MENTORING

RL: Do faculty have the responsibility to mentor student-athletes from urban and rural settings who are not typically acclimated to middle-class, mainstream culture?

MS: In an ideal world, faculty can reach out to these students. Nontenured faculty have to focus on their research and do not have the luxury of time. Tenured faculty have the luxury of time and can reach out. But unless you set up a reward system for faculty, it is always going to be ad-hoc. In terms of cultural heritage and good education, students from rural Indiana are more deprived than students from South Central. A lot of minority students will fall by the wayside unless universities go from idiosyncratic mentoring to a more institutionalized mentoring.

PB: When we think of the "faculty," the general faculty was encouraged to but not rewarded for mentoring. We have to have a group of people on campuses who have more interest and more focus to systemically help. I deal with race, gender, and national origin around the issues of equity. I deal with this on campus no matter where it comes from. There are students on campus with different experiences. We have white students who come from rural areas and small high schools who struggle trying to survive. If there are student-athletes that I have responsibility for, then I reach out and I do what I can to help them. The difficultly is greater for African-American students, and I put a little more interest and effort with them to do what I can. Someone has to have that interest.

When I talk to student-athletes who have an interest in coming here, I make it clear that my role as a faculty member here is to help them get an education. I am not a coach. Someone else has already evaluated their athletic skills. There is an agreement that they are going to use their athletic skills and ability in exchange for an opportunity to get a good education. If you think you are not getting the education, you need to let me know, because that is my responsibility. You need a group of people on campuses who will help. Someone is going to have to take responsibility since it cannot be left up to the "general faculty."

ESm: We get an overview of the problems with the data on graduation rates. Students who come from underrepresented groups, especially African Americans, are usually the ones going all-out to play a sport for the school. But too many leave the institution without a degree. That is an institution's problem, because it is a reciprocal relationship. African-American males, for example, are not getting their return. Someone has to step up and help them in the academic realm.

KH: I agree that it is an institutional problem, and I remind my institution every chance I get. I have not been successful in identifying a large-enough segment of the faculty to take this on.

MS: In Division III and small liberal arts colleges, mentoring is part of the job description and a very valuable part if the college does a good job with it. That is not so at Division I schools. At a faculty council meeting at Indiana one year, an administrator talked about mentoring all minority students. She asked how many faculty would be interested in doing this. I put my hand up with 3 others out of 450! This was the most active faculty on campus who give up their time for faculty council and many other things. I do not think it was racist. They do not have time. It was very evident that the university was not going to reward this service. All nontenured faculty, those who wanted to be promoted to professor, or want to get a new job at another university, are so plugged into the research at research institutions. The rewards for research are bountiful. The rewards for teaching and for service are minimal. The culture at research universities is deeply established. Division III is a very different world than Division IA.

ESm: It also extends beyond that into the student body. You would think this whole issue of the minority athlete and the need for support services comes out of the academic athletic union. When some students see an African-American male on campus they think two things: (1) He is an athlete, and (2) he is dumb. In the faculty meetings and administrative meetings I have attended over the years, I hear the same things. They see these students and start talking about SAT scores and what neighborhoods they come from. When Patrick Ewing's Georgetown team traveled, some fans threw bananas on the court and called him names. It goes well beyond the faculty and whether or not they are being paid. It is a societal issue about the place of people of color in general and in the sports area, which is primarily African-American athletes. There are still major stereotypes out there about whether they are academically able or whether they are athletically gifted from the time they are born. I have talked to faculty about how they hate to see these kids coming to classes. You go to the games and you see the same faculty out there cheering on the team. They are happy to have those free tickets. It is a big problem.

There is no institutional program to eliminate the problem. I have been in meetings where a group will come in and say that they need help with student-athletes, and no one raises their hand. The coaching staff feels they can let an athlete go who becomes ineligible or does something wrong off the playing field. They then go to some high school and get another "body." At Wake Forest there was an article in the paper about "ineligible athletes." It comes up every year. The coach, who just signed a million-dollar contract, said in the newspaper, "We have other guys." Here is a young man who has given four years of his life and ran into some difficulty in the classroom. The only thing the coach can say is "we have other guys."

PB: Several years ago I wrote an article on desegregation, and I did not give it a title. They kept calling me, wanting to know what to call it, and I finally settled on: "Can We Get There from Here?" It is clear to me that there are no easy answers to the questions posed. We can talk about faculty, but it is pretty clear that we are talking about universities, society, and students who are not athletes. It is a lot broader than that. Every time we solve a problem, we create three others. Those of us who are trying to correct these problems can't do it unless you want to tear it down and start over. The process of trying to fix it from here is very, very difficult. I do not know if we can get there from here.

GOOD NEWS WITH STUDENT-ATHLETES

KH: One of my favorite stories about student-athletes was in my first year at Michigan. The football team was headed for Indiana, and they were excused from my 1 p.m. class because the bus left at 2 p.m. Nonetheless, nine of the footballers came to the class and sprinted to the bus because they were interested in the class, their peers, and what I was trying to do. There are many times when they do not have any time and are looking for shortcuts, trying to get out of things. I tried to connect with student-athletes, usually with race or social class. The female student-athletes loved it when you attended their soccer game or softball game. Word spreads that their faculty member was at that particular event. I crossed racial lines with white football players because I was an offensive lineman. That encouraged office visits and more interaction.

MS: The most positive responses were from the female student-athletes. The female student-athletes still enrolled even after being advised not to take my courses because I did not give breaks to athletes or any other student. The female student-athletes who came were very good students. The discipline they learned in sports applied to class and their work. I got to know many of them over the years, and it has been a very positive experience. There is a composition component in my class, and I learned a great deal about them, their lives as a student-athletes, and college sports.

ESt: The reasons why I spend so much time writing and researching these issues is that the stories of many student-athletes are so inspiring. Recently, I have been deeply moved by the efforts of Jeremy Bloom, at the University of Colorado, and Ramogi Huma, founder of the Collegiate Athletes Coalition, to create an awareness of the inequities that college athletes encounter. Those two individuals represent everything that should be good about the relationship between athletics and higher education. They are independent thinkers moved to action by a sense of justice, equipped with the courage and personal fortitude to effect change in a system not just for themselves but for other athletes.

PB: Student-athletes have been the reason why I have stayed around so long. As a faculty representative, it is always difficult to know how you really are perceived. When students want someone to talk to who is not a part of the athletics department, I am often designated that person. They do not feel that they would be talking through me to the coach. Numerous student-athletes are very, very bright. They are so very busy trying to go to school and compete in their sport. They really have a lot more insight as to what they are doing, why they are doing it, and about the coaches and athletics. They changed my views and perceptions about what was going on that was certainly different than what I might have thought than if I had not met them.

ESm: The things that I think about are all of the cards, invitations to weddings, baby pictures, and personal messages. Letting them know that you are there for them and also learning from them. I taught a two-week course, and at the end a young lady stated, "I just have to tell you how good it feels to be a regular student for a change."

NOTE

1. The mission of the Drake Group is to help faculty and staff defend academic integrity in the face of the burgeoning college sport industry. It is a national network of college faculty that lobbies aggressively for proposals that ensure quality education for college athletes, supports faculty whose job security is threatened for defending academic standards, and disseminates information on current issues and controversies in sport and higher education.

CHAPTER 16

Student-Athletes' Forum

Lindsay Beddow Louisiana State University, Gymnastics
Keri Boyce University of Kentucky, Soccer
Zach Falconer Northeastern University, Football
Damone Jones Penn State University, Football
Morgan Marr University of Kentucky, Softball
Brian O'Leary University of Kentucky, Soccer
Charece Williams North Carolina State University, Volleyball
Sarah Wong University of Mississippi, Soccer

RL: Myles Brand proposed and the NCAA has adopted incentives and disincentives for graduation rates. What would be some good incentives for improving academics?

LB: I think that academic performance should be rewarded along with athletic performance. The term *student-athlete* implies that college athletes are both athletes and students; hence, one should not be rewarded above the other.

Many universities will reward student-athletes that do well academically at a separate banquet at the end of the year. From my experiences, the athletes that do not do well enough to get recognized are not even invited to attend the awards ceremony. If all athletes are invited to these banquets, they will see that their efforts off of the field can and will be rewarded, and it may motivate them to do better the next year. If athletic accomplishments can be rewarded in front of everyone, academic accomplishments should be rewarded as well.

Is there a way that academic performance could be factored into the BCS calculations? Instead of just looking at win/loss records and strength of schedule, they could also look at GPA and graduation rates when deciding which schools get to play for the big money bowls. Football should only be part of the equation, and this would be a way to reward the best student-athletes, not just the best athletes. This would also halt the criticism that NCAA football is modeled after the pros.

Money is the main driving force behind the way an athletic department conducts itself, which leads me to believe that incentives involving money will be the most effective. Rather than dividing the money from a bowl appearance equally among the schools in that conference, they could divide the money proportionate to the way each school performed academically each year. For example, in the SEC, Vanderbilt would get a bigger percentage of money than any of the other schools.

The NCAA should require schools to set benchmarks regarding graduation rates to be met within the next 5 years, 10 years, and so on. Schools are at different rates right now, so it would not be fair to reward schools that are able to graduate a specific percent (75 percent, for example). In that case, a school like Duke or Stanford would not have to work harder than what they are doing now, but for a school like Arkansas that number may seem unreachable.

Schools that fail to meet those benchmarks should be prohibited from hosting conference, regional, and national championships on campus that would normally generate money. This seems like it would get more people behind the movement to graduate more athletes. You could also reduce the number of scholarships a school can offer as a punishment for not graduating their student-athletes.

There are various incentives that I can think of to motivate schools to educate their players. Why not put their GPA on the TV screen along with their height, weight, and hometown? I think it would be upsetting to viewers watching their favorite running back out there with less than a 2.5 GPA. Schools would not want to face that criticism and would do things to correct the problem. Also, instead of getting stickers for their helmet for the number of tackles a player gets, why not put stickers on for how many A's the player gets? (I think some schools may already do this.)

BO: I think the NCAA has done a fairly good job in providing schools an incentive for increasing their graduation rates. Loss of scholarships is arguably the most important feature of this legislation. History has shown that a reduction in scholarships is usually followed by a downturn in the success of that individual team. Teams can overcome not having as big a budget as their rival or competitor, but if you cannot get the same amount of quality players, then the program will struggle. While the loss of revenue that could come with a postseason ban may be incentive to some institutions to exceed the academic progress rate, there are too many schools that operate in the red already to see how this would adversely affect their current practices.

MM: As incentives, you could provide additional scholarships to those teams that do well. However, more policing would need to be done to ensure that grades were being earned and not given, and teachers were not being bribed to give grades in order to receive more scholarships.

KB: One effective incentive for the schools could be a monetary incentive. This incentive would not be an increase in the number of scholarships allowed. However, it would be money that would go towards their academic support system for all student-athletes, or even money that would go towards improving the school as a whole.

MM: Should there be incentives for something we are expected to do anyway?

DJ: Because graduating its athletes is often tossed around as a priority, there should be no incentives for graduating its student-athletes. It's the school's responsibility to get a meaningful degree into the hands of its student-athletes.

RL: How about effective disincentives?

DJ: In order to rate a school fairly, the NCAA should require its member institutions to graduate its student-athletes at or above the same rate of the general student body—each respective school, not the association as a whole. Should a school not graduate its student-athletes at the prescribed rate, 50 percent of what it would normally receive from conference profit-sharing ventures. In the case of independents, a fine would be levied against a failing school equal to the average of other failing schools. That money would then go into the Student-athlete Opportunity Fund.

CW: A disincentive I feel would be effective is forcing schools to forgo a percentage of their portion in bowl revenue sharing. In conferences such as the ACC and the SEC, there is a lot of money in the pot due to BCS bowl bids and other bowls that teams in the conference attend. It makes sense that if a school is not following rules put in place in regard to academics or anything else, they should not have the ability to get such a large share of the bowl revenues. The money could be given to a fund, such as the NCAA Student-athlete Opportunities Fund.

KB: If the school has incredibly low graduation rates for a set amount of years, a restricted membership status for the institution in the NCAA might be the only option to get the school to comply quickly and make changes to improve their graduation rates.

ZF: Given the pressure on university administrators, athletic administrators, and coaches to win, any sanctions which threaten a university's ability to compete (by taking away scholarships) is bound to make them pay closer attention to the academic potential of the student-athletes that they're bringing in and to whether the student-athletes they have are graduating. However, the universities have a lot of leeway in policing themselves, and should a university be in violation, the disincentives take too long to kick in. More expedient levying of disincentives would make these sanctions more effective.

MM: You could decrease the number of scholarships available to those students entering. You could also take away coaches' incentives such as cars, tickets, contractual obligation that reduces the chance of removing him/ herself from the issue and going to another school (such as monetary stipulations), etcetera. If you do not hold the coaches responsible, it will be that much harder to filter it through the system.

RL: What will be the most significant issues influencing collegiate athletics in the next 5 to 10 years?

SW: The major issues from my point of view are the increase of athletes (especially football and basketball) leaving school early to go pro; the increasing trend of college athletics as a business; the battle of costs between university presidents/academic world versus the athletics departments (for example, the coaches' salaries versus the presidents'/ADs' salaries); the continued debate over academics versus athletics—are student-athletes really going to school for an education or are they going to school to try to get a pass to the next level in the pros? Other key issues will be poor decision-making (misrepresentation, substance abuse, etcetera) by college coaches who are under pressure and the lack of minority representation in Division I athletics.

CW: The most obvious issue is determining a national championship in football. Second are the football players challenging the NFL in order to enter the draft early. The third, a proposed salary cap on coaches' salaries, especially college football coaches.

MM: There are some key issues. The pressure to take supplements and/or performance enhancing drugs is growing, and the University of Washington softball program shows it is not just male athletes anymore. We will have to face the decision of whether to pay athletes and/or maintain an academic scholarship system. How will we fund the rising costs of competitive athletics departments? What will the results be of the increased pressure to push the envelope to get the best athletes? Will the ages in which one can go pro in the respective sports be lowered?

BO: Unfortunately, I think we will be discussing the same issues in 5 to 10 years as we are talking about now. Gambling, drug use, and academic fraud are and will still be big issues. Gambling is an issue that the NCAA has attempted to curtail but is probably facing an even tougher challenge today than ever before as gambling becomes more mainstream and accepted by the American public. Drug use, specifically steroids, seems to be becoming more and more prevalent as these drugs become harder to detect. With professional sports paying such large salaries, the incentive to do whatever it takes to be the best has been increased since even a decade ago. This leads college and high school kids to do whatever it takes to get one of those contracts. When it comes to academic fraud, I think we may see even more cases in the next 10 years than we have in the past. With the introduction of the Academic Performance Program, individuals may be more likely to participate in fraudulent activity in order to make sure that their team is above the 50 percent graduation rate requirement.

DJ: The biggest issues for college sports in the next 5 to 10 years will be directly tied to football and basketball, the premier revenue-generating sports. In football, it is likely that more true freshmen will play and will perform at high levels. The recent dominance of players like Maurice Clarett (Ohio State), Michael Hart and Chad Henne (Michigan), and Adrien Peterson (Oklahoma) illustrates that underclassmen can indeed perform at high levels. Due to the ephemeral nature of football, these players and others like them may want the opportunity to cash in on their NFL potential. After USC's Mike Williams and Clarett nearly won a challenge against the National Football League's strict rules about providing employment opportunities, there is a chink in the league's armor.

LB: The large amounts of money being generated by the schools with winning football programs is going to make it harder and harder not to pay the athletes that make all that money possible. As college sports becomes more and more like the pros, it will be more evident that the athletes aren't being fairly compensated for the amount of money they are generating.

It is also going to be harder and harder for the schools with smaller budgets and smaller football programs to keep up. The space between the haves and the have-nots is going to continue to grow, which will lead to more revenue sharing and even more accusations that college sports is a business.

ZF: The most significant issues influencing college athletics in the next 5 to 10 years will be containing costs and diversity (both in head coaching and athletic administration). Right now universities are allowed to spend as much as they can on athletics, and hence spending has spiraled out of control, with the average Division I university spending $27 million and Ohio State topping all universities at $85 million. Such large sums of money only serve to compromise the integrity of college athletics. In addition, they widen the gap between the haves and the have-nots, making it virtually impossible for most universities to compete on the highest levels. Instead of choosing a university based upon its academic offerings or campus life, most student-athletes now choose a school based upon whether it has state-of-the-art athletic facilities. And minority hiring in college athletics absolutely must improve. There's no plausible reason for such a lack of diversity.

KB: I think the most significant issues influencing collegiate athletics in the next 5 to 10 years will be the integrity of the coaches, and women and minorities in coaching roles and significant positions in college athletics departments.

There have been numerous college coaches who made many wrong ethical decisions in their careers, whether it is soliciting prostitutes, gambling on different games, drinking with students on campus, or giving money to their players. I am hoping that the integrity of college coaches does improve, but I feel like this is one issue that will not go away. Also, the number of minorities and women in coaching roles and positions in college athletics departments is a very important issue that will be very significant in the next 5 to 10 years. If these numbers do not even out, then the type of people that they hire under them will most likely be similar to themselves, which will severely influence college athletics.

RL: What are the most important issues for student-athletes?

DJ: The most important issue for student-athletes is the ongoing saga of "pay or not pay." The NCAA generously granted SAs [student-athletes] the right to work . . . for $2,000 per year. That's just under $5.50 a day. Although they are student-athletes and admittedly choose to participate in sports (as some pundits have argued), they are still entitled to be able to earn enough money for day-to-day expenses. For most athletes, that extra money comes from a family that can afford to send their son or daughter the money to get by. However, there are a number of SAs who come from low-income areas and families who can't afford to send extra money to school. Full scholarships don't pay for soap or toothpaste, or food after the dining hall is closed, or a calling card to say hello to folks at home 400 miles away.

BO: The number one issue for most student-athletes is money. While many student-athletes receive a monthly stipend, it is hardly enough to pay rent, utilities, and groceries. It is true that student-athletes are allowed to work, but it is very difficult to hold a job when you are participating in major college athletics. A typical day for me during undergrad included practice from 8 a.m. to anytime between 10 and 11 a.m. Then I would go to class from 12 p.m. to 2 or 3 p.m. before going to lift weights at 3:30. Then it would be back to class from 6 p.m. until 7:30 p.m. We played our games on Friday nights and Sunday afternoons for the most part, with the occasional Wednesday game included every season. If the games on the weekend were away from campus, we would usually leave Thursday morning and not return until late Sunday night, if not Monday morning. Include in that schedule time to study, and it is difficult to find an employer who is willing to hire you. This has led some student-athletes to enroll in welfare programs, which allow them to keep a roof over their head and food on the table.

CW: An important issue for student-athletes is having the ability to be paid. I feel that it is only fair that student-athletes are compensated for their many sacrifices. A demanding daily regimen does not allow student-athletes to work part-time jobs to take care of things they may need for success, happiness, or both. Many will argue that a scholarship should be fair payment for a student-athlete, but I disagree. If you have two students on scholarship, one athletic and one academic, there are obvious differences. An academic scholarship recipient does not have to practice three hours a day, which completely breaks down the body, making it difficult to study, miss important classes due to travel, graduate in 5 years, and has the opportunity to work a part-time job to support extracurricular activities or expenses not covered under scholarship such as car payments, insurance, or clothing. When I was a student-athlete, I rarely had money to go to the movies or go away for spring break. I barely had the money to pay my car note and insurance.

SW: I agree. Student-athletes need enough money to pay for rent, food, books, and other necessary things. In football and basketball, coaches put pressure on the advisors to find a way to make the student eligible to be on the field or on the court. Their livelihood depends on it, so of course, they are going to pressure the advisors. Perhaps if they kept the coaches from having close contact directly with the advisors, then the advisors would feel less pressure from the coaches. The students also need to be held accountable as well. They need to recognize if they are being pushed in a direction that does not suit their academic goals. The advisors could have more contact with the academic departments within the university, which could help determine which major is best for each student.

ZF: However, with all of the money being poured into universities and the athletic conferences due to their athletic participation (again at the Division I level), student-athletes need to better acquaint themselves with what monetary assistance they may be eligible for outside of their scholarships. Obviously, universities have a responsibility to make them more aware, but it is in student-athletes' interest to be proactive in acquiring this information. I am not suggesting that student-athletes ever be paid for playing a sport in college, but many universities have the financial flexibility to cover the costs for basic items such as clothing, food, or travel expenses, within limits. This could alleviate the problems that many universities are facing in terms of student-athletes taking improper payments from boosters.

Also, as long as the coaches are under the gun to win, they will consequently put pressure on academic advisors to keep their players eligible. One way to alleviate this problem is for coaches to recruit student-athletes who are better prepared for college (or better yet, their college) because, unfortunately, too often student-athletes are admitted to schools which they aren't academically suited for based upon their athletic abilities.

DJ: The misuse of athletes lends itself directly to the problems with not graduating them. The NCAA and its member institutions have had a history of exploiting its athletes. Again, some wouldn't consider it exploitation because of the scholarships the universities dole out, but that money, a portion of which is raised privately, is miniscule in comparison to what the association brings in from the postseason basketball tournament and the BCS. In line with those concerns is the way the scholarships themselves are structured. The four one-year scholarships create an atmosphere that allows coaches to not renew the scholarships of players who are underperforming. This is certainly not in line with the NCAA's moniker of "student-athlete." Athletic scholarships should be for 10 semesters (a semester should count as 12 credits or more for fall or spring, or 9 credits for a 12-week summer).

Graduating, rather than educating, SAs has been a problem for quite some time. If you peek inside of a football media guide, you can surely pick out the "football-friendly" majors at each school. They generally range from Sociology and Leisure Studies, to Criminal Justice and Liberal Arts. Don't believe that it's a coincidence that these players all love to study the same thing. Academic advisors are under constant pressure from the coaches to keep their athletes on the field. A coach can boast about graduation rates, but what is the true measure of academic success? High GPAs? Not in this day and age of inflated GPAs. Seventy-five percent graduation rate? Not when half of those guys have degrees that relegate them to entry-level jobs. Coaches have too much influence over the academic advisors. Coaches have too much power.

SW: Some athletes have the feeling that their coaches view the individual and the team as a means to their paycheck. Athletes should get more respect for the amount of time, energy, and hard work that goes into being a student-athlete. We need support from the university—so that we graduate no matter how long it takes. We need the support to miss practices if we need to be in class.

LB: Issues you face as a student-athlete vary as to whether or not your sport offers professional opportunities after college. In my sport, I knew there was nothing for me after college, so it was easy for me to put more focus on my education. In these sports, the coaches will in some ways be more lenient when it comes to missing practice to take a test. However, these student-athletes are still getting paid to be the best that they can be and don't want to let their coaches down. There were times when I would have to pick one or the other, and it was very hard when you are trying to do what's best for your future while trying to perform well for your university.

I have seen the way advisors work, and many of them feel like it is a lost cause to try and guide players in the right direction academically. They have lists of teachers that like football players, and then a list of those that don't, and that is how they place them in their classes. Many players do not come from a strong educational background and are used to having someone do everything for them. Many advisors do not care about the players as people and do not realize the impact that they could potentially have on the future of these student-athletes. The problem is that as soon as that player has lost his athletic eligibility, the advisor has a new crop of players to keep eligible and the athlete is in charge of his academics for usually the first time in his life.

There is also a lack of minority academic advisors. I know at the bigger schools with more money each player will be assigned to a mentor to meet with every week, aside from meeting with their advisor. More often than not, an African-American football player will be assigned to an attractive white female. Why? You could not have a bigger cultural gap between the two. How can someone mentor you that is nothing like you, that could not possibly imagine what you go through day in and day out? When asked why there were not more African-American mentors for the African-American student-athletes, the response of the athletics department was simply that it would be "too black." That makes me think about what I said earlier about why there are not more minority head coaches.

The one thing that comes to mind is the large amount of money that schools with big football programs spend on facilities. It is unnecessary to build a multimillion dollar training facility or academic center just to keep up with the other schools. It is amazing to see millions of dollars being used to add on to an already extravagant stadium, when the classrooms and the library are nearly falling apart.

MM: The pressure to be on the field as opposed to in the classroom was real. The inability to take certain classes because of scheduling conflicts and having to block off six hours a day for practice added to it. Many times these six hours were cutting it close, especially when you included time for conditioning and weight lifting and/or the hour or so of treatment necessary due to an injury. Then there was travel time as well as mandatory study hours.

At some point the student-athlete needs to be held accountable. I feel that, as a freshman, a career development course needs to be made required. Students across the board need to be made aware of the various career paths/options available to them upon graduation from the beginning. This course could be in the form of seminars in which guest speakers in various fields come and speak about their path to success. At the conclusion of this course, a major would need to be declared to complete the course and, the courses necessary should be laid out at that time. This way the student advisors would simply be there for encouragement and to aide the athletes in working out their schedule according to their practice schedule.

Colleges/universities need to establish a spending cap that is enforced across sports to stop the expensive expansions of stadiums and other high-end expenses that are not necessary to the success of the program. These need to be mandated by the NCAA and should be sport-specific. This may also aide in establishing a competitive balance within collegiate sports.

KB: Many student-athletes face the 20-hour rule, where we are only supposed to practice 20 hours a week, excluding any games we have. But, when you factor in the "optional" weight-lifting sessions and the extra individual practices (where groups of five to six players train one hour more once a week before practice), then it clearly comes out to more than 20 hours a week. I remember passing around the 20-hour sheets to sign each week, stating that we only practiced 20 hours, and everyone would just laugh it off, knowing full well we did way more than 20 hours. But, we were not about to complain, because we knew we would get yelled at by our coaches and, also, we were sure that the other teams were doing this as well. So to stay on the same level of everyone else, we felt like we had to comply with this.

MM: There is a real issue with "voluntary" practices. It is voluntary practice because if they were to make it mandatory, they would not be compliant with the 20-hour rule. However, you better be there or your playing time will be affected and possibly suspension off the team.

KB: Another major issue is being treated equally, both with regards to respect and monetarily, to every other team/sport at the school. Everyone who was on a full-ride knew how much their monthly check was, and soon the student-athletes found out how much bigger the checks were of the athletes on the other teams, like basketball, football, and baseball. Also, many of the athletes on the Olympic sports teams feel as if they are inferior to the "big-time" college sports (i.e., basketball, football, and sometimes baseball) simply due to the athletics directors who clearly show preference to the big-time sports.

Also, coaches' salaries need to be controlled. I think it is ridiculous that some college football and basketball coaches make the same amount if not more money than the university presidents. Yes, these coaches do a great job by winning and, in effect, bringing in a lot of money, but these salaries need to start being contained.

MM: The seclusion of the athletic culture was something I had to face. It is oftentimes hard to meet other students and/or join other organizations because of the reputation/stigma that athletes have amongst the student population as well as amongst professors. I only faced one antiathlete professor once, and I immediately dropped his course. I knew that regardless of the quality of the material that I handed in I was going to be graded unfairly. There would be no exceptions if I had to miss a class/quiz/exam due to a traveling date and/or a game.

CW: As an African-American student-athlete at a large predominately white university, I found it difficult to find others that I could relate to. The crazy thing is that I found some level of difficulty adjusting, and I grew up in a predominately white neighborhood and school system. I feel that African-American student-athletes are somewhat thrown into an environment which is not meant for them to thrive. Who can an African-American student-athlete talk to about where to get their hair cut/done or how to find a predominately black church, if that is what they are seeking? There is hardly any time in the athlete's schedule to venture outside of athletics to join a black students' board, or national association of black accountants, or a predominantly black sorority or fraternity. If athletics departments employed people in supervisory/influential positions, there is a chance that these people would recognize the culture shock for some African-American student-athletes and may put programs in place to help ease the transition. Ultimately, my thought is that athletics departments are not concerned about the overall well-being of student-athletes, and if they are, they really don't know how to assist these student-athletes to get to that "happy place."

RL: What should/can be done about the small number of minority head coaches and athletics directors in college athletics?

BO: I think the NFL has instituted a hiring process that the NCAA should look to follow. Granted, the requirement that teams in the NFL include minorities in their search and interview process for head coaches has its flaws. However, with more and more minorities being granted interviews, one would assume that, over time, we would start to see more and more minority head coaches. The NFL has already levied several fines for teams failing to follow this process. I think the NCAA would be wise to follow the NFL's lead, with a possible change in regards to the punishment for not meeting the criteria.

ZF: The BCA has taken a central role in addressing this issue by assembling lists of qualified minority candidates for universities trying to fill coaching vacancies. However, given the small number of minority head coaches and ADs, it appears that the NCAA must go a step further by mandating universities to make a good-faith effort in interviewing candidates of color. And should it be found that a university doesn't at least interview a minority candidate for an athletics position, the NCAA should levy sanctions (much in the same way the incentives and disincentives sanctions work). Minimally, this will give minority candidates an opportunity to introduce themselves to the higher-ups in college athletics. And given that many higher-ups in college athletics aren't familiar with the qualified minority candidates out there, this would give them the opportunity to demonstrate their talents.

CW: I feel that BCA is doing an excellent job of drawing attention to the fact that there are so few minority head coaches and athletics directors. However, university presidents are reluctant to hire minorities as athletics directors. Perhaps the NCAA could penalize those schools who do not interview or consider minority applicants. Schools tend to respond when they lose scholarships or bowl revenue. The effects of an increase in minorities in one of the two listed positions could be astronomical. I am sure there will be more and more African Americans who will aspire to hold these jobs, because all of a sudden they will be attainable. It is hard to have a dream when those who have control, power, or influence do not consider you as a viable candidate. Now these people will dream and act freely.

DJ: The problem with the lack of minority head coaches is a symptom of a larger societal problem. Notre Dame seemed not to care very much about a public relations fiasco when they released Ty Willingham. Some people wonder if Notre Dame should have been punished. The Irish had a chance to land arguably one of the best coaches in the college game right now in Urban Meyer. Is Urban Meyer a better football coach than Willingham? His teams seem to have done better, as evidenced by a 9-win campaign with Bowling Green, and a 10-win and undefeated season at the University of Utah. Even armed with those stats, it was stupid for the Fighting Irish to prematurely release Coach Willingham. With college football under ever-increasing scrutiny, the university, which has been a pillar of excellence in college football years, should have known better. That they made the decision in the face of the impending scrutiny shows either a severe insensitivity or a brazen disregard for the current state of racial hiring. If a spotlight school like Notre Dame can manage to make a brash decision, there's no measure in place to punish the others.

KB: I think that each school needs to make a point to thoroughly evaluate all of the candidates for coaching and athletics director positions that open up. When looking for college coaching candidates, each school must work with the Black Coaches Association to make sure that they consider every qualified candidate out there. The only thing that can be done is to make sure that people are not hired into these positions that are not qualified, but rather, each college needs to choose the best and most qualified candidate there is. I really feel like that is the only fair way to do it. They need to not take preference over a candidate if there is a "good ole' boys network" but instead hire the most qualified person.

LB: Promote more assistant coaches rather than buying another school's head coach when there are vacancies. LSU did well by promoting their assistant basketball coach, who is an African-American female.

MM: Just like the NBA has instituted the NBDL (National Basketball Development League), I feel that coaches and athletics directors need a similar program to develop their skills and fine-tune other attributes necessary to be successful in this field. Just because you were a phenomenal collegiate athlete does not mean that you have the business savvy or characteristic traits to be a coach. A league/program such as this would serve as a platform to provide individuals an opportunity to enter into the industry armed with the appropriate skills. More like a certification program, it would provide universities with a pool of candidates to choose from, as opposed to just being in the right place at the right time. This program should require a two-year minimum practicum in the field to gain the experience and to build a competitive résumé. This certification would then be necessary to hold a head-coaching position and/or athletics director role. It would put everyone on a level playing field, and you can determine your own destiny. NCAA could fund this program and also provide compliance courses to make sure that each individual is fully aware of all rules and regulations that they would eventually be expected to uphold.

CHAPTER 17

The NCAA in 2010

Daniel Boggan Jr. Former Sr. Vice President and
Chief Operating Officer, NCAA

The NCAA celebrated its 100th year in 2006. It is an organization that has grown to a place in America's culture that is synonymous with college athletic competition. Yet, there are contrasting pictures painted by supporters and critics. The supporters extol the virtues and importance of college athletics as part of the collegiate experience, whereas critics lament about the excessive time and effort spent by young women and men away from the classroom and the real purpose of college.

John Feinstein, in his book *The Last Amateurs*, maintains that college sports, and basketball in particular, "is about colleges chasing millions, no billions of dollars; it's about win at all costs." Is this a fair characterization of college athletics? The facts would suggest otherwise. I will come back to this later. The key question is about the future. If we look out to 2010, how will college athletics be viewed and how will the landscape of competition differ from what exists now? As we look back over the last seven years, major issues have come into play at the national level and many of them seem to be unsolvable within the current framework of athletic competition at the collegiate level. The problems that seem to recur each decade or two include the following:

- academic integrity of the individual athletics programs and the complex processes that support playing above getting one's degree.
- the commitment to sportsmanship and fair play.

- the overall well-being of the student-athletes, including concerns over the demands of playing and practice time and the minimum amount of time left for studying and classroom participation.
- the commercialism of "big-time" intercollegiate athletics as an enterprise that often warps the values of the university, e.g., the idea that entertainment provided through athletic programs is a legitimate collegiate purpose. This is particularly true for basketball (men's and women's), and for football.
- the internationalization of so much of college athletics, with the resulting effect of exporting scholarship dollars away from American youth and at the same time having to rethink the rules regarding the eligibility. It is clear that the U.S. system of precollege competition is so different from other countries. The current rules more often than not disadvantage domestic students when compared to the international student-athlete, who is often not in the same kind of high school–based athletic program. The international system does not have the trappings of the American precollege program and does not pretend to be about education; rather, it is about competition.
- the role of "big money" and "big paydays" for everyone except the student-athlete.
- the issue of who is in charge of intercollegiate athletics anyway.

I haven't mentioned winning and losing as an issue. In the real world every team that takes the field ought to be prepared to win or lose. There is a constant opportunity to learn from either outcome and to become better as a result of participating in the competition. This is the continuous-improvement model of American business. Teams and individuals should seek that exceptional performance each time they take the field, court, or pool, and hopefully proper execution will lead to victory. In the purist sense of athletic participation, we should always appreciate the effort, the desire, the teamwork, and the hard work that leads to the successful team and the outstanding individual performance.

There are discussions that take place on a recurring basis about the outcome of losing too often. Coaches and athletics directors fear this the most because the alumni, the administration, and the big boosters cannot stand the idea of losing too often or for too long. Thus, the pressure is on the coaches to win and can be a factor in driving much of the behavior in collegiate athletics that is then criticized by a large sector of the public. Most people do not want their college to cheat, or to pay the student-athletes illegally, or to violate the rules of recruiting, or to have the players on the team use illegal or banned performance enhancing substances. The conflict that every university faces is between those who believe that competition should be fair and within a set of principles and rules that everyone will live by, and those who look for ways to win no matter what. Besides, who is watching? Most of the time, no one. That group just does not want its team or coaches to get caught cheating.

How do we begin to sort out what the responsible and legitimate desired outcomes of intercollegiate athletic programs are? How do we begin to shape a vision of competition within the college scene that supports the student-athlete and his or her need to be successful beyond the final out, run, or last hurrah? How do we begin to align the needs of campus, conference, and national organization within a framework that supports amateur college athletics?

When the NCAA came into existence in 1906, there were serious concerns about student-athlete welfare. Safety was the paramount issue. The desire for a safe environment overrode the reckless abandon that was football at the turn of the 20th century. Unacceptable violence in football then and now is a recurring theme. How does the membership of the NCAA sharpen its vision and clarify the direction in which they want the NCAA to go? After all, while they may forget, the member institutions are the NCAA.

The violence of 1906 was epitomized by the flying wedge, a formation that led to the death of over 15 football players in 1905. The violence of 1996 was characterized through physical intimidation, unnecessary roughness, and verbal abuse. There was a team that best represented these practices, the Hurricanes of Miami. They were the Oakland Raiders of college football. The members decided to deal with the uncalled-for actions of many players and teams by rule. The football committee of the NCAA went to work and, to their credit, got rule changes enacted that slowed this behavior to almost a complete halt. The membership did this by being clear with the rules, redefining acceptable behavior, and strictly enforcing the new standards of conduct. There was also considerable community pressure to get these rules in place and enforced.

Because of those actions, player violence and trash talking has been lessened by consistent application of the rules and a demand for fair play. The problem in football in the '90s was eliminated for the most part by rule. What is instructive here is that community pressure and outrage created the pressure for meaningful change to occur. The public and the NCAA membership came to a conclusion that while college sports are often physical, as a society, wanton violence will not be tolerated. It was clear in 1906 and in 1996 that respect for competition, respect for one's opponent, and respect for the game are the foundation for sportsmanship and for a positive future for intercollegiate athletics.

College sports should be part of that which uplifts the spirit. It should occur, when on the fields of competition, all student-athletes give their best and the art form represented by the various teams is recognized for the excitement it creates and the communities that it builds. Sportsmanship and excellence are two pillars for building our athletics programs and may well serve as surrogates for civility and integrity in building strong communities. These are core values that we should try to always keep in front of us like guiding stars.

While player behavior is more under control, fan behavior in some colleges and universities is approaching the "anything-goes model." Uncontrolled violence in and around the stadium, arena, or playground is more likely to occur as a result of fan fanaticism. Like any other principle that has no concern with outcome, fanaticism can rule a mob. We saw it after bowl games in 2002, and after rival teams competed in 2003. Mobs have no conscience and usually turn destructive if they do not like an outcome—or sometimes even to celebrate a big win. Such behavior cannot become normative. The acts of denigrating the opposition stand in stark contrast to civil behavior and respect. Bad mouthing, name calling, trash talking, and verbally assaulting the opposing team borders on a hate crime and cannot be condoned. Alcoholic consumption coupled with the belief that one has the right to abuse, offend, threaten, and denigrate opposing team members is the height of negative sports behavior.

The public at large has to restate in no uncertain terms that this kind of behavior will not be tolerated because it fundamentally assaults and undermines the values that represent the best of the university and American values. After all, these competitions are supposed to be about creating the best environment for young women and men to grow and excel. We cannot expect our athletes to compete with restraint when mob or thuggish behavior surrounds the game. This culture of uncouthness and excessive violence must be stopped if the competitions that we cherish are to thrive. Our past would suggest that we must overcome this lack of basic restraints and the new style of fabricated hostility. However, we must be cognizant that this new strand of fan behavior has mutated to something worse than we have known before.

Let me now turn to this question: What do we want college athletics to look like in the year 2010? What are the positive outcomes that we hope to achieve by then? First and foremost, American college athletics should be the envy of such programs around the world. Student-athletes are, in fact, recognized first as students who participate in intercollegiate athletics. The member institutions of the NCAA are more focused on graduation, the academic success of students, and leadership development. Student-athlete graduation rates are even higher than they are now, and substantially higher than those of the student body. While winning is desired, it is not the only factor in a successful program.

Second, Title IX compliance will be a nonissue. The fact of equal athletics competition for women will not be perceived as a takeaway from men. The value of athletic participation is recognized as an important part of the college for all student-athletes. Women and men who coach support their teams without the unhealthy attribution that causes one gender to doubt the right of the other to have a fair share of the athletics department's resources.

Third, the cost of intercollegiate athletics is a model of fiscal responsibility and accountability. Athletics programs have developed a meaningful three- to five-year plan that can be funded, that is realistic, and that has parameters placed around each program within the overall context of campus resources.

These plans are reviewed and updated annually. The plans support gender and ethnic diversity at all levels within the department.

The welfare of student-athletes is the number-one priority on every campus when it comes to athletics. That commitment is felt across the campus. Academic departments believe that athletics is more than about game-day participation.

The coaching profession will have changed to the extent that ethnic minority groups and women acknowledge that positive change has occurred. Those who have been excluded from coaching acknowledge that the support of the NCAA president, the campus president or chancellor, and athletics directors is more than lip service.

The issue of pay for play has been put to rest because all constituents recognize the value of a legitimate college education delivered to the student-athlete in a timely manner. Parents are willing to advise their daughters and sons regarding the importance of education as a key to the future and as a vehicle for enhancing future success. The differentiation based on need is no longer a problem.

The direction athletics has taken reemphasizes the historic value of education and the role that athletics participation plays in our culture. As Charles Harris said in the November 9, 2000, issue of the *NCAA News*, "[W]hile we're charged with making athletics better, we're supposed to preserve the qualities that made athletics special in the first place so that the best values, the best qualities of the whole spirit of athletics competition are around 100 years from now."

- In 2010, the college and the high school community supports the ideal that we have an affirmative duty to make academic preparation stronger, athletics competition better, and fan behavior supportive and respectful (not demeaning and destructive). The refocusing on academic excellence, on athletic excellence, on personal and professional development, on community service and leadership, and on sportsmanship and ethical conduct are acknowledged as important to the strength of our campus community and relevant in strengthening our social fabric and in making social change.
- The NCAA, conferences, and the campus communities are aligned and moving forward together to make the student-athlete experience the best. The local community appreciates the values of education and athletic participation and the positive effect they have on the residents.
- The athletics departments are actively engaged in community service programs and have developed outreach strategies that help high school and younger students to see the possibilities that a college education offers. Those students are talking to the woman who is the college basketball star about her desire to be in the chief financial officer position, or the African-American football star whose plan is to get into education and become a principal of a high school.

The question now is: How do we get to that desired state?

First, there is the issue of alignment. The NCAA is a collection of colleges and universities. They must have a shared vision of what college athletics can be that is buttressed in academic preparation for its future participants. What we must accept is this: The seeds of the future are nourished in the present but were planted in the past. Our history is our strength and our problem. The NCAA members have to rededicate themselves to a new future based on core values that will stand the test of time. If, for instance, one goes to the website for an institution in Division I, II, or III, one is likely to find similar kinds of expressions about mission. As an example, here is one element of the Dartmouth College mission statement: It calls for "[a] devotion to a vital learning environment that relies on a faculty dedicated to outstanding teaching and scholarship; a talented and intellectually curious student body; a staff committed to the institution and its purposes; and alumni supportive of the pursuit of the highest ideals of teaching and learning." Each member institution has a similar call to purpose. Whether it is a land grant college or university, a private college or a small liberal arts college, the search for the best teaching, research, and service is still the soul of the university. The practical application of knowledge as a tool for improving the human condition is what we should be about every day. The notion of a better world, of stronger, more enlightened human communities through education, is a shared responsibility of our educational institutions.

The Knight Commission, in its first report, chided the NCAA membership for not graduating student-athletes at an acceptable level and for allowing college entrance standards of student-athletes to be lower than that of the regular student body. Finally, they concluded that presidential control needed to be asserted to right the ship of intercollegiate athletics.

Myles Brand, the new president of the NCAA, is one of their colleagues and understands the pressures of the university. In his first public address at the 2003 NCAA Convention he stated he would be using the following principles to help reframe a shared vision for the NCAA:

- Intercollegiate athletics must be integrated into the academic mission of colleges and universities.
- Presidential control of intercollegiate athletics is essential.
- The positive values of intercollegiate athletics should be addressed and reinforced.
- The integrity of intercollegiate athletics is and must remain paramount.
- Fair and just action within intercollegiate athletics must be achieved.

These need to be the shared goals activated through the support of every NCAA member. Dr. Brand also alerted the membership that he would push forward using two broad pillars as his guideposts: advocacy and reform. Since that speech, he has added a third pillar: accountability.

The principles are crucial. The goals are clear. The task at hand is strategic, not tactical. The intercollegiate community must pursue vigorously advocacy and reform and hold itself accountable for achieving five years from now what is identified as priorities today. Who is in charge now is also clear. At the NCAA national office it is a former president of a member institution. At the NCAA executive committee, the presidents are in charge. At the conference level, the presidents are in charge. Finally, at the campus level the presidents are in charge. Alignment at all three levels will cause the goals to be achieved. Failure to align campus, conference, and national goals will hinder the most meaningful changes. The current status quo will prevail. If the presidents choose to lead, then meaningful change can occur.

On issues of academic reform, the presidents have committed themselves in all three divisions to move aggressively to improve academic preparation, to respond to the needs of the student-athlete once they arrive on campus, and finally to put strong sanctions in place for failure. The academic reforms adopted in Division I envision incentives and disincentives to move forward the agenda of reform. Accountability is achieved through the loss of scholarships, and ultimately certain competitions.

Division II has strengthened its academic requirements and continues to review how to put more teeth in its sanctions. The division is moving toward a "graduation success" report that will provide an improved measure of academic outcomes and success for Division II student-athletes. The new method will better account for transfer student-athletes and those athletes who do not receive athletically related aid.

Division III already integrates its student-athletes into the overall campus requirements for the general student body. The Division III philosophy statement emphasizes that highest priority must be placed on the overall quality of a student's educational experience and the successful completion of the student's academic program. The Division III membership has adopted various rules and procedures to support these principles. Thus, student-athletes in this division are subject to the same admissions, initial eligibility, and continuous eligibility requirements applicable to the rest of the student body.

In Division I, where greater public scrutiny and abuse has been found, the issue of satisfactory progress has been revisited and new rules adopted. These will force more attention to student-athletes being on track to graduate if they are to remain eligible to play. A novel concept it is not, but it does speak to accountability. This is a good change if you believe that the promise of the college experience is the opportunity to get a good education, graduate, and be better prepared to deal with the rest of one's life. Though a college education is not the only way to become prepared for life, it is the foundation for a stronger, hopefully more informed, society.

Therefore, the focus should always be on what the true mission of the university or college is. Staying true to that basic purpose is what this effort of reform has to be about. The NCAA has a basic purpose statement within its constitution. It reads as follows:

> The competitive athletics programs of member institutions are designed to be a vital part of the educational system. A basic purpose of this Association is to maintain intercollegiate athletics as an integral part of the educational program and the athlete as an integral part of the student body and, by so doing, retain a clear line of demarcation between inter-collegiate athletics and professional sports. The NCAA leadership must be clear in maintaining that clear line of demarcation. The consequences of not doing so will lead to more discussions and demand for pay for play by the student-athlete.

There is a set of principles that support this basic purpose statement. If we were capable as human beings of living by principle alone, we would not need the hundreds of pages of rules. However, these principles ought to guide and inform the decision-making structure of the association. The members of the NCAA are supposed to use these principles in the day-to-day administration of their campus athletic programs and in setting policy for the future of their national organization.

President Carter talked about those core principles that should guide our way. He called them "unchanging principles." Dr. King called it the "moral compass" that guides our way. When Thomas Jefferson penned these famous words almost 230 years ago, "We hold these truths to be self-evident, that all men are created equal, and are endowed by their creator with certain in-alienable rights and among these are the right to life, liberty, and the pursuit of happiness," he issued a challenge to all Americans for all time. We have moved as a nation to include women and the African slave as a part of the promise of that American declaration. The statement represents a funda-mental set of core values for the American democracy that we know and cherish. The tragedy is that some people still do not believe that every American should be included when those fundamental beliefs are asserted. Even so, there is a need for:

- a shared vision,
- shared values,
- shared goals, and
- an understanding of our shared responsibility to one another.

To move forward as a society we must be able to create and hold on to a shared vision of America. There has to be a shared vision for the NCAA. Athletics is just one small component of American society. Education is much more fundamental to what we are and what we are to become. The American university was not created to be about sports, rather about how to nourish this democracy and its citizens. Yet college athletics can play a role in bringing us together as a people beyond race, class, and gender. It has a powerful pull for most of us.

In athletics within the NCAA, the members must come together and create that shared vision or reaffirm the existing one. The current set of principles has much of the "right stuff." If, for instance, you take principle 2.1 of the NCAA constitution as a case in point, it is very clear. It reads as follows: "It is the responsibility of each member institution to control its intercollegiate athletic program in compliance with the rules and regulations of the association. The institution's chief executive officer is responsible for the administration of all aspects of the athletics program, including the approval of the budget and the audit of all expenses."

The future of intercollegiate athletics will be framed around the issues of local control. The ultimate responsibility for the athletic program of each member institution is at the local level. This is one of the themes of both Knight Commission reports. The conclusions of the reports issued in 1991 and in 2001 are straightforward: CEO leadership is crucial to the NCAA and any successful reforms. Local campuses are where the successes and the failures are seen. The inability of the CEO or the athletics director to thwart academic fraud, or recruiting scandals, or sexual abuses by players are examples that we read about every year.

So what measures can be taken to deal with these lapses? Clearly one cannot legislate integrity, honesty, fairness, or a commitment to ethical conduct. And that is precisely the problem. The NCAA Constitution describes an ideal state for athletics. However, that state does not exist and will not without a rededication by all to those shared values and core principles. The Knight Commission's last report issued in June 2001, "A Call to Action: Reconnecting College Sports and Higher Education," is a terse reminder of how easy it is to stray from basic purpose "to maintain intercollegiate athletics as an integral part the educational program, and the student-athlete as an integral part of the student body." The words of the NCAA Constitution are on target. It is the actions at the local, regional, or national level that often betray the core values and the basic purpose.

If the rules were followed based on the current principles in the NCAA manual, the association would be much better off. Where conflict between principles might exist, then two other decision rules should be used: (1) Does the policy or rule support the student-athlete's success and development, and (2) is it consistent with the college or university's mission?

"A Call to Action" challenges the NCAA membership to do the right thing. The reconnecting of college sports and higher education must be a daily effort. It cannot be just a policy statement. It must be actualized by consistent deeds from all the responsible parties. At the local level and in the national roles as policy-makers, presidents, athletics directors, faculty athletics representatives, and all the staff must work to assure that the positive integration of athletics into academia occurs.

The fear expressed by the Knight Commission in its introduction is unsettling. The assertion that "the good name of the nation's academic enterprise is even more threatened today than when the Knight Commission published its first report a decade ago" is scary. The issue is easily assailed when "wrongdoing as a way of life seems to represent the status quo." Where, then, does the collegiate establishment turn? The answer is simple. The members of the NCAA must turn to one another and commit to doing what is right for the student-athlete and what is consistent with the higher calling of the purpose and mission of higher education.

The NCAA membership is in a unique place. The Knight Commission has issued its second report in 10 years. Cedric Dempsey, former president of the NCAA, presented a series of articles on key issues in college athletics called "The Will to Act." The new president, Myles Brand, with the support of the executive committee, has completed a new strategic plan. The plan's structure requires accountability at every level, and it involves participation by all constituencies. It affirms the value of college athletics and the leadership role of the presidents. Its strategies are designed to move the association forward based on core principles and a shared vision.

The stakes are huge. The future of college athletics as we now know it is up for redefinition. The issues that must be confronted will be addressed through the structure of the NCAA. The public and the student-athletes will be watching. The issues have not changed much, but the emphasis has. In 1906, when the NCAA came into being, safety was the key. The list is much longer now. Let's look at a few items on it.

1. *Safety/welfare of student-athletes.* How do we make sure that student issues are out in front? How do we make sure that we are not jeopardizing students' futures by failing to act? How do we make sure that the risk management issues that athletic competition brings are not overlooked?

2. *Academic integrity.* Why are institutions unable to stop academic fraud? Why are bogus courses allowed? Who is sending the message that if cheating is necessary to win, it's all right, so just do what you need to do to keep our athletes eligible.

3. *Cost of athletics.* What is a reasonable investment in the athletic program? What are the parameters that should be in place? Why should athletic cost be allowed to increase sometimes more than twice the rate of inflation? What is a fair way to compensate coaches? Why should they be the highest-paid employees in the academy?

4. *Initial eligibility/graduation rates.* What can and must be done to improve initial preparation for precollege student-athletes? How do we make sure that student-athletes are prepared for college work? What must we do to deliver on the promise that a scholarship represents more than an opportunity to compete, that it also provides an opportunity to obtain the keys to success in this society?

College athletics participation has caused high schools to prepare their student-athletes more richly and hopefully better. The high school community is a needed partner in creating an athletics culture in this country that supports the importance of education as a vehicle for achieving success and a better life if one gets one's degree. That is one reality that can be created. However, there is another—one that we must work to make sure does not come into existence. It could be that the headline for the Knight Commission report issued in 2011 reads, "The warning given in 2001 went unheard. The worst that was predicted has happened." What the NCAA membership has to assure is that the next report represents a different sentiment. The report states that the value of intercollegiate athletics, as part of the academy, is positively influenced by what comes from giving one's all in the classroom and on the field. There is a realization that effort in the classroom can produce excellence in learning. Hard work is an attribute that pays off academically and in athletic participation. Bill Bradley emphasizes that point in his work *Values of the Game.*

5. *Diversity: coaches and administration.* How can we provide equal opportunity to women and people of color in every part of athletics administration? How can we change the systems and processes that exclude people based on historical barriers and biases? How, for example, in 2002 can 26 percent of the assistant coaches in Division IA football be people of color but less than 4 percent hold positions as head coaches?

The need for principle-centered leadership and for decision-making is clear. The NCAA principles and core values should be the hallmark of every program. It is the dissonance between the principles and the reality that confuses many observers and alienates many athletes.

Finally, how does one change the perception that education is not fundamental to the pursuit of intercollegiate athletics? John Feinstein, in *The Last Amateurs*, points out that million-dollar contracts and poor graduation rates are likely to exist in some programs—if you are a winning coach. When Florida made it to the Final Four and then to the last game, "Billy Donovan was given a new contract worth more than $1.1 million annually in base salary." Feinstein goes on to say that "the graduation rate for the relevant period was 33% ... which hardly matters." The fact is that it does matter. The fact is that we should hold our coaches accountable for graduating the student-athletes they recruit. The promise of an education with a degree at the end of four or five years of college has to count as much or more than winning and losing.

For the NCAA of 2010, effective strategies are in place to move the members and the association to a place where the old questions have been answered and addressed. The Knight Commission issues a report in 2011 that applauds the NCAA membership for making the student-athlete experience a precious one—and one that has led to successful integration into the academy. Eligibility issues are no longer a problem, and the Knight Commission even addresses the issue of race.

CHAPTER 18

Recommendations

Richard E. Lapchick

T here are obviously many issues facing the leaders in college sport. The long list of recommendations in this final chapter will make that even more clear. I have taken this list from each author's statements in *New Game Plan*. The full text is, of course, in each chapter.

However, I will finish this book with the final vision presented and echoed by the athletics directors in their forum. They saw college sport as a change agent in society, especially regarding women and people of color. They believe sport provides more opportunities than any other part of our society. Dan Boggan echoed this when writing about a shared vision for the NCAA. He believes college athletics can play a role in bringing us together as a people beyond race, class, and gender.

As someone who has been involved with sport for three decades, I wholeheartedly agree. In spite of all of our problems, sport does regularly create that miracle where we come together as one people.

INTEGRITY AND ETHICS

Stoll and Beller had several recommendations to enhance ethical decision-making in college sport:

- Athletics departments should adopt a thorough mission statement that is directed toward ethics.

- Administrators and coaches need to adopt and value mission statements that are clear, lucid, moral, and important.
- Administrators and coaches should receive regular intensive education on moral reasoning and sport ethics.
- Athletics departments should have monthly discussion groups on the types of ethical issues that occur daily in college sport.
- Athletics needs a moral community and moral environment to keep on track and attached to a moral compass.

Student-athletes said that when it comes to integrity in college sport, you have to:

- look to the president, to yourselves, and to your parents for responsibility.
- have more open and accessible information to help schools to remain in check.
- instill ethical values in all associated with college sport; all would take formal classes in ethics.
- enact federal laws to punish boosters.
- have an NCAA rule under which a coach can be suspended for three to five years for a major violation.

Dan Boggan issued a "Call to Action" challenging the NCAA membership to do the right thing. It is the responsibility of each member institution to control its intercollegiate athletic program in compliance with the rules and regulations of the association. The reconnecting of college sports and higher education must be a daily effort and cannot be just a policy statement.

Boggan made the point from an NCAA perspective for the need for principle-centered leadership and decision-making. He contended that the NCAA principles and core values should be the hallmark of every program. It is the dissonance between the principles and the reality that confuses many observers and alienates many athletes.

COACHING ETHICS

Conference commissioners said the schools need to know the background of each coach if there was any questionable activity in that coach's profile.

The presidents recommended that they be involved with coaching hires. The president needs to:

- make a clear statement of values and expectations.
- not hire someone with a significant violation in his or her past.
- ask the right questions to be sure the student-athlete welfare is a high priority of the coach.
- see how well the coach and AD work together.

- see that the coach balances student-athlete welfare with wins and losses.
- get incentives in contracts for coaches with higher graduation rates and higher GPAs.

The athletics directors also felt strongly about coaching ethics and suggested:

- Do not hire someone with a major ethics violation.
- An ethics course is not enough; ethics must be part of the value system.
- The department must establish a culture of integrity and ethics, repeat the vision, and enforce it.
- Coaches know how to play by the rules of the game and need to extend it beyond the playing arena into their operations of coaching.

COST CONTAINMENT/FINANCES

John Gerdy made several recommendations to eliminate what he calls the "professional team" model being used in college sport.

- Eliminate athletic scholarships in favor of need-based institutional financial aid.
- Make freshman ineligible.
- Shrink the professional operation by cutting coaching and support staffs.
- Eliminate off-campus recruiting.
- Eliminate or significantly reduce the number of games played on weekdays.

Donna Lopiano made a series of cost-containment recommendations.

- *Contract limitations.* Approve national legislation to create one-year, renewable contracts for all coaches and staff in order to eliminate such practices as "buy-outs" and "golden parachutes."
- *Debt service and capital expenditures.* Require the approval of the faculty senate for major renovation or the building of new athletic facilities.
- *Recruiting reform.* Reform the current recruiting system. Consider allowing campus tryouts for prospective student-athletes (as is done in Division II) and other ways to restrict the excessive costs of off-campus recruiting.
- *Size of coaching staffs.* Reduce coaching staffs and base the number on a reasonable coach:student-athlete ratio.
- *Size of noncoaching staffs.* Limit the number of noncoaching personnel to a figure based on the number of student-athletes in the athletics department (e.g., employees in the areas of sports information, marketing, and promotions; administrative assistants; secretarial support; etc.).

- *Size of administrative staffs.* Eliminate administrative assistants in specific sports.
- *Excessive and unnecessary expenditures.* Prohibit football and men's basketball practices such as staying in hotels before home games; nonplayer travel parties to bowl and championship games; entertainment and other nonessential expenditures during preseason training periods, etc.
- *Scholarships.* For example, change "head-count" scholarships to "equivalency-based" scholarships and reassess scholarship limits in all sports to conform to commonly accepted team size. If football scholarships in Division IA were reduced from 85 to 65—using the 1999 average scholarship costs and applying a formula of 30 percent in-state student-athletes and 70 percent out-of-state student-athletes—there would be a savings of almost $300,000 each year.
- *Travel expenses.* Streamline all travel parties during the regular season by establishing maximum travel party limitations.
- *Number of competitions.* Reduce the length of seasons in appropriate sports, curtail the excessive number of competitions in some sports (e.g., softball and baseball), and consider reducing or eliminating institution-sponsored practice and competition in the off-season.
- *Sport budget limits.* Establish legislation to limit overall maximum expenditures (all-inclusive) on a per-sport basis, with differences in travel budgets based on geographical factors.
- *Roster limits.* Establish roster limits in every sport based on the number of athletes required to practice and compete.
- *Antitrust exemption.* Some have suggested that Congress should give schools a limited exemption from antitrust laws in order to tie the total recompense for head and assistant coaches to the top five full professors at the institutional or conference level or other justifiable salary levels.

Faculty recommended several ideas in this area.

- There should be a halt to salary escalation for coaches.
- Though they were drawn to more need-based scholarships, the faculty opposed John Gerdy's ideas because they believed ending athletic scholarships would hurt minority student-athletes. They thought there would be far better ways to cut costs.
- Faculty with expertise in accounting and finance should examine the finances of athletics to make sure that everything is on track.

Student-athletes made several recommendations with financial implications.

- Pay the athletes so they can live like other students.
- Increase funding for women.
- Impose a salary cap on the coaches.
- Keep athletics scholarships.

- Put a hold on facilities expansions.
- Do not put student-athletes up in hotels at home the night before a game.

The athletics directors made several points about finances.

- Private school athletics directors saw the need for the colleges to invest more in athletics to achieve a good balance.
- They also saw that raising all the money on the outside has limitations because it increases the potential booster influence.
- Several saw the need to downsize college athletics without additional revenues and thought that there could be a reduction in the number of scholarships.
- Several also argued for an agreement on the right number of sports for a school.
- None agreed with John Gerdy's idea of an end to athletic scholarships for varied reasons, the primary one of which was of the large number of student-athletes who have succeeded in life as a result of the opportunity to go to college on a scholarship. They also felt that scholarships were not a huge part of the budget and cuts elsewhere would be more realistic.

The presidents and conference commissioners also disagreed with Gerdy for the same reasons.

RACIAL HIRING PRACTICES

Richard Lapchick recommended several ways to increase opportunities for people of color and women for positions in college athletics.

- Continuously update the documentation of the diversity records of the department. Keep the information in the view of the public.
- Recognize that there are more than 48,000 professional positions in college sport at the 1,028 members of the NCAA. Opportunities exist off and on the playing field.
- For coaching and senior level positions, have a real search process that takes time to open the pool.
- Appoint a diverse search committee.
- Interview at least one person of color and one woman.
- Follow the university's affirmative action policies.
- Select the best person available after going through a process like this.
- Support the Black Coaches Association in their efforts to promote equal opportunity.

Fitz Hill elaborated on five recommendations to increase opportunities for African-American head coaches in football.

- *Address the problem.* In order to improve equal employment opportunities for African-American coaches, institutions must recognize that the current system used to select and hire football coaches at colleges and universities is flawed. Institutions must establish specific goals to address the core problems. When coaches do not recognize the reality of these problems, barriers become difficult to remove.
- *Specific hiring criteria needed.* When selecting coaches, most Division IA institutions lack specific hiring criteria and qualifications. A good starting point would be to define the term *qualified.* Currently, hiring practices deny African Americans opportunities to lead programs by failing to clearly define the qualifications necessary to become a Division IA football coach.
- *Identify and address racial barriers.* African Americans must be willing to speak up about problems and be courageous enough to risk their careers if they want to educate others about restrictive employment barriers.
- *Manage perceptions.* The perceptions of African-American football coaches can lead to minorities being pigeonholed in staff assignments with no potential for professional growth. African-American coaches must understand that some of their white colleagues will assume that the only reason they have their job is because of the color of their skin. One way African-American coaches can erase this stereotype is by seeking professional development and increasing their knowledge regarding the X's and O's of the game.
- *Honesty and frankness.* Many African-American coaches censor their true feelings as a simple means of survival. This reluctance to speak openly about inequities should not be confused with complacency. African-American coaches must be honest and frank and continue to educate others while striving to change unjust hiring practices.

The conference commissioners had several ideas regarding racial hiring practices.

- Create social gatherings to meet assistant coaches. When an AD calls, the commissioners will know the person and not just the name.
- Keep an expansive database of all assistants or people of color as well as NFL assistants.
- Create a minority internship program.
- Expand diversity of their own staff at the conference level.
- Include people of color in the interview process.
- Let search firms know that diversity is a priority.
- Have coaches mentor assistants.

The faculty recommendations for improving opportunities for people of color included making the faculty itself more diverse. In order to end the old boy's network across campus, they saw a clear need for more people of color on the faculty and a need to keep them happy so that they remain and do not feel isolated.

Athletics directors recommended the following in order to get more people of color in the pool for jobs in the athletics department:

- Make sure the search process includes people of color both on the search committee and in those interviewed.
- Include former student-athletes in the search.
- Emphasize with your department that diversity is good business so all will buy-in and understand.
- Look for colleges with great track records for developing talent in their search process.
- Serve on national conference committees to network and meet future hires.
- Regularly do diversity management training for the athletics department.

Regarding opportunities for people of color, student-athletes suggested:

- The NCAA should mandate interviews of people of color in the hiring process.
- More African Americans should be hired as assistants and graduate assistants.
- There needs to be an openness on the part of the athletics director and those hiring.
- Training should be provided for assistant coaches such as the National Basketball Development League.
- The creation of more diverse boards and presidents at the upper levels will create opportunities at the lower levels.

ACADEMICS

The conference commissioners said that the admissions offices needed to do a better job of identifying those who could graduate.

Student-athletes and athletics directors argued for a uniform standard to measure graduation rates.

The student-athletes proposed the following disincentives for schools with poor graduation rates:

- Lose revenue.
- Reduce scholarships.
- Enact postseason bans.
- Hold coaches responsible for poor graduation rates and reduce perks when they are low.
- Increase penalties if coaches leave after problems at the school so they can't just escape to another program.

The student-athletes proposed the following incentives for schools to encourage higher graduation rates:

- Have events that recognize athletes for academic achievements. Have all attend these events so even those who are not being honored see how responsive the community is to good academics.
- Do not use incentives because student-athletes should graduate and should not need incentives.
- Have the BCS rankings include academics as a factor.
- Divide conference revenue partially based on graduation rates.
- Cease hosting of regional, conference, or national championships on campuses of schools with poor graduation rates of student-athletes.
- Put the GPA of the student-athlete on television with his or her height, weight, hometown, and major.
- Add scholarships for schools with good rates, but police grades regarding inflation to make sure that people do not just change grades in order to increase the number of scholarships.

The presidents recommended freshman ineligibility to allow student-athletes time to prepare and adjust to college life.

Athletics directors recommended:

- Devote more attention on the front end to decrease the number of at-risk students admitted. Student-athletes agreed and put the onus on the coaches to recruit students who are prepared in high school for college.
- Recruit fewer junior college student-athletes because maximum support is needed.
- Demand post-eligibility support to increase graduation rates.

Faculty recommended that they should:

- Get the AAUP more involved with the governance of athletics.
- Be on more committees involved with athletics but secure release time in order to have the time available.
- Review the academic paths of student-athletes to make sure that they are on the right track.
- Control academics, including scheduling of classes.
- Identify specific faculty who would be seen by student-athletes as trusted mentors.
- Be advocates for student-athletes.
- Attend a wide variety of games to show support for student-athletes.
- Insist that the faculty athletics representatives be an independent voice and never be appointed by the athletics director.
- Advise student-athletes that they can come to faculty for help.

Dan Boggan argued for a stronger commitment to education. The members of the NCAA must turn to one another and commit to doing what is right for the student-athlete and consistent with the higher calling of the purpose and mission of higher education.

Boggan made the case that we should hold coaches accountable for graduating the student-athletes they recruit. The promise of an education with a degree at the end of four or five years of college has to count as much or more than winning and losing.

ACADEMIC ADVISORS

The conference commissioners and athletics directors said that academic advisors need more resources and equipment.

Regarding academic advisors, student-athletes suggested:

- Coaches should be kept away from advisors.
- Advisors should be involved with all academic programs on campus.
- Students should not accept guidance that runs counter to what they consider to be in their best interests.

GENDER EQUITY AND TITLE IX

Donna Lopiano made several recommendations to improve opportunities for girls and women in sport. In order to end gender discrimination in employment:

- Directly and immediately confront discriminatory practices. Doing this demands constant vigilance and perseverance.
- Make every effort to educate those overseeing the conduct of athletics programs—members of faculty athletics councils, college presidents and vice presidents, athletic directors—to the new forms of subtle discrimination that are undermining the ability of higher education to create an open, fair, and supportive employment environment for women in sport-related careers.
- Work against any effort to reduce participation opportunities for women, even in bad economic times.
- Develop women's sports as revenue-producers. There has been considerable debate as to whether women's athletics will ever be able to pay for itself. The real point is whether institutions are making every effort to ensure that men's and women's sports are doing all they can to produce any revenues that can contribute to defraying program expenses and eliminating unnecessary expenses.
- Promote coaching as a profession to all current athletes, both men and women. Each national sport governing body (NGB), coach's association, the USOC or the NCAA, NAIA, or NJCAA could produce an attractive "We Want You" brochure that presents male and female role-model coaches talking positively about their professional and volunteer activities. The seeds of coaching as a career possibility must be planted in the minds of female athletes. Along with encouraging our

athletes to consider a career in sport is the need to educate current coaches about how they affect the decisions of their athletes to pursue coaching.

- Insist on open and fair employment practices. Administrators need to act affirmatively to redistribute coaching opportunities fairly among women and minority groups. We cannot continue to permit athletics to operate as a "closed shop."
- Colleges and universities need to maintain data on numbers of coaches, administrators, and other professional positions by gender, race, and ethnic group and show comparative salaries and positions. That data can then be assembled, published, and reviewed each year. These organizational report cards send an important message about the importance of diversity and encourage accountability.
- Tenured faculty have the power to speak without concern for retribution and it is critical that they step forward to help women in the athletics trenches who have no such job security.
- Administrators who are doing the hiring have to be educated on the importance of marketplace hiring and how this practice actually increases the salary and pool of qualified candidates over the long term.
- Coaches and administrators have to establish new networks for minority and female recruiting because existing networks are predominantly white male. Employers should never accept the "no women applied" or "no minorities applied" excuse.
- Recognize the importance of and implement new employee orientation, support, and mentoring to ensure the retention of minority employees—be they women or racial minorities.
- Internships should be used to create test positions, especially in a bad economy. Every organization should have at least one, if not two or three, internship positions designated for women and minorities.
- Coaches need to be educated about the fact that what they say and do in front of their student-athletes influences their decisions about whether to make sport a career.
- Make scholarships in fee-charging junior programs or summer camps conducted by athletics departments a rule rather than the exception. Sport opportunity cannot be available only to youth who can afford it.
- Advocate for certification of coaches. Certification goes a long way toward preventing employment discrimination because it mandates objective criteria for weighing the basic qualifications of applicants.
- Recommend qualified women for positions. Males seldom criticize another male when it comes to whether that man is qualified for a job, and females must do the same.
- Female professionals must recognize that employment longevity is power. The longer a woman stays in her position, the more contacts she has and the greater support she develops. Doing good deeds in the community also generates power by providing a base of appreciative citizens outside of the institution.

- Speaking out against wrong is powerful and important. It is each individual's obligation to speak out against wrong if we want our educational institutions and athletic programs to exhibit integrity.
- No athletic department or sport organization employee or volunteer, athlete, parent, or fan should harass, threaten, slander (e.g., antigay slurs, pushing or shoving, property damage, graffiti directed at a particular person or group) a coach or athlete (or any person, for that matter) on the basis of sexual orientation.
- A coach or athlete's sexual orientation should not be a factor in determining his or her eligibility for teams, scholarships, coaching positions, or athletic or academic honors or awards.
- Coaches, athletes, other athletics department personnel, or students who participate in the harassment of lesbian or bisexual athletes or who contribute to a hostile environment for these athletes and coaches should be appropriately disciplined.
- Administrators should support coaches and athletes in addressing antigay incidents.

Regarding Title IX, student-athletes urged schools not to cut men's teams in order to add women's teams.

PERFORMANCE ENHANCING DRUGS

Yun-Oh Whang directed his recommendations for fighting performance enhancing drugs in college sports to several groups.

For everyone:

- Understand that college sport is not all about winning.
- Restore the true spirit of college sport to celebrate its athleticism, hard work, and discipline.
- Get involved! Be a watchdog for performance enhancing drug use and do whatever you can to help.

For the suppliers/distributors:

- Self-regulate the production and distribution of performance enhancing drugs.
- Invest in studies on the side-effects of performance enhancing drugs.
- Clearly show the ingredients on the labels of products.

For NCAA:

- Have more proactive education programs for the student athletes, and parents/guardians.
- Collaborate with professional sports leagues to keep the sport clean.

- Collaborate with K–12 institutions to educate administrators, coaches, and athletes.
- Implement tougher testing programs all across college athletics.
- Penalize the school and coaches/team doctors as well as the student-athlete when a violation is discovered.
- Trace the distribution route of the performance enhancing drug whenever a violation is found and make sure it is no longer accessible.

For the government:

- Implement a stricter regulation of dietary supplements.
- Penalize suppliers/distributors for deceptive labeling and advertising.

AGENTS

Fritz Polite made these recommendations for agents on campus:

- Establish a formal national governing body that would include high school and college administrators, coaches, student-athletes, parents, and state and local governments. The National Association of State Boards of Education (NASBE) has formed in hopes of monitoring and regulating high school athletics while focusing on issues of steroids, academic progress, and monitoring of high school expenses. No direct mention of agents was addressed.
- Formulate constructive and purposeful programs to support and promote student-athletes' continued participation in collegiate athletics.
- Provide better quality services to the student-athlete that foster a holistic approach to the continued development of the individual.
- Create a university task force with a major focus on agents. This could be in conjunction with compliance offices and university officials. It should be *proactive* rather than *reactive*.

STRUCTURE OF COLLEGE ATHLETICS

The athletics directors saw a need for:

- Decentralization of college sport away from the NCAA, with more responsibilities for conferences. The NCAA should continue to run championships and negotiate TV contracts.
- Giving student-athletes more of a voice and more input on reform issues.
- Modest stipends for student-athletes for living expenses. College sport cannot afford more than that modest support.
- More direct and open communications between the president and the athletics director.

The presidents agreed with the latter and said the athletics director should be part of the executive team so that he or she can better understand the university's mission and communicate it to the coaches. The president has to know what is going on.

The presidents emphasized a need to involve historically black colleges and universities (HBCUs) in the decision-making process because better decisions would be made this way and the HBCU's would be more likely to buy-in.

The presidents acknowledged the need to recognize and deal with the shift of power to conference commissioners.

Dan Boggan urged that the NCAA members rededicate themselves to a new future based on core values that will stand the test of time. The intercollegiate community must vigorously pursue advocacy and reform and hold itself accountable for achieving five years from now what are identified as priorities today. Alignment at all three levels will cause the goals to be achieved. Failure to align campus, conference, and national goals will hinder the most meaningful changes.

SPORTSMANSHIP

Conference commissioners had a sportsmanship summit and are now distributing a best-practices document along with the identification of the following problems commissioner's conferences must examine:

- how they manage events,
- how they deal with fans,
- how fans deal with student-athletes, and
- how coaches deal with student-athletes and fans.

Dan Boggan had sportsmanship high on his list for recommendations. College sport uplifts the spirit and this happens when on the fields of competition student-athletes give their best and are recognized for the excitement college sport creates and the communities that it builds. Sportsmanship and excellence are two pillars for building our athletics programs and may well serve as surrogates for civility and integrity in building strong communities. These are core values that we should try to always keep in front of us like guiding stars.

He also emphasized how fan violence can further corrupt sportsmanship. The public at large has to restate in no uncertain terms that fan violence will not be tolerated because it fundamentally assaults and undermines the values that represent the best of the university and American values. After all, these competitions are supposed to be about creating the best environment for young women and men to grow and excel. We cannot expect our athletes to compete with restraint when mob or thuggish behavior surrounds the game.

This excessive violence must be stopped. Our past would suggest that we must overcome this lack of basic restraints and the new style of fabricated hostility. However, we must be cognizant that this new strand of fan behavior has mutated to something worse than we have known before.

GAMBLING

The athletics directors saw gambling as a huge issue.

Bill Saum's recommendations regarding gambling in collegiate athletics followed the lead of NCAA president Myles Brand.

In 2004, in response to the findings of the NCAA's *2003 National Study on Collegiate Sports Wagering and Associated Health Risks*, President Myles Brand announced the formation of a national task force to further analyze the study's results and recommend strategies to counteract sports wagering among student-athletes. Dr. Brand said the task force's charge was to develop recommendations with a dual focus of ensuring the well-being of student-athletes as well as the integrity of intercollegiate athletics. The recommendations examined included expansion of education efforts, proposed NCAA legislation, and suggestions for legislation at the state and federal levels. The final report of the task force will focus on three main areas: compliance and policy, education, and law enforcement/coalition building.

Initiatives have been formulated to help educate the NCAA member institutions and student-athletes of the effects that sports wagering can have not only on their campuses but on student-athletes' lives. The task force proposed actions, include expanding background check programs for Division I officials in the sport of basketball, men's ice hockey, and baseball, all of which currently have betting lines in Las Vegas. A "best practices" document was also created to advise institutions on how they should try to combat the problem on each of their campuses.

The bulk of the action steps, however, occur in the educational area. This area proves to be an important part of deterring student-athletes from avoiding sports wagering based on the results of the study, educating them on how sports wagering can negatively affect their careers and lives.

The third area that the task force focused on is law enforcement and coalition building, with the primary emphasis being building relationships to foster awareness of this issue. An example and important recommendation would be to work with the National Federation of State High School Associations to educate high school student-athletes as well as parent organizations.

CONTRIBUTOR BIOGRAPHIES

Richard E. Lapchick is a human rights activist, a pioneer for racial equality, an internationally recognized expert on sports issues, a scholar and an author. He is often described as "the racial conscience of sport." He brought his commitment to equality and his belief that sport can be an effective instrument of positive social change to University of Central Florida where he accepted an endowed chair in August 2001.

Lapchick is a regular columnist for *The Sports Business Journal* and *ESPN.com*. He has written twelve books, more than 450 articles, and has given more than 2,600 public speeches. Lapchick has received eight honorary degrees. In 1993, he was named as the outstanding alumnus at the University of Denver where he got his Ph.D. in international race relations in 1973.

Lapchick was the American leader of the international campaign to boycott South Africa in sport for more than 20 years. He was among the 200 guests specially invited by Nelson Mandela to his inauguration.

Lapchick has been the recipient of numerous humanitarian awards including the Ralph Bunche International Peace Award. Lapchick was inducted into the Sports Hall of Fame of the Commonwealth Nations in the category of Humanitarian along with Arthur Ashe and Nelson Mandela. He received the "Hero Among Us Award" from the Boston Celtics in 1999 and was named as the Martin Luther King, Rosa Parks, Cesar Chavez Fellow by the State of Michigan in 1998. Lapchick was the winner of the 1997 "Arthur Ashe Voice of Conscience Award" from the Aetna Foundation. He also won the 1997

Women's Sports Foundation President's Award for work toward the development of women's sports. In 1995, the National Association of Elementary School Principals gave him their first award as a "Distinguished American in Service of Our Children."

Welch Suggs joined the Knight Foundation Commission on Intercollegiate Athletics as associate director in 2005. Previously he was the senior editor of the athletics section of the *Chronicle of Higher Education*, where he wrote about all types of off-the-field issues in college sports, including gender equity, finance, and the culture that has evolved in college athletics departments. He came to the *Chronicle* in 1998 from *Street & Smith's Sports Business Journal*, where he helped launch the magazine and covered college sports, women's sports, and stadium issues. He has also written for the *Dallas Business Journal*, the *Kansas City Star*, the *Columbia Missourian*, and the *Atlanta Journal-Constitution*, among other publications. His first book, *A Place on the Team: The Triumph and Tragedy of Title IX*, was published in 2005 by the Princeton University Press. A cum laude graduate of Rhodes College in Memphis, he lives in Washington, D.C.

Dr. John R. Gerdy teaches as a visiting professor in sports administration at Ohio University. He is also author of *The Successful College Athletic Program: The New Standard, Sports in School: The Future of an Institution*, and most recently, *Sports: The All-American Addiction*. Gerdy served as associate commissioner of the Southeastern Conference from 1989 to 1995 and as a legislative assistant at the NCAA from 1986 to 1989. He earned a masters in sports administration and a Ph.D. in higher education from Ohio University. A 1979 graduate of Davidson College, he achieved All-American honors in basketball. Davidson retired his jersey in 1979 and they inducted him into its Hall of Fame in 1994. He also played professionally in the Continental Basketball Association. He resides on a farm in Conestoga, Pennsylvania, with his wife and two children.

Dr. Sharon K. Stoll serves as the director of the Center for ETHICS* at the University of Idaho. Dr. Stoll is considered one of the leading authorities in competitive moral education intervention techniques for college-age adults in America. Also professor of physical education, Dr. Stoll is a distinguished faculty member and winner of a prestigious University of Idaho Outreach Award in 2000 and a University of Idaho Teaching Award in 1992. A former public school teacher, coach, and athlete, Dr. Stoll holds a Ph.D. in sport philosophy from Kent State University and is the creator and director of one of the few programs in America that is directed toward moral education with competitive populations. The program at the University of Idaho includes a minor in sport ethics at the undergraduate level, a master's degree in sport science, and a Ph.D. in education.

Dr. Jennifer M. Beller is an associate professor in educational psychology in the Department of Educational Leadership and Counseling Psychology at Washington State University. She is considered one of the leading authorities in measurement and evaluation of moral development and moral reasoning of competitive populations in America today. Dr. Beller was the winner of Eastern Michigan University's Scholarly Recognition Award in 1996 and was named one of the leading scholars in the university's 150-year history. She recently co-authored a paper that won the Conference Paper of the Year Award for the American Society of Engineering Education. Dr. Beller holds a doctorate in sport philosophy and ethics from the University of Idaho and teaches courses in sport ethics, statistics, and research design within WSU's College of Education.

Dr. Fitzgerald Hill was the head football coach at San Jose State University from 2001 to 2004. Entering the 2004 season, Hill was one of only five African-American head coaches in Division IA football and one of two head football coaches at this level who had earned a doctoral degree. In 1997, he earned his Ed.D. in higher education from the University of Arkansas. His doctoral dissertation, *Examining the Barriers Restricting Employment Opportunities Relative to the Perceptions of African American Football Coaches at NCAA Division I-A Colleges and Universities*, is an objective review of the plight of African Americans in the college-football coaching profession. Hill has given speeches and oral presentations across the country on this subject. A veteran of Operation Desert Shield and Desert Storm, he was awarded a bronze star for service to his country. In 2005 he became a visiting scholar at the University of Central Florida's DeVos Sport Business Management Program. He was named President of Arkansas Baptist College in 2006.

Donna A. Lopiano is one of the nation's foremost advocates for women and girls in sport. A Hall of Fame softball player, she became athletics director at the University of Texas, where she helped propel a top-notch women's program. Lopiano has served as the executive director of the Women's Sports Foundation and has written and spoken extensively on the issue of gender and sport. She helped dramatically expand the success of women's sport at Texas and also expand the role and scope of the Women's Sports Foundation.

Bill Saum is the NCAA's director of agent, gambling, and amateurism activities, a position he has held since November 1998. For two years prior to his promotion to director, he was the NCAA's representative for agent and gambling issues. Saum was an NCAA enforcement representative from April 1988 to September 1996, investigating possible rules violations by member institutions.

Saum earned an undergraduate degree in education from the University of Dayton in 1981. He earned his master's degree in sports administration from Bowling Green State University.

Before joining the NCAA, Saum was an assistant football coach and assistant dean of students at Defiance College in Defiance, Ohio; assistant football coach and educator at Rittman High School in Rittman, Ohio; assistant football coach and head track coach at Heidelberg College in Tiffin, Ohio; and graduate assistant football coach at Bowling Green State University in Bowling Green, Ohio.

Dr. Yun-Oh Whang joined the faculty at Kansas State University after teaching sports marketing at the University of Central Florida for four years. He earned his Ph.D. in marketing from the University of Southern California with emphasis on consumer behavior. His research interests include consumer information processing, cultural issues in marketing, sports marketing, and e-commerce. As an entrepreneur, Dr. Whang's industry experience includes CEO and president of StarLight Computing, Inc. in Seoul, Korea, and president of StarLight Multimedia Production in St. Louis, Missouri. He also provided consulting services for various companies (including Avante Global, Samsung Electronics, and Microsoft) on marketing strategy and sporting event sponsorship issues, and he was involved in a number of training programs for executives and marketing managers.

Dr. Fritz G. Polite is an assistant professor and associate director of the Institute for Diversity and Ethics in Sport in the DeVos Sport Business Management Program, College of Business, the University of Central Florida (UCF). Polite has played, coached, and managed professionally as well as published/presented internationally in the areas of sociocultural aspects of sport, hiring practices, and brand vertical extension. He has 25 years of experience in sports, management, coaching, teaching, and business. Prior to joining UCF, Polite was the program director for the Florida State University's (FSU) Partnership for Enhancing Education Resources program, an after-school mentoring program funded by AT&T that provided tutoring, mentoring, academic support, and career counseling for at-risk youth. He played and coached professionally (American Football) in Germany, Switzerland, and Italy. Dr. Polite also served six years in the U.S. Army as an orthopedic specialist.

Charles S. Farrell has had a distinguished career as a journalist and social activist. Charles was an editor of the sports section for the *Washington Post* and was the sports editor at the *Chronicle of Higher Education* when he won the Excellence in Sports Journalism Award for Print from Northeastern University's Center for the Study of Sport in Society. He joined the center and led the College Student-Athlete Project, a self-evaluative program to assess how the mission of the university was matched by the performance of the athletics department on 22 college campuses. After leaving the center, Charles joined the Reverend Jesse Jackson as the head of Rainbow Sports, which fought for social change, particularly on racial issues in college and professional sport. He is a member of many organizations and continues to write about the issues still confronting sport. He is currently a principal and the senior consultant to Sports Perspectives International.

PRESIDENTS

John DiBiaggio became the 11th president of Tufts University on August 1, 1992. Prior to that appointment, he served as president of Michigan State University from 1985 to 1992, and as president of the University of Connecticut from 1979 to 1985. Dr. DiBiaggio chose to join Tufts University in 1992 because of its commitment to excellence in education, to the ethic and practice of public service and active citizenship, and to a global perspective that fosters solution-oriented scholarship and research.

Among his achievements at Tufts is the establishment of the University College of Citizenship and Public Service, which integrates the theory and application of active citizenship in courses throughout Tufts's undergraduate, graduate, and professional programs. As one who has held a lifelong commitment to volunteering, Dr. DiBiaggio has served as president of the board of the American Council on Education; as chairman of the National Campus Compact; and on the boards of the American Film Institute, the NCAA Foundation, and the blue ribbon Knight Foundation Commission on Intercollegiate Athletics.

Joe Crowley served as president at the University of Nevada for 22 years. Crowley earned his B.A. in political science from the University of Iowa in 1959, his M.A. in social science from Fresno State in 1963, and his Ph.D. in political science from the University of Washington in 1967. He was a professor in the university's department of political science and served as chair of that department and the university's faculty senate.

Crowley has served on many campus, community, and professional organizations, including the Economic Development Authority of Western Nevada (EDAWN), United Way of Northern Nevada, Channel 5 Public Television, Sierra Arts Foundation, Reno Rotary Club, the Commission on Colleges of the Northwest Association of Schools and Colleges, the NCAA Council, and the NCAA Presidents Commission. In January 1995, he completed a two-year term as president of the NCAA. The author or editor of numerous books and articles, Crowley writes on educational policy, environmental policy, and the presidential nominating process. *No Equal in the World: An Interpretation of the Academic Presidency* was published in 1994. *In the Arena: The NCAA's First Century* was published in 2006.

John C. Hitt became the 4th president of the University of Central Florida on March 1, 1992, after 19 years of administrative experience and a distinguished academic career. A native of Houston, Texas, he graduated cum laude in 1962 from Austin College in Sherman, Texas, earning a bachelor of arts degree in psychology. He completed his M.S. in 1964 and his Ph.D. two years later, both in physiological psychology, at Tulane University. His graduate study was supported by fellowships from the Danforth Foundation and the National Science Foundation.

Dr. Hitt serves on the boards of the Greater Orlando Chamber of Commerce, the Economic Development Commission of Mid-Florida, SunTrust N.A., the Winter Park Health Foundation, and United Arts, among others. He is also a member of the Florida Council of 100 and the Florida High-Tech Corridor Council. Dr. Hitt is past president of the Florida Association of Colleges and Universities and served on the Presidents Commission of the NCAA until its restructuring in 1997.

W. Roger Webb became the 19th president of the University of Central Oklahoma, July 1997. Dr. Webb is a native of eastern Oklahoma and received a bachelor of arts degree from Oklahoma State University and a juris doctorate degree from the University of Oklahoma College of Law. Following his service as Oklahoma Commissioner of Public Safety from 1974 to 1978, Roger Webb served as president of Northeastern State University for 19 years, 1978 to 1997. His leadership has been reflected in his active participation in city, state, and national offices he has held during his career. Dr. Webb was named to the Oklahoma Higher Education Hall of Fame in 1995. He served as president/chairmen of Oklahoma Academy for State Goals, and presided as state chairman of Oklahoma Homecoming '90.

President Webb serves on the board of directors for American Association of State Colleges and Universities, National Consortium of Academics and Sports, and Lambda Chi Alpha. He currently serves on the board of directors for the Oklahoma Business Roundtable and the Governor's International Roundtable. He serves on the Executive Committee of the Oklahoma Academy and the executive committee of Leadership Oklahoma. He is also active in the Oklahoma City and Edmond communities, serving on the board of advisors for Oklahoma City Chamber of Commerce, board of directors of Oklahoma Metro United Way, and the board of directors of Edmond Medical Center (Hospital Board).

CONFERENCE COMMISSIONERS

Jim Delany has served as commissioner of the Big 10 Conference since 1991. He received his undergraduate degree in political science from the University of North Carolina in 1970 and juris doctorate degree from the University of North Carolina School of Law in 1973. At UNC, Delany was a three-year member of the varsity basketball team, serving as tri-captain in 1970. As a Tarheel, Delany twice participated in the NCAA Final Four competition. Delany's distinguished career in administering intercollegiate athletics began at the NCAA, where he was employed as an enforcement representative from 1975 to 1979. For the next decade, he served as commissioner of the Ohio Valley Conference, where he oversaw the growth and enhancement of OVC athletic programs for men and women.

Active in the community, Delany has coached several youth teams and has been associated with Special Olympics and YMCA endeavors at various times. During his tenure as Big 10 commissioner, Delany has led the Big 10 through significant periods of change and growth that have helped the conference maintain its preeminent position as one of the nation's leaders in providing quality athletic and academic experiences for young people.

Mike Slive has served as the Southeastern Conference commissioner since 2002. Slive graduated from Dartmouth College with a bachelor of arts degree in 1962. He earned a juris doctorate from the University of Virginia Law School in 1965 and an L.L.M. from the Georgetown University Law Center in 1966.

Prior to joining the SEC, Slive was the commissioner of Conference USA. Presently, Slive is the chair of the first NCAA Infractions Appeals Committee and the National Letter of Intent Appeals Committee. He is also chair of the board of directors of NCAA Football USA and the president of the Collegiate Commissioners Association (CCA). Furthermore, Slive was named to the executive committee of the National Association of Collegiate Directors of Athletics (NACDA) and serves on the board of advisors of the Marquette Sports Law Institute.

Patty Viverito is in her 13th season as senior associate commissioner of the Missouri Valley Conference. She is also in her 20th year directing the Gateway Football Conference as its commissioner. Viverito earned her bachelor's degree from Northern Illinois and her master's in sports management from the University of Massachusetts at Amherst. In 1994, she received the Harold J. VanderZwaag Distinguished Alumnus Award from Massachusetts.

A nationally respected administrator, Viverito has served on the prestigious NCAA Executive Committee and NCAA Council and was chair of the NCAA Committee for Women's Athletics. Viverito recently completed service as a member of the CCA Executive Committee, the chair of the Division IAA

Subcommittee of CCA, and as a consultant to the NCAA Football Oversight Committee.

Chris Monasch has spent his entire career in college athletics, serving in various leadership capacities for more than 24 years, and has a résumé that touches some 30 institutions. He has led both the America East and Northeast Conferences, as well as served in different athletic administration capacities at Fordham and Seton Hall Universities. He has experience with such complex issues as NCAA governance, compliance, and academic support and is known as a visionary administrator. Monasch is a St. John's alumnus, graduating with a B.S. in athletic administration in 1981.

Monasch spent eight years as commissioner of the America East Conference, leading that organization in implementing an NCAA compliance program, developing a marketing program, and organizing the league television network. Monasch also created a student athletic advisory committee to address and restructure its NCAA governance process to empower the league's presidents as its chief governing body. Monasch also oversaw the addition of four new members to the conference and brought the conference to the highest level of athletic success in its history.

In addition to his degree from St. John's, Monasch holds a master of arts in communication from Fordham University (1984) and a juris doctorate from Seton Hall University (1993). Monasch was named as the new athletics director at St. John's University in 2005.

Kevin L. Weiberg was named Big 12 Conference commissioner in 1998. Weiberg earned a bachelor of science degree in education from Kansas State University in 1978 and master of science degree in athletics administration from Western Illinois University in 1979. Prior to joining the Big 12 Conference, Weiberg worked in conference operations for almost 10 years at the Big 10 Conference, beginning as associate commissioner/chief operations officer before being promoted to deputy commissioner.

During Weiberg's tenure in the Big 12 he has renewed and enhanced the conference's commitment to student-athlete academic performance and has revised its policies in the areas of sportsmanship and rules compliance. He has been instrumental in initiating the Group of Six conference reform discussions that have helped produce significant momentum within the NCAA system for national academic reform.

Daniel Boggan Jr., was the former senior vice-president and chief operating officer for the National Collegiate Athletic Association (NCAA). Dan graduated from Albion College in 1967 with a B.A. in history and sociology, and a master's in social work in 1968 from the University of Michigan.

Dan has worked in four different areas. From 1986–70, he served as a social worker and was the Director of the west campus at Starr Commonwealth for Boys. He then spent 16 years from 1970 through 1986 as a senior manager starting as assistant city manager in Jackson, Michigan and ending as city manager in Berkeley, California. From 1986–94, he served as vice-chancellor for business and administrative services at the University of California, Berkeley. In 1994, he became the NCAA's group executive director for eduation services. In January 1996 he was promoted to senior vice-president and chief operating officer of the NCAA. He retired in 2004.

Always active in the community, Boggan was one of the founders of the National Forum for Black Public Administrators (NFBPA) and its president from 1990–91.

Dan was selected as the Outstanding Public Administrator for the NFBPA in 1987. He also received an honorary doctorate of public service degree from Albion College in 1995. He was selected the 2002 National Sports Administrator of the Year by the Black Coaches Association.

He is married and has four children.

ATHLETICS DIRECTORS

Clarence Underwood served as director of intercollegiate athletics at Michigan State University from 1999 to 2002. Underwood began his MSU career as a student, earning a bachelor's degree in physical education in 1961. He also received a master's degree and a Ph.D. from MSU. Prior to being named athletics director, Underwood served as interim athletics director and senior associate athletics director.

Since retiring in 2002, Underwood has worked part-time in the Michigan State admissions office and put much of his time toward charitable pursuits, which include serving on the Sparrow Foundation board of directors and helping develop Coaches for Kids during its inception in 1999.

Don DiJulia began his second stint as director of athletics at Saint Joseph's University in 1988. He first led the Hawks' athletic program from 1976 to 1981, before taking the positions of East Coast Conference commissioner (1981–83) and Metro-Atlantic Athletic Conference commissioner (1984–88). Today, he is the assistant vice president/athletics director at SJU. During the past 13 years at the university, DiJulia has added five new programs, overseen the building of a new weight training facility, and spearheaded athletics fundraising for additional facility renovations. This includes the planning and construction of the $5 million athletics and recreation complex. A former NACDA executive committee member (1995–98), he has stressed the importance of the student-athlete by creating an Athletics Director's Honor Roll and senior scholar-athlete awards. DiJulia also has been active on the regional and national levels by serving his second term as Atlantic-10 Conference president and hosting numerous league championships and the 2000 NCAA Women's Basketball Final Four.

Dan Guerrero became director of athletics for UCLA in 2002. Previously, Guerrero served as Cal State Dominguez Hills director of athletics and athletics director for the University of California, Irvine. Guerrero received his bachelor's degree from UCLA in 1974, where he played second base for four years on the men's baseball team. He received a master's degree in public administration from Cal State Dominguez Hills.

Among his accomplishments, Guerrero has been inducted in the UCLA Baseball Hall of Fame, named a 1999 Sports Ethics Fellow by the Institute for International Sport, and named Cal State Dominguez Hills 2003 Alumnus of the Year.

Bill Byrne joined Texas A&M University as athletics director after successful tenures at Oregon and Nebraska. He was in his 11th year as the director of athletics at the University of Nebraska before he came to Texas A&M. The 23-sport Cornhusker program under his watch earned ratings among the nation's best. When Byrne arrived in Lincoln, the athletics department was operating with a $2.5 million deficit; he left the program on firm financial ground, winning 92 championships on a $44.5 million budget. Nine of the 23 Nebraska sports finished in the top 25 in the 2001–02 school year, and Nebraska finished among the top 25 in the NACDA Directors' Cup every year since the cup's inception.

Byrne received the prestigious John L. Toner Award in 2002 from the National Football Foundation, signifying the director of athletics who demonstrates superior administrative abilities and dedication to college athletics, especially collegiate football. Byrne served as president of NACDA from 1991–92, and spent nine years on the NACDA executive committee. He currently serves on numerous NACDA committees. He received a bachelor's degree in business in 1967, then continued at Idaho State to earn an MBA in 1971.

FACULTY

Dr. Percy Bates has been a faculty member at the University of Michigan since 1965. He has served as an assistant dean, has been chairperson of special education in the department of education in Washington, D.C., and is presently a member of the Secretary of Education's Title IX Commission on Opportunities in Athletics. Dr. Bates has worked with dozens of school districts, assisting them with assessing educational programs as well as dealing with equity, gender, and desegregation issues that teachers and administrators encounter on a day-to-day basis. Percy is the UM Faculty Athletics Representative and is very active with the UM and National Student Athlete Advisory.

Murray Sperber is widely recognized as the nation's foremost critic and commentator on the subject of college sports and culture, and is in constant demand by the media. He is the chairman of the National Alliance for Collegiate Athletic Reform (NAFCAR), an intercollegiate faculty committee advocating reform in athletic policy. A professor of English and American studies at Indiana University, Bloomington, his previous books include *College Sports, Inc.*; *Onward to Victory: The Crises That Shaped College Sports*; and *Shake Down the Thunder: The Creation of Notre Dame Football.*

Dr. Earl Smith is a research scientist in the social and behavioral sciences. He is currently the Distinguished Rubin Professor of American Ethnic Studies and professor and chairman, department of sociology, at Wake Forest University in Winston-Salem, North Carolina. Professor Smith obtained his bachelor's degree from SUNY and his masters and doctorate from the University of Connecticut in Storrs, Connecticut.

Professor Smith is an active scholar with an interest in issues related to social justice. He has a range that spans several disciplines and topics, including but not limited to sociology, economics, and anthropology. His topical interests include issues related to crime, urbanization, higher education, health, and the institution of sport.

Dr. C. Keith Harrison conducts research and teaches at Arizona State University in the College of Education, Division of Educational Leadership and Policy Studies. He is also in the process of consulting with the department of athletics at ASU and various academic units to develop an undergraduate certificate for Leadership and Ethics in Sport.

Dr. Harrison established the Paul Robeson Research Center for Leadership, Academic, and Athletic Prowess at the University of Michigan, Ann Arbor, in 1998 while on the faculty in sport management. Dr. Harrison has published numerous peer-review articles and book chapters on intercollegiate athletics, diversity in sport, and representations of athletes in mass media. He has lectured nationally and internationally about his research.

In addition to his duties at ASU, Dr. Harrison is also scholar-in-residence at Rush Philanthropic's Hip Hop Summit Action Network (HSAN). Dr. Harrison has created and co-produced five educational documentaries. He is also the author of the *Hiring Report Card* published by the Black Coaches Association.

Dr. Ellen Staurowsky received her undergraduate degree in health and physical education from Ursinus College, master's degree in sport psychology from Ithaca College, and doctorate in sport management from Temple University. Since 1992, Dr. Staurowsky has worked at Ithaca College. Dr. Staurowsky has presented on nearly 100 occasions to learned societies, professional associations, and conferences, from the local through international levels, on topics relating to gender equity and Title IX, pay equity and equal employment opportunity, the exploitation of athletes, the faculty role in reforming college sport, representation of women in sport media, and the misappropriation of American Indian imagery in sport. In addition to publications in scholarly journals, her critiques and analyses on a variety of issues have appeared in *Street & Smith's Sports Business Journal*, the *NCAA News*, *Athletic Management*, and *News from Indian Country*. In 1998, she co-authored a book along with Allen Sack from the University of New Haven entitled *College Athletes for Hire: The Evolution and Legacy of the NCAA Amateur Myth*.

Staurowsky has won numerous national awards. She has served on various committees of the North American Society for Sport Sociology (NASSS) since 1996. She is one of the founding members of the Drake Group (a group of faculty committed to intercollegiate athletic reform), and she currently serves on the Drake Group's executive committee. In 2002, she received the Ithaca College Faculty Award for Excellence in Scholarship. She is a recent past president of the North American Society of Sport Sociology.

STUDENT-ATHLETES

Lindsay Beddow is currently a student in the DeVos School of Sport Business Management at the University of Central Florida. Originally from Tampa, Florida, Lindsay did her undergraduate studies at Louisiana State University on a full gymnastics scholarship. While working toward her degrees in psychology and sociology, Lindsay also received All-SEC honors on the uneven bars and received NCAA Academic All-American honors in each of her four years on the gymnastics team. Now at UCF, Lindsay works as a graduate assistant for Richard Lapchick at the Institute for Diversity and Ethics in Sport and also works at the UCF SABRE Center, which provides academic support for student-athletes. After she graduates, Lindsay wants to pursue a career doing either community relations in professional sports or academic advising for student-athletes.

Keri Boyce graduated from the DeVos Sport Business Management Program at the University of Central Florida in May 2005. While at UCF, she was a graduate assistant for Richard Lapchick, worked game nights for the Orlando Magic, and completed an internship with the Orlando Magic. Originally from Birdsboro, Pennsylvania, Keri attended the University of Kentucky on a full athletic scholarship, where she obtained a bachelor of business administration in marketing and graduated summa cum laude. At Kentucky, she was a member of the women's soccer team and was named cocaptain her senior year. She received SEC Freshman of the Year honors and All-SEC honors, and she was National Player of the Week. She was also named to the dean's list, SEC

Academic Honor Roll, and Athletic Director's Honor Roll. She currently works for the NCAA.

Zachary Falconer, a native of Boston, holds an undergraduate degree in organizational communications from Northeastern University (NU). At NU he was a cocaptain of the football team during his senior year and a three-time All-Atlantic-10 selection at outside linebacker. He was also voted the team's most valuable player (MVP) in his senior year. In the spring of 2000 he was signed by the Oakland Raiders. After a brief stint with the Raiders, Falconer enrolled in the Athletes in Service to America (AIS) Program, an Americorp Program operated through Northeastern University's Center for the Study of Sport in Society. Falconer was then hired as a training specialist for the Mentors in Violence Prevention Program in January of 2001. The multiracial, mixed-gender program is the first large-scale attempt to enlist high school, collegiate, and professional athletes in the fight against all forms of men's violence against women. Falconer graduated from the University of Central Florida's DeVos Sport Business Management Program in the spring of 2005. He aspires to one day be a leader in the sports industry. He currently works for the Orlando Magic.

Damone Jones is currently a master's candidate in the DeVos Sport Business Management Program. In the fall semester, he worked in the office of academic support for student-athletes with the football team. During that term, the football team had its best academic performance since the Golden Knights became a Division IA program. Damone did his undergraduate work at the Pennsylvania State University, where he earned a B.S. in recreation and parks management, with minors in English and business. Also, he was on the football team for five seasons, earning two letters and starting for one season.

Morgan Marr, a native of Vienna, Virginia, received a full athletic scholarship to attend the University of Kentucky in the fall of 1999 to pitch for the Wildcats. She graduated summa cum laude with a B.B.A. in marketing after three years of course work. Upon graduation she worked in the advertising department at Nike in Beaverton before entering the DeVos Sport Business Management Program at the University of Central Florida in the fall of 2002. Throughout the program she worked with the NFL in New York City, the Tampa Bay Buccaneers, and Axcess Sports and Entertainment in Jacksonville, Florida. She graduated in May 2004 with an M.B.A. as well as a master of sport business management, while maintaining a 3.9 GPA, serving as a graduate research assistant for Dr. Richard Lapchick and Dr. Bill Sutton, and serving as a pitching coach for the UCF Golden Knights softball team. She currently is employed by the Atlanta Hawks, Atlanta Thrashers, and Philips

Arena working in the marketing, advertising, and branding department and as the stage manager for the Atlanta Hawks.

Brian O'Leary is currently a master's candidate in the DeVos Sport Business Management Program at the University of Central Florida. He is originally from Lexington, Kentucky, and received a B.B.A. in marketing from the University of Kentucky. During his four years at UK, Brian was a four-time letter winner and ranks first on the school's all-time saves and shutouts lists. He was twice named to the Southeastern Conference Honor Roll. Brian's soccer career continued after college with the Cincinnati Riverhawks of the A-League and with FC Viikingit in Helsinki, Finland, of the Finnish First Division. During high school, Brian was voted the Kentucky Male Soccer Player of the Year and was selected to the NSCAA All-American team as well as being a Gatorade All-American.

Charece Williams graduated cum laude with a B.S. in business management from North Carolina State University. Charece was a two-time captain, team most valuable player, and four-year starter of the North Carolina State women's volleyball team. She served as president of the Student-Athlete Advisory Committee, as a member of the Chancellor's Liaison Committee, and on the Council on Athletics. Charece's community involvement includes mentoring students at a local middle school and serving as keynote speaker at local Raleigh schools. She also was also honored as N.C. State's representative at the NCAA Leadership Conference and as a CP&L Community Champion; she earned the Atlantic Coast Conference Top Six for Service Award; and she was awarded an N.C. State Woman of the Year Award.

Charece received an M.B.A. and as well as a master of science in sport business management through the DeVos Sport Business Management Program at the University of Central Florida. She currently works for Disney's Wide World of Sports.

Sarah Wong grew up in Vancouver, Canada. She earned a four-year soccer scholarship at the University of Mississippi. She graduated with a marketing degree and moved to Indianapolis, where she worked at the NCAA in branding, broadcasting, and promotions. Sarah was part of the inaugural class of the DeVos Sport Business Management Program at the University of Central Florida, where she worked as a graduate assistant for Richard Lapchick. Sarah went to work for Wilson Sporting Goods in Chicago after she graduated, but she currently works as a sales manager for corporate sports and events with Maui Jim Sunglasses.

INDEX